Theodore F. Seward

The Tonic Sol-Fa Music Reader

A course of instruction and practice in the tonic sol-fa method of teaching singing, with a choice collection of music suitable for day schools and singing schools

Theodore F. Seward

The Tonic Sol-Fa Music Reader
A course of instruction and practice in the tonic sol-fa method of teaching singing, with a choice collection of music suitable for day schools and singing schools

ISBN/EAN: 9783337218577

Printed in Europe, USA, Canada, Australia, Japan

Cover: Foto ©Thomas Meinert / pixelio.de

More available books at **www.hansebooks.com**

THE

TONIC SOL-FA MUSIC READER

REVISED AND IMPROVED.

A COURSE OF INSTRUCTION AND PRACTICE IN THE

TONIC SOL-FA METHOD OF TEACHING SINGING,

WITH A

CHOICE COLLECTION OF MUSIC SUITABLE FOR DAY SCHOOLS AND SINGING SCHOOLS.

By THEODORE F. SEWARD AND B. C. UNSELD.

APPROVED BY JOHN CURWEN.

The Biglow & Main Co., Publishers,

135 FIFTH AVENUE, NEW YORK. LAKESIDE BUILDING, CHICAGO

FOR SALE BY BOOKSELLERS AND MUSIC DEALERS GENERALLY.

PREFACE TO THE FIRST EDITION.

The Tonic Sol-fa System is presented by the authors of this book to the American public, in the firm belief that the introduction of the system will mark a new era in the musical history of this country. The Tonic Sol-fa System presents two widely different characteristics, either one of which ought to commend it to all who are interested in music. Together they constitute an absolute demand for recognition. These characteristics are:

First.—*It removes three-fourths of the difficulties of music from the path of the beginner; and,*

Second.—*It leads to far greater intelligence and appreciation in the advanced stages of study and practice.*

A scholarly American musician has recently written concerning Tonic Sol-fa: —"It is not only a method of making music easy, but for making it more truly and profoundly understood."

The Tonic Sol-fa System is often called, by those who use it, "the natural method." The steps of progression are so easy and natural that both teachers and pupils find a pleasure in the study that they never realized before. It is so simple as to bring about a new departure in the teaching of music, in the following respect —*Those who know a little about music can teach that little without being compelled to master the whole science beforehand, as is necessary with the staff notation.* In this way a new class of teachers is developed wherever the Tonic Sol-fa System is introduced, viz.: persons of education and culture who love music, but who have heretofore been deterred by its technical difficulties from devoting themselves to it. It has been a common experience in England for such persons to begin teaching the first steps by the Sol-fa method, and, becoming interested, they have gone on studying and teaching till they were led to devote themselves exclusively to music, and became among its most intelligent exponents and successful workers.

Try the system fairly. Do not omit the best points and fancy you know all about Sol-fa. The various devices and expedients presented in the system are not matters of theory, but the outgrowth of years of actual trial and experience by many of the best teachers of Great Britain.

It is important to state that the "Tonic Sol-fa Music Reader," is published with the full sympathy and approval of Mr. Curwen, the founder of the system. The first steps were submitted to him for examination and were returned approved, with but few and unimportant changes. Since the recent death of Mr. Curwen, his son, Mr. J. Spencer Curwen, who takes his place in directing the movement in England, has examined and approved the MS.

Orange, N. J.

THEO. F. SEWARD,
B. C. UNSELD.

PREFACE TO THE NEW EDITION.

When the Reader was first issued, in 1880, the Tonic Sol-fa system was almost unknown in America. It is now an acknowledged factor in our national education. Mr. Louis A. Russel, in the preface to his "Method of Solfeggio," says, "In America there has been no new thought or method in sight-singing for the last 20 years which cannot be traced more or less directly to Mr. Curwen's influence."

The advocates of the Staff Method cannot dismiss Tonic Sol-fa with a word, as they were able to do ten years ago. But their present attitude is, perhaps, as far as their influence extends, even more injurious to the interests of musical education. They freely acknowledge the merits of the system, but claim that its advantages can be secured by a direct application to the staff. This is a fatal fallacy. The blessing of Tonic Sol-fa to the world is in its notation. The devices which grow out of the notation can no more be educationally applied to the staff than the methods of modern arithmetic can be applied to the Roman system of numerals. The transforming power of Tonic Sol-fa is in its natural and philosophical method of representing the beautiful realities of the tone world.

The educational part of this book—the method proper—is drawn from Mr. Curwen's various published works, but mainly from "The Standard Course." The authors claim no originality except in the manner of presentation. It has been prepared with great care, taking in every valuable point of the system, but rearranging and condensing for the special adaptation of the method to the musical needs of this country. The "Standard Course," which is Mr. Curwen's most complete setting forth of the system, includes full instructions in vocal training, harmony, musical form, etc, etc. The "Tonic Sol-fa Music Reader" presents only the facts of time and tune, for the use of elementary classes. Part I, embracing the first four Steps of the method, contains the instructions and exercises needed to prepare pupils for the Junior and Elementary Certificates. Part II, embracing the Fifth and Sixth Steps and an introduction to the Staff notation, furnishes the material necessary for the preparation for the Intermediate Certificate. The two parts are also bound together in a complete edition.

New York, Jan., 1890.

THEO. F. SEWARD,
B. C. UNSELD.

The Certificates of the Tonic Sol-fa College.

Steps of the Method.

A great advantage of the Tonic Sol-fa method is that it is really a *system*, from beginning to end. One of the most useful features of the method is the arrangement of the course of instruction in a series of graded steps. The close of each step is intended as a point at which the work should be revised, and the standing of each pupil ascertained before proceeding to the next. Anything which is left dimly understood or imperfectly practiced in one step, is only a legacy of so much confusion, weakness and discouragement handed over to the next. How many *lessons* will be required to teach each step it is difficult to say, without knowing the kind of class. The teacher should be guarded against hurry rather than delay.

The Certificates.

The Tonic Sol-fa movement has been distinguished from all other efforts to promote music among the people by its System of Certificates, issued by the Tonic Sol-fa College of London. It is a complete system of examination upon an extensive scale. The special object of these certificates is to save the pupil from one-sidedness, and to secure an equality of progress in tune, time, memory, etc., as well as to promote private study and discipline at home. They insure an "all-roundness" of training and serve as a stimulus to the pupil. For the *true* pupil they find out (what he wants to know) his *weak places*, show him in what direction *self-teaching* is specially demanded, and give him the *confidence* of knowing that he has really and satisfactorily reached a certain stage. The ambition to obtain them promotes such an amount of home-work that it fully four-folds the work of the teacher.

American Tonic Sol-fa College.

THE AMERICAN TONIC SOL-FA ASSOCIATION AND COLLEGE OF MUSIC (Post office address, New York, N. Y.) was incorporated in 1889 under the laws of the State of New York. It acts in affiliation with the Tonic Sol-fa College of London, and its certificates are recognized as equivalent to its own. Information as to organization, postal courses, examinations, etc., may be obtained by writing to the above address.

Below are the requirements of the first two certificates.* The questions in Theory of the Second Grade are here omitted because of lack of space, but may be obtained from the College at 2 cents per copy, plus postage.

Manner of Teaching.

It is hardly necessary to say that the ways of presenting the various subjects in this book are not to be followed mechanically. They are illustrations of the manner in which the topics may be treated, but every teacher will have his own way of carrying out the details. See *Manual for Teachers of the School Series* (price, 12 cents, by mail) for other ways of teaching the various topics. One of the leading characteristics of this system is that so little time needs to be occupied with theory. "We learn to do by doing" is the grand motto of the Tonic Sol-faist. The new devices of the system—the Modulator, Manual Signs, Time-names, and even the doctrine of Mental Effects are all expedients for leading the student to *practice* more, to *think* more, to *remember* better; in other words, to increase his musical intelligence.

Requirements for the First Grade or Preparatory Certificate.

Examiners.—Those who hold the Second Grade or a higher certificate, with Theory, and who have been appointed to examine by the College of Music.

1. *Memory.*—Bring on separate slips of paper the names of three tunes, and *sol-fa* from memory, while pointing it on the modulator, one of these tunes chosen by lot.

2. *Time.*—*Taatai* once, and then *laa* on one tone in perfectly correct time, any of the rhythms Nos. 1, 3, 4, 5, 7, 9 or 11 (see pp. 107-8) which the Examiner may select. [Two attempts allowed; a different test to be given for the second trial.]

3. *Modulator.*—*Sol-fa* or *laa* from the Examiner's pointing on the modulator, a voluntary, moving at the rate of M.60, consisting of at least twenty-four tones, including leaps to any of the tones of the scale, but neither transition nor the minor mode.

4. *Tune.*—*Sol-fa* or *laa* at sight, from the tonic sol-fa notation, a phrase of eight tones, all in the common major scale, and no tones shorter than a pulse.

5. *Ear Test.*—The key-tone having been given, tell the sol-fa names of the tones of the Doh chord sung to *laa* or played in any order, also the phrases fah me and te_1 doh.

First Grade Musical Theory.

Answer any two or more of the following Questions, put by the Examiner:

1. Name the tones of the scale and their mental effects.
2. Name the tones of the Doh chord; of the Soh chord; of the Fah chord.
3. Name the little steps of the scale.
4. What is the time name of an undivided pulse?
5. What is the time name of a pulse divided into halves? into quarters?
6. Write in two-pulse measure an exercise of two measures: (*a*) In primary form. (*b*) In secondary form.
7. Write in three-pulse measure an exercise of two measures: (*a*) In primary form. (*b*) In secondary form.

Requirements for the Second Grade or Elementary Certificate.

Examiners.—Those who hold the Third Grade, or a higher certificate, with Theory, and who have been appointed to examine by the College of Music.

Before examination, Candidates must satisfy the Examiner that they hold the First Grade Certificate.

1. *Memory.*—Bring on separate slips of paper the names of six tunes, and *sol-fa* from memory, while pointing it on the modulator, one of these tunes chosen by lot.

2. *Time.*—*Taatai* at first sight and then *laa* in perfectly correct time, a test which may contain any of the quarter-pulse divisions. [Two attempts allowed; a different test to be given for the second trial.]

3. *Modulator.*—(*a*) Sing to *laa* to the Examiner's pointing on the modulator, a voluntary, including leaps to any of the tones of the scale, but neither transition nor the minor mode. (*b*) *Sol-fa* or *laa* a voluntary, containing transition of one remove in each direction.

4. *Tune.*—Pitch the key-tone by means of a given C; *sol-fa* once, then sing to *laa*, a sight test in tune containing leaps to any tones of the scale; but neither transition, nor minor mode, nor any divisions of time less than a full pulse.

Candidates may *laa* instead of *sol-faing* the test.

5. *Ear Test.*—Tell the notes of a phrase of three tones in smooth melodic progression. The Examiner will give the key-tone and sing the test to *laa*, or play it upon an instrument. [Two attempts allowed; a different test to be given for the second trial.]

The College will supply to the examiner the texts to be used in Nos. 2, 4 and 5

NOTE.—The registration fee for this Certificate is 15 cents, which is exclusive of Examiner's fee. Registration fee stamp may be purchased from the Examiner.

Mental Effects and Manual Signs of Tones in Key.

Note.—*The diagrams show the right hand as seen by pupils sitting in front of the teacher towards his left hand. The teacher makes his signs in front of his ribs, chest, face and head, rising a little as the tones go up, and falling as the tones go down.*

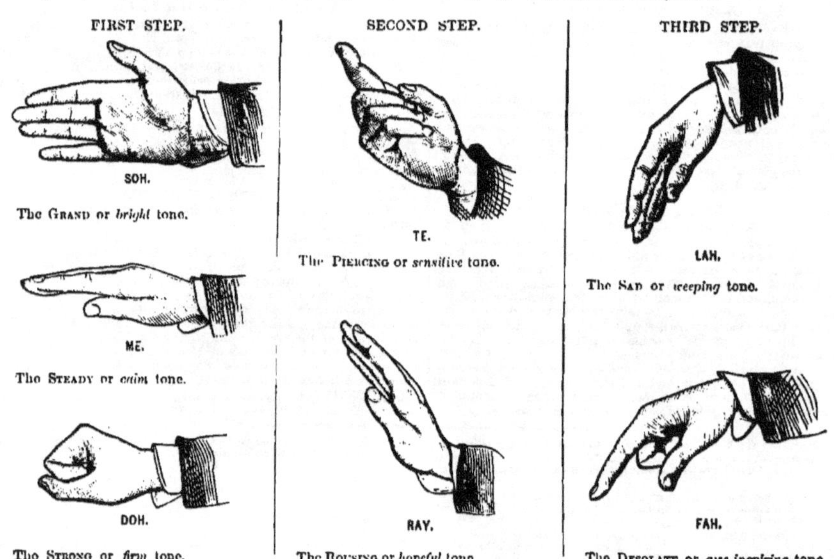

Mental Effects.—Some teachers are, at first, inclined to ignore this doctrine of the Sol fa method, but it is a subject eminently worthy of the profoundest study. Mental effects are difficult to perceive because they *are mental*. Let not the teacher be discouraged if he does not at once grasp the whole matter. *The perception of mental effect is cumulative*, the more the subject is studied the plainer it becomes. The practice of teaching by mental effect has become so important in the Tonic Sol-fa method that the teacher cannot take too much pains to master it. *He should remember that these effects exist, whether he recognizes them or not*, and it is certainly wiser to utilize than to ignore them. The pamphlet "Studies in Mental Effects" furnishes a large variety of examples.

Note.—*These proximate verbal descriptions of mental effect are only true of the tones of the scale when sung slowly—when the ear is filled with the key, and when the effect is not modified by harmony.*

Finger-Signs for Time,

As seen from the pupil's (not the teacher's) point of view.

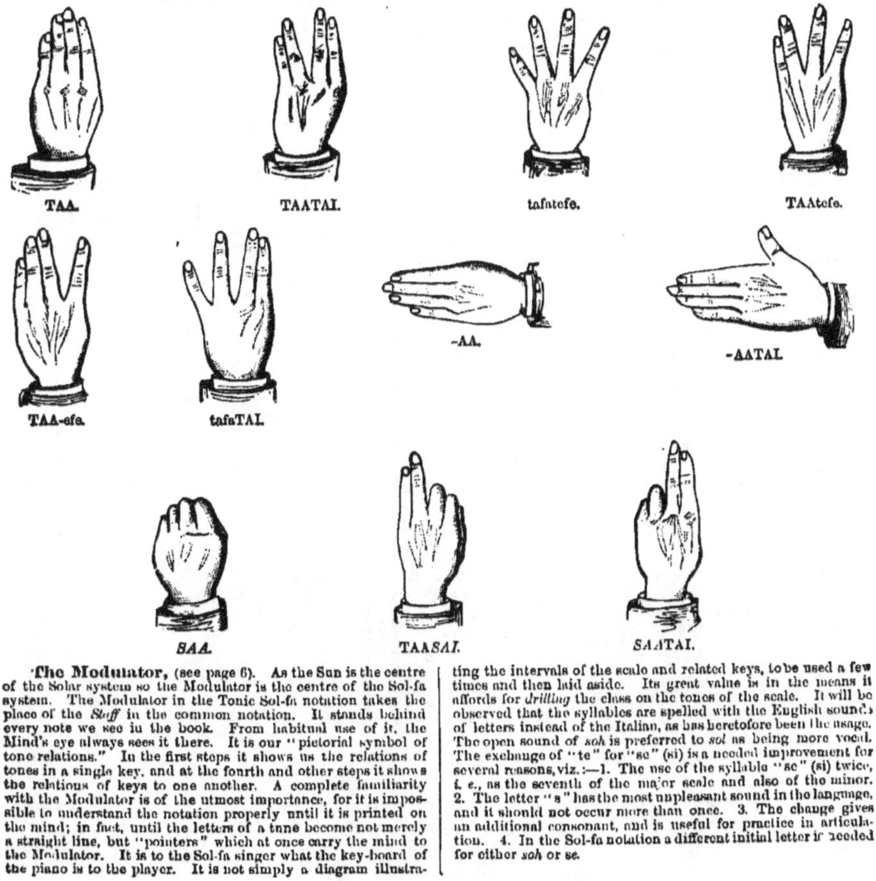

TAA. TAATAI. tafatefe. TAAtefe.

TAA-efe. tafaTAI. -AA. -AATAI.

SAA. TAA*SAI.* *SA*A*TAI.*

The Modulator, (see page 6). As the Sun is the centre of the Solar system so the Modulator is the centre of the Sol-fa system. The Modulator in the Tonic Sol-fa notation takes the place of the *Staff* in the common notation. It stands behind every note we see in the book. From habitual use of it, the Mind's eye always sees it there. It is our "pictorial symbol of tone relations." In the first steps it shows us the relations of tones in a single key, and at the fourth and other steps it shows the relations of keys to one another. A complete familiarity with the Modulator is of the utmost importance, for it is impossible to understand the notation properly until it is printed on the mind; in fact, until the letters of a tune become not merely a straight line, but "pointers" which at once carry the mind to the Modulator. It is to the Sol-fa singer what the key-board of the piano is to the player. It is not simply a diagram illustrating the intervals of the scale and related keys, to be used a few times and then laid aside. Its great value is in the means it affords for *drilling* the class on the tones of the scale. It will be observed that the syllables are spelled with the English sounds of letters instead of the Italian, as has heretofore been the usage. The open sound of *soh* is preferred to *sol* as being more vocal. The exchange of "te" for "se" (si) is a needed improvement for several reasons, viz.:—1. The use of the syllable "se" (si) twice, *i. e.*, as the seventh of the major scale and also of the minor. 2. The letter "s" has the most unpleasant sound in the language, and it should not occur more than once. 3. The change gives an additional consonant, and is useful for practice in articulation. 4. In the Sol-fa notation a different initial letter is needed for either *soh* or se.

Notation of Time.

The long heavy bar indicates a strong accent; the short, thin bar (|) a medium accent, and the colon (:) a weak accent.

Time is represented by the space between the accent marks. The space from one accent mark to the next represents a Pulse. (*Beat, or Part of the measure.*) The space between the strong accent marks (long bars) represents a measure.

Two-Pulse Measure.	Three-Pulse Measure.	Four-Pulse Measure.	Six-Pulse Measure.
‖ : ‖	‖ : : ‖	‖ : | : ‖	‖ : : | : : ‖

The Tonic Sol-fa Method makes use of a system of *Time-names* to aid in the study of time. The Pulse is the unit of measurement, and a tone one pulse long is named TAA.

| d :d | d :d ‖
TAA TAA TAA TAA

The continuation of a tone through more than one pulse is indicated by a dash, and the time-name is obtained by dropping the consonant.

| d :d | d :— | d :— | — :— ‖
TAA TAA TAA - AA TAA - AA - AA - AA

A pulse divided into halves—half-pulse tones—is named TAATAI, and is indicated in the notation by a dot in the middle.	| d .d :d .d ‖ TAATAI TAATAI
A tone continued into the first half of the next pulse—a pulse-and-a-half tone—is named and indicated thus:	| d :— .d ‖ TAA -AA TAI
A pulse divided into quarters is named *tafatefe*, and is represented by a comma in the middle of each half-pulse.	| d,d.d,d :d .d ‖ ta-fa-te-fe TAATAI
A pulse divided into a half and two quarters is named TAAtefe.	| d .d,d :d .d,d ‖ TAA - te-fe TAA - te-fe
A pulse divided into three quarters and a quarter is named TAA-efe, and is indicated by a dot and comma.	| d .,d :d .,d ‖ TAA -efe TAA -efe
Thirds of a pulse are named TAATAITEE, and represented by commas turned to the right.	| d ‚d ‚d :d ‚d ‚d ‖ taa-tai-tee taa-tai-tee
Silences (Rests) are named by substituting the letter S for T or f, thus: a full pulse silence is named *SAA*; a half pulse silence is named *SAA* on the first half of a pulse and *SAI* on the second half. Quarter pulse silences are named *sa* on the first half and *se* on the second. Silences are indicated by the absence of notes in the pulse divisions, *i. e.* vacant space.	| d : ‖ TAA *SAA* | d . : .d ‖ TAA *SAI SAA* TAI | d,d.d, : ,d.d,d ‖ ta-fa-te-*se* *sa*-fa -te -fe

The Modulator.

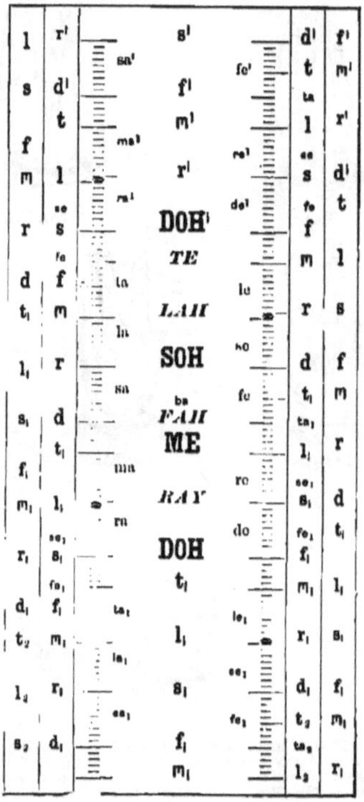

l	r'		s'		d'	f'
		sa'		fe'	t	m'
s	d'		f'		ta	
	t		m'		l	r'
f		ma'		re'	se	
m	l		r'		s	d'
		ra'		de'		
	se				fe	t
r	s		DOH'		f	
	fe		*TE*		m	l
d	f	ta		le		
t_1	m		*LAH*		r	s
		la		ba		
l_1	r		SOH		d	f
		sa	ba	fe	t_1	m
s_1	d		*FAH*		ta_1	
	t_1		ME		l_1	r
f_1		ma		re	se_1	
m_1	l_1		*RAY*		s_1	d
		ra		de	fe_1	t_1
	se_1					
r_1	s_1		DOH		f_1	
	fe_1		t_1		m_1	l_1
d_1	f_1	ta_1		le_1		
t_2	m_1		l_1		r_1	s_1
		la_1		se_1		
l_2	r_1		s_1		d_1	f_1
		sa_1		fe_1	t_2	m_1
s_2	d_1		f_1		ta_2	
			m_1		l_2	r_1

Note.—AA has the sound of *a* in *father*; AI, as in *aid*; *e*, as in *effect*.

Minuter divisions of the pulse, sixths, eighths, ninths, are seldom used except in instrumental music. In the Sol fa notation no distinction is made between $\frac{2}{4}$, $\frac{2}{2}$, $\frac{3}{4}$, $\frac{3}{2}$ etc., there being but one way of writing the different *varieties* of measure.

THE TONIC SOL-FA MUSIC READER.

PART I.—Instructions and Exercises in the First, Second, Third and Fourth Steps. Covering the Junior and Elementary Certificates.

FIRST STEP.

To recognize and produce the tones Doh, Me, Soh; the upper octave of Doh, and the lower octave of Soh. To recognize and produce the strong and weak accent, and the simplest divisions of time, viz:—the Pulse, the half-pulse, two-pulse measure and three-pulse measure.

The first lesson may begin by practicing a familiar tune, or by a few appropriate remarks by the teacher, after which he may say—

You may listen to me and be ready to sing the examples I give you.

He sings a tone which he considers in his own mind as *Doh*, the first tone of the scale, at about the pitch of D or E, clearly and firmly to the syllable *laa*

You may all sing it.—

The Dash ——— will signify that a command is obeyed or a question answered. It may be necessary to repeat the example several times before the voices blend well.

NOTE.—The teacher should never sing *with* his pupils, but give examples or patterns carefully which they are to imitate. They should listen while he sings, and he listen while they sing. Mr. Curwen says, "The first art of the pupil is to *listen well*. He that listens best, sings best." After this tone is sung correctly, the teacher may say—

Listen to me again—

He now sings a tone a fifth higher, *Soh*, the fifth tone of the scale, to the syllable *laa*. The pupils imitate.

Now sing these two tones, after me, just as I sing them.

He sings the two tones in succession, to laa, in any order he chooses, but varies the manner of producing them; making them sometimes loud, sometimes soft, long or short; *changing the pitch of Doh frequently*, sometimes singing C and G, sometimes E and B, or D and A, etc., the pupils imitating each pattern. See examples below—Exs. 1 to 4.

SOH

We will now learn the names of these two tones—The lower tone is called *Doh*—What is it called?—The upper tone is called *Soh*—What is it called?

NOTE.—In giving out a new fact or principle the teacher should always question the pupils, that they may not only hear it stated but be led to state it themselves. The teacher, as he gives the names, writes or "prints" them on the blackboard, *Soh* above *Doh*, leaving considerable space between them.

DOH

Now we will sing the tones to their names; repeat after me the tones I give you.

The following exercises are specimens of patterns which the teacher may give. The upright lines indicate how much of each exercise may be given as a pattern. The horizontal dash—shows that the tone should be prolonged.

1. Keys **D, F** and **C.**

|d d d — |s s s — |d d . s s d — ||

2.

|s s s — |d d d — |s s d s d ||

3.

|d d s — |s s d — |d d s s d ||

4.

|d — s — d — |s — d — s s d — ||

You may now sing as I point to the names on the blackboard and without a pattern from me.

They sing, to his pointing, exercises similar to those given above.

Sing again as I point, but this time sing the tones to laa.

He points to the names, they sing to laa. In all these exercises the teacher will frequently change his keytone, lest the pupils be tempted to try to sing by *absolute pitch* instead of giving their attention to the *relation* of tones.

Now I will sing *Doh* and you may sing the *Soh* to it.

He sings *Doh* and then gives them a signal to sing *Soh*.

I will take a different *Doh* and you may give me the *Soh* to it.

He takes a different pitch for *Doh* and they sing the *Soh* to it. This he does several times, always changing the keytone.

You may now name the tones as I sing them, I will sing to laa, and when I sing the lower tone, say *Doh*, and when I sing the upper tone say *Soh*.

He sings the two tones in various successions, the pupils

calling out "Doh," "Soh," etc. It may be well for him to sing each tone several times and not to change too quickly—for instance d d d d s s s d d s s d s d s s d, etc.

Name them once more, and if I sing a different tone from these two, one that is neither *Doh* nor *Soh*, you may say *New-tone.*

He sings as before, the class calling out the names, and after keeping them a little while in expectation, he sings the third tone of the scale—*Me*—(of course, to *laa*), which the pupils at once detect. It is better to let the new tone come in after *Soh*, thus, d - s — m.

Is the new tone higher or lower than *Doh?*	
Is it higher or lower than *Soh?*	**SOH**
The name of the new tone is *Me.*	
What is its name?	**ME**
Where shall I write it on the board?	
See diagram.	**DOH**
Imitate the patterns I give you.	

He patterns the following, or similar examples, singing to the names, which the pupils repeat. A narrower type and somewhat altered form is given to the letter m (m), for convenience in printing.

5. Keys D, F and C.

|d s m — |m s d — |d s m s d ||

6.

|d m d — |s m s — |m d m — |m s m — ||

7.

|s d m — |m d s — |s s m s d ||

8.

|d m s — |s m d — |d s m d ||

Now sing as I point.

The teacher should drill the class thoroughly on these three tones, singing them first to the names and afterward to laa.

The pitch should be changed frequently.

Thus far we have been studying the names and relative positions of these three tones, but now I want to call your attention to the most important and most interesting thing about them, and that is their characters, or the effects or impressions they produce upon the mind. One of them is a strong, firm tone; another is a bright, clear, grand tone; and another is a gentle, peaceful, calm tone. I want you to find out the character of each tone for yourselves. You may listen to me and, as I sing, give your attention specially to *Doh*, and then tell me which of these characters it has; whether it is calm and peaceful, or clear and grand, or strong and firm.

Teacher sings the following phrases or something similiar, bringing out strongly the character of *Doh*:

|d :— |d :d |m :m |d :— |d :m |s :m |s :s |d :— ||

Is *Doh* calm and peaceful, or clear and grand, or strong and firm?

Now listen to *Soh* and tell me what character it has.

Teacher sings the following phrase:

|d :d |m :d |s :s |s :— |s :m |d :m |s :s |s :— ||

What kind of a tone is *Soh?*

Now listen to *Me.*

Teacher sings the following phrase:

:d |m :d |m :s |m :— |m :m |s :m |d :s |m :— ||

What is the character of *Me?*

What kind of tone is *Doh?—Soh? Me?*

I call your attention to these characters or mental effects of the tones not as a mere matter of curiosity, but as a real help in singing them. As you try to sing a tone, think of its mental effect and that will help you to sing it correctly.

Let us now learn to sing the tones from signs representing their mental effects. The strong, firm tone is represented by the closed hand thus, (see manual signs). All make it.

What kind of a tone is indicated by this sign?

What is its name?

The bright, clear, grand tone is represented by the open hand thus—. All make it.

What kind of a tone does this sign indicate?

What is its name?

And this sign (open hand, palm downwards), represents the calm, peaceful tone. All make it.

What kind of a tone is indicated by this sign?

And this?—and this?—etc., etc., etc.

Give me the sign for the strong tone.

The sign for the grand tone.

The sign for the calm tone—Grand tone.—Strong tone, etc.

You may sing the tones as I indicate them by the signs. Think of their mental effects as you sing them.

The teacher will give a good drill with the hand-signs, pupils singing to the sol-fa names and also to laa.

Listen to me and when I sing the grand tone, instead of telling me its name, you may give me its sign.

Teacher sings the tones to laa, and each time he sings *soh* the pupils make the sign.

Now give me the sign for the calm tone when you hear it.

Teacher sings as directed above, pupils make the sign.

Now give the sign for the strong tone.

Teacher and pupils as directed as above.

Now give the sign for each tone as I sing.

Teacher sings to laa, pupils giving the sign for each tone.

I will indicate the tones in yet another way. I will let d stand for *Doh*, m for *Me* and s for *Soh*.

Teacher writes the following exercise or a similar one.

d d s s m m d

You may sing the lesson as written and you will be singing from the Tonic Sol-fa Notation.

The following exercises may now be written upon the board and practiced, or they may be sung from the book.—first to the syllables and then to laa. "Key C," "Key G," etc., will tell the teacher where to pitch his *Doh*. Although there is no indication of time in these exercises, they all have a melodic form and should be sung with a rhythmic flow. They may be sung as fast or as slow as the teacher likes; he can indicate the time by gentle taps on the table.

9. Key D.
d d m d m m s m s s m m s m d

10. Key F.
d m s s m d s s m m s s m s d

11. Key C.
d s m s d d m s m d m m s m d

12. Key E.
s m d m s s s m s m d m s s d

13. Key G.
m d s m m d s m m m s s m s d

14. Key E.
m m m d m m m s m m s m d m d

15. Key C.
d s m d m d s m d m d s m s d

16. Key D.
d m s m s m d s m s d s d m d

The upper octave of *Doh* may now be taught by the same process as that used for *Me*. When the pupils have discovered the new tone the teacher may proceed as follows:

Is the new tone higher or lower than *Doh?*

Is it higher or lower than *Me?*

Higher or lower than *Soh?*

The name of the new tone is *Doh*. What is its name?

You may think it strange that we have two tones with the same name, but it will be explained a little later in the course

NOTE.—The nature of octaves can be better explained after the complete scale has been taught

Where shall I write it on the board?

I need not write it in full; the first letter will be sufficient.

Teacher writes a d in the proper place.

In writing, the Upper *Doh* is indicated by the figure 1 placed at the top of the letter thus, d', and is called *One-Doh*. While we are practicing this new tone I want you to be thinking about its mental effect; compare the Upper *Doh* with the lower and notice whether it has the same effect, or if it is stronger or firmer.

Let the new tone be practiced in connection with the others, first by patterns from the teacher, and then from the teacher's pointing. Then let the teacher by questioning develop the fact that its mental effect is the same as the lower *doh*, only stronger or more positive. The manual sign for d' is the same as for d with the hand raised. The following exercises are given as specimen patterns for the teacher. Sing them first to the sol-fa syllables, and afterwards to laa.

d'

SOH

ME

DOH

Exercise 17 consists of short phrases, intended as patterns, to be given by the teacher.

17. Keys C and D.

| d m s d^1 | d^1 s m d | d^1 s d^1 — | d^1 s m — | m d^1 s — | s m d^1 — |

| d^1 m s — | s d^1 m — | m d d^1 — | d^1 d m — | m d^1 d | d d^1 s m d |

After a thorough drill upon the tones by pattern, from the Modulator, Hand-Signs, and so on, the following exercises may be written upon the blackboard and practiced or they may be sung from the book.

18. Key D.

d d m m d m s s d^1 d^1 s m s m d

19. Key C.

d s m s d^1 s d^1 s m m s s m s d^1

20. Key C.

d^1 s m m d^1 m s s d^1 m s m s d^1 d

21. Key D.

d m s d^1 d^1 s s m d m s m d^1 s d

d^1 SOH ME DOH s_1

The teacher may now explain the lower octave of *Soh* by simply stating that as we have an Upper *Doh*, so we may also have a Lower *Soh*. It is indicated in the notation by the figure 1 placed at the bottom of the letter thus s_1, and is called *Soh-One*. Its mental effect is the same, only somewhat subdued. The hand sign for s_1 is the same as for s with the hand lowered. Let *Soh-One* be practiced after the same manner as that pursued with the *One-Doh*, only taking a higher pitch for the key tone.

The following exercises are patterns for the teacher.

22. Keys F, A and G.

| d s_1 d — | d m s_1 d | d s_1 m d |

| d m s s_1 d | d s_1 s m d |

The class is now ready to practice the following exercises.

23. Key F.

d s_1 d m s s m d d s_1 d m s s_1 d

24. Key A.

d d m d s_1 s_1 m d m m s m d s_1 d

25. Key G.

m m d s_1 s s m d s m d s_1 m s_1 d

26. Key F.

s s m d s_1 s_1 m d s s m d s_1 s d

TIME AND RHYTHM.

NOTE.—The Tonic Sol-fa treatment of the subject of Time (Rhythmics), differs essentially from that which has usually prevailed in this country. Here the *measure* has been regarded as the standard or unit. In the Sol-fa method, the *pulse*, which corresponds to our *beat* or *part of the measure*, is treated as the unit; and time is measured by a regular recurrence of accent. This is undoubtedly the true philosophy. In fact some prominent teachers in this country have already developed this theory in their later works. There are several ways in which this subject may be presented to a class. The following will serve as an illustration of one way, which the teacher may vary, or condense or enlarge as he may deem best. For another method, see *Teacher's Manual of the Tonic Sol-fa School Series*, published by Biglow & Main.

Listen to me, I will sing a familiar tune, and as I sing I wish you to observe that their will occur in your minds, at regular intervals, a throb or pulsation of some kind that keeps time with the music.

The teacher sings to laa a familiar tune, such as "Haste thee, Winter,"—

|d :d |s :s |l :l |s :—|f :f |m :m |r :r |d :—|| etc.

or "Vesper Hymn,"—

|m :s |f :s |m :s |r :s |m :s |f :r |d :t_1 |d :—||

bringing out the strong accent.

Those who noticed the throbs or pulsations may hold up hands.

I will sing again and will indicate these pulsations by taps upon the table, and you may indicate them by some motion of your hands.

He sings again, giving a tap for each *strong* accent, the pupils making, perhaps, a downward motion of the hand.

These throbs or heavy tones are called accents. What are they called?

I will sing again and you will notice that after each of these accents there occurs a second pulsation, but of less force.

He sings again, giving a heavy tap for the strong accent and a light tap for each weak accent.

How many noticed the light throbs?

The heavy pulsations are called strong accents, and the light ones are called weak accents.

How many kinds of accents have we?

I will sing again and you may indicate every accent, strong or weak, by some motion of your hand.

The pupils may be directed to make a downward motion for the strong accent and an upward motion for the weak accent. These motions are not absolutly essential and they are not intended as an exercise in beating time, but merely as a means for the pupils to show to the teacher that they recognize the accents.

Listen again—this time I will occasionally stop singing to show you that the accents may go on in the mind without the music.

In this exercise the teacher will occasionally stop singing for a measure or two but keeps on tapping in regular time.

I will now show you that the accents will move quickly or slowly as the music goes fast or slow.

Teacher illustrates this.

You learn from all these examples that time in music is measured by regularly recurring accents.

How is time measured in music?

The time from one strong accent to the next strong accent is called a Measure.

What is it called?

What is a Measure?

The time from any accent, strong or weak, to the next, is called a Pulse.

What is it called? What is a Pulse?

Listen to me.

He sings a number of measures to laa, two tones to each measure, accenting distinctly, thus, LAA *laa*, LAA *laa*, etc.

After each strong pulse how many weak pulses were there?

Yes, they were regularly STRONG, *weak*, STRONG, *weak*, etc.

Listen again.

This time he accents the first in every three, thus, LAA *laa laa*, LAA *laa laa*, etc.

How many weak pulses followed each strong pulse?

Yes, they were regularly STRONG, *weak*, *weak*, STRONG, *weak*, *weak*, etc.

Different arrangements of the order of accents makes different kinds of measure.

What makes different kinds of measure?

A measure consisting of two pulses, one strong and one weak, is called Two-pulse measure. What is it called?

A measure consisting of three pulses, one STRONG and two *weak*, is called Three-pulse measure. What is it called?

Listen to me, and tell me which kind of measure you hear.

Teacher sings a number of measures to laa, accenting distinctly, changing occasionally from two-pulse to three-pulse measure and back again, the pupils calling out "two-pulse," "three-pulse," at each change. Or he may sing a familiar tune in each kind of measure and require the pupils to tell which kind of measure the tune is in.

NOTE.—In the Standard Course of the tonic Sol-fa Method the pupils are not taught to beat time until the Fourth Step. Mr Curwen says—"Pupils should not be allowed to "beat" time until they have gained *a sense* of time. * * * Because no one can well learn two things at once, and, consequently, those who try to do so are constantly found beating to their singing instead of singing to an independent, steady beat. * * * *Beating* time can be of no use—is only a burden to the pupil in *keeping* time, till it has become almost automatical, until "the time beats itself" and you know that your beating *will* go right whatever becomes of the voice. Then, and not till then, the beating becomes *an independent test* of the singing."

American teachers, however, are so accustomed to teaching counting and beating time from the beginning that the teacher may introduce it here if he prefers—not as a test in singing, but as a separate exercise as a means or a help in developing the sense of time. In two-pulse measure the countings are *one* two, *one* two, etc., and the motions of the hand are *down* up, *down* up, etc. In three-pulse measure the countings are *one* two three, *one* two three, etc., and the motions are *down* left up, *down* left up, etc., or *down* right up, etc.

In practicing exercises in time it is useful to have names for the different lengths. The time-name of a tone one pulse long is Taa.

The "aa" is pronounced as "a" in father.

You may sing in two-pulse measure, one tone to each pulse, thus, Taa taa, Taa taa, etc.

If preferred by the teacher, the syllable Traa may be used for the strong accent. Let this be kept going until all get into the "swing" of the rhythm—alternate measures may then be sung by the teacher and class, or by two divisions of the class, being careful to keep a steady rate of movement. Then let it be done with a different rate.

Let us try two-pulse measure again, but this time begin with the weak pulse, thus, taa Taa, taa Taa, etc.

Let this be practiced as above.

When the measure begins with a strong pulse it is called the Primary Form of the measure. What is it called?

When is a measure in the Primary Form?

When the measure begins with a weak pulse it is called the Secondary Form. What is it called? When is a measure in the Secondary Form?

Three-pulse measure may next be practiced with the same process as that just given to the two-pulse measure, or it may be defered until later.

I will now write a number of pulses on the blackboard and you may sing them as I direct.

Teacher writes thus:—

Taa Taa Taa Taa Taa Taa Taa Taa

You may sing them in two-pulse measure commencing with a strong pulse.—

Teacher indicates the time by a gentle tap of the pointer on each pulse.

Again, commencing with a weak pulse.

Teacher, if he chooses, may have them sung in three-pulse measure.

You see that as the exercise now stands there is nothing on the board to tell us which are the strong and which are the weak pulses. In the Sol-fa notation an upright bar (|) shows that the pulse following it is to have the strong accent; the weak accent is indicated by two dots (:) and the Double Bar (||) shows the end.

Teacher while he is making the above statement inserts the accent marks as follows:—

| Taa : taa | Taa : taa | Taa : taa | Taa : taa ||

What does the bar indicate?

How is the weak accent indicated?

What does the double bar show?

The accent marks are placed at equal distances of space and thus represent the equal divisions of time.

The space from one accent mark to the next, strong or weak, represents the time of a pulse, and the space between the bars represents the time of a measure.

What represents the time of a pulse?

What represents the time of a measure?

You may now sing the exercise as written.

After it is sung correctly, at different rates of movement, the teacher will write an exercise, beginning with the weak pulse, thus:—

: taa | Taa : taa | Taa : taa | Taa : taa | Taa ||

Let this be practiced at different rates of movement from the teacher's patterns. Then each exercise should be sung to laa, teacher writing an "l" under each *taa*. Then erasing the "ls" and putting a d in each pulse, sing *doh*. Then again with the following or similiar successions:

| Taa : taa | Taa : taa | Taa : taa | Taa : taa ||
| d : d | s : s | m : m | d : d ||

Teacher will next erase the Sol-fa notes, leaving the taas.

I will sing the exercise, and if I make a mistake, you may say wrong.

Teacher sings it the first time correctly; second time with wrong accent, and the third time he makes a mistake in the second measure—prolonging the tone through both pulses, at which the pupils will say "wrong."

Which measure was wrong?

How many tones are indicated in the second measure?

How many did I sing?

Was it a long tone or a short tone? How long was it?

Yes, I continued the tone through the second pulse—made it two pulses long. It is called a two-pulse tone. What is it called?

When a tone is continued from one pulse to the next the continuation is indicated by a horizontal line, thus, — The time-name for continuations is obtained by dropping the consonant, thus, Taa-aa.

The teacher, as he makes these statements, changes the second and fourth measure so they appear thus:—

| Taa : taa | Taa : -aa | Taa : taa | Taa : -aa ||

Teacher pointing to the continuation mark, asks:—

What does this horizontal line indicate?

How are the time-names for continuations obtained?

How long must this tone be?

What is the time-name of a two-pulse tone?

A convenient short name for two-pulse tones is Twos. What will be a good short name for one-pulse tones?

In the lesson now on the blackboard what kind of tones are required in the first and third measures? *Ones.*

In the second and fourth? *Twos.*

I will sing the lesson first and then you may try it.

If the pupils fail to prolong the tones their full length, the vowel AI (as in "aid") may be added thus, | TAA-AI: -AA-AI. When the lesson has been sung correctly to the time-names and at different rates, it should be sung to laa, the teacher indicating laa by an l under the time-names.

Then he may change the measures so as to obtain the following or similar rhythms. Each exercise should be sung several times—to the time-names to laa—and at different rates of speed. They may also be sung in tune, the teacher writing the Sol-fa letters under the time-names as has been already suggested.

27.

TAA	TAA	TAA	TAA	TAA	-AA	TAA	-AA
|l	:l	|l	:l	|l	:—	|l	:— ‖

28.

TAA	-AA	TAA	TAA	TAA	TAA	TAA	-AA
|l	:—	|l	:l	|l	:l	|l	:— ‖

29.

\|l :— \|l :— \|l :l \|l :— ‖

30.

\|l :— \|l :l \|l :— \|— :— ‖

31.

:l \|l :l \|l :l \|l :— \|— ‖

32.

:l \|l :— \|l :l \|l :— \|— ‖

It is not important to *dwell* on the *secondary* forms of the measure or on three-pulse measure at this point. To practice three-pulse measure the teacher will write the following exercise on the board:

| TAA :TAA :TAA | TAA :TAA :TAA | TAA :TAA :TAA | TAA :TAA :TAA |

Let it be sung with clear accent to the time-names and to the laa; then the teacher will change the measures so as to obtain the following rhythms. Each exercise should be sung to the time-names, to laa, etc.

33.

TAA	TAA	TAA	TAA	-AA	-AA	TAA	TAA	TAA	TAA	-AA	-AA
|l	:l	:l	|l	:—	:—	|l	:l	:l	|l	:—	:— ‖

34.

\|l :l :l \|l :— :l \|l :l :l \|l :— :— ‖

35.

\|l :— :l \|l :— :l \|l :l :l \|l :— :— ‖

36.

The pupils are now prepared to take up the following lessons. It will be observed that here is an abundance of exercises, but the teacher must not feel compelled to dwell upon *all* that are here given, he selects only such as his class may require. A bright, smart class may sing through all of these exercises to advantage, while a dull, slow class will positively need them.

Two-part Singing.—It is at first very difficult for pupils to sing independently one of another. The simplest form of two-part singing is that in which one divison of the class repeatedly strikes the same tone ("tolls the bell"), while another divison sings the tune as in exercise 37. Each part should be sung seperately by all the class before singing the two together. These early exercises are best suited for those classes in which the voices are all of the same sort, that is, all men's voices, or else all woman's or children's voices. If, however, the class is a mixed one, the ladies may take one part and the gentlemen the other, or, better still, half the gentlemen and half the ladies may sing each part. As soon as an exercise is sung, it should be sung over again, exchanging the parts.

The teacher will explain that Braces are used both at the beginning and ending of lines to show what parts of the music may be sung together.

The teacher may explain that music is naturally divided into short portions or *phrases*. Just before beginning a phrase is, *musically considered*, the best place to take breath. Where words are sung, the breath must be taken with reference to the sense of the words. More on this subject in the following steps. The dagger (†) shows where breath may be taken.

37. KEY D.

d :d	m :m	s :s	m :—	† d^1 :d^1	s :m	s :s	d :— ‖
d :d	d :d	d :d	d :—	d :d	d :d	d :d	d :— ‖

38. KEY D.

d :m	s :m	s :m	d^1 :—	† d^1 :s	m :s	s :m	d :— ‖
d :d	d :—	m :m	m :—	m :m	m :m	d :d	d :— ‖

39. KEY F.

d :—	m :—	s :s	m :—	† m :—	d :—	s :m	d :— ‖
d :d	d :d	m :m	d :—	d :d	m :d	s_1 :s_1	d :— ‖

40. KEY C.

d :d	m :m	s :s	d^1 :s	† d^1 :s	m :—	† m :s	d :— ‖
Great and	good is	God our	Fa - ther,	Great and	good,	great and	good.
Trees and	birds and	flow'rs de -	clare Him	Great and	good,	great and	good.
d :d	d :d	m :m	m :m	m :m	d :—	d :m	d :— ‖

41. KEY D. Round for four parts.

d^1 :s	m :d	m :s	d^1 :d^1	† * s :s	s :s	s :—	s :— †
Join in	sing - ing	Hal - le -	lu - jah!	Hal - le -	lu - jah!	A - -	men.

m :—	m :—	† m :m	m :m	d :m	s :m	d :—	d :— ‖
A - -	men,	Hal - le -	lu - jah!	Hal - le -	lu - jah!	A - -	men.

When the first division reaches the note under the asterisk (*) the second division strikes in at the beginning; the third division begins when the second has reached the asterisk, and so on

42. KEY D.

| d :d :d | m :m :m | d :m :s | d' :— :— | d' :d' :d' | s :s :s | d' :s :m | d :— :— ||
| d :d :d | d :— :— | m :m :m | m :— :— | m :m :m | m :— :— | m :m :m | d :— :— ||

43. KEY C.

| d :d :d | m :— :— | m :m :m | s :— :— | s :s :s | d' :d' :d' | s :s :s | d :— :— ||
| d :— :d | d :— :— | d :— :d | m :— :— | m :— :m | m :— :m | m :— :m | d :— :— ||

44. KEY G. Round in four parts.

:s_1	d :— :d	s_1 :— :s_1	m :— :m	d :— :m
Now	sing a -	loud, your	voic - - es	raise ! To

s :m :d	s :m :d	s_1 :— :s_1	d :—	
join in the	cho - rus of	grate - - - ful	praise.

Half-pulse Tones may now be taught, or if the teacher prefers, they may be transfered to the next step.

The following lesson may be written on the board,

|l :l |l :l |l :l |l :l ||

and after it is sung correctly the teacher may say:

I will sing the lesson and if I make a mistake you may say wrong.

He may sing it correctly the first time; with wrong accent the second, and the third time be sings two tones in the first pulse of the second measure at which the pupils will say "wrong."

Which measure was wrong?

Which pulse of that measure?

How many tones are indicated in that pulse?

How many did I sing?

Two tones sung in the time of one pulse are called Half-pulse Tones or Halves.

What are they called?

The time-name of the first half is TAA—of the second half TAI. What is the time-name of the first half? Second half?

The sign for an equally divided pulse is a dot in the middle, thus, | . :

The teacher changes the measures to obtain the following rhythms. They should be practiced carefully—from the teacher's patterns—to the time-names—to laa, etc.

The Finger Signs for time (TAA, TAATAI and TAA-AA) may be introduced here with good effect. These signs are generally given with the left hand, to distinguish them from the Hand Signs for Tune, which are chiefly given with the right. Of course the teacher may use his right hand if he finds it easier. The back of the hand is toward the pupils, and the thumb should not be seen, for we never divide a pulse into five equal parts. The time may be marked either by slight forward and backward movements of the hand, or by the right hand tapping the pulses on the top of the left or beating Time in the regular way close by.

The Time Chart also affords a most excellent means for drilling a class in time. It is to Time what the modulator is to Tune.

45.

TAA TAA	TAA - TAI TAA	TAA TAA	TAA -AA
l :l	l .l :l	l :l	l :— ||

46. KEY D.

TAA TAA	TAA - TAI TAA	TAA - TAI TAA - TAI	TAA -AA
l :l	l .l :l	l .l :l .l	l :— ||
d :m	s .s :m	s .s :m .m	d :— ||
d :s	m .s :d	m .d :s .m	d :— ||

47. KEY F.

TAA - TAI TAA	TAA - TAI TAA	TAA - TAI TAA - TAI	TAA - TAI TAA	
l .l :l	l .l :l	l .l :l .l	l .l :l	
s_1 .d :d	s_1 .d :d	s .m :s .m	d .d :d	

Taatai-ing in tune.—By "taataing" is meant singing an exercise (on one tone) to the time-names, just as "Sol-fa-ing" is singing to the Sol-fa syllables. "Taataing in tune" is singing the *tune* to the time-names. Mr. Curwen says, "*Laaing* on *one* tone helps to form that *abstract* idea of a rhythm which is desired. But such an idea is never truly established until the ear can recognize a rhythm as the *same*, though all the various *disguises* which different tune-forms put upon it. To learn the abstract you must recognize it in *many* concretes * * * As a help to this distinct conception of rhythm, it is useful to *taatai* each time-exercise on various tune-forms."

After the above time-exercises have been sung to the time-names and to laa, let them be sung to the *tunes* printed under each, and lastly let the tunes be sung to the time names.

Exercises 48 to 52 introduce half-pulse tones in two-pulse measure. Each exercise should be *taataid* on one tone to secure correct rhythm.

48. KEY D.

|d .m :m |d .m :m |s :s |m :— |m .s :s |m .s :s |d^1 :s |d^1 :— ||
|d :d |d :d |d .m :m |d :— |m :m |m :m |m .s :s |m :— ||

49. KEY C.

|d :d |m :d |s .s :m .s |d^1 :— |† d^1 .s :m .s |d^1 :m |s :s |d :— ||
|d :d .d |d :d .d |m .m :m .m |m † :m .m |m :m .m |d :d .d |m .m :s .s |d :— ||

50. KEY D.

|d .d :d .d |m .m :m .m |s .m :d .m |s :— |m .m :m .m |s .s :s .s |d^1 .s :m .s |d :— ||
|d .d :d .d |d .d :d .d |m .m :m .m |s :— |d .d :d .d |m .m :m .m |m .m :m .m |d :— ||

51. KEY G. Round in four parts. T. F. S.

|d .d :d .d |d .d :d .d |* m .m :m .m |m .m :m .m |
What a clat - ter! What's the mat - ter! John-ny's gone and spilt the bat - ter

|s .s :s .s |s :s_1 |s :s_1 |s :— ||
On my nice new clothes, oh, dear! oh, dear!

52. KEY G. Round in three parts.

|d :d |s_1 :s_1 |m :— |d :— |* m :m |d :d |s :— |m :— |
Roam-ing o - ver mead - ows, Sing - ing ev - er gai - - ly,

|s .s :s .s |s :s |s_1 .s_1 :s_1 .s_1 |s_1 :s_1 ||
Tra la la la la la Tra la la la la la.

Modulator Voluntaries.—At every lesson the teacher should drill the class in following his pointing on the Modulator, *without a pattern.* This exercise is called a *Voluntary.* The pupils must be taught to follow promptly, and to hold the tones as long as the pointer stays on a note. The teacher must be careful not to vary from the "Step" at which the class is engaged; that is, in the first step he must use only the tones d m s d' s, ; in the second step he may use the tones d m s t r and their replicates, but not f and l. The *Step Modulators* are recommended for the early work, as they prevent the teacher going out of the step in which the class is studying. The teacher must follow his own fancy in his voluntaries, taking care to adapt them to the capacity of his class, not to make them too difficult nor too easy, but progressive as his pupils gain facility. He should make them as beautiful and attractive as he can, introducing snatches of familiar tunes now and then; and above all things he must avoid falling into self-repeating habits, that is, constantly repeating favorite phrases which the pupils come to know by heart. The teacher is recommended to *practice* his voluntaries at home; write them down, if necessary, and commit them to memory. See the pamphlet, "Hints for Voluntaries."

The Time Chart is intended to be used for *time-voluntaries* in the same way that the Modulator is used for tune-voluntaries.

The Hand-Signs, in connection with mental effects, are to be used at every lesson. *The Finger-Signs for Time* are also considered very useful for exercises in time.

Mental Effects should be frequently reviewed, accompanied with fresh illustrations. It is only in this way the impression can be deepened. The perception of mental effect is at first very dim, but it is cumulative, and the more attention given to it the clearer and stronger it becomes. See pamphlet, "Studies in Mental Effects."

Ear Exercises.—At every lesson the teacher will exercise his class in naming the tones he sings. There are several ways in which this may be done. First way, teacher sings several tones to figures and requires the pupil to tell him to which figure or figures he sung s or m, etc. Thus, "Tell me to which figure I sing s"—

Sings d m m s d— or d d m d s m d— or m d s m, etc.
1 2 3 4 5 — 1 2 3 4 5 6 7 — 1 2 3 4

"Tell me to which figure I sing d"—

Sings s m s d m— or m s d m d s m. etc.
1 2 3 4 5 — 1 2 3 4 5 6 7

The same process is given to other tones. Another way, the teacher sings the tones to laa and the pupils make the manual sign for the tone required. Again, the teacher gives the key-tone and chord and after a slight pause sings to *laa, lo, loo, lai* or any vowel either d m s d' or s, and requires the pupils to tell him what tone he sung, thus:—

|d :— |s :m |d :— |s (loo) :— ||

Again, the teacher sings to laa and the pupils name or give the hand signs for all the tones. Again, the teacher sings two or three or four or more tones to laa, as, d m d s, etc., which the pupils repeat after him, first to laa, then to the Sol-fa syllables. When the pupils can do this quite readily they will then be required to simply give the names without singing the tones. The teacher may then sing to different vowels, as,

s m s d
lo lo lai laa

and the pupils give the names.

In *time* ear-exercises the teacher sings two, three or four measures on one tone to laa, and requires the pupils to tell him the length of the tones in each measure, or they may *Taatai* or write what the teacher sings. Again the teacher *sol-fas* a short exercise which the pupils *taatai in tune.* It is a great advantage when the answers to these ear-exercises can be *written* by the pupils and afterward examined by the teacher or his assistants. The answers should come from *all* the pupils, not merely from a few. See pamphlet, "Hints for Ear Exercises."

Writing Exercises.—Notation is best taught by writing, and the thing *noted* is more quickly and easily practiced when the notation is clear and familiar to the mind. Hence the value of the writing exercises. The teacher instructs his pupils to draw on slate or paper four (or eight or sixteen) measures in the primary (or secondary) form, thus:—

| : | : | : | : | etc., or : | : | : | : | ||

and then dictates the notes to be written in each pulse, or he may write them on the blackboard for the pupils to copy.

Dictation.—The time-names furnish a means of dictating, by very brief orders, *one pulse at a time,* "Accent," "Time," and "Tune" at once. The following example would be dictated thus: "Prepare four two-pulse measures, secondary form." "TAA *soh-one,*" "TAA *doh,*" "TAATAI *me doh,*" "TAA *soh-one,*" "TAA *doh,*" "TAATAI *me doh,*" "TAA *soh,*" "TAA *doh.*"

:s, |d :m .d |s, :d |m .d :s |d ||

Pointing from Memory.—At the close of each lesson the pupils should take pride in showing their teacher how many of the previous exercises they can point on the Modulator and Sol-fa from memory. Musical memory should be cultivated from the first, because it will greatly facilitate the progress of the pupil in future steps, and will be of constant service in after life. To encourage this exercise the pupils should be provided with small modulators upon which they can practice pointing at home. Where it is feasible the whole class should be supplied with "Hand Modulators" and point and sing together, holding their modulators in such way that the teacher can overlook all.

Writing from Memory.—Pupils should also be well practiced in writing tunes from memory. Even where it is difficult for a whole class to point on their modulators from memory at the same moment, so as to be seen by the teacher, it is not difficult to engage a whole class at the same moment in writing from memory the tunes they have learned. At the close of every lesson, one or two of the exercises should be chosen for the memory exercise of the next meeting. The pupil (at home) should copy that exercise six or ten times from the book, until he finds by testing himself that he can write it from memory.

Keep within the Step.—The teacher must fully understand that in all these exercises he must keep within the step at which the class is engaged. All the topics of the step should be mastered before the next step is entered. For instructions in *Voice Training,* Breathing, etc., belonging to this Step, the teacher will consult the Standard Course.

QUESTIONS FOR WRITTEN OR ORAL EXAMINATION.

DOCTRINE.

1. What are the first three tones you have learned thus far?
2. Which of these is the lowest tone? The next higher? The highest?
3. Which is the more important, the relative position of these tones or their mental effects?
4. What is the mental effect of *Doh*? Of *Me*? Of *Soh*?
5. How are these mental effects represented to the eye?
6. Besides the hand-signs and the modulator what other way have we of indicating or writing the tones?
7. What letter represents *Doh*? *Me*? *Soh*?
8. What is this method of musical notation called?
9. What other tones have you learned beside *Doh*, *me*, *soh*?
10. What is the mental effect of *one-doh*?
11. What is its hand-sign?
12. How is it indicated in the notation?
13. What is the mental effect of *soh-one*?
14. What is its hand-sign?
15. How is it indicated in the notation?
16. How is time in music measured?
17. How many kinds of accents have you learned?
18. What is the time from one strong accent to the next strong accent called?
19. What is the time from any accent to the next called?
20. Is there but one order of arrangment of accents or may there be different arrangements?
21. What do different arrangements of accents produce?
22. How many kinds of measure have you learned and what are they?
23. What is the order of accents in two-pulse measure? Three pulse measure?
24. When is a measure in its primary form? Secondary?
25. How is the strong accent indicated in the notation? The weak accent?
26. What represents the time of a pulse? Of a measure?
27. What is the time-name of a one-pulse tone?
28. How is the strong accent indicated in the time-names?
29. When a tone is continued from one pulse into the next, how is the continuation marked?
30. How are the time-names for continuations obtained?
31. When two tones are sung in the time of one pulse, what are they called?
32. What is the time-name of the first half of a pulse? The second?
33. How are half-pulse tones indicated in the notation?
34. How is the end of an exercise indicated?

PRACTICE.

35. Sing to *laa* the *Soh* to any *Doh* the teacher gives.
36. Sing in the same manner the *Soh-one*.
37. Sing in the same manner the *One-Doh*.
38. Sing in the same manner the *Me*.
39. Sing in the same manner *Soh* to any *One-Doh* the teacher gives.
40. Sing in the same manner the *Me*.
41. Sing in the same manner the *Doh*.
42. Taatai the upper part in one of the Exs. 48, 49, or 50.
43. Taatai in tune one of the Exs. 48, 49, or 50, but not the same as in the last requirement, chosen by the teacher.
44. Point on the modulator from memory any one of the Exs. 40, 41, 42, 44, chosen by the teacher.
45. Write from memory another of these exercises.
46. From any phrase (belonging to this step), sung to figures, tell your teacher, or write down which figure was sung to *Me*.
47. Ditto *Soh*.
48. Ditto *Doh*.
49. Ditto Soh_1.
50. Having heard the chord, tell or write down which tone was sung to *laa*
51. Follow the teacher's pointing on the modulator in a new voluntary, containing *Doh*, *Me*, *Soh*, Doh^1, and Soh_1, TAA, TAA-AA and TAATAI.
52. Write from dictation and afterwards sing a similar exercise.

This tune properly belongs in the Third Step but is inserted here on account of space.

53. KEY F. DENNIS. S. M. NAEGELI.

:m	m :d :m	r :t_1 :r	d : :d	d :l_1 :d	d :s_1 :d	t_1 :— :r
:d	d :s_1 :d	t_1 :s_1 :s_1	s_1 :— :s_1	l_1 :f_1 :l_1	s_1 :m_1 :s_1	s_1 :— :t_1
1. How	gen - - tle	God's com -	mands, How	kind His	pre - - cepts	are! Come,
2. Be -	neath His	watch - - ful	eye His	saints se -	cure - - ly	dwell; The
3. His	good - - ness	stands ap -	proved, Un -	changed from	day to	day; I'll
:s	s :m :s	s :r :f	m :— :m	f :d :f	m :d :m	r :— :s
:d	d :— :d	s_1 : :s_1	d :— :d	f_1 :— :f_1	d :— :d	s_1 :— :s_1

r :t_1 :r	d :m :s	s :r :f	m :s :l	s :m :f	m :d :r	d :— ‖
t_1 :s_1 :s_1	s_1 :d :d	t_1 :— :r	d :— :d	d :— :d	d :s_1 :s_1	s_1 :— ‖
cast your	bur - - dens	on the	Lord, And	trust His	con - - stant	care.
hand which	bears all	na - ture	up, Shall	guard His	chil - - dren	well.
drop my	bur - - den	at His	feet, And	bear a	song a -	way.
s :r :f	m :s :m	r :s :s	s :m :f	m :s :l	s :m :f	m :— ‖
s_1 :— :s_1	d :— :d	s_1 :— :s_1	d :— :d	d :— :f_1	s_1 :— :s_1	d :— ‖

SECOND STEP.

In addition to the tones **d, m, s, d'** *and* **s,** *to recognize and produce Ray and Te. To distinguish and produce the medium accent and the four-pulse and six-pulse measures. The whole-pulse silence, half-pulse tones in three-pulse measure, pulse-and-a-half tones and quarter-pulse tones in their simplest forms.*

To introduce *Ray* and *Te* the teacher may proceed somewhat as follows. After reviewing the tones already taught, and a short drill from the Modulator or hand-signs, he may say:—

Name the tones I sing and if I sing a different tone from those you have learned, one that is not **d, m,** or **s,** you may say *new tone.*

The teacher sings the tones to *laa,* pupils calling out "Doh," "Soh," and so on, and after keeping them a moment or two in expectation he sings *Ray* the second tone of the scale (of course, to *laa*), which the pupils at once detect as a new tone.

Is the new tone higher or lower than *Doh?*

Is it higher or lower than *Me?*

If the answers are not prompt and correct the exercise must be repeated.

The name of the new tone is *Ray.*

He writes it on the board or shows it on the Modulator.

As we have an upper *Doh* so also we can have an upper *Ray,* and there is also an upper *Me* and an upper *Soh.* They are called *one-Ray, one-Me* and *one-Soh.*

He writes them on the board or shows them on the modulator.

Name the tones again, and if I sing a tone you have not heard before, say *new tone.*

He sings the tones to laa as before, pupils calling out the names, and after a moment or two he sings *Te,* the seventh tone of the scale. He questions the class as to the position of the new tone, writes its name on the board or shows it on the modulator, and also its lower octave. See diagram. He then patterns and points on the modulator such exercises as these—

m'
r'
DOH'
TE
SOH
ME
RAY
DOH
t,
s,
m,

54. Key C.

{|d :m |s :—|s :t |r' :—|r' :t |s :d'|s :m |d :—||

55. Key F.

{|d :m |s :m |s, :t, |r :t, |s, :s |m :s |d :—||

56. Key A.

{|d :m |d :s, |t, :r |t, :s, |d :s, |m :s, |d :—||

57. Key F.

{|s :m |d :m |s :r |t, :r |s :m |s :s, |d :—||

58. Key D.

{|m :d |m :s |r :t, |r :s |m :s |r :s |d :—||

The teacher next brings up in review the mental effects of *doh, me* and *soh,* and then proceeds to develope the mental effects of *ray* and *te,* somewhat as follows:

Now give your attention to the mental effect of *ray* in the examples I shall sing, and notice first whether *ray* gives a feeling of rest, of satisfaction, or whether it is the reverse of that, is restless, expectant, unsatisfied.

Teacher sings in any key suited to his voice, the following exercises, making a slight pause before the last tone.

|d' :s |m :s |d' :r' |r' :— ||

All sing it.—

Are you satisfied to stop on that tone or do you expect something else?

Listen again.

Teacher sings.

|d' :s |m :s |d' :r' |m' :— ||

All sing the same.—

Is that as satisfactory as the former or more so?

Listen again.

Teacher sings.

|d' :s |m :s |m' :r' |r' :— ||

All sing it.—

Satisfactory or expectant?

Listen again.

Teacher sings.

|d' :s |m :s |m' :r' |d' :— ||

All sing it.—

Satisfactory or expectant?

You learn from these examples that *ray* is a restless, moving, expectant tone, that it leans upon *doh* or *me.* But listen again and notice whether it has a depressing, desponding, hopeless effect, or whether it is hopeful, rousing, animating.

Teacher sings the following which the pupils may repeat.

:s .d' |r' :d' .t |d' :s .d' |r' :m' .r' |d' ||

What is its effect, depressing and hopeless, or hopeful, rousing, animating?

It will be well to sing the exercise again, substituting *doh* for *ray*, thus,

:s .d' |d' :d' .t |d' :s .d' |d' :m'.d' |d' ||

and again with *ray* as at first; this will produce a contrast that will make *ray* stand our very clearly. The following examples will illustrate the mental effect of *te*. The teacher may use them in his own way, to show that *te* is a restless tone, with an intense longing for *doh*, an urgent, sharp, sensitive piercing effect.

|d :m |s :d' |t :— |d' :— ||

:d' |s :m |r :t |t :— |d' ||

In the following exercise m and s are substituted for t to produce a contrast.

:d' |s :m |r :m |m :— |d' ||

Sing it again with t and then as follows—

:d' |s :m |r :s |s :— |d' ||

and finally with t as above.

The manual sign for the rousing, hopeful tone is this —. All make it.—

The sign for the sensitive, piercing tone is this —, pointing up to *doh*, the tone to which it so strongly leans. All make it.—

The teacher now proceeds to drill the class thoroughly in the new tones by means of the modulator, hand-signs, ear-exercises, etc., during which practice he will have the tones d m s sung together as a chord.

This may be done by dividing the class into three sections, one section to sing *doh*, another *me*, and another *soh*. First let *doh* and *soh* be sung together, then *doh* and *me*; then *me* and *soh*, and then *doh*, *me* and *soh* all at once. The teacher will explain that when tones are combined in this way, the combination is called a chord. This particular chord, formed of the tones of d m s is called the chord of DOH, or Tonic Chord. The chord of DOH may be taught in the first step, if the teacher prefers. The tones s t r' should next be combined in the same way. They form the chord of SOH, or Dominant Chord. The class is now prepared to take up the study of the following exercises:

59. KEY F. Round for three parts.

|d :d |m :r |d :t, |d :— |m :m |s :s
After labor we shall find, Music will re-

|m :r |m :— |s :m |d :t, |d :s, |d :— ||
lieve the mind, And our hearts to-geth-er bind.

60. KEY G. Round for four parts.

|s, :s, |d :d |s, :s, |d :d |r :— |m :— |r :— |m :—
Scotland's burn-ing, Scot-land's burn-ing; Look out, Look out;

|s :— |s :— |s :— |s :— |t, :r |d :d |t, :r |d :d ||
Fire! Fire! Fire! Fire! Pour on wa-ter, pour on wa-ter.

61. KEY D. Round for three parts. A. L. C.

|d :t, |d :— |r :r |m :— |m :r |m :d
"Here I go, sure and slow," Says the tur-tle

|d :t, |d :— |s .s :s |s .d' :m |s .s :s .s |d' :— ||
down be-low. "Not so I, swiftly fly," Sings the bird on high.

62. KEY C. Round for four parts. T. F. S.

|s .s :m |s .s :r |m .m :d |r .s :s .s
Hur-ry now, hur-ry now, Come a-long, Won't you hur-ry?

|d' :— |t :— |d' :s |s :— ||
No, no; Wait a while.

Tuning Exercises are designed for the purpose of teaching voices singing different parts *to study one another*, and to chord well together. To some extent this is done in every exercise, but it requires also separate study. The teacher, in these exercises endeavors to secure from the class a uniformly clear, *soft* tone—making a signal to any one whose voice is so prominent as to stand out from the rest,—and to maintain the perfect *tuning into each other* of all the parts of the chord. For some time the accord of the voices will be very rough and imperfect, but *soft singing* and listening will amend the fault. The exercises may be sung from the book, but a better plan is to sing them from the blackboard, as in this way a correct position of the pupil is secured, and the teacher can readily call the attention of all, in a moment, to any point in the exercise. Ex. 63 may be sung as follows—By three sections of women's voices, one section singing the first part, another the second and another the third. When moderately well done, the parts should be exchanged, those who sang the first part taking the second, the second taking the third and the third the first. At the next change the same process is repeated. The exercise may then be sung in the same manner by three sections of men's voices. Boys whose voices have not changed will sing with the women. Again, let all the men sing the third part, and two sections of women take the first and second; again, all the women sing the first part, and the men in two sections taking the second and third. Again, all the women sing the second part, and the men in two sections the first and third.

To be sung first to the sol-fa syllables, then to *laa* and to *loo*.

TUNING EXERCISES.

63. Keys F and G.

1st.	d :—	m :—	s :s	m :—	s :—	— :—	m :s	s :—
2d.	d :—	m :—	m :m	d :—	s :—	m :—	d :m	m :—
3d.	d :—	— :—	d :d	d :—	s :—	m :—	d :s_1	d :—

For the following exercises in four parts the class should be divided into four sections, two sections of ladies taking the two upper parts and two sections of gentlemen taking the two lower parts. This division of the voices must not be considered as a final classification into Soprano, Contralto, Tenor and Base. That will come later in the course. The top line is the Soprano (marked S), the next lower is the Contralto (C); the next below the Contralto is Tenor (T), and the lowest is the Base (B).

64. Key C.

Sing first as written. Second time, Soprano and Tenor change parts. Third time, Soprano and Contralto change parts, Contralto singing d t_1 d instead of d' t d'.

S.	d :—	s :m	d :—	m :—	s :—	d' :—	d' :t	d' :—
C.	d :—	s :m	d :—	m :—	— :—	— :—	m :r	m :—
T.	d :—	s :m	d :—	m :—	s :—	— :—	s :s	s :—
B.	d :—	s :m	d :—	— :—	— :—	— :—	s :s	d :—

65. Key F.

First as written. Second time, Soprano take Tenor, Tenor take Contralto, singing s instead of s_1, Contralto take Soprano. Third time, Soprano and Contralto change parts. Soprano singing s instead of s_1.

d :—	s_1 :m	d :—	m :—	s_1 :—	d :—	d :t_1	d :—
d :—	s_1 :m	d :—	m :—	s_1 :—	— :—	s_1 :s_1	s_1 :—
d :—	s_1 :m	d :—	m :—	— :—	— :—	m :r	m :—
d :—	s_1 :m	d :—	— :—	— :—	— :—	s_1 :s_1	d :—

66. Key C.

First as written. Second time, Soprano and Tenor change parts. Third time, Soprano take Contralto—Contralto take Tenor, singing t_1 instead of t—Tenor take Soprano.

d :—	m :d	s :—	:	:	s :—	s :s	s :—
d :—	m :d	s :—	:	r :—	— :—	m :r	m :—
d :—	m :d	s :—	t :—	— :—	— :—	d' :t	d' :—
d :—	m :d	s :—	— :—	— :—	— :—	s :s	d :—

67. Key F.

First as written. Second time, Soprano take Tenor—Tenor take Contralto, singing s instead of s_1, Contralto take Soprano. Third time Soprano and Contralto change parts, Soprano singing s instead of s_1.

d :—	m :d	s_1 :—	t_1 :—	— :—	— :—	d :t_1	d :—
d :—	m :d	s_1 :—	:	:	s_1 :—	s_1 :s_1	s_1 :—
d :—	m :d	s_1 :—	:	r :—	— :—	m :r	m :—
d :—	m :d	s_1 :—	— :—	— :—	— :—	s_1 :s_1	d :—

Breathing Places.—It was taught in the first step that the best places to take breath, *musically considered*, are at the beginning of the musical phrases. But the sense of the words is of more importance than musical phrasing. It frequently happens that the phrasing of the words and phrasing of the music do not agree. In such cases breath must be taken where it will not destroy the sense of the words. In the following example the musical phrasing would allow a breath to be taken at the dagger (†), and this would suit the first verse; but it would not do for the second verse; and the breathing places neither of the first nor second verses would answer for the third.

KEY G.

d	:s_1 .s_1	d	:–	.d †	r	:t_1	d	:—
1. Light	of the	world,		O	Sav -	iour	dear!	
2. Son	of the	Fa	-	ther	Lord	most	high.	
3. Je -	sus is	from		the	proud	con -	cealed.	

To take breath before a strong pulse the time of the breath must be taken from the end of the previous weak pulse; to take breath before a weak pulse the time of it may be taken from the beginning of the same pulse. It is not only convenient but necessary to take breath before all long sustained tones or long connected phrases.

It is recommended that before singing the words of a tune they should be studied separately. The teacher may read the portion of words from one breathing place to another, which the pupils are to repeat after him and mark the breathing place with pencil. In this exercise particular attention should be given to pronunciation; the vowels should be clear and pure and the consonants sharp and distinct.

Expression is such a use of *loudness* and *softness* in singing as tends to make the music more expressive. Even in the earliest steps, pupils enjoy thus embellishing their music. Here it is enough to draw attention occasionally to what is indeed the chief part of expression—that which is suggested by the words. First there must be fixed the *medium* or normal degree of force proper to the *general sentiment* of the piece,—then whatever words are printed in the common type are to be sung with that appropriate medium force, whatever words are printed in SMALL CAPITALS are to be sung louder, and whatever words are printed in *italics* are to be sung more *softly*. Many of the pieces in this book are left to be marked by the pupils under the direction of the teacher. A single line drawn under the words by pen or pencil will indicate italics, and a double line small capitals.

SWELL THE ANTHEM.

68. KEY G.

SOPRANO.	d	:d	d	:s_1	d	:m	s	:—	s	:s	s	:m	r	:d	t_1	:—
CONTRALTO.	s_1	:s_1	s_1	:m_1	s_1	:d	t_1	:—	t_1	:t_1	d	:d	t_1	:d	s_1	:—
	1. Swell	the	an -	them,	raise	the	song;		Prais -	es	to	our	God	be -	long;	
	2. Hark!	the	voice	of	na -	ture	sings,		Prais -	es	to	the	King	of	kings;	
TENOR.	m	:m	m	:d	s	:m	r	:—	r	:r	m	:s	s	:m	r	:—
BASE.	d	:d	d	:d	m	:d	s_1	:—	s_1	:s_1	d	:d	s_1	:s_1	s_1	:—

d	:d	d	:s_1	d	:m	s	.—	s	:s	s.	:m	r	:r	d	:—
s_1	:s_1	s_1	:m_1	s_1	:d	t_1	:—	t_1	:t_1	d	:d	d	:t_1	d	:—
Saints	and	an -	gels	join	to	sing,		Prais -	es	to	the	heav'n -	ly	King.	
Let	us	join	the	cho -	ral	song,		And	the	grate -	ful	tones	pro -	long.	
m	:m	m	:d	s	:m	r	:—	r	:r	m	:s	s	:s	m	:—
d	:d	d	:d	m	:d	s_1	:—	s_1	:s_1	d	:d	s_1	:s_1	d	:—

ff 69. KEY F.

				f				*m*				*p*			
s	:s	s	:m	d	:m	s	:—	d	:m	s	:—	d	:m	s	:—
TRY	THE	ECH -	OES	AS	WE	GO,		as	we	go,		*as*	*we*	*go,*	
f				*m*				*p*				*pp*			
m	:m	m	:r	d	:r	m	:—	d	:r	m	:—	d	:r	m	:—
HEAR	THEM	AN -	SWER	soft	and	low,		*Soft*	*and*	*low,*		*soft*	*and*	*low.*	

The Slur is a horizontal line drawn under two or more notes and shows that one syllable of the words is to be sung to as many notes as are thus connected.

CHEERFUL LABOR.

70. Key D.

d :m :s	d' :— :s	s :t :r'	d' :— :—	d' :s :d'	d' :s :m
d :d :m	m :— :s	s :r :r	m :— :—	m :m :m	m :m :d
1. Let us, dear	broth - - ers,	Cheer-ful - ly	toil;	Nev - er from	la - bor, No,
2. Rich is the	treas - - ure	Now to be	won;	Toil in full	meas-ure Till
m :s :d'	s :— :d'	t :r' :t	d' :— :—	s :d' :s	s :d' :s
d :d :d	d :— :m	s :s :s	d :— :—	d :d :d	d :d :d

s :r :m	d :m :s	d' :s :d'	d' :s :m	s :r :m	d :— :—
t, :t, :t,	d :— :—	m :m :m	m :m :d	t, :t, :t,	d :— :—
nev - er re -	coil, ...	Nev - er from	la - bor, No.	nev - er re -	coil.
time shall be	done.	Toil in full	meas - ure Till	time shall be	done.
s :s :s	m :— :—	s :d' :s	s :d' :s	s :s :s	m :— :—
s, :s, :s,	d :— :—	d :d :d	d :d :d	s, :s, :s,	d :— :—

LONGINGS.

71. Key E♭. B. C. U.

m .m :d .m	s :m	r .r :d .r	m :—	m .m :d .m
d .d :d .d	d :d	t, .t, :d .t,	d :—	d .d :d .d
1. Pur-er yet and	pur - - er	I would be in	mind,	Dear-er yet and
2. *Calmer yet and*	*calm - - er*	*Tri - al bear, and*	*pain,*	*Sur - er yet and*
3. Quicker yet and	quick - er	Ev - er on - ward	press,	Firm-er yet and
s .s :m .d	m :s	s .s :m .s	s :—	s .s :m .d
d .d :d .d	d :d	s, .s, :s, .s,	d :—	d .d :d .d

s :m	r .r :m .r	d :—	r .r :t, .r	s :r
d :d	t, .t, :t, .t,	d :—	t, .t, :s, .t,	t, :t,
dear - - er	Ev - 'ry du - ty	find;	Hop - ing still and	trust - - ing
sur - - er	*Peace at last to*	*gain;*	*Suff - 'ring still and*	*do - - - ing*
firm - - er	Step as I pro-	gress;	Oft these earn - est	long - - ings,
m :s	s .s :s .s	m :—	s .s :r .r	r :s
d :d	s, .s, :s, .s,	d :—	s, .s, :s, .s,	s, :s,

m .m :d .m	s :—	r .r :t, .r	s :r	m .m :r .r	d :—
d .d :d .d	t, :—	t, .t, :s, .t,	t, :t,	d .d :t, .t,	d :—
God with-out a	fear,	Pa - tient-ly be -	liev - - ing	He will make all	clear.
To his will re -	*signed,*	*And to God sub-*	*du - - ing*	*Heart, and will, and*	*mind.*
Swell within my	breast,	Yet their in - ner	mean - ing	Ne'er can be ex -	pressed.
s .s :m .d	r :—	s .s :r .r	r :s	s .s :s .s	m :—
d .d :d .d	s, :—	s, .s, :s, .s,	s, :s,	d .d :s, .s,	d :—

The Medium Accent should now be explained. One or more of the following tunes may be sung by the teacher (to *laa*), first in two-pulse measure with every other accent strong and heavy, and then in four-pulse measure by changing every alternate strong accent into a medium. It may be well to let the pupils imitate the teacher's examples.

```
:s, |d  :d  |m  :m |r  :d  |r  :m  |r  :d  |m  :r  |d  ||
|d  :d  |r  :r  |m :m |r  :r  |m :s |f  :m |r  :r |d  :— ||
|m  :s  |f  :s  |m :s  |r  :s  |m :s  |f  :r  |d  :t, |d  :— ||
```

Also the following, first in three-pulse measure, as written, and then in six-pulse measure by changing every alternate strong accent into a medium.

```
|m :— :m |m :— :d |r :— :r |r :— :— |m :— :m |s :— :f |
|m :— :— |r :— :— |d :— :— ||     or     |s, :s, :s, |s, :s, :s, |
|s, :d :r |m :— :— |r :r :r |r :r :d |m :m :r |d :— :— ||
```

Also the following time-exercises may be written on the blackboard and sung first as written, and then with every other strong accent made medium.

```
TWO-PULSE MEASURE.
FOUR-PULSE MEASURE.     |1     :1     |1     :1     |1     :1     |1     :1     ||

THREE-PULSE MEASURE.
SIX-PULSE MEASURE.      |1   :1   :1   |1   :1   :1   |1   :1   :1   |1   :1   :1   ||
```

When the pupils have distinguished the medium accent and can produce it, the teacher will explain that the medium accent changes two two-pulse measures into a four-pulse measure, and two three-pulse measures into a six-pulse measure. In four-pulse measure the accents are arranged in the order **strong**, *weak*, MEDIUM, *weak* (as in the words "**mo**-*men*-TA-*ry*," "**plan**-*e*-TA-*ry*"). In six-pulse measure the accents are arranged in the order **strong**, *weak*, *weak*, MEDIUM, *weak*, *weak* (as in the words "**spir**-*it*-*u*-AL-*i*-*ty*," "**im**-*mu*-*ta*-BIL-*i*-*ty*"). The medium accent is indicated in the notation by a short, thin bar. In the time-names the medium accent is indicated, when necessary (as in dictation exercises), by the letter L, thus, TLAA, TLAATAI, etc. In Taataing, the L is not useful. The teacher must not expect too great a nicety of distinction at first. The finer points both of time and tune require much practice.

The following time-exercises may now be practiced from the teacher's pattern, first with the time-names and then to *laa*.

It will be well in exercises 72 and 74 to sing each measure four times, as a separate exercise, before singing the four measures continuously. In exercises 73 and 75 the portions marked off by the dagger (†) should be treated in the same way. Additional time-exercises are obtained by Taataing the rounds and tunes on one tone.

72.

```
|1   :1    |1   :1    |1   :—    |1   :1    |1   :—    |1   :—    |1   :—    |—   :—    ||
 TAA  TAA   TAA  TAA   TAA - AA   TAA  TAA   TAA - AA   TAA - AA   TAA - AA  - AA - AA
```

73.

```
                                                     †
:1   |1   :—    |1   :1    |1   :—    |—   :1    |1   :1    |1   :1    |1   :—    |—    ||
TAA   TAA - AA   TAA  TAA   TAA - AA  - AA  TAA   TAA  TAA   TAA  TAA   TAA - AA- AA
```

74. First slowly, beating six times to the measure, then quickly, beating twice.

```
|1   :1   :1   |1   :1   :1   |1   :—   :—   |1   :—   :—   |1   :1   :1   |1   :—   :1   |1   :—   :—   |—   :—   :—   ||
 TAA  TAA  TAA  TAA  TAA  TAA  TAA - AA - AA  TAA - AA - AA  TAA  TAA  TAA  TAA - AA  TAA  TAA - AA - AA - AA - AA - AA
```

75.

```
                                                            †
:1   |1   :—   :1   |1   :1   :1   |1   :—   :—   |1   :—   :1   |1   :1   :1   |1   :—   :1   |1   :—   :—   |—   :—   ||
TAA   TAA - AA  TAA  TAA  TAA  TAA  TAA - AA - AA  TAA - AA  TAA  TAA  TAA  TAA  TAA - AA  TAA  TAA - AA - AA - AA - AA
```

76. KEY E♭. Round in four parts.

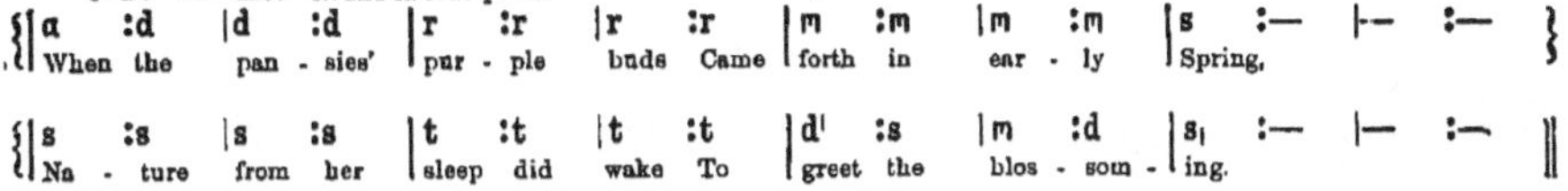

d :d	d :d	r :r	r :r	m :m	m :m	s :—	— :—
When the	pan - sies'	pur - ple	buds Came	forth in	ear - ly	Spring,	
s :s	s :s	t :t	t :t	d' :s	m :d	s, :—	— :— ‖
Na - ture	from her	sleep did	wake To	greet the	blos - som -	ing.	

77. KEY F. Round in four parts.

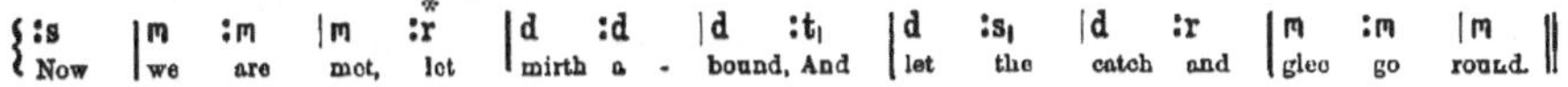

:s	m :m	m :r	d :d	d :t,	d :s,	d :r	m :m	m ‖
Now	we are	met, let	mirth a -	bound, And	let the	catch and	glee go	round.

78. KEY C. Round in four parts.

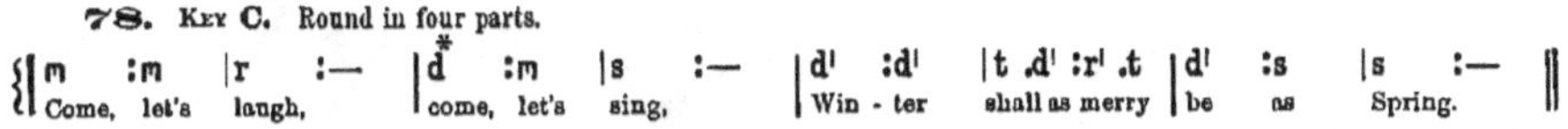

m :m	r :—	d :m	s :—	d' :d'	t .d' :r' .t	d' :s	s :— ‖
Come, let's	laugh,	come, let's	sing,	Win - ter	shall as merry	be as	Spring.

79. KEY G. Round in four parts.

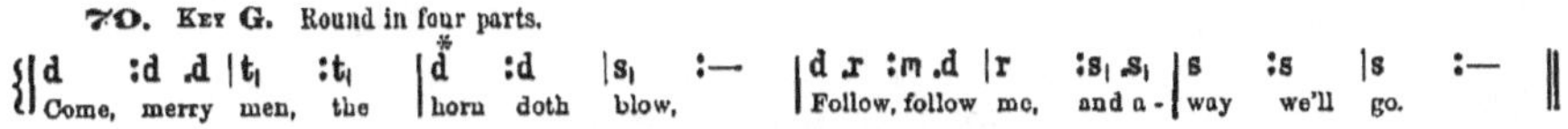

d :d .d	t, :t,	d :d	s, :—	d .r :m .d	r :s, .s,	s :s	s :— ‖
Come, merry	men, the	horn doth	blow,	Follow, follow	me, and a -	way we'll	go.

HAPPY HOME.

80. KEY C. B. C. U.

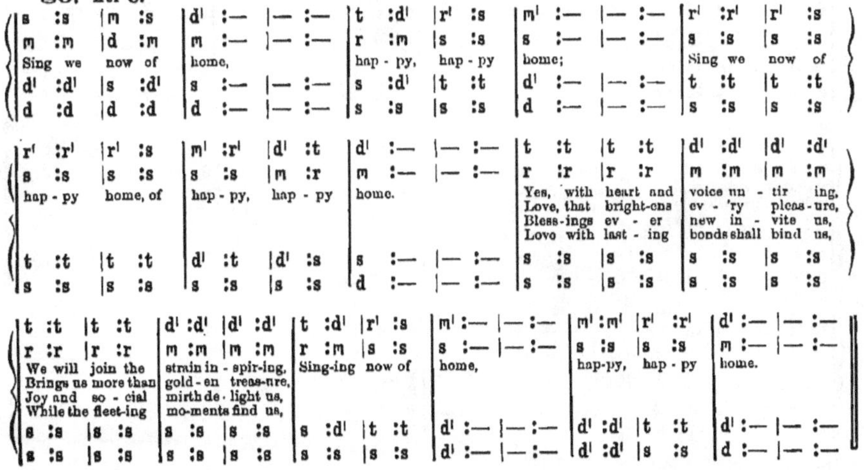

s :s	m :s	d' :—	— :—	t :d'	r' :s	m' :—	— :—	r' :r'	r' :s
m :m	d :m	m :—	— :—	r :m	s :s	s :—	— :—	s :s	s :s
Sing we	now of	home,		hap - py,	hap - py	home;		Sing we	now of
d' :d'	s :d'	s :—	— :—	s :d'	t :t	d' :—	— :—	t :t	t :t
d :d	d :d	d :—	— :—	s :s	s :s	d :—	— :—	s :s	s :s

r' :r'	r' :s	m' :r'	d' :t	d' :—	— :—	t :t	t :t	d' :d'	d' :d'
s :s	s :s	s :s	m :r	m :—	— :—	r :r	r :r	m :m	m :m
hap - py	home, of	hap - py,	hap - py	home.		Yes, with Love, that Bless-ings Love with	heart and bright-ens ev - er last - ing	voice un - ev - 'ry new in - bonds shall	tir ing, pleas - ure, vite us, bind us,
t :t	t :t	d' :t	d' :s	s :—	— :—	s :s	s :s	s :s	s :s
s :s	s :s	s :s	s :s	d :—	— :—	s :s	s :s	s :s	s :s

t :t	t :t	d' :d'	d' :d'	t :d'	r' :s	m' :—	— :—	m' :m'	r' :r'	d' :—	— :— ‖
r :r	r :r	m :m	m :m	r :m	s :s	s :—	— :—	s :s	s :s	m :—	— :—
We will Brings us Joy and While the	join the more than so - cial fleet-ing	strain in - gold - en mirth de - mo-ments	spir-ing, treas-ure, light us, find us,	Sing-ing	now of	home,		hap-py,	hap - py	home.	
s :s	s :s	s :s	s :s	s :d'	t :t	d' :—	— :—	d' :d'	t :t	d' :—	— :—
s :s	s :s	s :s	s :s	s :s	s :s	d' :—	— :—	d' :d'	s :s	d :—	— :—

81. Key C. Round in two parts.

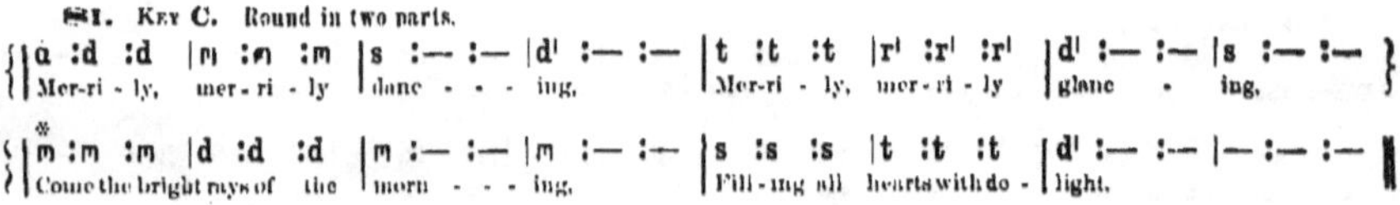

d :d :d | m :m :m | s :— :— | d' :— :— | t :t :t | r' :r' :r' | d' :— :— | s :— :—
Mer-ri-ly, mer-ri-ly dance - - - ing, Mer-ri-ly, mer-ri-ly glanc - ing.

m :m :m | d :d :d | m :— :— | m :— :— | s :s :s | t :t :t | d' :— :— | — :— :—
Come the bright rays of the morn - - - ing, Fill-ing all hearts with de - light.

82. Key G. Round in two parts.

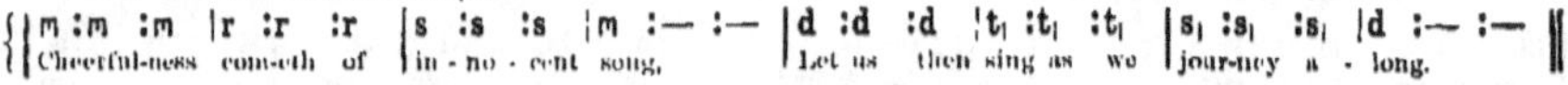

m :m :m | r :r :r | s :s :s | m :— :— | d :d :d | t_1 :t_1 :t_1 | s_1 :s_1 :s_1 | d :— :—
Cheerful-ness com-eth of in - no - cent song, Let us then sing as we jour-ney a - long.

83. Key D. Round in four parts.

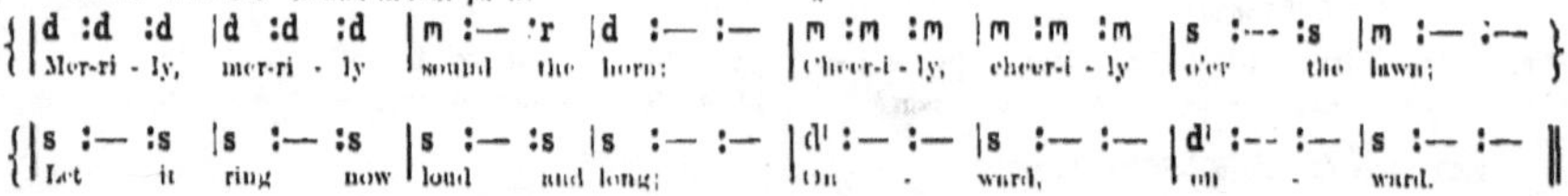

d :d :d | d :d :d | m :— :r | d :— :— | m :m :m | m :m :m | s :— :s | m :— :—
Mer-ri-ly, mer-ri-ly sound the horn; Cheer-i-ly, cheer-i-ly o'er the lawn;

s :— :s | s :— :s | s :— :s | s :— :— | d' :— :— | s :— :— | d' :— :— | s :— :—
Let it ring now loud and long; On - ward, on - ward.

BOUNDING SO MERRILY ONWARD.

84. Key G. Arr. from H. R. Palmer.

m :m :m | m :m :m | s :— :— | m :— :— | r :r :r | r :d :r | m :— :— | — :— :—
d :d :d | d :d :d | d :— :— | d :— :— | t_1 :t_1 :t_1 | t_1 :d :t_1 | d :— :— | — :— :—
1. Bound-ing so mer-ri-ly on - - ward, Happy, light-heart-ed and free;
2. Pleasure comes not for to - mor - - row, Let us en - joy it to - day;
s :s :s | s :s :s | m :— :— | s :— :— | s :s :s | s :m :s | s :— :— | — :— :—
d :d :d | d :d :d | d :— :— | d :— :— | s_1 :s_1 :s_1 | s_1 :s_1 :s_1 | d :— :— | — :— :—

𝄋 FINE.

m :m :m | m :m :m | s :— :— | m :— :— | r :r :r | r :m :r | d :— :— | — :— :—
d :d :d | d :d :d | d :— :— | d :— :— | t_1 :t_1 :t_1 | t_1 :t_1 :t_1 | d :— :— | — :— :—
Roaming thro' woodland and mead - ow, Glad mer-ry hunters are we;
D. S. While thro' each rocky sur - round - ing, Ech-o our notes will pro - long.
Fling to the winds ev - 'ry sor - row, While thro' the woodlands we stray;
D. S. Na-ture pre-pares a col - la - tion, None but her lov - ers can know.
s :s :s | s :s :s | m :— :— | s :— :— | s :s :s | s :s :s | m :— :— | — :— :—
d :d :d | d :d :d | d :— :— | d :— :— | s_1 :s_1 :s_1 | s_1 :s_1 :s_1 | d :— :— | — :— :—

D. S.

t_1 :t_1 :t_1 | d :d :d | r :— :— | s_1 :— :— | d :d :d | r :r :r | m :— :— | — :— :—
s_1 :s_1 :s_1 | m_1 :m_1 :m_1 | s_1 :— :— | s_1 :— :— | s_1 :s_1 :s_1 | s_1 :s_1 :s_1 | s_1 :— :— | — :— :—
O - ver the val - ley re - sound - ing, Fling we our glad hap - py song,
Joy comes with each in - spir - a - - tion, Paint-ing the cheeks with a glow;
r :r :r | d :d :d | t_1 :— :— | t_1 :— :— | d :d :d | t_1 :t_1 :t_1 | d :— :— | — :— :—
s_1 :s_1 :s_1 | s_1 :s_1 :s_1 | s_1 :— :— | s_1 :— :— | m_1 :m_1 :m_1 | s_1 :s_1 :s_1 | d :— :— | — :— :—

Silent Pulse.—The following exercises include the practice of the one-pulse silence. The teacher may explain this in his own way. A very good way is th a which two-pulse tones, and half-pulse tones were taught in the first step—that is, by singing a simple time-exercise and making a mistake, passing over a pulse in silence, the pupils calling out, *wrong*, etc. The time-name of a silent pulse is *SAA*, and to further distinguish the silence names they are printed in *italics*. In taataing, the silent pulses are to be passed in a whisper—that is, the time-name *SAA* is to be whispered. Some teachers prefer the name [TAA] placed in brackets or printed in italics, *Taa*, and sung in a whisper. The teacher must not allow the pupils to exaggerate the hissing sound of the S. The silent pulses may at first be passed in a whisper, but they should finally be done in absolute silence, the pupils being told to close the lips firmly and *think* the name. The following exercises should be Taataied and *laa-ed* on one tone and then taataid in tune:

85. KEY D.

TAA :TAA	TAA :*SAA*	TAA :TAA	TAA :*SAA*	TAA :*SAA*	TAA :*SAA*	TAA :TAA	TAA :*SAA*
d :d	d :	m :m	m :	s :	s :	m :s	d' :
Now we	sing,	now we	rest;	Sing,	rest,	do your	best.

86. KEY A.

d :	s, :	d :s,	d :	d :d	t, :t,	d :t,	d :
March,	march,	march a -	long,	Brave - ly	for - ward	all day	long.

87. KEY F.

d :d	*SAA* :*SAA*	m :m	:	s :	m :	:s, .s,	d :
On - ward,		Up - ward,		March,	march,	forward	march.

88. KEY G. Round in four parts. U.

d :	s, :	d :s,	d :	d :d	t, :t,	d :t,	d :
March,	march,	march a -	way,	Who are	read - y	for the	fray;
m :m	r :r	m :r	m :	s :s	s :s	s, :s,	:s
Fal - ter	not for	foe - man's	ire,	Now make	read - y,	aim and	shoot.

89. KEY C. Round in two parts. T. F. S.

s :d' :	s :d' :	t :t :t	d' :— :	s :m :d	s :m :d	r :r :r	m :— :
Cuc-koo	cuc-koo,	list to the	song;	Sweetly it	floats o'er the	meadows a -	long.

90. KEY C.

f :d' | t : | *m* :t | d' : | *p* :d' | t : | *pp* :t | d' : | :
Who's THERE? I'm sure I heard a sound;

: | *m* :s | s : | *p* :d | d : | *pp* :s | s : | *f* :d | m :s
Don't speak, keep still, hush, hush, O YES, 'TIS

f :d' | d' : | :d' | d' : | :d' | r' :t | d' :— | —
AH YES, who sing this lit - tle song.

d' : | :d' | s : | :s | m :m | r :s | d :— | —
WE who sing, who sing this lit - tle song.

SWEET EVENING HOUR.

91. KEY F. *p* *m* *p* A. L. COWLES.

|m :— |d :m |r :— |— : |s :— |r :s |m :— |— : |d :d |d :d

|d :— |s_1 :d |t_1 :— |— : |t_1 :— |s_1 :t_1 |d :— |— : |d :d |d :d

1.Sweet even - ing hour, Sweet even - ing hour, Sun - set's gold - en

2.Calm even - ing hour, Calm even - ing hour, Shades of night are

|s :— |m :s |s :— |— : |r :— |s :s |s :— |— : |m :m |m :m

|d :— |d :d |s_1 :— |— : |s_1 :— |s_1 :s_1 |d :— |— : | : | :

m

|r :— |r :— |m :— |d :m |r :— |— :s |m :r |d : | : | :d

|t_1 :— |t_1 :— |d :— |s_1 :d |t_1 :— |— : | : | :m |r :d |t_1 :d

glo - - ry Fades in the west, And now once more his la - bor o'er, The

steal - - ing O'er vale and hill, The flow - ers close, the birds re - pose, All

|s :— |s :— |s :— |m :s |s :— |— : | : | : | : | :m

| : | : |d :— |d :d |s_1 :— |— : | : | : | : | :d

p

|m :— |m :r |d :— |— : |s :— |r :s |m :— |— : |r :— |m :r |d :— |— : ||

|d :— |d :t_1 |d :— |— : |t_1 :— |t_1 :t_1 |d :— |— : |t_1 :— |t_1 :t_1 |d :— |— : ||

toi - - ler may rest. Sweet evening hour, Sweet evening hour.

na - - ture is still. Calm evening hour, Calm evening hour.

|s :— |s :s |m :— |— : | : | : | : | : |s :— |s :s |m :— |— : ||

|d :— |s_1 :s_1 |d :— |— : | : | : |d :— |m :d |s_1 :— |s_1 :s_1 |d :— |— : ||

Sweet evening,

Calm evening,

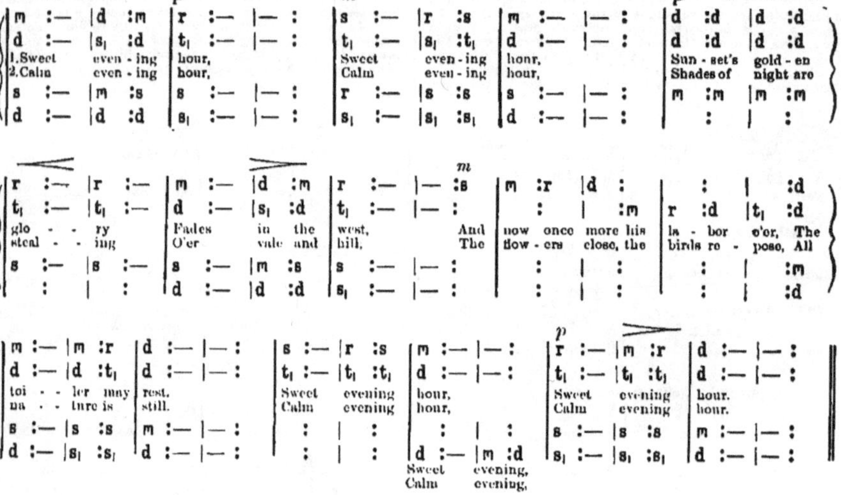

OVER THE SNOW.

92. KEY E. R. S. TAYLOR.

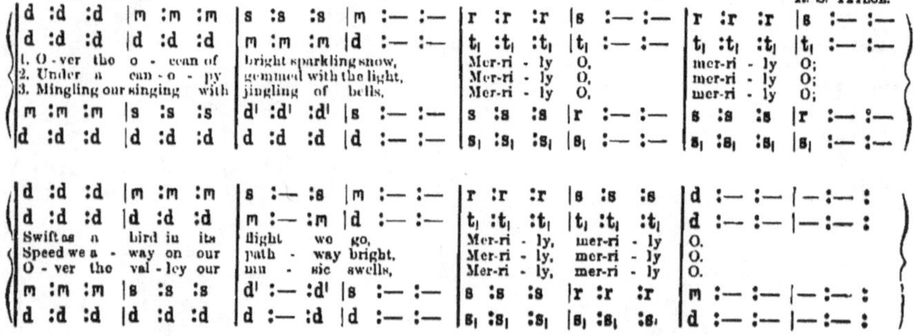

|d :d :d |m :m :m |s :s :s |m :— :— |r :r :r |s :— :— |r :r :r |s :— :—

|d :d :d |d :d :d |m :m :m |d :— :— |t_1 :t_1 :t_1 |t_1 :— :— |t_1 :t_1 :t_1 |t_1 :— :—

1. O - ver the o - cean of bright sparkling snow, Mer-ri - ly O, mer-ri - ly O;

2. Under a can - o - py gemmed with the light, Mer-ri - ly O, mer-ri - ly O;

3. Mingling our singing with jingling of bells, Mer-ri - ly O, mer-ri - ly O;

|m :m :m |s :s :s |d^1 :d^1 :d^1 |s :— :— |s :s :s |r :— :— |s :s :s |r :— :—

|d :d :d |d :d :d |d :d :d |d :— :— |s_1 :s_1 :s_1 |s_1 :— :— |s_1 :s_1 :s_1 |s_1 :— :—

|d :d :d |m :m :m |s :— :s |m :— :— |r :r :r |s :s :s |d :— :— |— :— :

|d :d :d |d :d :d |m :— :m |d :— :— |t_1 :t_1 :t_1 |t_1 :t_1 :t_1 |d :— :— |— :— :

Swift as a bird in its flight we go, Mer-ri - ly, mer-ri - ly O.

Speed we a - way on our path - way bright, Mer-ri - ly, mer-ri - ly O.

O - ver the val - ley our mu - sic swells, Mer-ri - ly, mer-ri - ly O.

|m :m :m |s :s :s |d^1 :— :d^1 |s :— :— |s :s :s |r :r :r |m :— :— |— :— :

|d :d :d |d :d :d |d :— :d |d :— :— |s_1 :s_1 :s_1 |s_1 :s_1 :s_1 |d :— :— |— :— :

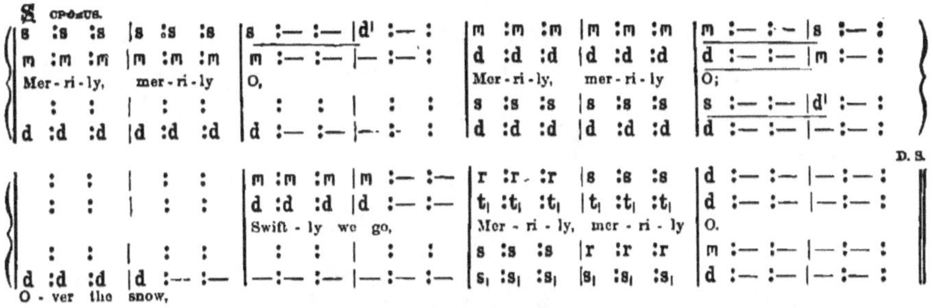

𝄋 CHORUS.

s :s :s	s :s :s	s :— :—	d' :— :	m :m :m	m :m :m	m :— :—	s :— :
m :m :m	m :m :m	m :— :—	— :— :	d :d :d	d :d :d	d :— :—	m :— :
Mer - ri - ly, mer - ri - ly	O,			Mer - ri - ly, mer - ri - ly	O;		
: :	: :	: :	: :	s :s :s	s :s :s	s :— :—	d' :— :
d :d :d	d :d :d	d :— :—	— :— :	d :d :d	d :d :d	d :— :—	— :— :

D. S.

: :	: :	m :m :m	m :— :—	r :r :r	s :s :s	d :— :—	— :— :
: :	: :	d :d :d	d :— :—	t, :t, :t,	t, :t, :t,	d :— :—	— :— :
		Swift - ly we go,		Mer - ri - ly, mer - ri - ly		O.	
: :	: :	: :	: :	s :s :s	r :r :r	m :— :—	— :— :
d :d :d	d :— :—	— :— :—	— :— :—	s, :s, :s,	s, :s, :s,	d :— :—	— :— :
O - ver the snow,							

STILL LIKE DEW.

93. KEY F. B. C. UNSELD.

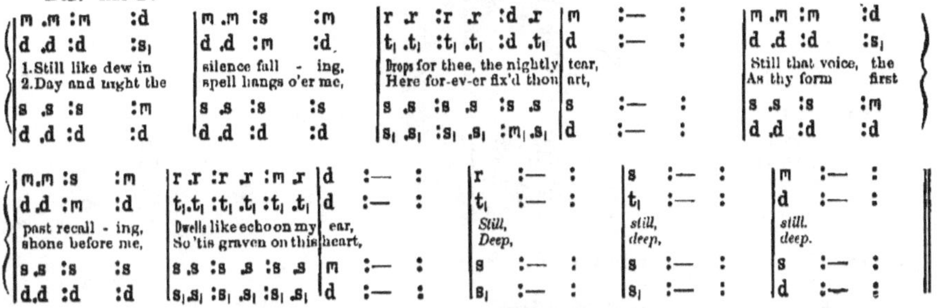

m .m :m :d	m .m :s :m	r .r :r .r :d .r	m :— :	m .m :m :d
d .d :d :s,	d .d :m :d	t, .t, :t, .t, :d .t,	d :— :	d .d :d :s,
1. Still like dew in	silence fall - ing,	Drops for thee, the nightly	tear,	Still that voice, the
2. Day and night the	spell hangs o'er me,	Here for-ev-er fix'd thou	art,	As thy form first
s .s :s :m	s .s :s :s	s .s :s .s :s .s	s :— :	s .s :s :m
d .d :d :d	d .d :d :d	s, .s, :s, .s, :m, .s,	d :— :	d .d :d :d

m .m :s :m	r .r :r .r :m .r	d :— :	r :— :	s :— :	m :— :
d .d :m :d	t, .t, :t, .t, :t, .t,	d :— :	t, :— :	t, :— :	d :— :
past recall - ing,	Dwells like echo on my	ear,	*Still,*	*still,*	*still.*
shone before me,	So 'tis graven on this	heart,	*Deep,*	*deep,*	*deep.*
s .s :s :s	s .s :s .s :s .s	m :— :	s :— :	s :— :	s :— :
d .d :d :d	s, .s, :s, .s, :s, .s,	d :— :	s, :— :	s, :— :	d :— :

ff 94. KEY C. 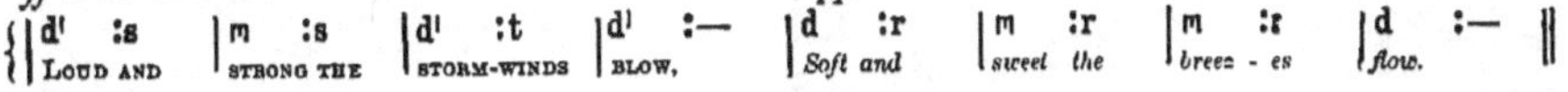 *pp*

| d' :s | m :s | d' :t | d' :— | d :r | m :r | m :r | d :— |
| LOUD AND | STRONG THE | STORM-WINDS | BLOW, | *Soft and* | *sweet the* | *breez - es* | *flow.* |

pp 95. KEY G. *ff*

| d :d | s, :s, | d :t, | d :— | m :m | s :m | d :r | d :— |
| *Soft and* | *sweet the* | *breez - es* | *flow,* | LOUD AND | STRONG THE | STORM - WINDS | BLOW. |

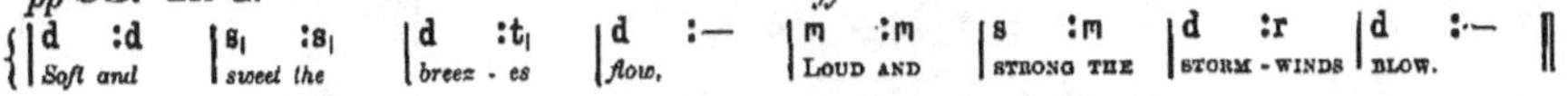

Pulse and half tones may be taught as follows. The teacher writes the following exercises on the board:

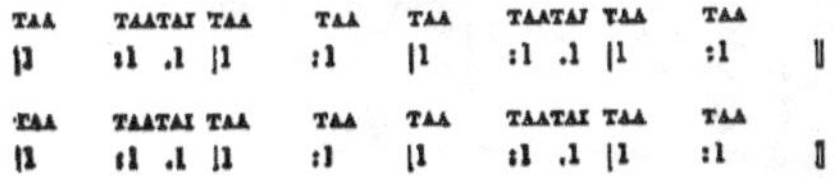

| TAA | TAATAI TAA | TAA | TAA | TAATAI TAA | TAA |
| 1 | :1 .1 | 1 | :1 | 1 | :1 .1 | 1 | :1 ||

| TAA | TAATAI TAA | TAA | TAA | TAATAI TAA | TAA |
| 1 | :1 .1 | 1 | :1 | 1 | :1 .1 | 1 | :1 ||

And when they are sung correctly he changes the second one to

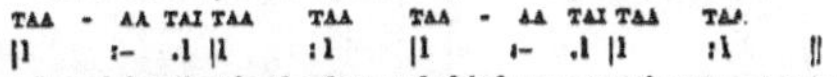

| TAA - AA TAI TAA | TAA | TAA - AA TAI TAA | TAA |
| 1 :- .1 | 1 | :1 | 1 :- .1 | 1 | :1 ||

and explains that in the first and third measure the tones are to be continued from the first pulse into the first half of the second, making the tone a pulse and a half long. The exercise is then to be taataid and laa-ed from the teacher's pattern. The two exercises may then be sung alternately.

The following exercises are to be taataid and laaed on one tone and taataid in tune:

96. Key G.

```
|TAA    TAA TAI |TAA    TAA  |TAA - AA TAI |TAA    TAA  |TAA - AA TAI |TAA - AA TAI |TAA TAI TAA TAI |TAA - AA ||
|l     :l  .l   |l     :l    |l    :-  .l  |l     :l    |l    :-  .l  |l    :-  .l  |l   .l  :l  .l  |l    :—   ||
|d     :d  .r   |m     :m    |d    :-  .r  |m     :m    |m    :-  .r  |m    :-  .r  |m   .r  :d  .t, |d    :—   ||
```

97. Key D.

```
|l   :-  .l |l    :l   |l   :l  .l |l   :—   |l   :-  .l |l  .l  :l  .l |l   :l   |l   :—  ||
|m   :-  .r |d    :m   |s   :m  .s |d'  :—   |t   :-  .t |d' .s  :m  .d |m   :r   |d   :—  ||
```

98. Key F.

```
|TAA - - AA  TAI TAA |TAA   TAA   TAA |TAA - AA  TAI TAA TAI |TAA  -AA   SAA ||
|l       :-  .l  :l  |l     :l    :l  |l    :-   .l  :l  .l  |l    :—    :   ||
|d       :-  .r  :m  |s     :m    :d  |t,   :-   .d  :m  .r  |d    :—    :   ||
```

99. Key G.

```
:l  .l |l   :-  .l  :l  .l  |l   :l    :l  .l |l   :-  .l  :l  .l |l   :—  ||
:d  .r |m   :-  .r  :d  .t, |d   :s,   :s, .d |t,  :-  .t, :d  .r |d   :—  ||
```

100. Key F. Round for three parts.

```
                                                 *                      U.
|s       :-  .s |s    :-  .s |m   .r    :d  .t, |d    :—   |m    :-  .m |m    :-  .r  |
 Sing        we  now       a  mer-ry,    mer-ry  lay,        Let      us  all        be

|d   .t,  :d   .r  |m   :   |d   :d   |d     :d   |s,   :s,   |d    :—   ||
 hap-py    while we  may,     As   we    jour - ney  on    our    way.
```

A. S. Kieffer.

GENTLE SPRING IS HERE AGAIN.

101. Key G.

B. C. Unseld.

```
|s,  :-  .s, |d   :d   |r    :d  .r   |m   :—   |s    :-  .s  |s    :m    |r   :—   |d   :  |
|m,  :-  .m, |s,  :d   |t,   :d  .t,  |d   :—   |d    :-  .d  |d    :d    |t,  :—   |d   :  |
 1. Gen  - the spring is   here  a  -  gain,     Bring - ing mirth and     glad - - - ness;
 2. Years  a - go   her    gen - tle   voice,    Filled  my  heart with    pleasure - - ure,
 3. All    a - lone she    calm - ly   sleeps,   Un  -  der-neath  the     wil - - - - low;
|d   :-  .d  |m   :m   |s    :s       |s   :—   |m    :-  .m  |m    :s    |s   :—   |m   :  |
|d   :-  .d  |d   :d   |s,   :m, .s,  |d   :—   |d    :-  .d  |d    :d    |s,  :—   |d   :  |

|s,  :-  .s, |d   :d   |r    :d  .r   |m   :—   |s    :-  .s  |s    :m    |r   :—   |d   :  |
|m,  :-  .m, |s,  :d   |t,   :d  .t,  |d   :—   |d    :-  .d  |d    :d    |t,  :—   |d   :  |
 And     the sing - ing   birds have   come,     Chas - ing gloom and      sad - - - ness,
 And     life's lot was   full  of     joy,      With  this sin - gle      treas - - - ure;
 And     the hare - bells mute - ly    weep.     Tears  up - on  her       pil - - - low;
|d   :-  .d  |m   :m   |s    :s       |s   :—   |m    :-  .m  |m    :s    |s   :—   |m   :  |
|d   :-  .d  |d   :d   |s,   :m, .s,  |d   :—   |d    :-  .d  |d    :d    |s,  :—   |d   :  |
```

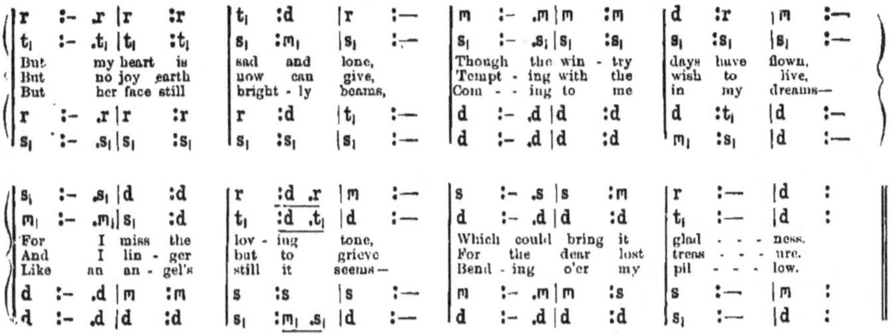

r :- .r |r :r |t_1 :d |r :— |m :- .m |m :m |d :r |m :—
t_1 :- .t_1 |t_1 :t_1 |s_1 :m_1 |s_1 :— |s_1 :- .s_1 |s_1 :s_1 |s_1 :s_1 |s_1 :—
But my heart is | sad and lone, | Though the win - try | days have flown,
But no joy earth | now can give, | Tempt - ing with the | wish to live,
But her face still | bright - ly beams, | Com - - ing to me | in my dreams—
r :- .r |r :r |r :d |t_1 :— |d :- .d |d :d |d :t_1 |d :—
s_1 :- .s_1 |s_1 :s_1 |s_1 :s_1 |s_1 :— |d :- .d |d :d |m_1 :s_1 |d :—

s_1 :- .s_1 |d :d |r :d .r |m :— |s :- .s |s :m |r :— |d :
m_1 :- .m_1 |s_1 :d |t_1 :d .t_1 |d :— |d :- .d |d :d |t_1 :— |d :
For I miss the | lov - ing tone, | Which could bring it | glad - - - ness.
And I lin - ger | but to grieve | For the dear lost | treas - - - ure.
Like an an - gel's | still it seems— | Bend - ing o'er my | pil - - - low.
d :- .d |m :m |s :s |s :— |m :- .m |m :s |s :— |m :
d :- .d |d :d |s_1 :m_1 .s_1 |d :— |d :- .d |d :d |s_1 :— |d :

BANISH SORROW.

202. Key E. B. C. U.

:m .m |m :- .m :d .m |s :m :m .m |r :- .r :s .r |m :— :m .m |m :- .m :d .m
:d .d |d :- .d :d .d |d :d :d .d |t_1 :- .t_1 :t_1 .t_1 |d :— :d .d |d :- .d :d .d
1 Ban-ish | all desponding | sor - row, Tho' the | skies may frown to- | day; Shall not | sun - shine with to-
2 Here's a | hand for ev - 'ry | broth - er, Working | stout - ly, climbing | slow, Here's a | will to help each
3 Join we, | then, in bravest | cho - rus, Sing-ing | all our pains to | rest While the | heav'n gleams kind-ly
:s .s |s :- .s :m .s |m :s :s .s |s :- .s :r .s |s :— :s .s |s :- .s :m .s
:d .d |d :- .d :d .d |d :d :d .d |s_1 :- .s_1 :s_1 .s_1 |d :— :d .d |d :- .d :d .d

s :m :m .m |r :- .s :s .t_1 |d :— :m .m |r :- .t_1 :d .r |m :d :m .m
d :d :d .d |t_1 :- .t_1 :t_1 .s_1 |s_1 :— :d .d |t_1 :- .s_1 :s_1 .t_1 |d :d :d .d
mor - row, O'er its | a - - - - zure beauty | play? Life must | bring its toils and | trou - bles, But the
oth - - er, In the | doubt we all must | know. Hopes are | cheered and loads are | light - ened By the
o'er us, Light and | joy shall make us | blest. Strength shall | stoop to lift the | weak - est, Love the
m :s :s .s |s :- .s :r .r |m :— :s .s |s :- .r :s .s |s :m :s .s
d :d :d .d |s_1 :- .s_1 :s_1 .s_1 |d :— :d .d |s_1 :- .s_1 :m_1 .s_1 |d :d :d .d

r :- .t_1 :d .r |m :— :m .m |m :- .m :d .m |s :m :m .m |r :- .s :s .t_1 |d :—
t_1 :- .s_1 :s_1 .t_1 |d :— :d .d |d :- .d :d .d |d :d :d .d |t_1 :- .t_1 :t_1 .s_1 |s_1 :—
heart that fears and | faints, Makes the | heavy - y bur-den | dou - ble, Heap-ing | care with vain com- | plaints.
mag - ic of a | word, Dusk - y | day by smiles are | bright ened, Ere the | friend - ly tone is | heard.
low - liest grief shall | see, Pride no | more shall spurn the | meek - est; Broth-ers | firm and true are | we.
s :- .r :s .s |s :— :s .s |s :- .s :m .s |m :s :s .s |s :- .s :r .r |m :—
s_1 :- .s_1 :m_1 .s_1 |d :— :d .d |d :- .d :d .d |d :d :d .d |s_1 :- .s_1 :s_1 .s_1 |d :—

Quarter-pulse tones are to be taught next. The method for doing this need not be described—the same process pursued with half-pulse tones may be used or they may be taught at once by pattern from the Time Chart or Finger-signs or from the exercises below. They are named *tafatefe*. They are indicated in the notation by a comma in the middle of each half-pulse, thus, |1 ,1 .1 ,1 :
ta fa te fe

Exercises to be taatald and laa-ed and taatald in tune.

103. KEYS C, G.

TAA TAI ta - fa - te - fe | TAA TAI TAA | ta - fa - te - fe TAA TAI | ta - fa - te - fe TAA
1 .1 :1 ,1 .1 ,1	1 .1 :1	1 ,1 .1 ,1 :1 .1	1 ,1 .1 ,1 :1
d .d :m ,m .m ,m	d .m :s	s ,s .s ,s :m .s	s ,s .s ,s :d^1
d .t_1 :d ,r .m ,r	d .t_1 :d	r ,d .t_1 ,d :r .r	m ,r .d ,r :m

ta - fa - te - fe TAA TAI | ta - fa - te - fe TAA | ta - fa - te - fe ta - fa - te - fe | TAA TAI TAA
| 1 ,1 .1 ,1 :1 .1 | 1 ,1 .1 ,1 :1 | 1 ,1 .1 ,1 :1 ,1 .1 ,1 | 1 .1 :1 ‖
| d^1 ,d^1 .d^1 ,d^1 :t .t | d^1 ,d^1 .d^1 ,d^1 :s | s ,s .s ,s :m ,m .m ,m | s .t :d^1 ‖
| m ,r .d ,t_1 :d .s_1 | d ,t_1 .d ,r :m | m ,r .d ,r :m ,r .d ,r | d .t_1 :d ‖

104. KEY G. Round in three parts. A. L. C.

| d :d | d :d | t_1 .t_1 :t_1 | d .d :d | * m :m | m :m | r .r :s | m .m :m |
One, two, three, four, keep the time, keep the time, One, two, three, four, Voices chime, voices chime,

| s ,s .s ,s :s .m | d .m :s | s_1 ,s_1 .s_1 ,s_1 :s_1 .s_1 | d :— ‖
Tra la la la la la la la la, Tra la la la la la la

105. KEY D. Round in three parts.

| d :d .d | r :r .r | m :r | d :— |
Come with the reap - ers this sun ny morn,

| * m :m | s :s | s .s :s .s | m :— |
Hear them sing a - mong the yel - low corn,

| s ,s .s ,s :s | t ,t .t ,t :t | d^1 ,d^1 .d^1 ,d^1 :d^1 .t | d^1 :— ‖
Merri - ly they sing, mer-ri - ly they sing, Tra la la la la la la.

106. KEY F. Round in four parts. U.

| d ,d .d ,d :m .m | r .r :m | * m ,m .m ,m :s .s | t_1 .t_1 :d |
Mer-ri - ly the bells are ring - ing near; Cheeri-ly the birds are sing - ing here.

| s ,s .s ,s :s .s | s ,s .s ,s :s | d ,d .d ,d :d .d | s_1 ,s_1 .s_1 ,s :d ‖
Listen to the bells! how merri - ly they ring! Listen to the birds! how cheeri-ly they sing.

A. S. KIEFFER.

LOVELY MAY.

107. KEY C.

B. C. UNSELD.

```
| s   .s   :s    | s ,s .s ,s :s             | s   .m   :s   .d'  | d'    :t    |
| m   .m   :m    | m ,m .m ,m :m             | m   .d   :m   .m   | m     :r    |
1. Love-ly  May,   mer-ry, mer-ry May!        Bird - lets now are    sing  -  ing: -
2. Hap-py   May,   mer-ry, mer-ry May!        With our  songs we     greet    thee;
3. Balm-y   May,   mer-ry, mer-ry May!        How  we   love  thy    glad  -  ness;
| d'  .d'  :d'   | d',d' .d' ,d' :d'         | d'  .s   :d'  .s   | s     :s    |
| d   .d   :d    | d ,d .d ,d :d             | d   .d   :d   .d   | s     :s    |
```

```
| r'  .r'  :r'   | r',r' .r' ,r' :r'         | m'  .r'  :d'  .t   | d'    :—    |
| s   .s   :s    | s ,s .s ,s :s             | s   .s   :m   .r   | m     :—    |
Ev - ery - where,  thro' the balmy air,       Songs of  pleas - ure  ring!
On   the   hill,   by the shining rill        Now   we  wel - come   thee.
Buds and   flow'rs thro' the sunny hours     Ope  their scent - ed  leaves.
| t   .t   :t    | t ,t .t ,t :t             | d'  .t   :d'  .s   | s     :—    |
| s   .s   :s    | s ,s .s ,s :s             | s   .s   :s   .s   | d     :—    |
```

```
| s   .s   :m   .m   | s   .s   :d'  | t ,t .t ,t :r'     | d',d' .d' ,d' :m'  |
| m   .m   :d   .d   | m   .m   :m   | r ,r .r ,r :r      | m ,m .m ,m :m      |
Wel - come, wel - come, love - ly May,  Merry, merry May,    merry, merry May;
| d'  .d'  :s   .s   | d'  .d'  :s   | s ,s .s ,s :s      | d',d' .d' ,d' :d'  |
| d   .d   :d   .d   | d   .d   :d   | s ,s .s ,s :s      | d ,d .d ,d :d      |
```

```
| s   .s   :m   .m   | s   .s   :m'  | m',m' .m' ,m' :r' ,r' .r' ,r' | d'   :—  ||
| m   .m   :d   .d   | m   .m   :s   | s ,s .s ,s :s ,s .s ,s        | m    :—  ||
Wel - come, wel - come, love - ly May,  Merry, merry, merry, merry      May.
| d'  .d'  :s   .s   | d'  .d'  :d'  | d',d' .d' ,d' :t ,t .t ,t     | d'   :—  ||
| d   .d   :d   .d   | d   .d   :d   | s ,s .s ,s :s ,s .s ,s        | d    :—  ||
```

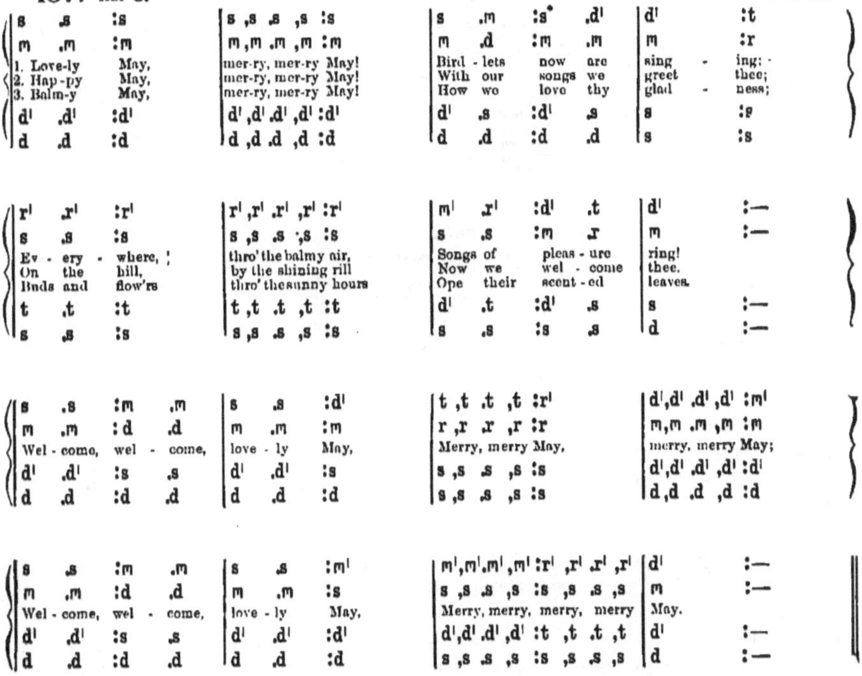

Modulator Voluntaries, EAR EXERCISES, DICTATION, *Pointing* and *Writing from Memory*, as described in the first step are to be practiced regularly at every lesson. Pulse-and-a-half tones, quarter pulse tones and silences, as in the following example—

```
|d   :-  .r |m   :   |m,m.m,m: m  .r   |d   :—   ||
```

would be dictated thus, "TAAA d," "—AATAI r," "TLAA m," "*SAA*," "tafatefe m m m m," "TAATAI m r," "TLAA-AA d."

Certificates.—Pupils now begin to make up their list of three tunes for the Junior School Certificate or six tunes for the Elementary Certificate. No tune of less than eight four-pulse measures or sixteen two-pulse measures should be accepted. For instructions in *Voice Training, Breathing, Harmony*, etc., belonging to this step, the teacher will consult the Standard Course.

QUESTIONS FOR WRITTEN OR ORAL EXAMINATION.

DOCTRINE.

1. What two new tones have you learned in this step?
2. What is the relative position of *Ray* to *Doh?*
3. What is the relative position of *Te* to *Doh?*
4. What is the mental effect of *Ray?*
5. What is the mental effect of *Te?*
6. What is the manual sign for *Ray?* For *one-Ray?*
7. What is the manual sign for *Te?* For *Te-one?*
8. What chord is formed of the tones d m s?
9. What chord is formed of the tones s t r?
10. What new kind of accent have you learned in this step?
11. How is the medium accent indicated in the notation?
12. How is the medium accent indicated in the time-names?
13. What two new kinds of measure have you learned in this step?
14. What is the order of accents in four-pulse measure?
15. What is the order of accents in six-pulse measure?
16. What is the time-name for a silent pulse?
17. How is it indicated in the notation?
18. What is the time-name of a pulse-and-a-half tone?
19. How is it indicated in the notation?
20. What is the time-name of four quarter-pulse tones?
21. What is the time-name of the first quarter of a pulse? The second? The third? The fourth?
22. How are quarter pulses indicated in the notation?

PRACTICE.

23. Sing to *laa* the *Ray* and the *Te*, to any *Doh* the teacher gives.
24. Ditto the *Ray'* and *Te* to any *Doh'*.
25. Taatai from memory any one of Exs. 85 to 89, 90 to 99, chosen by the teacher.
26. Taatai the upper part of one of the Exs. 103 or 107, chosen by the teacher.
27. Taatai-in-tune the upper part of Exs. 102 or 107, chosen by the teacher.
28. Point on the Modulator (sol faing) any one of the following four Exs. 60, 61, 78, 79, chosen by the teacher.
29. Write from memory any other of these exercises chosen by the teacher.
30. Follow the teacher's pointing in a new voluntary, containing *Doh*, *Me*, *Soh*, *Te* and *Ray*, but no difficulties of time.
31. From any phrase (belonging to this step) sung to figures, tell your teacher (or write down) which figure was sung to *Ray*,—to *Ray'*,—to *Te*,—to *Te*,.
32. Having heard the tonic chord, tell your teacher (or write down) which tone (*Doh*, *Me*, *Soh*, *Te* or *Ray*) was sung to *laa*. Do this with two different tones.
33. Taatai any Rhythm of at least two measures belonging to this step which the teacher shall *laa* to you. He will first give you the measure and rate of movement by taataing two plain measures and marking the accent by *r* and *l* without beating time, but the two measures you have to copy he will simply *laa* on one tone.
34. Taatai-in-tune any Rhythm of at least two measures, belonging to this step, which after giving the measure and rate as above, the teacher may sol-fa to you.

---

pp **108.** KEY C.

m :m :m	f :f :m	r :m :f	m :— :—
Wand - 'ring in	*dark - ness and*	*grop - ing our*	*way;*

ff d' :d' :d'	r' :r' :d'	t :d' :r'	d' :— :— ‖
LIGHT WILL BE	WEL - COME, YES,	WEL - COME THE	DAY.

p **109.** KEY D.

d .d :d	r .r :r	*m* m .d :r .m	f :—	*f* s .s :s
Soft - ly now,	*soft - ly now,*	Lightly raise the	song;	LOUDER NOW,

l .l :l	*ff* t .s :l .t	d' :—	*ff* d' .d' :d'	t .t :t
LOUDER NOW,	LOUD AND VER - Y	STRONG.	LOUD AND STRONG,	LOUD AND STRONG,

f l .d' :t .l	s :—	*m* f .f :f	m .m :m	*p* r .f :m .r	d :— ‖
NOW LESS LOUD AND	STRONG.	Soft-er now,	soft-er now,	*Soft-ly end our*	*song.*

THIRD STEP.

The prominent topics of the Third Step are as follows—The tones FAH *and* LAH, *completing the Scale. The Standard Scale. To pitch tunes. Classification of voices. The Metronome. The Half-pulse Silence. Various combinations of Quarter-pulses. Modification of mental effects.*

```
s'
f'
m'
r'
DOH'
TE
LAH
SOH
FAH
ME
RAY
DOH
t,
l,
s,
```

The tones *Fah* and *Lah* are now to be taught. The method for doing this need not be described, the same process which was used for r and t will be used for the new tones, see p. 19. The mental effect of *Fah*, a gloomy, serious, desolate tone, and of *Lah*, a sorrowful, weeping tone, may be shown by the following examples.

KEY C OR D.

```
|d  :s  |m  :d  |f  :—  |d  :—  ||
|d' :m  |s  :d' |f  :—  |m  :—  ||
|d  :m  |r  :s  |f  :—  |m  :—  ||
```

KEY G.

```
|d  :s  |m  :d  |{f  :—  |d  :—  ||
                 {f, :—  |d  :—  ||
```

KEY C OR D.

```
|d  :m  |s  :m  |l  :—  |s  :—  ||
|d  :m  |s  :m  |d' :t  |l  :—  ||
```

KEY G.

```
|d  :m  |r  :l, |d  :t, |l, :—  ||
|d  :r  |m  :d  |l, :—  |s, :—  ||
```

After the mental effects of the new tones are developed and their appropriate hand-signs taught, the tones are then to be thoroughly practiced, from the modulator, hand-signs, ear exercises, etc. The chord of FAH, or *Sub-Dominant*, consisting of the tones f l d', may be brought out. See chords of DOH and SOH, page 20. The chord of *Seven-Soh* (⁷S) or *Dominant Seventh*, consisting of the tones s t r f, although belonging to the Fourth Step, may be taught at this point.

The following exercises should be carefully taught by pattern from the modulator.

110. KEY C.

```
{|d :m :s |f :l :d' |s :t :r' |d' :— :— |r' :t :s |d' :l :f |s :r :m |d :— :— ||
```

111. KEY C.

```
{|d  :m  |s  :m  |f  :l  |d' :l  |s  :t  |r' :t  |d' :—  |—  :—  }
{|d' :s  |m  :s  |d' :l  |f  :l  |d' :s  |t  :r' |d' :—  |—  :—  ||
```

112. KEY A.

```
{|d :m :d |l, :f, :l, |s, :t, :r |d :— :— |d :s, :m, |d :l, :f, |r :t, :s, |d :— :— ||
```

113. KEY G.

```
{|d  :s, |m  :d  |d  :l, |f  :l, |s, :t, |r  :f  |m  :—  |—  :—  }
{|m  :d  |s, :d  |f  :d  |l, :d  |t, :r  |f  :t, |d  :—  |—  :—  ||
```

The Scale. After the tones **d r m f s l t d'** have been sung in successive order, the teacher will explain that this series of tones is called the Scale. Each tone of the scale differs from the others in pitch. By "pitch" is meant the highness or lowness of tones. It may be observed that the eighth tone above or below any given tone has the same, mental effect and the same name. The two tones are so nearly alike in character that the ear accepts them as relatively the same notwithstanding the difference of pitch. They are Replicates or Octaves one of the other. The word octave sometimes means *a set* of eight tones, sometimes the eighth tone and sometimes the difference of pitch or distance between the two tones. The teacher will question the class thoroughly in regard to the scale—"Which is the third tone?" Me. "The fifth tone?" Soh. "The second tone? "Ray -and so on; also questions in regard to the mental effects and hand-signs. He will explain that **d m** and **s** are readily distinguished as the strong, bold tones of the scale, and **r f l** and **t** as the leaning tones: **t** and **f** have the strongest leaning or leading tendency, **t** leading upward to **d** and **f** leading downward to **m**. The most important tone of the scale, the strongest, most restful, the governing tone, is called the Key-tone. A key tone, with the tones related to it or belonging to it, is called a key. A distinction is made between "key" and "scale." A Key is a family of related tones consisting of a key-tone with six related tones and their replicates. A scale is the tones of a key arranged in successive order, ascending or descending. The intervals of the scale, large and small steps, etc., will be explained in the Fourth Step.

The Standard Scale. The teacher will show by practical examples that the scale may be sung at different pitches. Any conceivable pitch may be taken as the key-tone, and the other related tones will readily take their proper places. It is necessary to have one particular scale of pitch as a standard from which all the others are to be reckoned. This scale is called The Standard Scale (commonly known as Natural Scale). The particular degree of pitch which is taken as the key-tone of the Standard Scale is named C, *Ray* is D, *Me* is E, *Fah* is F, and so on, as shown in the diagram. These pitch-names (letters) of the Standard Scale should be thoroughly committed to memory. The correct pitch of this scale may be obtained from a piano or organ, or any of the common musical instruments properly tuned, or, for ordinary vocal purposes from a C' tuning-fork. It is a great advantage to have one tone in absolute pitch fixed on the memory, and it is more easy to do this than is commonly supposed. The teacher will frequently ask the pupils to sing C' (which in a man's voice is really C) and then tests them with the tuning-fork. In this way the power of recollection is soon developed. In estimating the chances of certainty, however, we should always bear in mind that any bodily or mental depression has a tendency to flatten even our recollection. Any pitch of the Standard Scale may be taken as a key tone. A scale or key is named from the letter taken as the key-tone. The different keys are indicated in the notation by the signatures "Key C," "Key G," and so on.

To pitch tunes. Up to this point the teacher has fixed the pitch of the key-tone. The pupils themselves should now learn to do it in turn. The pupil strikes the C' tuning-fork, and taking the tone it gives, sings down the scale to the tone he wants. This tone he swells out, and then repeats it to the syllable *doh*, and perhaps sings the scale or chord of DOH to confirm the key. Further instructions on pitching tunes in the Fourth Step.

d'—C'
t—B

l—A

s—G

f—F
m—E

r—D

d—C

114. KEY G. Round in three parts.

d :d	f :m	r :s	m :—	d :d	l_1 :d	t_1 :t_1	d :—	d :d	f_1 :f_1	s_1 :s_1	d :—
Come, now,	let us	mer-ry	be,	Fill our	souls with	mirth and	glee,	Hearts and	voi-ces	all a-	gree.

115. KEY B♭. Round in four parts.

:s_1	d :d	r :r	m :m	d :d	l_1 :l_1	t_1 :t_1	d :—	—
If	hap - pi -	ness has	not her	seat And	cen - tre	in the	breast,	
:s_1	f_1 :f_1	f_1 :f_1	m_1 :s_1	d :s_1	l_1 :f_1	r_1 :s_1	d_1 :—	—
We	may be	wise or	rich or	great, But	nev - er	can be	blest.	

116. KEY D. Round in two parts. T. F. S.

m :m	f :m	m :m	f :m	m :m	f :m	d :r	m :
If the	weath - er	keeps so	storm - y,	and the	rain comes	down like	that,
s :s	l :s	s :s	l :s	s :s	l :s	m :s	d' :
I shall	nev - er	have the	priv - i -	lege of	wear - ing	my new	hat.

117. KEY F. Round in three parts. T. F. S.

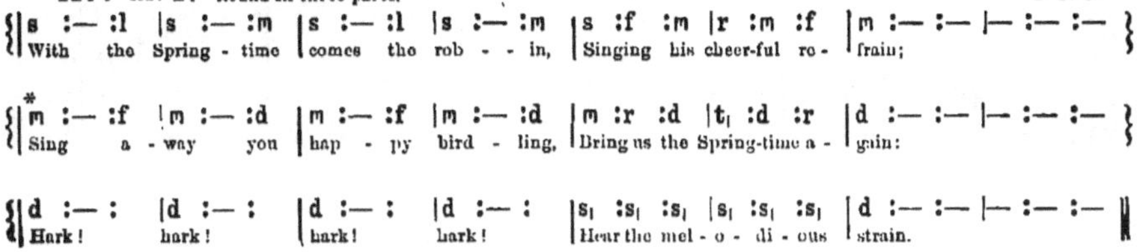

| s :— :l | s :— :m | s :— :l | s :— :m | s :f :m | r :m :f | m :— :— | — :— :— |
With the Spring - time | comes the rob - - in, | Singing his cheer-ful re - | frain;

| * m :— :f | m :— :d | m :— :f | m :— :d | m :r :d | t_1 :d :r | d :— :— | — :— :— |
Sing a - way you | hap - py bird - ling, | Bring us the Spring-time a - | gain:

| d :— : | d :— : | d :— : | d :— : | s_1 :s_1 :s_1 | s_1 :s_1 :s_1 | d :— :— | — :— :— ‖
Hark! hark! | hark! hark! | Hear the mel - o - di - ous | strain.

118. KEY C. T. F. S.

:s | l :s | m :s | l :s | m :s | l :l | t :t | d' :— | — |
1.O sweet to me the gen - tle spring, When earth is robed in flowers,
2.The plow - man drives his shin - ing share A - cross the mel - low lea.
:m | f :m | d :m | f :m | d :m | f :f | r :r | m :— | — |

:d' | t :l | s :d' | t :l | s :l | s :m | f :s | m :— | — ‖
And beau - ti - - ful the sum - mer time, With all its leaf - y bowers.
And lays the fur - rows broad and fair, As waves up - on the sea.
:m | s :f | m :m | s :f | m :f | m :d | r :m | d :— | — ‖

119. KEY G. T. F. S.

| m :— :m | s :— :m | d :— :d | m :— :d | l_1 :— :d | f :— :l_1 | s_1 :d :m | r :— :— |
All that now so dark ap - pears, While earth's dark shad - ows dim the sight,
| d :— :d | m :— :d | m_1 :— :m_1 | s_1 :— :m_1 | f_1 :— :l_1 | l_1 :— :f_1 | m_1 :s_1 :d | t_1 :— :— |

| m :— :m | s :— :m | d :— :d | m :— :d | l_1 :— :d | f :— :l_1 | s_1 :m :r | d :— :— ‖
All our doubts and all our fears Will be made clear in heav - en's light.
| d :— :d | m :— :d | m_1 :— :m_1 | s_1 :— :m_1 | f_1 :— :l_1 | l_1 :— :f_1 | m_1 :s_1 :f_1 | m_1 :— :— ‖

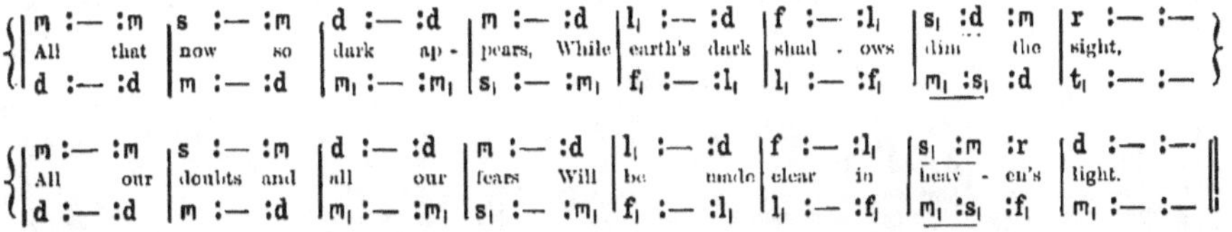

Tuning Exercises.—See page 21. To be *Solfa-ed, laa-ed* and then sung very softly to *loo*.

Sing Ex. 120 first as written. Second time, Soprano take the Tenor, Tenor take the Contralto, singing d' instead d, Contralto take the Soprano. Third time Soprano and Contralto change parts, Soprano singing d' instead of d. In the key G the Tenor and Contralto change parts, Contralto singing l_1 instead of l, and Base will take f_1 instead of f.

120. KEYS C, E♭ AND G.

| d :— | m :d | f :— | : | : | f :— | f :f | m :— ‖
| d :— | m :d | f :— | : | d :— | — :— | d :d | d :— ‖
| d :— | m :d | f :— | l :— | — :— | — :— | l :l | s :— ‖
| d :— | m :d | f :— | — :— | — :— | — :— | f :f | d :— ‖

121. KEY C. Sing only as written.

| d :— | m :d | s :— | : | : | f :— | m :r | m :— ‖
| d :— | m :d | s :— | : | r :— | — :— | d :t_1 | d :— ‖
| d :— | m :d | s :— | t :— | — :— | — :— | d' :s | s :— ‖
| d :— | m :d | s :— | — :— | — :— | — :— | s :s_1 | d :— ‖

122. KEY E♭.

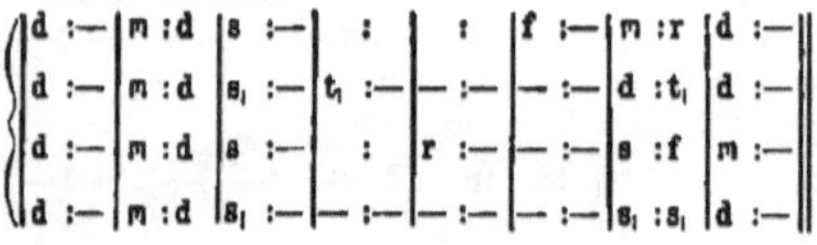

d :—	m :d	s :—	:	:	f :—	m :r	d :—
d :—	m :d	s_1 :—	t_1 :—	— :—	— :—	d :t_1	d :—
d :—	m :d	s :—	:	r :—	— :—	s :f	m :—
d :—	m :d	s_1 :—	— :—	— :—	— :—	s_1 :s_1	d :—

123. KEY F.

d :—	m :d	s :—	:	r :—	— :—	d :t_1	d :—
d :—	m :d	s_1 :—	t_1 :—	— :—	— :—	d :s_1	s_1 :—
d :—	m :d	s :—	:	:	f :—	m :r	m :—
d :—	m :d	s_1 :—	— :—	— :—	— :—	s_1 :s_1	d :—

COMING NIGHT.

124. KEY F. M. 86. B. C. U.

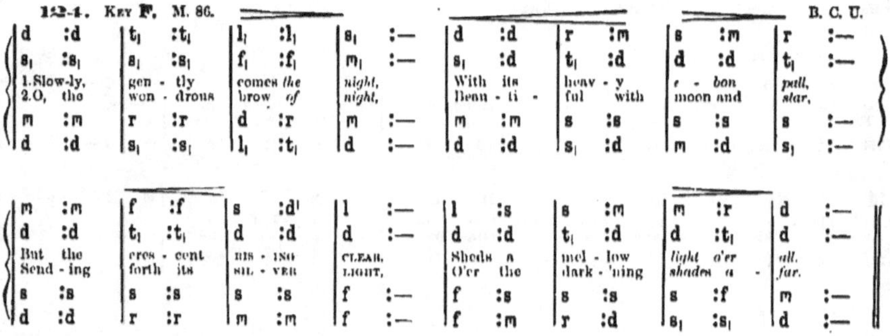

d :d	t_1 :t_1	l_1 :l_1	s_1 :—	d :d	r :m	s :m	r :—
s_1 :s_1	s_1 :s_1	f_1 :f_1	m_1 :—	s_1 :d	t_1 :d	d :d	t_1 :—
1. Slow-ly,	gen - tly	comes *the*	*night,*	With its	heav - y	*e - bon*	*pall,*
2. O, the	won - drous	brow *of*	*night,*	Beau - ti -	ful with	moon and	*star,*
m :m	r :r	d :r	m :—	m :m	s :s	s :s	s :—
d :d	s_1 :s_1	l_1 :t_1	d :—	d :d	s_1 :d	m :d	s_1 :—

m :m	f :f	s :d^1	l :—	l :s	s :m	m :r	d :—
d :d	t_1 :t_1	d :d	d :—	d :d	t_1 :d	d :t_1	d :—
But the	cres - cent	RIS - ING	CLEAR,	Sheds a	mel - low	*light o'er*	*all,*
Send - ing	forth its	SIL - VER	LIGHT,	O'er the	dark - 'ning	*shades a -*	*far.*
s :s	s :s	s :s	f :—	f :s	s :s	s :f	m :—
d :d	r :r	m :m	f :—	f :m	r :d	s_1 :s_1	d :—

SILENT VALE.

p **125.** KEY E♭. M. 76. B. C. U.

s :s	l :l	s :m	s :m	d :d	r :r	*m* m :s	r :—	s :s	l :l
d :d	d :d	d :d	d :d	d :d	t_1 :t_1	d :d	t_1 :—	d :d	d :d
1. *Si - lent*	*vale! where*	love and	pleas - ure	Ev - er	round our	cot - tage	flow'd;	Beauteous	as the
2. *Fare ye*	*well, ye*	loft - y	shad - ows,	Which have	shield-ed	oft our	head;	Still be	green ye
m :m	f :f	m :s	m :s	l :m	s :s	s :s	s :—	m :m	f :f
d :d	d :d	d :d	d :d	l_1 :l_1	s_1 :s_1	d :m	s :—	d :d	d :d

d^1 :l	s :m	s :s	d :d	m :r	d :—	*p* f :f	l :l	m :m	s :—
d :d	d :d	d :d	d :d	d :t_1	d :—	d :d	d :d	d :d	d :—
WESTERN	EVENING,	Love-ly	as the	*sun-lit*	*cloud,*	*Peaceful*	*as the*	*ves - per*	*bell,*
LOVE - LY	MEADOWS,	Fields with	bright-est	*flow'rs be*	*spread;*	*Fields where*	*oft the*	*ves - per*	*song,*
l :f	m :s	m :m	m :m	s :f	m :—	l :l	f :f	s :s	m :—
d :d	d :d	d :d	l_1 :l_1	s_1 :s_1	d :—	f :f	f :f	d :d	d :—

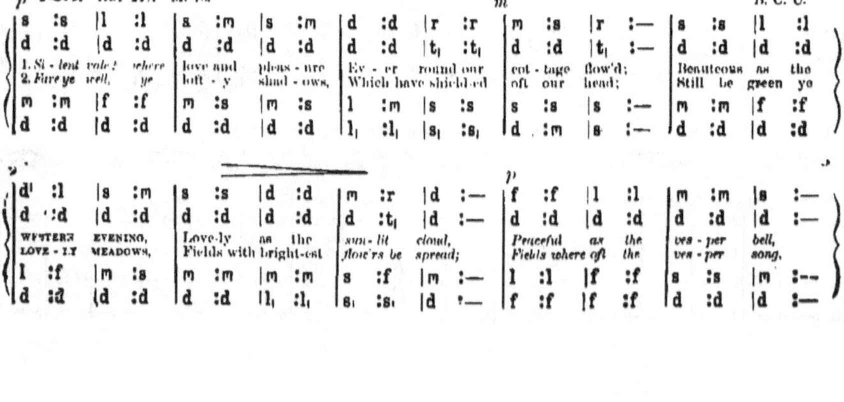

m ... *p*

| s :m \|s :m | d :r \|m :— | s :m \|s :m | s :— \|s :— | s :— \|— :— ‖
| d :d \|d :d | d :t₁ \|d :— | d :d \|d :d | d :— \|t₁ :— | d :— \|— :— ‖
Thee we bid a | long fare - well, | Thee we bid a | *long fare* - | *well.*
Swelled in ech - oes | sweet and long, | Thee we bid a | *long fare* - | *well.*
| m :s \|m :d | m :s \|s :— | m :s \|m :s | m :— \|r :— | m :— \|— :— ‖
| d :d \|d :d | l₁ :s₁ \|d :— | d :d \|d :d | s₁ :— \|s₁ :— | d :— \|— :— ‖

SONG OF THE AUTUMN.

126. KEY C. M. 76. Words and Music by H. R. PALMER, by per.

| d' :d' :d' \|t :t :t | l :l :l \|s :s :s | f :f :f \|m :m :m | r :— :— \|— :— :—
| m :m :m \|s :s :s | f :f :f \|m :m :m | r :r :r \|d :d :d | t₁ :— :— \|— :— :—
1.Beauti - ful morning, the | au-tumn a - dorn-ing, Oc - | to - ber's as pleasant as | May;
2.Let us be straying, no | time for de - lay - ing, Oc - | to - ber's as pleasant as | May;
| s :s :s \|s :s :s | s :l :t \|d' :d' :d' | s :s :s \|s :s :s | s :— :— \|— :— :—
| d :d :d \|d :d :d | d :d :d \|d :d :d | t₁ :t₁ :t₁ \|d :d :m | s :— :— \|— :— :—

| r' :r' :r' \|d' :d' :d' | t :t :t \|l :l :l | s :s :s \|l :l :l | s :— :— \|s :l :t
| f :f :f \|m :m :m | r :r :r \|m :m :m | r :r :r \|r :r :r | r :— :— \|r :m :f
Long tho' the shadows Thrown | out on the meadows, The | for - ests are ro - sy and | gay; Mer - ri - ly
Nuts we will gath - er To | cheer wintry weather; A - | way to the for- ests, a - | way; Cheerful - ly
| t :t :t \|d' :d' :d' | r' :r' :r' \|d' :d' :d' | t :t :t \|d' :d' :d' | t :— :— \|t :d' :r'
| s :s :s \|s :s :s | s :s :s \|d :d :d | r :r :r \|r :r :r | s :— :— \|f :m :r

| d' :d' :d' \|t :t :t | l :l :l \|s :s :s | f :f :f \|m :m :m | r :— :— \|— :— :—
| m :m :m \|s :s :s | f :f :f \|m :m :m | r :r :r \|d :d :d | t₁ :— :— \|— :— :—
birds are now filling the | air with their trilling, Let | us be as joy - ful as | they;
squirrels are chipping in | time with our tripping. They | of - fer to show us the | way;
| m' :r' :d' \|s :s :s | s :l :t \|d' :d' :d' | s :s :s \|s :s :s | s :— :— \|— :— :—
| d :d :d \|d :d :d | d :d :d \|d :d :d | l₁ :t₁ :d \|r :m :f | s :— :— \|— :— :—

| r' :r' :r' \|d' :d' :d' | t :t :t \|l :l :l | s :l :s \|f :m :r | d :— :— \|— :— :— ‖
| f :f :f \|m :m :m | r :r :r \|m :m :m | r :r :r \|t₁ :t₁ :t₁ | d :— :— \|— :— :— ‖
Fling a-way sor - row, Ne'er | grieve for the morrow, Oc - | to - ber's as pleasant as | May.
Fling a-way sor - row, Ne'er | grieve for the morrow, Oc - | to - ber's as pleasant as | May.
| t :t :t \|d' :d' :d' | r' :r' :r' \|d' :d' :d' | t :t :t \|s :s :f | m :— :— \|— :— :— ‖
| s :s :s \|s :s :s | s :s :s \|d :d :d | r :r :r \|s₁ :s₁ :s₁ | d :— :— \|— :— :— ‖

MOTHER, CHILDHOOD, FRIENDS AND HOME.

127. Key F. M. 76. CHESTER G. ALLEN.

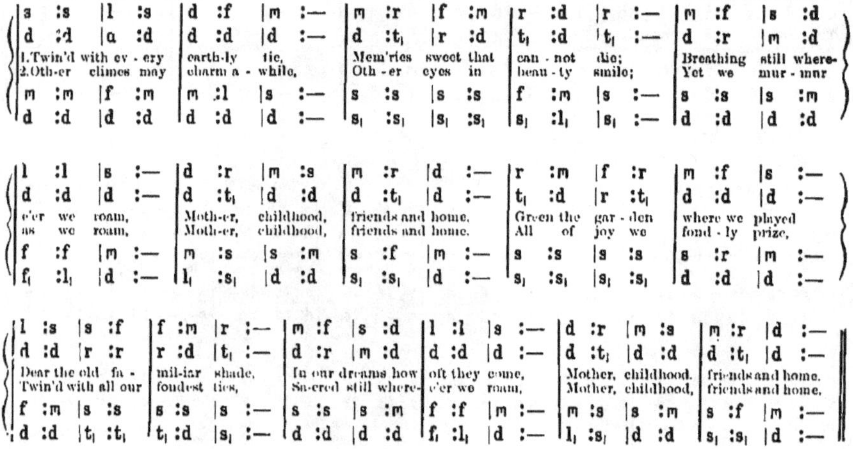

|s :s |l :s |d :f |m :— |m :r |f :m |r :d |r :— |m :f |s :d
|d :d |d :d |d :d |d :— |d :t, |r :d |t, :d |t, :— |d :r |m :d
1.Twin'd with ev - ery | earth-ly tie, | Mem'ries sweet that | can - not die; | Breathing still where-
2.Oth-er climes may | charm a - while, | Oth - er eyes in | beau - ty smile; | Yet we mur - mur
|m :m |f :m |m :l |s :— |s :s |s :s |f :m |s :— |s :s |s :m
|d :d |d :d |d :d |d :— |s, :s, |s, :s, |s, :l, |s, :— |d :d |d :d

|l :l |s :— |d :r |m :s |m :r |d :— |r :m |f :r |m :f |s :—
|d :d |d :— |d :t, |d :d |d :t, |d :— |t, :d |r :t, |d :d |d :—
e'er we roam, | Moth-er, childhood, | friends and home. | Green the gar - den | where we played
as we roam, | Moth-er, childhood, | friends and home. | All of joy we | fond - ly prize,
|f :f |m :— |m :s |s :m |s :f |m :— |s :s |s :s |s :r |m :—
|f, :l, |d :— |l, :s, |d :d |s, :s, |d :— |s, :s, |s, :s, |d :d |d :—

|l :s |s :f |f :m |r :— |m :f |s :d |l :l |s :— |d :r |m :s |m :r |d :— ‖
|d :d |r :r |r :d |t, :— |d :r |m :d |d :d |d :— |d :t, |d :d |d :t, |d :— ‖
Dear the old fa - | mil-iar shade, | In our dreams how | oft they come, | Mother, childhood. | friends and home.
Twin'd with all our | foudest ties, | Sa-cred still where- | e'er we roam, | Mother, childhood, | friends and home.
|f :m |s :s |s :s |s :— |s :s |s :m |f :f |m :— |m :s |s :m |s :f |m :— ‖
|d :d |t, :t, |t, :d |s, :— |d :d |d :d |f, :l, |d :— |l, :s, |d :d |s, :s, |d :— ‖

THE WAYSIDE WELL.

128. Key D. B. C. UNSELD.

|s .s :m .m |f .f :r |r .m :f .s |l :s |s .s :m .m
|m .m :d .d |r .r :t, |t, .d :r .m |f :m |m .m :d .d
1.Oh! the pret - ty | way-side well, | Wreath'd a-bout with | ros - es, | When be-guiled with
2 Treads the drov-er | on the sward, | Comes the la - b'rer | to thee, | Free as gen - tle -
3 Fair the greet-ing | face as - cends, | Like a na - iad | daugh - ter, | When the pea - sant
|d' .d' :s .s |s .s :s |s .s :s .d' |d' :d' |d' .d' :s .s
|d .d :d .d |s, .s, :s, |s, .s, :s, .s, |d :d |d .d :d .d

|f .f :r |r .s :t .s |l :s |f .f :r .r |m .f :s
|r .r :t, |t, .t, :r .r |r :r |r .r :t, .t, |d .r :m
sooth-ing spell, | Wea-ry foot re - | pos - es; | With a wel - come | fresh and green,
man or lord, | From his steed to | woo thee; | Thou from parch-ing | lips dost earn,
las - sie bends, | To the trem-bling | wa - ter; | When she leans up - | on her pail,
|s .s :s |s .s :s .s |d' :t |t .t :s .s |s .s :d'
|s, .s, :s, |s, .s, :s, .t, |r :s |s .s :s, .s, |d .d :d

l .l :d' .l	l :s	d' .d' :s .s	m .f :s	l .s :m .d	r :d ‖
f .f :l .f	f :m	m .m :m .m	d .r :m	f .m :d .d	t, :d ‖
Wave thy bor - der	grass - es,	By the dust - y	trav-'ler seen,	Sigh-ing as he	pass - es.
Many a murmured	bless - ing,	And en - joy - est	in thy turn,	In - no - cent ca -	ress - ing
Glanc-ing o'er the	mead - ow,	Sweet shall fall the	whispered tale,	Soft the doub-le	shad - ow.
d' .d' :d' .d'	d' :d'	s .s :d' .d'	s .s :d'	t .d' :s .m	f :m ‖
f .f :f .f	d :d	d .d :d .d	d .d :d	s, .s, :s, .s,	s, :d ‖

MUSIC EVERYWHERE.

120. KEY G. M. 90. CHESTER G. ALLEN, by per.

d .d :t, .l,	s, :d	r .r :d .t,	d :—	d .d :t, .l,
m, .m, :s, .f,	m, :s,	l, .l, :s, .s,	s, :—	m, .m, :s, .f,
1. Mu-sic in the	spring - time,	Wak-ing up the	flowers;	Mu - sic in the
2. Mu-sic in the	rain - drops,	Fall-ing in the	night;	Mu - sic in the
d .d :d .d	d :m	f .f :m .r	m :—	d .d :d .d
d .d :d .d	d :d	f, .f, :s, .s,	d :—	d .d :d .d

s, :d	r .r :d .t,	d :—	r .m :r .d	t, :d
m, :s,	l, .l, :s, .s,	s, :—	t, .d :t, .l,	s, :s,
green trees,	Mu - sic in the	bowers;	Mu - sic in the	cot - - tage.
young birds,	When the day is	bright;	Mu - sic in the	crick - et,
d :m	f .f :m .r	m :—	s .s :s .r	r :m
d :d	f, .f, :s, .s,	d, :—	s, .s, :s, .s,	s, :s,

r .m :f .m	r :—	d .d :t, .l,	s, :d	r .r :d .t,	d :— ‖
t, .d :r .d	t, :—	s, .s, :s, .f,	m, :s,	l, .l, :s, .s,	s, :— ‖
Mu-sic in the	lea,	Mu-sic in the	south wind,	Mu-sic o'er the	sea.
Chirping loud and	clear,	Mu-sic in the	spring time,	Mu-sic all the	year,
s .s :s .s	s :—	m .m :d .d	d :m	f .f :m .r	m :— ‖
s, .s, :s, .s,	s, :—	d .d :d .d	d :d	f, .f, :s, .s,	d :— ‖

130. KEY D. CRESCENDO AND DIMINUENDO.

p				*m*			
d :r	m :r	m :f	s :—	s :s	l :s	l :t	d' :—
See the	*sun* in	glo - ry	rise	From the	o - cean's	HEAV - ING	BREAST,

f				*m*			
d' :t	l :s	l :l	s :—	s :f	m :f	m :r	d :— ‖
THEN MOVE	O'ER the	bound-less	skies,	Sink - ing	soon *be -*	*neath the*	*West.*

SKATING GLEE.

131. KEY C. M. 100 beating twice. A. S. KIEFFER.

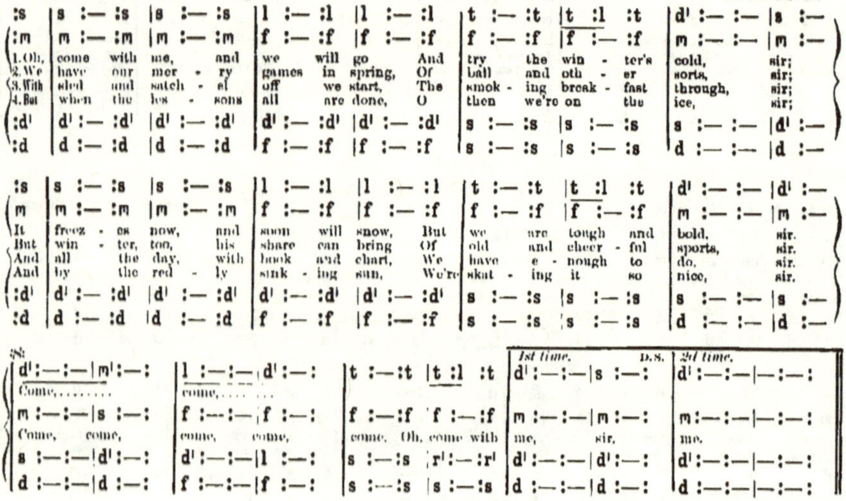

:s	s :— :s	s :— :s	l :— :l	l :— :l	t :— :t	t :l :t	d' :— :—	s :—
:m	m :— :m	m :— :m	f :— :f	f :— :f	f :— :f	f :— :f	m :— :—	m :—
1. Oh,	come with	me, and	we will	go And	try the	win - ter's	cold,	sir;
2. We	have our	mer - ry	games in	spring, Of	ball and	oth - er	sorts,	sir;
3. With	sled and	satch - el	off we	start, The	smok - ing	break - fast	through,	sir;
4. But	when the	les - sons	all are	done, O	then we're	on the	ice,	sir;
:d'	d' :— :d'	d' :— :d'	d' :— :d'	d' :— :d'	s :— :s	s :— :s	s :— :—	d' :—
:d	d :— :d	d :— :d	f :— :f	f :— :f	s :— :s	s :— :s	d :— :—	d :—

:s	s :— :s	s :— :s	l :— :l	l :— :l	t :— :t	t :l :t	d' :— :—	d' :—
m	m :— :m	m :— :m	f :— :f	f :— :f	f :— :f	f :— :f	m :— :—	m :—
It	freez - es	now, and	soon will	snow, But	we are	tough and	bold,	sir.
But	win - ter,	too, his	share can	bring Of	old and	cheer - ful	sports,	sir.
And	all the	day, with	book and	chart, We	have e -	nough to	do,	sir.
And	by the	red - ly	sink - ing	sun, We're	skat - ing	it so	nice,	sir.
:d'	d' :— :d'	d' :— :d'	d' :— :d'	d' :— :d'	s :— :s	s :— :s	s :— :—	s :—
:d	d :— :d	d :— :d	f :— :f	f :— :f	s :— :s	s :— :s	d :— :—	d :—

:S:

						1st time.	D.S.	2d time.	
d' :— :—	m' :— :	l :— :—	d' :— :	t :— :t	t :l :t	d' :— :—	s :— :	d' :— :—	— :— :
Come,........		come,......							
m :— :—	s :— :	f :— :—	f :— :	f :— :f	f :— :f	m :— :—	m :— :	m :— :—	— :— :
Come,	come,	come,	come,	come. Oh,	come with	me,	sir.	me.	
s :— :—	d' :— :	d' :— :—	l :— :	s :— :s	r' :— :r'	d' :— :—	d' :— :	d' :— :—	— :— :
d :— :—	d :— :	f :— :—	f :— :	s :— :s	s :— :s	d :— :—	d :— :	d :— :—	— :— :

LO! THE GLAD MAY MORN.

132. KEY D. M. 120. *Brightly.* From the GERMAN.

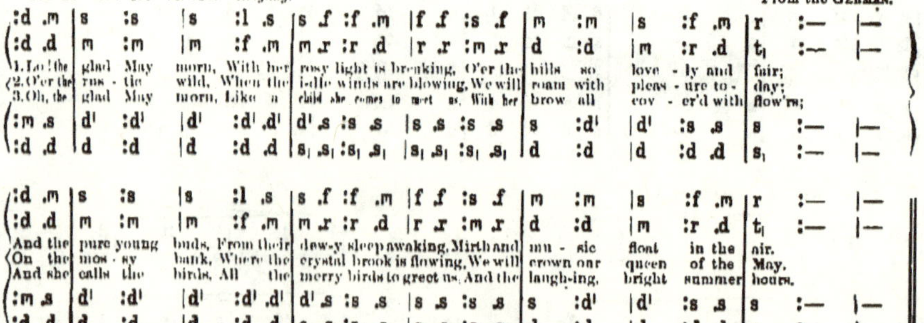

:d .m	s :s	s :l .s	s .f :f .m	f .f :s .f	m :m	s :f .m	r :—	—
:d .d	m :m	m :f .m	m .r :r .d	r .r :m .r	d :d	m :r .d	t_1 :—	—
1. Lo! the	glad May	morn, With her	rosy light is	breaking, O'er the	hills so	love - ly and	fair;	
2. O'er the	rus - tic	wild, When the	idle winds are	blowing, We will	roam with	pleas - ure to -	day;	
3. Oh, the	glad May	morn, Like a	child she comes to	meet us, With her	brow all	cov - er'd with	flow'rs;	
:m .s	d' :d'	d' :d' .d'	d' .s :s .s	s .s :s .s	s :d'	d' :s .s	s :—	—
:d .d	d :d	d :d .d	s_1 .s_1 :s_1 .s_1	s_1 .s_1 :s_1 .s_1	d :d	d :d .d	s_1 :—	—

:d .m	s :s	s :l .s	s .f :f .m	f .f :s .f	m :m	s :f .m	r :—	—
:d .d	m :m	m :f .m	m .r :r .d	r .r :m .r	d :d	m :r .d	t_1 :—	—
And the	pure young	buds, From their	dew-y sleep	awaking, Mirth and	mu - sic	float in the	air.	
On the	mos - sy	bank, Where the	crystal brook is	flowing, We will	crown our	queen of the	May.	
And she	calls the	birds, All the	merry birds to	greet us, And the	laugh-ing,	bright summer	hours.	
:m .s	d' :d'	d' :d' .d'	d' .s :s .s	s .s :s .s	s :d'	d' :s .s	s :—	—
:d .d	d :d	d :d .d	s_1 .s_1 :s_1 .s_1	s_1 .s_1 :s_1 .s_1	d :d	d :d .d	s_1 :—	—

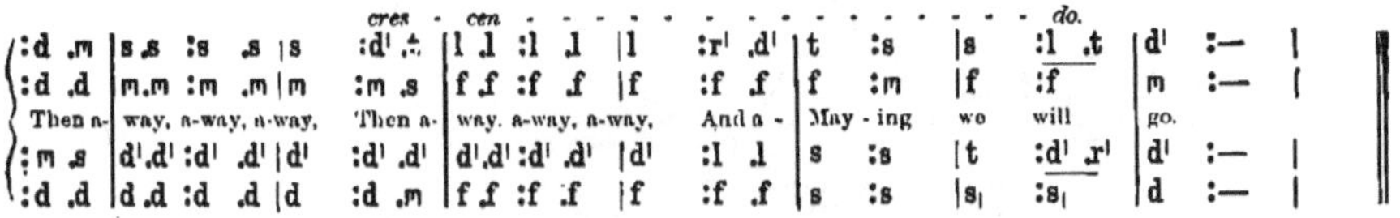

cres - cen - - - - - - - - - - - - - - - - - do.

:d .m	s .s :s .s | s	:d' .t	l .l :l .l | l	:r' .d'	t :s	s :l .t	d' :—
:d .d	m .m :m .m | m	:m .s	f .f :f .f | f	:f .f	f :m	f :f	m :—
Then a-	way, a-way, a-way,	Then a-	way, a-way, a-way,	And a -	May - ing	we will	go.
:m .s	d'.d' :d' .d' | d'	:d' .d'	d'.d' :d' .d' | d'	:l .l	s :s	t :d' .r'	d' :—
:d .d	d .d :d .d | d	:d .m	f .f :f .f | f	:f .f	s :s	s, :s,	d :—

MERRILY THE CUCKOO.

133. KEY D. M. 80. CHESTER G. ALLEN.

s ,s .s ,s :s .m	d' .l :s	r .m :f .l	s :m
m ,m .m ,m :m .d	m .f :m	t, .d :r .f	m :d
1.Merri-ly the cuck - oo	in the vale	To the morn is	sing - ing,
2.Pleasantly the sun, with	gold - en light,	Wakes the earth to	glad - ness,
d' ,d' .d' ,d' :d' .s	s .d' :d'	s .s :s .t	d' :s
d ,d .d ,d :d .d	d .d :d	s, .s, :s, .s,	d :d

s ,s .s ,s :s .m	d' .l :s .d'	t .s :l .t	d' :d' .s
m ,m .m ,m :m .d	m .f :m .m	f .f :f .f	m :m .m
Cheeri-ly the ech - o's	fair - y tale By	sil - ver fount is	ring - ing. A -
Happi - ly we roam till	dew - y night With -	out a thought of	sad - ness. A -
d' ,d' .d' ,d' :d' .s	s .d' :d' .d'	r' .t :d' .r'	d' :s .s
d ,d .d ,d :d .d	d .d :d .d	s .s :s .s	d :d .d

f .m :r .l	s .f :m .s	f .m :r .l	s .f :m
r .d :t, .f	m .r :d .m	r .d :t .f	m .r :d
way, a - way, with	foot - steps free, We'll	chase the shad - ows	o'er the lea:
way, a - way, with	foot - steps free, We'll	chase the shad - ows	o'er the lea:
s .s :s .t	d' .d' :d' .s	s .s :s .t	d' .d' :d'
s, .s, :s, .s,	d .d :d .d	s, .s, :s, .s,	d .d :d

𝄋 D.S.

s ,s .s ,s :s	l ,l .l ,l :l	l .r' :d' .t	d' :—
m ,m .m ,m :m	f ,f .f ,f :f	f .f :m .r	m :—
Merri - ly we go,	Merri-ly we go,	None so gay as	we.
Merri - ly we go,	Merri-ly we go,	None so gay as	we.
d' ,d' .d' ,d' :d'	d',d' .d' ,d' :d'	l .l :s .s	s :—
d ,d .d ,d :d	f ,f .f ,f :f	f .r :s .s,	d :—

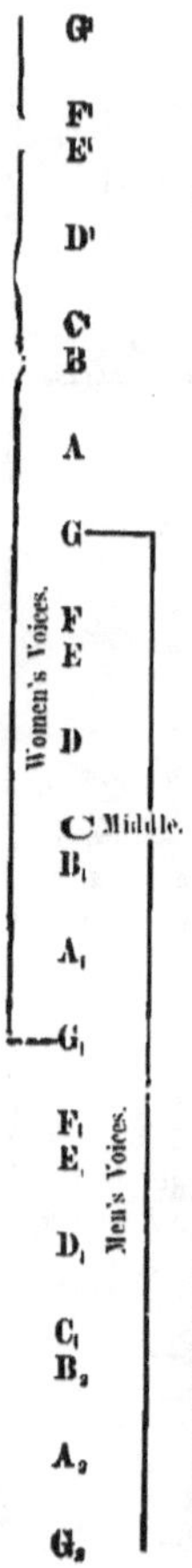

Classification of Voices. The teacher may now proceed to a more definite classification of the voices. He will first explain the difference of pitch between the voices of men and the voices of women. This may be done by having the women sing the scale of C several times alone, and then let the men sing it alone. Most of the men will think they sang the same tones the ladies sang. To prove they did not, let the ladies sing d (C) and sustain it, while the men sing from *their* d up to d', when they reach their d' they will be in exact unison with the ladies. It will thus be seen that the voices of men are naturally an octave lower than the voices of woman. This pitch C, which was just sung in unison, and which stands high in a man's voice and low in a woman's—is called middle C. It is about the middle tone of the usual vocal compass and is common to nearly all musical instruments. The diagram on the left will show the usual vocal compass, male and female. The teacher may find it useful to draw this diagram on the blackboard and have the tones sung at their proper pitch to his pointing. Let all begin at Middle C, the voices of the men and women in exact unison, then, as the teacher points, sing up the scale together. At G the men will stop, many of them will have to stop before reaching that tone, the woman continue up to G'. Then, descending, the men will join in at G (at the proper pitch) and together descend to to G_1, at this tone the women will stop, the men continuing down to G_2. Returning upwards, the women will join in at G_1 and so on.

G' F' E' D' C' B A G F E D C Middle. B_1 A_1 G_1 F_1 E_1 D_1 C_1 B_2 A_2 G_2

Women's Voices. Men's Voices.

131. KEY C.

LADIES.	d	:d	d	:d	d	:d	d	:d
	Now	our	voic -	es	all	a -	nit -	ed;
GENTLEMEN.	d'	:d'	d'	:d'	d'	:d'	d'	:d'
	m	:m	s	:s	d'	:d'	t	:—
	Let	us	see	why	they	a - -	gree:	
	d'	:d'	t	:t	l	:l	s	:—
	t	:t	d'	:s .f	m	:f	s	:m
	'Tis	be - -	cause	when	first	we	start -	ed
	s	:f	m	:r	d	:r	m	:d
	s	:f	m	:r	d	:d	d	:—
	We	were	sing -	ing	Mid -	dle	C.	
	m	:f	s	:l .t	d'	:d'	d'	:—

The teacher may next examine the women's voices and classify them into high voices called Soprano and low voices, called Contralto. The high voices of men are called Tenor—the low voices of men are called Base. Each voice should be examined individually. To examine the women's voices the teacher gives G (first G above middle C) as a key-tone and requires the pupil to sing the scale, first upward as high as she can go, and then downward as low as she can go. If the fuller, more beautiful and more easily produced tones of her voice lie above G it may be classed as a high voice. If the best tones lie below G, then it may be called a low voice. The men's voices may be examined in the same way by taking G_1 (first G_1 below middle C), as a key-tone. It is the *quality* of the voice, not the compass, that decides the question. Cultivation may afterwards make a difference, but this simple mode of classification will answer for the present purpose. The diagram on the right shows the usual easy compass of the different voices.

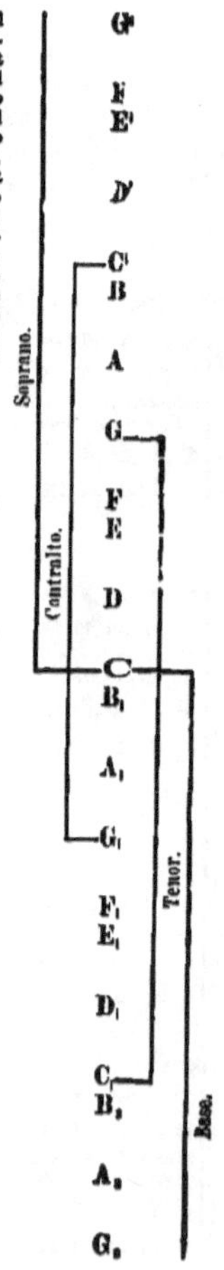

G' F' E' D' C' B A G F E D C B_1 A_1 G_1 F_1 E_1 D_1 C_1 B_2 A_2 G_2

Soprano. Contralto. Tenor. Base.

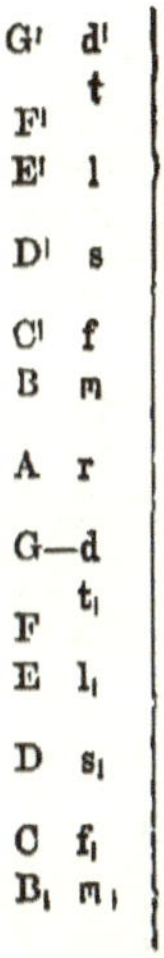

G' d'
t
F'
E' l
D' s
C' f
B m
A r
G—d
t_1
F
E l_1
D s_1
C f_1
B_1 m_1

Octave Marks. The pitch of the key-tone of any key is always taken from the unmarked octave of the Standard Scale, and this *doh*, whatever pitch it may be, with the six tones above it are without octave marks. For instance, for the key G, the unmarked G of the Standard Scale is taken as *doh*, this *doh* with the six tones above, **r m f s l t**, are without octave mark; the scale below would have the lower octave mark. This may be illustrated by the following diagram. To save the unnecessary multiplicity of octave marks, both in writing and printing, the Tenor and Base parts are always written an octave higher than they are sung. In quoting octave marks, as in dictation, the upper octave marks are distinguished by naming them before the note, the lower by naming them after—thus, C' is "one-C," d' is "*one-doh,*" G_1 is "G-one," s_1 is "*soh-one.*" It will help the memory to notice that the higher comes first. Thus, we say that the easy Base Compass is, as above, "from G-two to C," that of Contralto "from the G-one to one-C," that of the Tenor "from C-one to unmarked F," that of the Soprano "from unmarked C to one-F."

135. KEY C.

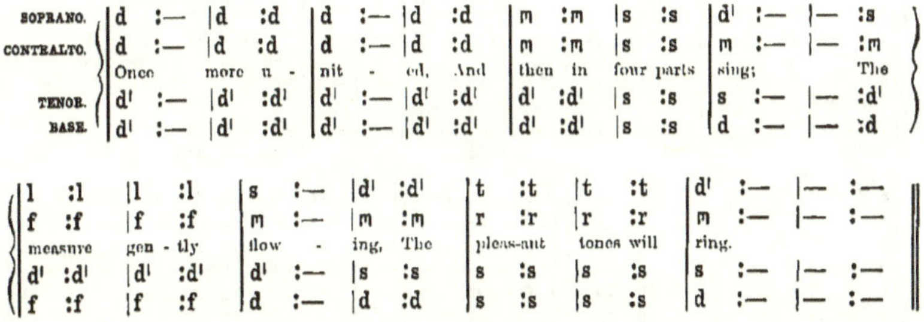

SOPRANO. |d :— |d :d |d :— |d :d |m :m |s :s |d' :— |— :s
CONTRALTO. |d :— |d :d |d :— |d :d |m :m |s :s |m :— |— :m
Once more u - nit - ed, And then in four parts sing; The
TENOR. |d' :— |d' :d' |d' :— |d' :d' |d' :d' |s :s |s :— |— :d'
BASE. |d' :— |d' :d' |d' :— |d' :d' |d' :d' |s :s |d :— |— :d

|l :l |l :l |s :— |d' :d' |t :t |t :t |d' :— |— :— ‖
|f :f |f :f |m :— |m :m |r :r |r :r |m :— |— :— ‖
measure gen - tly flow - ing, The pleas-ant tones will ring.
|d' :d' |d' :d' |d' :— |s :s |s :s |s :s |s :— |— :— ‖
|f :f |f :f |d :— |d :d |s :s |s :s |d :— |— :— ‖

Unison really means two or more voices singing the same identical tone, as in the first two measures of No. 135, but it is generally used to mean that men and women sing the same part, *i. e.*, the men an octave lower than the women, as in the first two measures of No. 136.

SONGS OF PRAISE.

136. KEY C. H. R. PALMER.

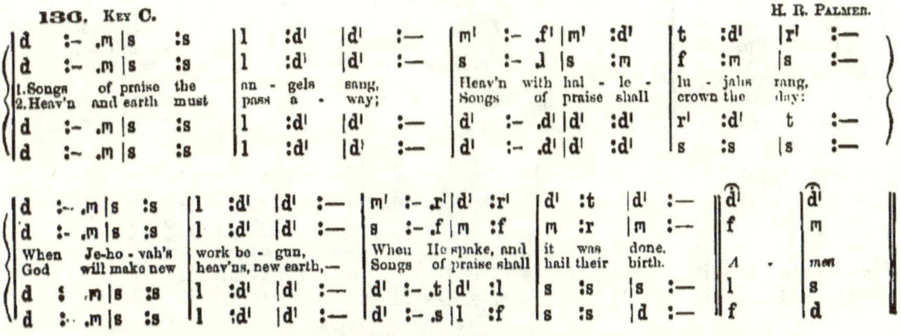

|d :- .m |s :s |l :d' |d' :— |m' :- .f' |m' :d' |t :d' |r' :—
|d :- .m |s :s |l :d' |d' :— |s :- .l |s :m |f :m |s :—
1. Songs of praise the an - gels sang, Heav'n with hal - le - lu - jahs rang,
2. Heav'n and earth must pass a - way; Songs of praise shall crown the day:
|d :- .m |s :s |l :d' |d' :— |d' :- .d' |d' :d' |r' :d' |t :—
|d :- .m |s :s |l :d' |d' :— |d' :- .d' |d' :d' |s :s |s :—

|d :- .m |s :s |l :d' |d' :— |m' :- .r' |d' :r' |d' :t |d' :— ‖d' |d' ‖
|d :- .m |s :s |l :d' |d' :— |s :- .f |m :f |m :r |m :— ‖f |m ‖
When Je-ho - vah's work be - gun, When He spake, and it was done. A - men
God will make new heav'ns, new earth,— Songs of praise shall hail their birth.
|d : .m |s :s |l :d' |d' :— |d' :- .t |d' :l |s :s |s :— ‖l |s ‖
|d :- .m |s :s |l :d' |d' :— |d' :- .s |l :f |s :s |d :— ‖f |d ‖

CHRISTMAS SONG.

137. KEY C. L. M. GORDON, by per.

m :— |s :— |f :— |s :— |r :— |s :— |m :— |d :— |m :— |s :—
Sweet the chim - ing, Still the tim - ing, Glad - ness
d :— |m :— |r :— |r :— |r :— |t_1 :— |d :— |d :— |d :— |m :—
d :r |m :f |s :l |t :d' |t :l |s :f |m :r |d :t_1 |d :r |m :f
Stee-ple bells with joy-ful chim-ing, Stee-ple clocks with care-ful tim-ing, Ush-er in the
d :— |— :— |r :— |— :— |s_1 :— |— :— |d :— |— :— |d :— |— :—
Sweet bells chim - ing, Glad

s :— |s :— |r :— |s :— |d :— |— :— |s :— |s :— |s :— |s :—
fill ing all the air. Chil - dren sing - ing,
r :— |r :— |r :— |t_1 :— |d :— |— :— |r :r |f :f |m :f |s :m
Chil-dren's voi-ces car-ols sing-ing,
s :l |t :d' |t :l |s :f |m :— |— :— |t :t |r' :r' |d' :r' |m' :d'
Christmas rhym-ing on the si-lent air.
r :— |— :— |s_1 :— |— :— |d :— |— :— |s :— |s :— |d :— |d :—
hearts mak - ing. Chil - dren sing - ing.

s :— |s :— |s :— |s :— |m :— |s :— |f :— |s :— |r :m |f :s |l :t |d' :—
An - gels wing - ing. Ti - dings bring - ing, Peace and gladness ev - ery - where.
r :r |f :f |m :f |s :m |d :— |m :— |r :— |r :— |r :m |f :s |l :t |d' :—
An-gel bands thro' heaven winging, To the earth glad ti-dings bringing, Peace and gladness ev - ery - where.
t :t |r' :r' |d' :r' |m' :d' |d :r |m :f |s :l |t :d' |t :l |s :f |m :r |d :—
s :— |s :— |d :— |d :— |d :r |m :f |s :l |t :d' |t :l |s :f |m :r |d :—
An - gels wing - ing.

NEVER SAY FAIL.

138. KEY D. CHESTER G. ALLEN.

:m |m :— |d :m |s :— |m :s |l :d' |t :l |s :— |— :s |l :— |f :l
:d |d :— |d :d |m :— |d :m |f :l |s :f |m :— |— :m |f :— |d :f
1. Keep work - ing, 'tis wis - er than sit - ting a - side, And dream - ing, and
2. With eyes ev - er o - pen, a tongue that's not dumb, A heart that will
3. In life's ros - y morn - ing, in man - hood's fair pride, Let this be your
:s |s :— |m :s |d' :— |s :d' |d' :— |d' :d' |d' :— |— :d' |l :— |l :d'
:d |d :— |d :d |d :— |d :d |f :— |f :f |d :— |— :d |f :— |f :f

s :— |m :s |s :— |f :m |r :— |— :d |d :m |s :l |s :— |m :s
m :— |d :m |r :— |r :d |t_1 :— |— :d |d :m |s :l |s :— |m :s
sigh - ing and wait - ing the tide; In life's earn - est bat - tle those
nev - er to sor - row suc - cumb; You'll bat - tle and con - quer, the
mot - to your foot - steps to guide; In storm and in sun - shine, what-
d' :— |s :s |s :— |s :s |s :— |— :d |d :m |s :l |s :— |m :s
d :— |d :d |t_1 :— |t_1 :d |s_1 :— |— :d |d :m |s :l |s :— |m :s

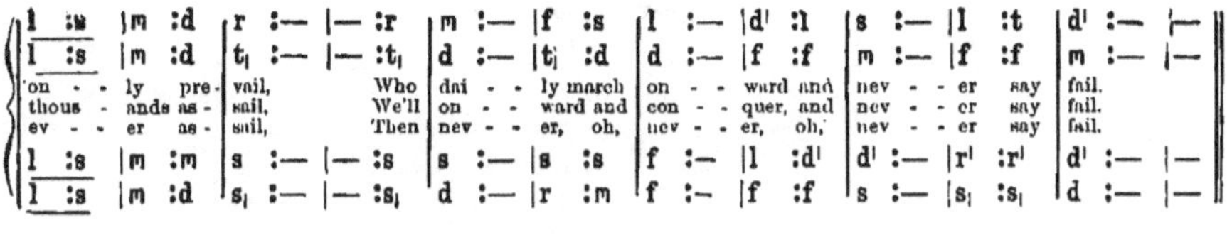

l :s |m :d |r :— |— :r |m :— |f :s |l :— |d' :l |s :— |l :t |d' :— |—

l :s |m :d |t, :— |— :t, |d :— |t, :d |d :— |f :f |m :— |f :f |m :— |—

on - - ly pre - | vail, Who | dai - - ly march | on - - ward and | nev - - er say | fail.

thous - ands as - | sail, We'll | on - - ward and | con - - quer, and | nev - - er say | fail.

ev - - er as - | sail, Then | nev - - er, oh, | nev - - er, oh, | nev - - er say | fail.

l :s |m :m |s :— |— :s |s :— |s :s |f :— |l :d' |d' :— |r' :r' |d' :— |—

l :s |m :d |s, :— |— :s, |d :— |r :m |f :— |f :f |s :— |s, :s, |d :— |—

MORNING HYMN.

139. Key C. T. F. Seward.

:d |m :— |m :f |s :— |m :s |l :— |— :l |d' :— |t :l |s :— |s :m

:d |d :— |d :r |m :— |d :m |f :— |— :f |l :— |s :f |m :— |m :d

1.Our | Fa - ther we | thank thee for | sleep, For | qui - et and | com - fort and

2 Our | voic - es would | ut - ter thy | praise, Our | hearts would o'er - | flow with thy

3.So | long as thou | deem - est it | right, That | here on the | earth we should

:m |s :— |s :d' |d' :— |s :d' |d' :— |— :d' |d' :— |d' :l |d' :— |d' :s

:d |d :— |d :d |d :— |d :d |f :— |— :f |f :— |f :f |d :— |d :m

r :— |— :d |m :— |m :f |s :m |f :s |l :— |— :l |s :— |d' :m'

t, :— |— :d |d :— |d :r |m :d |r :m |f :— |— :f |m :— |m :s

rest, We | thank thee for | lov - ing to | keep Thy | chil - dren from

love, O | teach us to | walk in thy | ways, And | fit us to

stay, We | pray thee to | guard us by | night, And | help us to

s :— |— :m |s :— |s :d' |d' :— |d' :d' |d' :— |— :d' |d' :— |d' :s

s, :— |— :d |d :— |d :d |d :— |d :d |f :— |— :f |s :— |s :s

r' :— |d' :t |d' :— |— :d' |d' :— |t :l |d' :— |t :l |s :— |m :f

f :— |m :r |m :— |— :m |l :— |s :f |l :— |s :f |m :— |d :r

be - - ing dis - | tressed. O | bow in their | weak - ness can | crea - tures re -

meet thee a - | bove. The | heart's pure af - | fec - tion is | all we can

serve thee by | day. And | when all the | days of our | earth - life are

s :— |s :s |s :— |— :d' |d' :— |d' :d' |d' :— |d' :d' |s :— |s :d'

s, :— |s, :s, |d :— |— :d |f :— |f :f |f :— |f :f |d :— |d :d

s :— |— :d' |m' :— |r' :d' |m' :— |r' :d' |t :— |l :t |d' :— |—

m :— |— :m |s :— |f :m |s :— |f :m |r :— |d :r |m :— |—

pay Thy | fath - er - ly | kind - ness by | night and by | day.

give; In | love's pure de - | vo - tion O | help us to | live.

past, Re - | ceive us in | heav - en to | praise thee at | last.

d' :— |— :d' |d' :— |s :s |d' :— |s :s |s :— |s :s |s :— |—

d :— |— :d |d :— |d :d |d :— |d :d |s, :— |s, :s, |d :— |—

HOW SWEET TO HEAR.

140. KEY D. T. F. SEWARD.

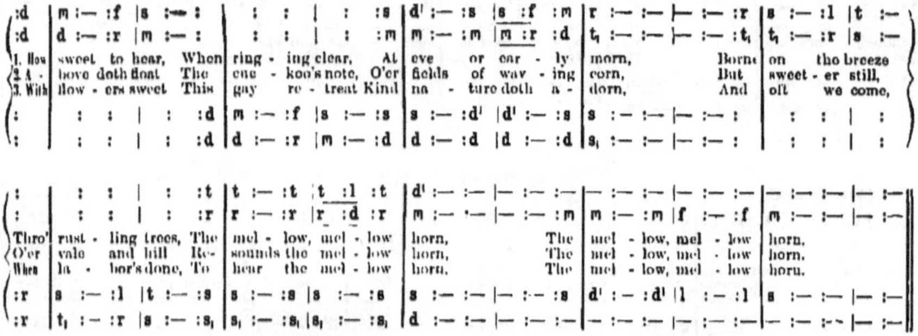

:d |m :— :f |s :— : | : : | : :s |d' :— :s |s :f :m |r :— :— |— :— :r |s :— :l |t :—
:d |d :— :r |m :— : | : : | : :m |m :— :m |m :r :d |t, :— :— |— :— :t, |t, :— :r |s :—

1. How sweet to hear, When ring - ing clear, At eve or ear - ly morn, Borne on the breeze
2. A - bove doth float The cuc - koo's note, O'er fields of wav - ing corn, But sweet - er still,
3. With flow - ers sweet This gay re - treat Kind na - ture doth a - dorn, And oft we come,

: | : : | : :d |m :— :f |s :— :s |s :— :d' |d' :— :s |s :— :— |— :— : | : : | :
: | : : | : :d |d :— :r |m :— :d |d :— :d |d :— :d |s, :— :— |— :— : | : : | :

: | : : | : :t |t :— :t |t :l :t |d' :— :— |— :— :— |— :— :— |— :— :— |— :— :— |— :—
: | : : | : :r |r :— :r |r :d :r |m :— :— |— :— :m |m :— :m |f :— :f |m :— :— |— :—

Thro' rust - ling trees, The mel - low, mel - low horn, The mel - low, mel - low horn.
O'er vale and hill Re- sounds the mel - low horn, The mel - low, mel - low horn.
When la - bor's done, To hear the mel - low horn, The mel - low, mel - low horn.

:r |s :— :l |t :— :s |s :— :s |s :— :s |s :— :— |— :— :s |d' :— :d' |l :— :l |s :— :— |— :—
:r |t, :— :r |s :— :s, |s, :— :s, |s, :— :s, |d :— :— |— :— :— |— :— :— |— :— :— |— :— :— |— :—

141. KEY D.

m *p*

|s :f |m :— |f :m |r :— |r :m |f :f |s :f |m :—
Fall - ing leaves, fall - ing leaves, Tell how sad - ly na - ture grieves;
|m :r |d :— |r :d |t, :— |t, :d |r :r |m :r |d :—

p *f* *m* *p*

|m :f |s :s |l :t |d' :— |d' :l |s :— |s :f |m :—
While the au - tumn breez - es blow, Soft and low, soft and low.
|d :r |m :m |f :f |m :— |m :f |m :— |m :r |d :—

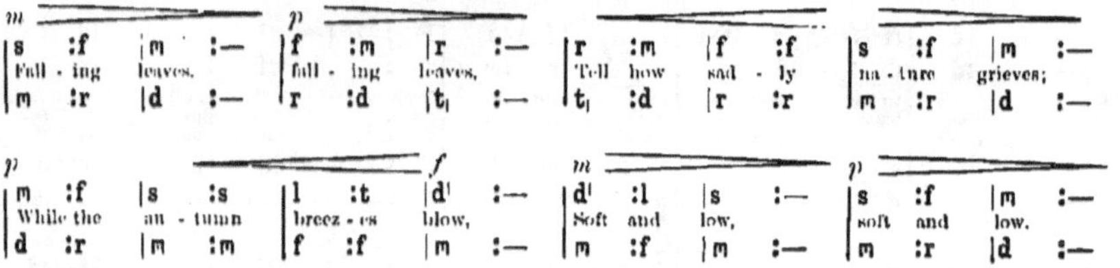

142. KEY D. STACCATO AND LEGATO.

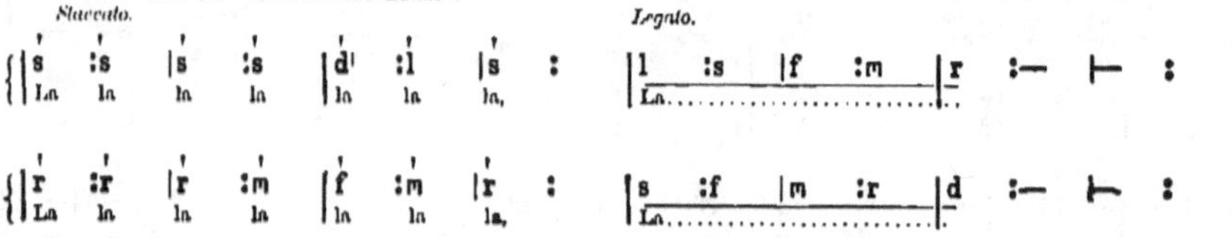

Staccato. *Legato.*

|s :s |s :s |d' :l |s : |l :s |f :m |r :— |— :
La la la la la la la, La........................

|r :r |r :m |f :m |r : |s :f |m :r |d :— |— :
La la la la la la la, La........................

143. KEY A.

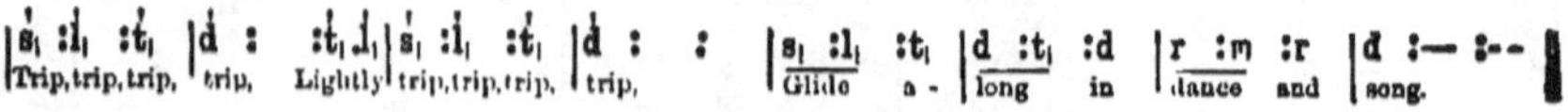

|s, :l, :t, |d : :t, .l, |s, :l, :t, |d : : |s, :l, :t, |d :t, :d |r :m :r |d :— :—
Trip, trip, trip, trip, Lightly trip, trip, trip, trip, Glide a - long in dance and song.

MY MOUNTAIN HOME.

144. KEY D. M. 90, beating twice. Words and Music by A. S. KIEFFER, by per.

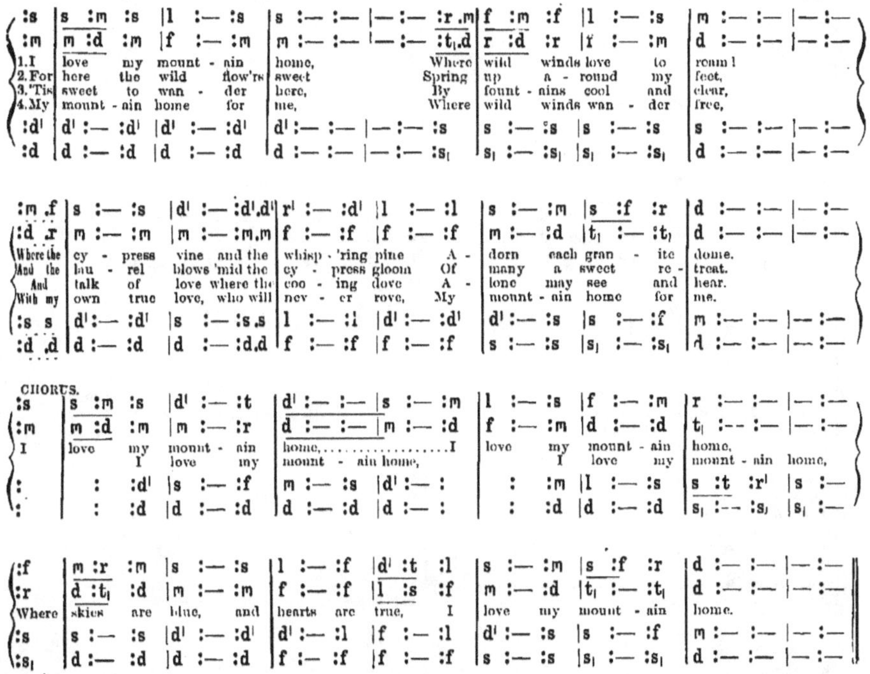

:s |s :m :s |l :— :s |s :— :— |— :— :r.m |f :m :f |l :— :s |m :— :— |— :—
:m |m :d :m |f :— :m |m :— :— |— :— :t₁.d |r :d :r |r :— :m |d :— :— |— :—
1.I love my mount - ain home, Where wild winds love to roam!
2.For here the wild flow'rs sweet Spring up a - round my feet,
3.'Tis sweet to wan - der here, By fount - ains cool and clear,
4.My mount - ain home for me, Where wild winds wan - der free,
:d' |d' :— :d' |d' :— :d' |d' :— :— |— :— :s |s :— :s |s :— :s |s :— :— |— :—
:d |d :— :d |d :— :d |d :— :— |— :— :s₁ |s₁ :— :s₁ |s₁ :— :s₁ |d :— :— |— :—

:m.f |s :— :s |d' :— :d'.d' |r' :— :d' |l :— :l |s :— :m |s :f :r |d :— :— |— :—
:d.r |m :— :m |m :— :m.m |f :— :f |f :— :f |m :— :d |t₁ :— :t₁ |d :— :— |— :—
Where the cy - press vine and the whisp - 'ring pine A - dorn each gran - ite dome.
And the lau - rel blows 'mid the cy - press gloom Of many a sweet re - treat.
And talk of love where the coo - ing dove A - lone may see and hear.
With my own true love, who will nev - er rove, My mount - ain home for me.
:s.s |d' :— :d' |s :— :s.s |l :— :l |d' :— :d' |d' :— :s |s :— :f |m :— :— |— :—
:d.d |d :— :d |d :— :d.d |f :— :f |f :— :f |s :— :s |s₁ :— :s₁ |d :— :— |— :—

CHORUS.

:s |s :m :s |d' :— :t |d' :— :— |s :— :m |l :— :s |f :— :m |r :— :— |— :—
:m |m :d :m |m :— :r |d :— :— |m :— :d |f :— :m |d :— :d |t₁ :— :— |— :—
I love my mount - ain home,..................I love my mount - ain home,
I love my mount - ain home, I love my mount - ain home,
: | : :d' |s :— :f |m :— :s |d' :— : | : :m |l :— :s |s :t :r' |s :—
: | : :d |d :— :d |d :— :d |d :— : | : :d |d :— :d |s₁ :— :s₁ |s₁ :—

:f |m :r :m |s :— :s |l :— :f |d' :t :l |s :— :m |s :f :r |d :— :— |— :— ||
:r |d :t₁ :d |m :— :m |f :— :f |l :s :f |m :— :d |t₁ :— :t₁ |d :— :— |— :— ||
Where skies are blue, and hearts are true, I love my mount - ain home.
:s |s :— :s |d' :— :d' |d' :— :l |f :— :l |d' :— :s |s :— :f |m :— :— |— :— ||
:s₁ |d :— :d |d :— :d |f :— :f |f :— :f |s :— :s |s₁ :— :s₁ |d :— :— |— :— ||

145. KEY C. Round for two parts. T. F. S.

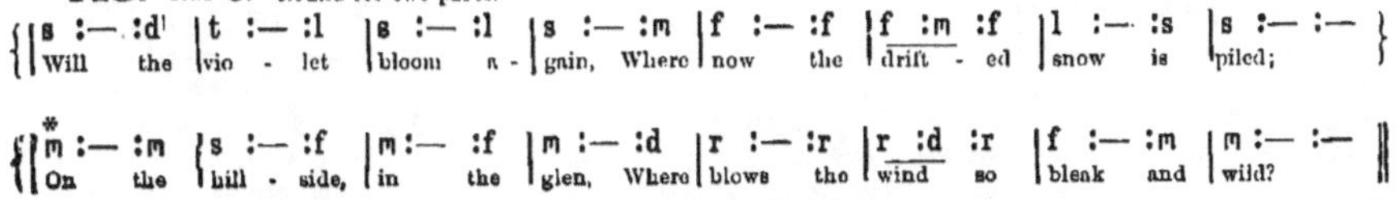

|s :— :d' |t :— :l |s :— :l |s :— :m |f :— :f |f :m :f |l :— :s |s :— :—
Will the vio - let bloom a - gain, Where now the drift - ed snow is piled;

|*m :— :m |s :— :f |m :— :f |m :— :d |r :— :r |r :d :r |f :— :m |m :— :— ||
On the hill - side, in the glen, Where blows the wind so bleak and wild?

SUNSHOWER.

146. KEY A. M. 72. T. W. DENNINGTON, by per.

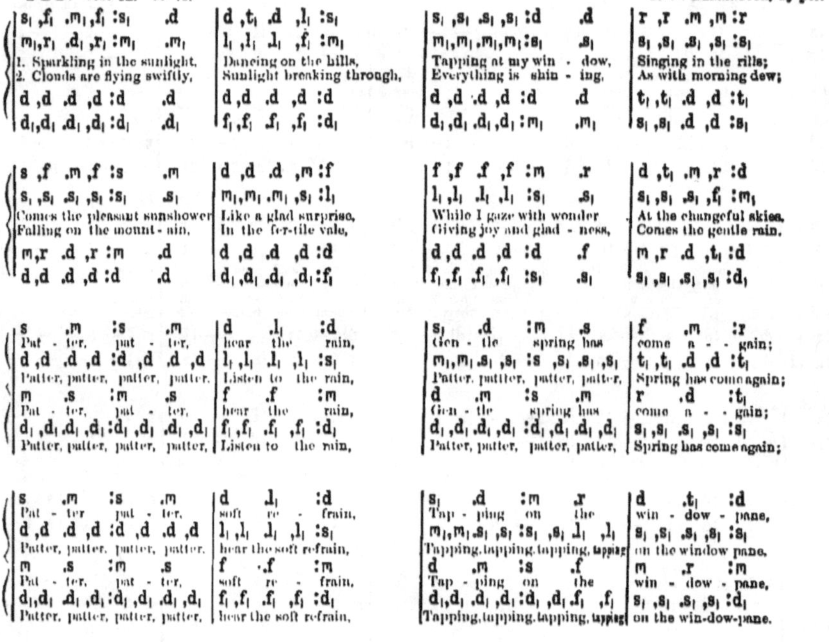

s_1 ,f_1 .m_1 ,f_1 :s_1 .d	d ,t_1 .d ,l_1 :s_1	s_1 ,s_1 .s_1 ,s_1 :d .d	r ,r .m ,m :r
m_1,r_1 .d_1 ,r_1 :m_1 .m_1	l_1 ,l_1 .l_1 ,f_1 :m_1	m_1,m_1 .m_1,m_1 :s_1 .s_1	s_1 ,s_1 .s_1 ,s_1 :s_1
1. Sparkling in the sunlight,	Dancing on the hills,	Tapping at my win - dow,	Singing in the rills;
2. Clouds are flying swiftly,	Sunlight breaking through,	Everything is shin - ing,	As with morning dew;
d ,d .d ,d :d .d	d ,d .d ,d :d	d ,d .d ,d :d .d	t_1 ,t_1 .d ,d :t_1
d_1,d_1 .d_1 ,d_1 :d_1 .d_1	f_1 ,f_1 .f_1 ,f_1 :d_1	d_1 ,d_1 .d_1 ,d_1 :m_1 .m_1	s_1 ,s_1 .d ,d :s_1

s ,f .m ,f :s .m	d ,d .d ,m :f	f ,f .f ,f :m .r	d ,t_1 .m ,r :d
s_1 ,s_1 .s_1 ,s_1 :s_1 .s_1	m_1,m_1 .m_1 ,s_1 :l_1	l_1 ,l_1 .l_1 ,l_1 :s_1 .s_1	s_1 ,s_1 .s_1 ,f_1 :m_1
Comes the pleasant sunshower	Like a glad surprise,	While I gaze with wonder	At the changeful skies.
Falling on the mount - ain,	In the fer-tile vale,	Giving joy and glad - ness,	Comes the gentle rain.
m,r .d ,r :m .d	d ,d .d ,d :d	d ,d .d ,d :d .f	m ,r .d ,t_1 :d
d ,d .d ,d :d .d	d_1 ,d_1 .d_1 ,d_1 :f_1	f_1 ,f_1 .f_1 ,f_1 :s_1 .s_1	s_1 ,s_1 .s_1 ,s_1 :d_1

s .m :s .m	d .l_1 :d	s_1 .d :m .s	f .m :r
Pat - ter, pat - ter,	hear the rain,	Gen - tle spring has	come a - - gain;
d ,d .d ,d :d ,d .d ,d	l_1 ,l_1 .l_1 ,l_1 :s_1	m_1,m_1 .s_1 ,s_1 :s ,s_1 .s_1 ,s_1	t_1 ,t_1 .d ,d :t_1
Patter, patter, patter, patter.	Listen to the rain,	Patter, patter, patter, patter,	Spring has come again;
m .s :m .s	f .f :m	d .m :s .m	r .d :t_1
Pat - ter, pat - ter,	hear the rain,	Gen - tle spring has	come a - - gain;
d_1 ,d_1 .d_1 ,d_1 :d_1 ,d_1 .d_1 ,d_1	f_1 ,f_1 .f_1 ,f_1 :d_1	d_1 ,d_1 .d_1 ,d_1 :d_1 ,d_1 .d_1 ,d_1	s_1 ,s_1 .s_1 ,s_1 :s_1
Patter, patter, patter, patter,	Listen to the rain,	Patter, patter, patter, patter,	Spring has come again;

s .m :s .m	d .l_1 :d	s_1 .d :m .r	d .t_1 :d
Pat - ter pat - ter,	soft re - frain,	Tap - ping on the	win - dow - pane,
d ,d .d ,d :d ,d .d ,d	l_1 ,l_1 .l_1 ,l_1 :s_1	m_1,m_1 .s_1 ,s_1 :s_1 ,s_1 .l_1 ,l_1	s_1 ,s_1 .s_1 ,s_1 :s_1
Patter, patter, patter, patter.	hear the soft refrain,	Tapping, tapping, tapping, tapping	on the window pane,
m .s :m .s	f .f :m	d .m :s .f	m .r :m
Pat - ter, pat - ter,	soft re - frain,	Tap - ping on the	win - dow - pane,
d_1,d_1 .d_1 ,d_1 :d_1 ,d_1 .d_1 ,d_1	f_1 ,f_1 .f_1 ,f_1 :d_1	d_1,d_1 .d_1 ,d_1 :d_1 ,d_1 .f_1 ,f_1	s_1 ,s_1 .s_1 ,s_1 :d_1
Patter, patter, patter, patter,	hear the soft refrain,	Tapping, tapping, tapping, tapping	on the win-dow-pane.

147. KEY D. Round for three parts.

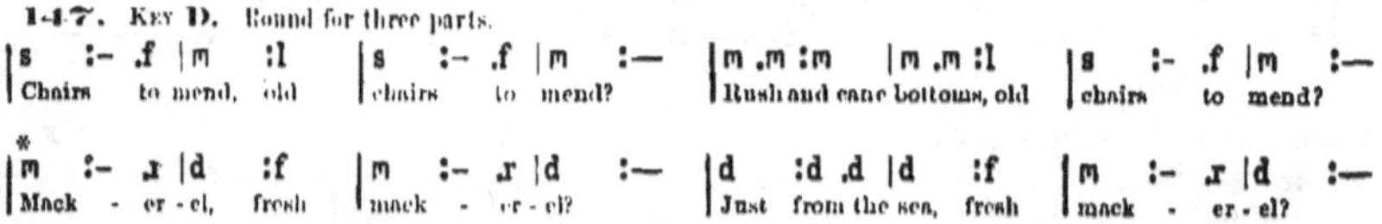

s :- .f | m :l	s :- .f | m :—	m .m :m | m .m :l	s :- .f | m :—
Chairs to mend, old	chairs to mend?	Rush and cane bottoms, old	chairs to mend?
* m :- .r | d :f	m :- .r | d :—	d :d .d | d :f	m :- .r | d :—
Mack - er - el, fresh	mack - er - el?	Just from the sea, fresh	mack - er - el?
d .d :d .d | d .d :d .d	d :d | d^1 .d^1 :d^1 .d^1	d :d^1 | d :d^1	d .d :d .d | d^1 .d^1 :
Here's a chance for bargains with your	cast - off clothing and your	old hats, old boots.	rags and empty bottles.

148. KEY A. M. 72. **SERENADE.**

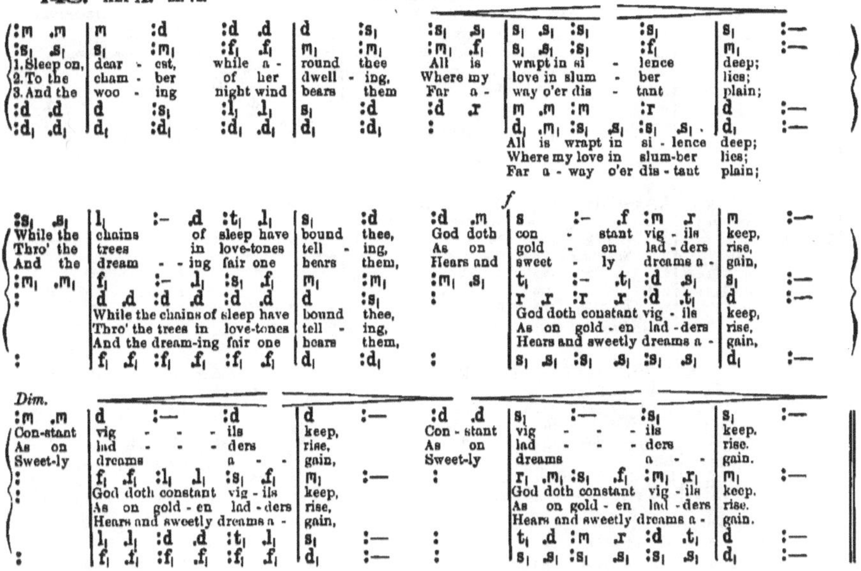

```
:m  .m  |m     :d      :d  .d   |d      :s,     :s,  .s,  |s, .s, :s,     :s,     |s,     :—
:s, .s, |s,    :m,     :f, .f,  |m,     :m,     :m,  .f,  |s, .s, :s,     :f,     |m,     :—
1.Sleep on, dear - est, while a - round thee   All is      wrapt in si  -  lence    deep;
2.To the    cham - ber  of her    dwell - ing, Where my    love in slum -  ber      lies;
3.And the   woo - ing   night wind bears them   Far a -    way o'er dis -  tant     plain;
:d  .d  |d     :s,     :l,  .l, |s,     :d      :d   .r   |m  .m  :m      :r      |d      :—
:d, .d, |d,    :d,     :d,  .d, |d,     :d,     :         |d, .m, :s, .s, :s, .s, |d,     :—
                                                           All is wrapt in si - lence deep;
                                                           Where my love in slum-ber lies;
                                                           Far a - way o'er dis - tant plain;
```

```
                                                          f
:s, .s, |l,    :-  .d  :t,  .l, |s,     :d      :d   .m   |s   :-  .f  :m   .r   |m     :—
While the chains   of   sleep have bound thee,   God doth   con  -  stant vig - ils  keep,
Thro' the trees    in   love-tones tell - ing,   As on      gold  -  en   lad - ders rise,
And the   dream - - ing fair one  hears them,    Hears and  sweet -  ly  dreams a - gain,
:m, .m, |f,    :-  .l,  :s,  .f, |m,     :m,     :m,  .s,  |t,  :-  .t, :d   .s,  |s,    :—
:       |d .d  :d  .d   :d   .d  |d      :s,     :         |r .r :r  .r :d   .t,  |d     :—
         While the chains of sleep have bound thee,         God doth constant vig - ils keep,
         Thro' the trees in love-tones  tell - ing,         As on gold - en lad - ders rise,
         And the dream-ing fair one     hears them,         Hears and sweetly dreams a - gain,
:       |f, .f, :f, .f, :f, .f, |d,     :d,     :         |s, .s, :s, .s, :s, .s, |d,   :—
```

Dim.

```
:m  .m  |d     :—      :d       |d      :—      :d  .d    |s,     :—      :s,     |s,     :—
Con-stant vig  - - -   ils      keep,           Con - stant vig  - - -    ils      keep.
As on     lad  - - -   ders     rise,           As on      lad  - - -     ders     rise.
Sweet-ly  dreams     a - -      gain,           Sweet-ly   dreams      a - -       gain.
:       |f, .f, :l, .l, :s, .f, |m,     :—      :         |r, .m, :s, .f, :m, .r, |m,   :—
         God doth constant vig - ils keep,                  God doth constant vig - ils keep.
         As on gold - en lad - ders rise,                   As on gold - en lad - ders rise.
         Hears and sweetly dreams a - gain,                 Hears and sweetly dreams a - gain.
:       |l, .l, :d  .d  :t,  .l, |s,     :—      :         |t, .d :m  .r  :d  .t, |d     :—
:       |f, .f, :f, .f, :f,  .f, |d,     :—      :         |s, .s, :s, .s, :s, .s, |d,   :—
```

149. KEY A♭. **EVAN. C. M.** W. H. HAVERGAL.

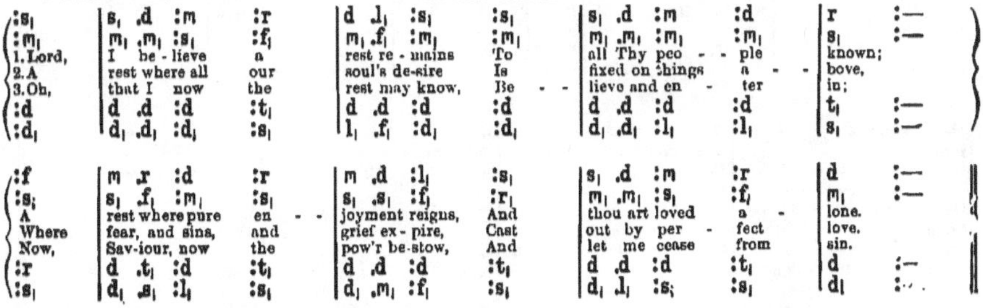

```
:s,     |s, .d  :m      :r      |d  .l, :s,     :s,     |s, .d  :m      :d      |r      :—
:m,     |m, .m, :s,     :f,     |m, .f, :m,     :m,     |m, .m, :m,     :m,     |s,     :—
1.Lord,  I be - lieve   a        rest re - mains To      all Thy peo - - ple     known;
2.A      rest where all our      soul's de-sire  Is      fixed on things a - -   bove,
3.Oh,    that I now     the      rest may know,  Be - -  lieve and en -  ter     in;
:d      |d  .d  :d      :t,     |d  .d  :d      :d      |d  .d  :d      :d      |t,     :—
:d,     |d, .d, :d,     :s,     |l, .f, :d,     :d,     |d, .d, :l,     :l,     |s,     :—
```

```
:f      |m  .r  :d      :r      |m  .d  :l,     :s,     |s, .d  :m      :r      |d      :—
:s,     |s, .f, :m,     :s,     |s, .s, :f,     :r,     |m, .m, :s,     :f,     |m,     :—
A        rest where pure en - -  joyment reigns, And     thou art loved  a -     lone.
Where    fear, and sins, and     grief ex - pire, Cast   out by per -    fect    love.
Now,     Sav-iour, now  the      pow'r be-stow,  And     let me cease     from    sin.
:r      |d  .t, :d      :t,     |d  .d  :d      :t,     |d  .d  :d      :t,     |d      :—
:s,     |d, .s, :l,     :s,     |d, .m, :f,     :s,     |d, .l, :s,     :s,     |d,     :—
```

CANON. NOW THE EVENING FALLS.

150. KEY B♭. M. 104. May be sung in two, three or four parts. BEETHOVEN.

$m\ :r\ \vert d\ :t_1$	$l_1\ :—\ \vert —\ :t_1.d$	$r\ :d\ \vert t_1\ :l_1$	$s_1\ :—\ \vert —\ :l_1.t_1$	$d\ :t_1\ \vert l_1\ :—$
Now the eve - ning	falls, The	bird of twi - light	calls Our	footsteps home,
$:\ \vert\ :$	$l_1\ :s_1\ \vert f_1\ :m_1$	$r_1\ :—\ \vert —\ :m_1.f_1$	$s_1\ :f_1\ \vert m_1\ :r_1$	$d_1\ :—\ \vert —\ :r_1.m_1$
	Now the eve - ning	falls, The	bird of twi - light	calls Our
$:\ \vert\ :$	$:\ \vert\ :$	$:\ \vert\ :$	$m\ :r\ \vert d\ :t_1$	$l_1\ :—\ \vert —\ :t_1.d$
			Now the eve - ning	falls, The
$:\ \vert\ :$	$:\ \vert\ :$	$:\ \vert\ :$	$:\ \vert\ :$	$l_1\ :s_1\ \vert f_1\ :m_1$
				Now the eve - ning

$—\ :l_1\ \vert r\ :d$	$t_1\ :—\ \vert —\ :d.r$	$m\ :r\ \vert d\ :t_1$	$l_1\ :—\ \vert —\ :t_1.d$	$r\ :d\ \vert t_1\ :l_1$
No long - er	roam, For	now the eve - ning	falls, The	bird of twi - light
$f_1\ :m_1\ \vert r_1\ :—$	$—\ :r_1\ \vert s_1\ :f_1$	$m_1\ :—\ \vert —\ :f_1.s_1$	$l_1\ :s_1\ \vert f_1\ :m_1$	$r_1\ :—\ \vert —\ :m_1.f_1$
foot - steps home,	No long - er	roam, For	now the eve - ning	falls, The
$r\ :d\ \vert t_1\ :l_1$	$s_1\ :—\ \vert —\ :l_1.t_1$	$d\ :t_1\ \vert l_1\ :—$	$—\ :l_1\ \vert r\ :d$	$t_1\ :—\ \vert —\ :d.r$
bird of twi - light	calls Our	foot-steps home,	No long - er	roam, For
$r_1\ :—\ \vert —\ :m_1.f_1$	$s_1\ :f_1\ \vert m_1\ :r_1$	$d_1\ :—\ \vert —\ :r_1.m_1$	$f_1\ :m_1\ \vert r_1\ :—$	$—\ :r_1\ \vert s_1\ :f_1$
falls, The	bird of twi - light	calls Our	foot-steps home,	No long - er

$s_1\ :—\ \vert —\ :l_1.t_1$	$d\ :t_1\ \vert l_1\ :—$	$—\ :l_1\ \vert r\ :d$	$t_1\ :—\ \vert —\ :d.r$	$m\ :r\ \vert d\ :t_1$
calls Our	foot-steps home,	No long - er	roam, For	now the eve - ning
$s_1\ :f_1\ \vert m_1\ :r_1$	$d_1\ :—\ \vert —\ :r_1.m_1$	$f_1\ :m_1\ \vert r_1\ :—$	$—\ :r_1\ \vert s_1\ :f_1$	$m_1\ :—\ \vert —\ :f_1.s_1$
bird of twi - light	calls Our	foot-steps home,	No long - er	roam, For
$m\ :r\ \vert d\ :t_1$	$l_1\ :—\ \vert —\ :t_1.d$	$r\ :d\ \vert t_1\ :l_1$	$s_1\ :—\ \vert —\ :l_1.t_1$	$d\ :t_1\ \vert l_1\ :—$
now the eve - ning	falls, The	bird of twi - light	calls Our	foot - steps home,
$m_1\ :—\ \vert —\ :f_1.s_1$	$l_1\ :s_1\ \vert f_1\ :m_1$	$r_1\ :—\ \vert —\ :m_1.f_1$	$s_1\ :f_1\ \vert m_1\ :r_1$	$d_1\ :—\ \vert —\ :r_1.m_1$
roam, For	now the eve - ning	falls, The	bird of twi - light	calls Our

$l_1\ :—\ \vert —\ :t_1.d$	$r\ :d\ \vert t_1\ :l_1$	$s_1\ :—\ \vert —\ :l_1.t_1$	$d\ :t_1\ \vert l_1\ :—$	$—\ :l_1\ \vert r\ :d$
falls, The	bird of twi - light	calls Our	foot-steps home,	No long - er
$l_1\ :s_1\ \vert f_1\ :m_1$	$r_1\ :—\ \vert —\ :m_1.f_1$	$s_1\ :f_1\ \vert m_1\ :r_1$	$d_1\ :—\ \vert —\ :r_1.m_1$	$f_1\ :m_1\ \vert r_1\ :—$
now the eve - ning	falls, The	bird of twi - light	calls Our	foot - steps home,
$—\ :l_1\ \vert r\ :d$	$t_1\ :—\ \vert —\ :d.r$	$m\ :r\ \vert d\ :t_1$	$l_1\ :—\ \vert —\ :t_1.d$	$r\ :d\ \vert t_1\ :l_1$
No long - er	roam, For	now the eve - ning	falls, The	bird of twi - light
$f_1\ :m_1\ \vert r_1\ :—$	$—\ :r_1\ \vert s_1\ :f_1$	$m_1\ :—\ \vert —\ :f_1.s_1$	$l_1\ :s_1\ \vert f_1\ :m_1$	$r_1\ :—\ \vert —\ :m_1.f_1$
foot-steps home,	No long - er	roam, For	now the eve - ning	falls, The

$t_1\ :—\ \vert —\ :d.r$	$m\ :r\ \vert d\ :t_1$	$l_1\ :l_1\ \vert l_1\ :t_1$	$d\ :—\ \vert —\ :—$
roam, For	now the eve - ning	falls, No long - er	roam.
$—\ :r_1\ \vert s_1\ :f_1$	$m_1\ :—\ \vert —\ :f_1.s_1$	$l_1\ :s_1\ \vert f_1\ :—$	$m_1\ :—\ \vert —\ :—$
No long - er	roam, No	long - er	roam.
$s_1\ :—\ \vert —\ :l_1.t_1$	$d\ :t_1\ \vert l_1\ :—$	$—\ :l_1\ \vert l_1\ :s_1$	$s_1\ :—\ \vert —\ :—$
calls Our	foot - steps home,	No long - er	roam.
$s_1\ :f_1\ \vert m_1\ :r_1$	$d_1\ :—\ \vert —\ :r_1.m_1$	$f_1\ :m_1\ \vert r_1\ :s_1$	$d_1\ :—\ \vert —\ :—$
bird of twi - light	calls, No	long - er......	roam.

EVENING PRAYER.

151. Key A♭. J. H. Tenney.

s_1 :- .s_1 :s_1 .d	m :— :r	d :— :—	d :t_1 :l_1	s_1 :— :
m_1 :- .m_1 :s_1 .s_1	s_1 :— :f_1	m_1 :— :—	l_1 :s_1 :f_1	m_1 :— :
1. God, who madest	earth and	heaven,	Dark - ness and	light,
2. Guard us when we	sleep or	wake,	And when we	die,
d :- .d :d .m	d :— :t_1	d :— :—	d :d :d	d :— :
d_1 :- .d_1 :m_1 .d_1	s_1 :— :s_1	d_1 :— :—	f_1 :f_1 :f_1	d_1 :— :

s_1 :- .s_1 :s_1 .d	m :— :r	d :— :—	r :d :t_1	d :— :t_1 .d
m_1 :- .m_1 :s_1 .s_1	s_1 :— :f_1	m_1 :— :—	l_1 :s_1 :f_1	m_1 :— :s_1 .s_1
Who the day for	toil has	given,	For rest the	night: May thine
Wilt thou then in	mer - cy	take	Our souls on	high? When the
d :- .d :d .m	d :— :t_1	d :— :—	f :m :r	d :— :r .d
d_1 :- .d_1 :m_1 .d_1	s_1 :— :s_1	l_1 :— :—	f_1 :s_1 :s_1	d_1 :— :s_1 .m_1

r :- .r :m .r	r :d :d .r	m :- .m :f .m	m :r :r .r
s_1 :- .s_1 :s_1 .f_1	f_1 :m_1 :m_1 .f_1	s_1 :- .s_1 :s_1 .s_1	s_1 :s_1 :s_1 .s_1
an - gel guard de -	fend us, Slumber	sweet thy mercy	send us, Ho - ly
last dread call shall	wake us, Do not	thou, our Lord, for -	sake us, But to
t_1 :- .t_1 :d .t_1	d :d :d .d	d :- .d :r .d	d :t_1 :t_1 .t_1
s_1 :- .s_1 :s_1 .s_1	d_1 :d_1 :d_1 .d_1	d :- .d :t_1 .d	s_1 :s_1 :s_1 .s_1

		f :m :r	d :— :—
r :- .r :d .r	m :d :	l_1 :s_1 :s_1	s_1 :— :—
s_1 :- .s_1 :s_1 .s_1	s_1 :l_1 :	f_1 :s_1 :f_1	m_1 :— :—
dreams and hopes at -	tend us	This live - long	night.
reign in glo - ry	take us	With thee on	high.
t_1 :- .t_1 :d .t_1	d :d :	d :d :t_1	d :— :—
s_1 :- .f_1 :m_1 .r_1	d_1 :f_1 :	f_1 :m_1 :r_1	d_1 :— :—
	Small notes for second verse.	l_1 :s_1 :s_1	d_1 :— :—

152. Key F. Round for three parts. T. F. S.

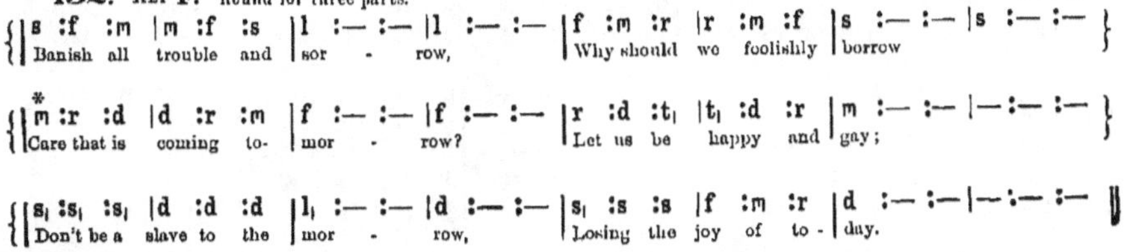

s :f :m	m :f :s	l :— :—	l :— :—	f :m :r	r :m :f	s :— :—	s :— :—
Banish all	trouble and	sor -	row,	Why should we	foolishly	borrow	
* m :r :d	d :r :m	f :— :—	f :— :—	r :d :t_1	t_1 :d :r	m :— :—	— :— :—
Care that is	coming to-	mor -	row?	Let us be	happy and	gay;	
s_1 :s_1 :s_1	d :d :d	l_1 :— :—	d :— :—	s_1 :s :s	f :m :r	d :— :—	— :— :—
Don't be a	slave to the	mor -	row,	Losing the	joy of to -	day.	

WAKE THE SONG OF JUBILEE.

153. KEY D. M. 112. *Boldly, without dragging.* CHESTER G. ALLEN, by per.

|d' :t |d' :-.l |s :-.f |m :— |r :m |f :l |s :m |r :— |s :-.s |s :—
|m :f |s :-.f |m :-.r |d :— |t_1 :d |r :f |m :d |t_1 :— | : | :m
Wake the song of ju - bi - lee, Let it ech - o o'er the sea, Wake the song of
|s :s |s :-.d' |d' :-.s |s :— |s :s |s :s |s :s |s :— | : | :d'
|d :r |m :-.f |s :-.s_1 |d :— |f :m |r :t_1 |d :m |s :— |s :-.s |s :—

|— :— |— :— |s :-.s |s :s |— :— |— :— |d' :t.l |s :m |l :s.f |m :
|r :m |f :r | : | : |r :m |f :r |d' :t.l |s :m |l :s.f |m :
ju - bi - lee, Let it ech - o o'er the sea, Wake the song of ju - bi - lee,
|t :d' |r' :t | : | : |t :d' |r' :t |d' :t.l |s :m |l :s.f |m :
|— :— |— :— |s :-.s |s :s |— :— |— :— |d' :t.l |s :m |l :s.f |m :

|f :s |l :r' |d' :t |d' :— ‖ *p* : | : | : | : | *p* : | :
|d :d |d :f |m :f |m :— ‖ d :r |m :-.f |m :r |d :— |f :m |l :s
Let it ech - o o'er the sea; Now is come the promised hour, Je - sus reigns with
|l :s |f :l |s :s |s :— ‖ m :s |d' :-.l |s :f |m :— |l :s |f :m
|f :m |f :r |s :s_1 |d :— ‖ : | : | : | : | : | :

| : | : |*p* t :d' |r' :t |d' :r' |m' :— |*p* d' :t |l :r' |d' :t |d' :—
|f :m |r :— |r :m |f :r |s :s |s :— |m :s |f :f |m :f |m :—
sovereign pow'r. All ye na - tions join and sing, Christ is Lord and King of kings.
|t :d' |t :— |s :s |s :s |s :t |d' :— |d' :d' |d' :l |s :s |s :—
| : | : |s :s |s :s |m :s |d' :— |d :m |f :f |s :s_1 |d :—

|*f* d' :s |l :t |d' :r' |m' :— |*ff* d' :t |l :r' |d' :t |d' :— |s :-.s |s :s
|m :m |f :f |m.s :s |s :— |m :s |f :f |m :f |m :— | : | :
Let it sound from shore to shore, Je - sus reigns for - ev - er - more. All ye na - tions
|s :d' |d' :s |s :t |d' :— |d' :d' |d' :l |s :s |s :— | : | :
|d :d |f :r |d.m :s |d' :— |d :m |f :f |s :s_1 |d :— |s :-.s |s :s

|s :— |— :— |s :-.s |s :s |s :— |— :— |d' :t.l |s :m |l :s.f |m :—
|r :m |f :r | : | :m |r :m |f :r |d' :t.l |s :m |l :s.f |m :—
join and sing. Je - sus is the King of kings. Let it sound from shore to shore.
|t :d' |r' :t | : | :d' |t :d' |r' :t |d' :t.l |s :m |l :s.f |m :—
|s :— |— :— |s :-.s |s :s |s :— |— :— |d' :t.l |s :m |l :s.f |m :—

| f :s | l :r' | d' :t | d' :— ‖ : | : | : | : | : | : |
| d :d | d :f | m :f | m :— ‖ : | : | : | : | : | : |
Je - sus reigns for ev - er - more.
| l :s | f :l | s :s | s :— ‖ : | : | : | : | : | : |
| f :m | f :r | s :s_1 | d :— ‖ *mezzo.* d :r | m :d | f :m .r | d :— | l_1 :t_1 | d :m |
Now the des - ert lands re - joice, And the isl - ands

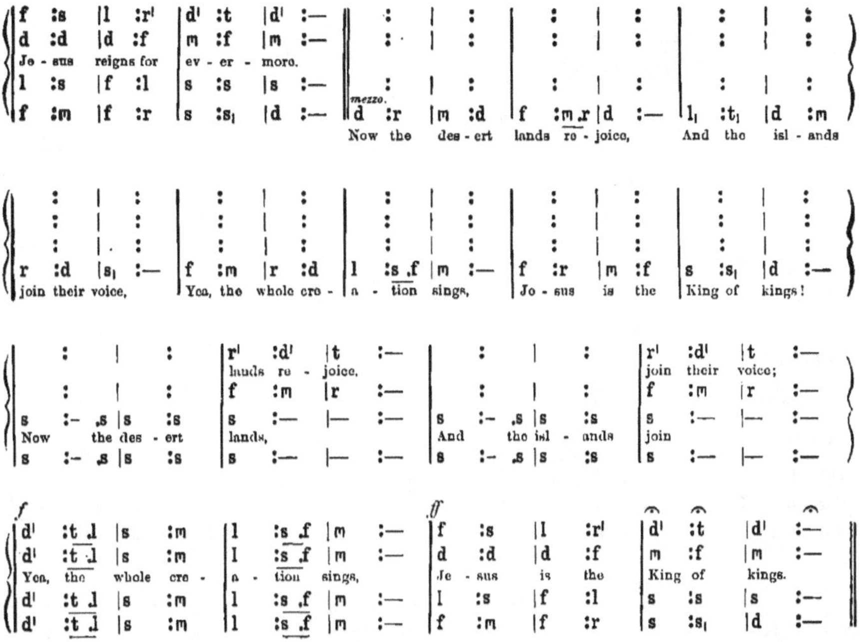

:	:	:	:	:	:	:	:	:	:
:	:	:	:	:	:	:	:	:	:
:	:	:	:	:	:	:	:	:	:
r :d	s_1 :—	f :m	r :d	l :s .f	m :—	f :r	m :f	s :s_1	d :—
join their voice, Yea, the whole cre - a - tion sings, Je - sus is the King of kings!

| : | : | r' :d' | t :— | : | : | r' :d' | t :— |
lands re - joice. join their voice;
| : | : | f :m | r :— | : | : | f :m | r :— |
| s :- .s | s :s | s :— | — :— | s :- .s | s :s | s :— | — :— |
Now the des - ert lands, And the isl - ands join
| s :- .s | s :s | s :— | — :— | s :- .s | s :s | s :— | — :— |

f *ff*
| d' :t .l | s :m | l :s .f | m :— | f :s | l :r' | d' :t | d' :— ‖
| d' :t .l | s :m | l :s .f | m :— | d :d | d :f | m :f | m :— ‖
Yea, the whole cre - a - tion sings, Je - sus is the King of kings.
| d' :t .l | s :m | l :s .f | m :— | l :s | f :l | s :s | s :— ‖
| d' :t .l | s :m | l :s .f | m :— | f :m | f :r | s :s_1 | d :— ‖

THE LORD'S PRAYER.

154. KEY F.

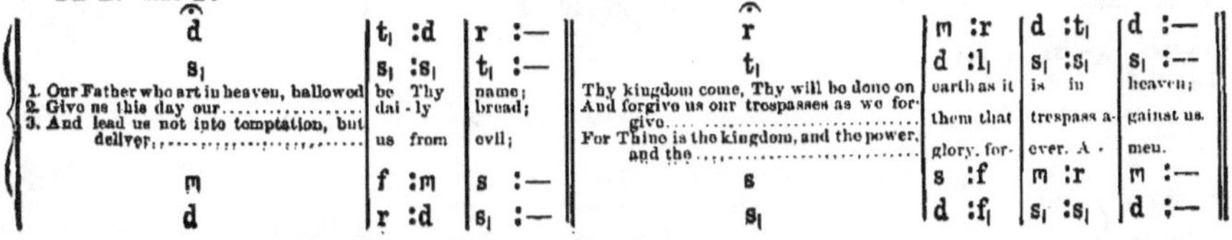

| d | t_1 :d | r :— ‖ r | m :r | d :t_1 | d :— ‖
| s_1 | s_1 :s_1 | t_1 :— ‖ t_1 | d :l_1 | s_1 :s_1 | s_1 :— ‖

1. Our Father who art in heaven, hallowed | be Thy | name; ‖ Thy kingdom come, Thy will be done on | earth as it | is in | heaven;
2. Give us this day our.................. | dai - ly | bread; ‖ And forgive us our trespasses as we forgive.............................. | them that | trespass a- | gainst us.
3. And lead us not into temptation, but deliver........................ | us from | evil; ‖ For Thine is the kingdom, and the power, and the.............................. | glory, for- | ever. A - | men.

| m | f :m | s :— ‖ s | s :f | m :r | m :— ‖
| d | r :d | s_1 :— ‖ s_1 | d :f_1 | s_1 :s_1 | d :— ‖

The Metronome is an instrument for regulating the rate of movement in a piece of music. It is a pendulum which can be made to swing at various rates per minute. M. 60 (Metronome 60), in the Tonic Solfa notation means, "Let the *pulses* of this tune move at the rate of 60 in a minute." In the case of very quick six-pulse measure, the metronome rate is made to correspond, not with pulses, but with half measures—"beating twice in the measure."

A cheap substitute for the costly clockwork metronome is a string with a weight attached to one end—a common pocket tape-measure is the most convenient. The following table gives the number of inches of the tape required for the different rates of movement. The number of inches here given is not absolutely correct, but is near enough for ordinary purposes.

M. 50........	Tape 56 inches.
M. 56........	" 47 "
M. 60........	" 38 "
M. 66........	" 31 "
M. 72........	" 27 "
M. 76........	" 24 "
M. 80........	" 21 "
M. 88........	" 17 "
M. 96........	" 13½ "
M. 120........	" 8½ "

Remembering M. 60. Just as it is useful to remember one tone in absolute pitch, so also, is it useful to remember one rate of movement. The rate of M. 60 is to be fixed in the mind as a standard; then twice that speed, M. 120; or a speed half as fast again, M. 90, are easily conceived. To fix M. 60 in the mind, the teacher will frequently ask the pupils to begin *Taataing* at what they consider to be that rate, and then test them with the metronome. The recollection of rate of movement is, like the recollection of pitch, affected by temperament of body or mood of mind. But these difficulties can be conquered, so that depression of either kind shall not make us sing too slowly.

Sustaining the Rate of Movement. The power of sustaining a uniform speed is one of the first and most important musical elements. To cultivate this faculty the teacher requires the pupils to taatai on one tone a simple measure, thus:

| TAA :TAA | TAA :TAA ||

repeating it steadily six or eight times *with* the metronome, so as to get into the swing. He then stops the metronome while they continue taataing for several measures, then starts it again, on the first pulse of the measure, and the class can see immediately whether the rate has been sustained.

The Half-Pulse Silence is indicated by the blank space between the dot (which divides the pulse into halves) and the accent mark. It is named *SAA* on the first half of the pulse, and *SAI* on the second half, thus:

| .l :or |l .
SAA TAI TAA *SAI*

In taataing, the silent half-pulses are passed, by whispering the time-name.

155. KEY F.

TAA TAI TAA *SAI* | TAA TAI TAA *SAI* | TAA *SAI* TAA *SAI* | TAA - AA

l .l :l .	l .l :l .	l . :l .	l :—	
m .r :d .	f .m :r .	m . :d .	s :—	
d .r :m .	r .m :f .	m . :s .	d :—	

156. KEY D.

TAA TAI *SAA* TAI | TAA TAI *SAA* TAI | TAA *SAI* *SAA* TAI | TAA - AA

l .l : .l	l .l : .l	l . : .l	l :—	
d .d : .r	m .m : .f	s . : .f	m :—	
m .m : .r	d .d : .t_1	d . : .r	d :—	

157. KEY D.

TAI | TAA TAA TAI | TAA *SAA* TAI | TAA TAI TAA TAI | TAA *SAA* TAI | TAA TAI TAA TAI | TAA *SAA* TAI | TAA TAA TAI |

.l |l :l .l |l : .l |l .l :l .l |l : .l |l .l :l .l |l : .l |l :l .l |l . : . ||
.s |d^1 :s .m |d : .d |m .m :d .m |s : .s |d^1 .d^1 :s .s |m : .m |d :m .s |d^1 . : . ||

158. KEY A.

TAI TAA TAI | TAA -AA TAI TAA TAI | TAA -AA TAA TAA TAI | TAA TAA TAA TAI | TAA -AA

.l :l .l |l :– .l :l .l |l :– .l :l .l |l :l :l .l |l :– . ||
.s_1 :s_1 .s_1 |d :– .t_1 :l_1 .t_1 |d :– .t_1 :d .r |m :d :r .t_1 |d :– . ||

159. KEY D. Round in two parts.

|d^1 .d^1 :d^1 . |t .t :t . |d^1 .t :l .s |l .t :d^1 . |
Mer - ry May, mer - ry May, How I love the mer - ry May:

|*d .d :d . |r .r :r . |m . :m . |f .f :m . ||
Mer - ry May, mer - ry May; Yes, yes, mer - ry May.

YES, OR NO.

100. KEY G. M. 96. LOWELL MASON.

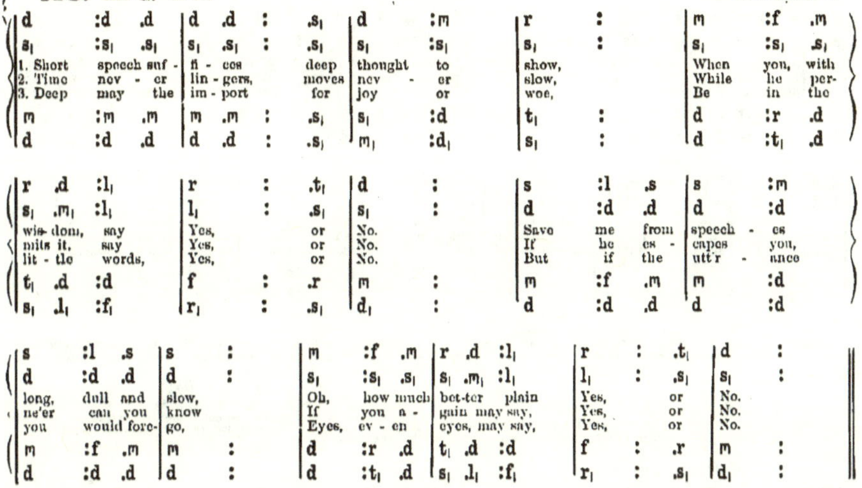

d :d .d	d .d : .s_1	d :m	r :	m :f .m
s_1 :s_1 .s_1	s_1 .s_1 : .s_1	s_1 :s_1	s_1 :	s_1 :s_1 .s_1
1. Short speech suf -	fi - ces deep	thought to	show,	When you, with
2. Time nev - er	lin - gers, moves	nev - er	slow,	While he per-
3. Deep may the	im - port for	joy or	woe,	Be in the
m :m .m	m .m : .s_1	s_1 :d	t_1 :	d :r .d
d :d .d	d .d : .s_1	m_1 :d_1	s_1 :	d :t_1 .d

r .d :l_1	r : .t_1	d :	s :l .s	s :m
s_1 .m_1 :l_1	l_1 : .s_1	s_1 :	d :d .d	d :d
wis-dom, say	Yes, or	No.	Save me from	speech - es
mits it, say	Yes, or	No.	If he es -	capes you,
lit - tle words,	Yes, or	No.	But if the	utt'r - ance
t_1 .d :d	f : .r	m :	m :f .m	m :d
s_1 .l_1 :f_1	r_1 : .s_1	d_1 :	d :d .d	d :d

s :l .s	s :	m :f .m	r .d :l_1	r : .t_1	d :
d :d .d	d :	s_1 :s_1 .s_1	s_1 .m_1 :l_1	l_1 : .s_1	s_1 :
long, dull and	slow,	Oh, how much	bet-ter plain	Yes, or	No.
ne'er can you	know	If you a -	gain may say,	Yes, or	No.
you would fore-	go,	Eyes, ev - en	eyes, may say,	Yes, or	No.
m :f .m	m :	d :r .d	t_1 .d :d	f : .r	m :
d :d .d	d :	d :t_1 .d	s_1 .l_1 :f_1	r_1 : .s_1	d_1 :

ROBBINS. C. M.

101. KEY B♭. DARIUS E. JONES.

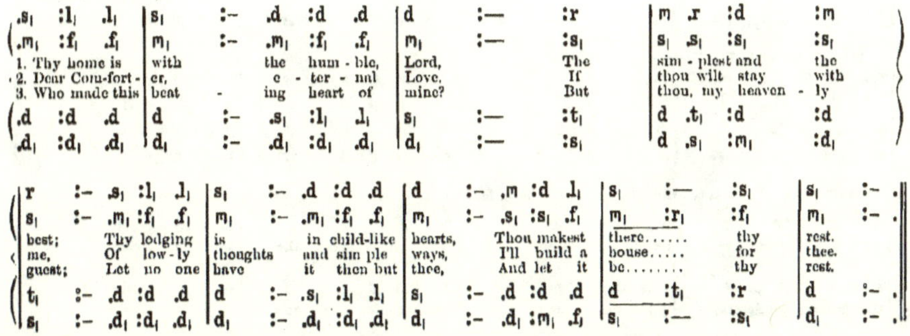

.s_1 :l_1 .l_1	s_1 :– .d :d .d	d :— :r	m .r :d :m
.m_1 :f_1 .f_1	m_1 :– .m_1 :f_1 .f_1	m_1 :— :s_1	s_1 .s_1 :s_1 :s_1
1. Thy home is	with the hum - ble,	Lord, The	sim - plest and the
2. Dear Com-fort -	er, e - ter - nal	Love, If	thou wilt stay with
3. Who made this	beat - ing heart of	mine? But	thou, my heaven - ly
.d :d .d	d :– .s_1 :l_1 .l_1	s_1 :— :t_1	d .t_1 :d :d
.d_1 :d_1 .d_1	d_1 :– .d_1 :d_1 .d_1	d_1 :— :s_1	d .s_1 :m_1 :d_1

r :– .s_1 :l_1 .l_1	s_1 :– .d :d .d	d :– .m :d .l_1	s_1 :— :s_1	s_1 :– .
s_1 :– .m_1 :f_1 .f_1	m_1 :– .m_1 :f_1 .f_1	m_1 :– .s_1 :s_1 .f_1	m_1 :r_1 :f_1	m_1 :– .
best; Thy lodging	is in child-like	hearts, Thou makest	there...... thy	rest.
me, Of low-ly	thoughts and sim ple	ways, I'll build a	house..... for	thee.
guest; Let no one	have it then but	thee, And let it	be........ thy	rest.
t_1 :– .d :d .d	d :– .s_1 :l_1 .l_1	s_1 :– .d :d .d	d :t_1 :r	d :– .
s_1 :– .d_1 :d_1 .d_1	d_1 :– .d_1 :d_1 .d_1	d_1 :– .d_1 :m_1 .f_1	s_1 :— :s_1	d_1 :– .

KEOKUK. C. M.

102. Key C. Wm. B. Bradbury.

.s	s .s :s .s	s :d'	t : .t	d' .l :s .f	m : .m	m .m .m .s	s .f :f .r
.m	m .m:r .r	d :s	s : .f	m .f :m .r	d : .d	d .d :d .m	m .r :r .t_1
1. Ye	trembling souls, dis-	miss your	fears, Be	mercy all your	theme, Mer-	cy which like a	river flows In
2. Fear	not the powers of	earth and	hell, Those	powers will God re-	strain; His	arm shall all their	rage repel, And
3. Fear	not the want of	out - ward	good: For	His He will pro-	vide; Grant	them supplies of	daily food, And
.d'	d' .d':t .t	d' :m'	r' : .r'	d' .d' :d' .s	s :	:	:
.d	d .m:s .f	m :d	s : .s	l .f :s .s_1	d :	:	:

r .r :s .f	m : .s	s .s :d' .d'	m' :d'	d' :l	s .s :s .t	d' :–
t_1 .t_1 :t_1 .r	d : .m	m .m :s .s	s :s	l :f	m .m :r .f	m :–
one perpetual	stream; Mer-	cy which like a	riv - er	flows In	one perpetual	stream.
make their efforts	vain; His	arm shall all their	rage re-	pel, And	make their efforts	vain.
all they need be-	side; Grant	them supplies of	dai - ly	food, And	all they need be-	side.
:	: .d'	d' .d' :m' .m'	d' :d'	d' :d'	d' .d' :t .r'	d' :–
:	: .d	d .d :d .d	d :m	f :f	s .s :s .s	d :–

A pulse divided into two quarters and a half, is named tafaTAI. A half and two quarters are named TAA-tefe. They are indicated thus:

| l ,l .l
tafa TAI

| l .l ,l :
TAA tefe

A pulse divided into three quarters and a quarter is named TAA-efe. The quarter-pulse continuation, like all other continuations, is properly represented by a dash, (a) but in order to save space the dash is omitted and the dot and comma placed close together, (b).

(a) | l .- ,l :
TAA - efe

(b) | l .,l :
TAA - efe

The time-name TAA-efe must not be pronounced TAA-efe, the intervening "e" is not to be sounded, but the "AA" continued up to the "f" thus, TAA-afe or TAA-fe.

103. Keys D, G. TafaTAI.

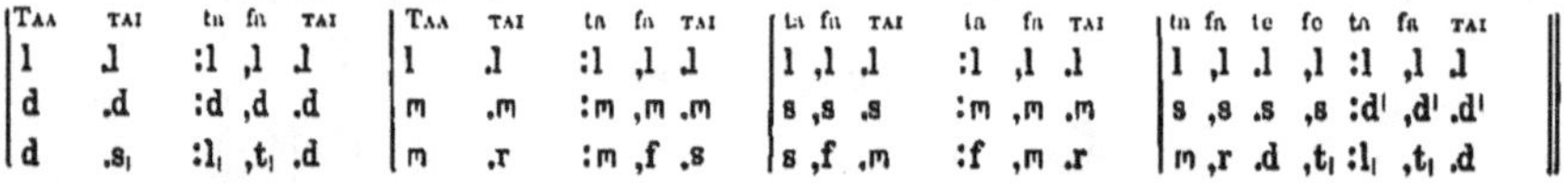

TAA TAI ta fa TAI	TAA TAI ta fa TAI	ta fa TAI ta fa TAI	ta fa te fe ta fa TAI
l .l :l ,l .l	l .l :l ,l .l	l ,l .l :l ,l .l	l ,l .l ,l :l ,l .l
d .d :d ,d .d	m .m :m ,m .m	s ,s .s :m ,m .m	s ,s .s ,s :d' ,d' .d'
d .s_1 :l_1 ,t_1 .d	m .r :m ,f .s	s ,f .m :f ,m .r	m ,r .d ,t_1 :l_1 ,t_1 .d

104. Keys D, F. TAAtefe.

TAA te fe TAA TAI	TAA te fe TAA	TAA te fe TAA te fe	ta fa te fe TAA
l .l ,l :l .l	l .l ,l :l	l .l ,l :l .l ,l	l ,l .l ,l :l
s .s ,s :d' .s	m .d ,m :s	d' .s ,s :d' .s ,s	m ,m .m ,m :d
m .m ,r :d .s_1	d .d ,r :m	m .r ,m :f .m ,f	s ,f .m ,r :d

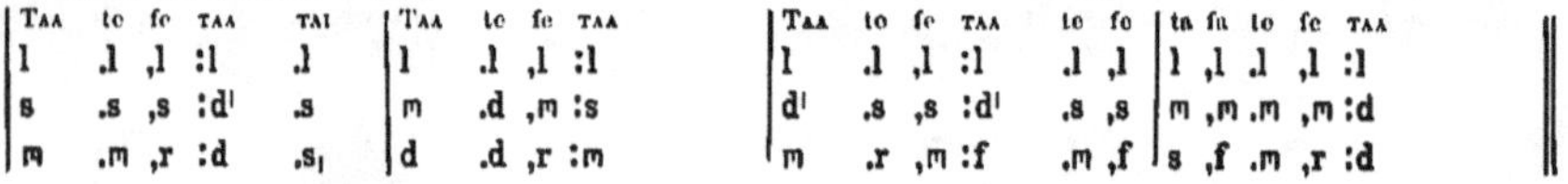

105. Key F. Halves and Quarters. Round in four parts.

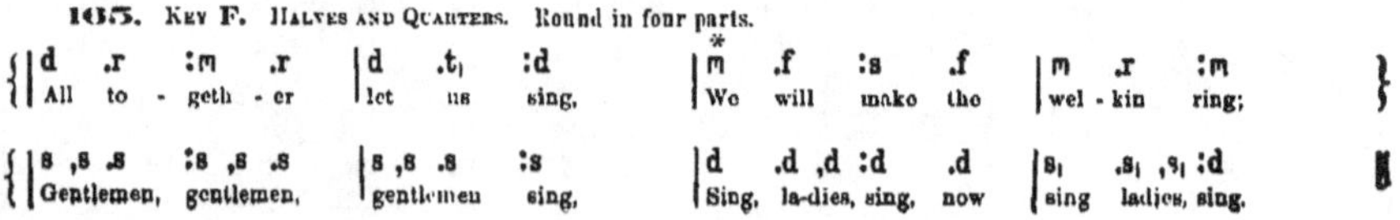

d .r :m .r	d .t_1 :d	* m .f :s .f	m .r :m
All to - geth - er	let us sing,	We will make the	wel - kin ring;
s ,s .s :s ,s .s	s ,s .s :s	d .d ,d :d .d	s_1 .s_1 ,s_1 :d
Gentlemen, gentlemen,	gentlemen sing,	Sing, la-dies, sing, now	sing ladies, sing.

166. Keys C, A. Taa-efe

TAA TAI	TAA te fe	TAA TAI	TAA	TAA TAI	TAA- efe	TAA TAI	TAA
l .l	:l .l ,l	l .l	:l	l .l	:l .,l	l .l	:l
m .m	:d .d ,m	s .s	:s	s .s	:m .,s	d' .d'	:d'
d .t,	:d .d ,r	m .f	:s	d .t,	:d .,r	m .r	:d

l .,l	:l .l	l .,l	:l	l .,l	:l .,l	l .l	:l
d' .,d'	:s .s	m .,m	:d	d .,d	:m .,m	s .s	:d'
m .,r	:d .r	d .,l,	:s,	s, .,l,	:t, .,d	r .m	:d

167. Keys F, C.

l :l .,l	l :l	l :l .,l	l :—	l :l .,l	l :l	l :—	— :
d :d .,r	m :s	d :m .,m	r :—	t, :t, .,d	r :m	d :—	— :
s :l .,s	m :s	d' :r' .,d'	l :—	s :s .,s	l :t	d' :—	— :

168. Key G. Round for three parts.

m :m .,m	m .m :m .m	r :s .,f	m :—	d :d .,d	d .d :d .d
Bim, bome, the	bells are ring-ing,	Come, come a -	way;	Hark! to their	distant ring-ing,

t, :m .,r	d :—	s :s,	d :—	s :s,	d :—
Come, come a -	way.	Bim, bome,	bell,	Bim, bome,	bell.

169. Key D. Round for four parts.

d. :d.	d. :d.	d .,r :m .f	m .r :d	m .,f :s .l	s .f :m	d' :—	d' :—
Tick, tock,	tick, tock,	Hear the clock, it	seems to say,	One more hour is	pass'd away,	Ding,	dong.

ANTWERP. L. M.

170. Key A. T. F. Seward.

d :s, .,s,	d :— .d	r :t,	d :—	m :d .,r	m :— .m	f :m	r :—
m :m, .,m,	m, :— .m,	f, :f,	m, :—	s, :m, .,f,	s, :— .s,	s, :s,	s :—
1. Light of the soul,	O	Sav - iour	blest!	Soon as thy pres -	ence	fills the	breast,
2. Son of the Fa -	- ther	Lord most	high:	How glad is he	who	feels thee	nigh;
3. Je - sus is from	the	proud con -	cealed,	But ev - er - more	to	babes re -	vealed,
d :d .,d	d :— .d	t, :r	d :—	d :s, .,s,	d :— .d	r :d	t, :—
d :d .,d	d :— .d	s, :s,	d, :—	d, :d, .,d,	d, :— .d	t, :d	s, :—

r :t, .,d	r :— .m	f .s :m .f	r :—	m .r :f .m	s .f :m .r	d :t,	d :—
s, :s, .,s,	s, :— .s,	s, :s,	s, :—	s, .f, :l, .s,	s, :s, .l,	s, :f,	m, :—
Darkness and guilt	are	put to	flight,	All then is	sweet - ness	and de -	light.
Come in thy hid -	- den	maj - es -	ty,	Fill us with love,	fill	us with	thee.
Through him unto	the	Fa - ther	be	Glo - ry and praise	o - -	ter - nal -	ly,
t, :s, .,l,	t, :— .d	r .m :d .r	t, :—	d :d .d	m .r :s .f	m :r	m :—
s, :s, .,s,	s, :— .s,	s, :s,	s, :—	d, :d, .d,	d, .r, :m, .f,	s, :s,	d, :—

OH! THE SPORTS OF CHILDHOOD.

171. KEY C. *Smoothly; in swinging style.* M. 104. O. R. BARROWS.

m | *p* | *f*
s .,l :s .,f |m :d' | s .,l :s .,f |m :d' | r' .,d' :t .,l |s :r'
m .,f :m .,r |d :m | m .,f :m .,r |d :m | f .,f :f .,f |f :f
1. Oh, the sports of child - hood! | *Roaming thro' the wild - wood,* | RUN-NING O'ER THE MEAD - OWS,
2. Swaying in the sun - beams, | *Floating in the shad - ow,* | SAIL-ING ON THE BREEZ - ES,
3. Oh, the sports of child - hood! | *Roaming thro' the wild - wood,* | SING-ING O'ER THE MEAD - OWS,
d' .,d' :d' .,d' |d' :s | d' .,d' :d' .,d' |d' :s | t .,d' :r' .,d' |t :t
d .,d :d .,d |d :d | d .,d :d .,d |d :d | s .,s :s .,s |s :s

| *m* | *p*
d' :l .,d' |s :— | s .,l :s .,f |m :d' | s .,l :s .,f |m :d'
m :f .,f |m :— | m .,f :m .,r |d :m | m .,f :m .,r |d :m
HAP - PY AND FREE; | How my heart's a - beat - ing, | *Thinking of the greet - ing,*
HAP - PY AND FREE; | Chas-ing all our sad - ness, | *Shout-ing in our glad - ness,*
HAP - PY AND FREE; | But my heart's a - beat - ing, | *For the old time greet - ing,*
d' :d' .,l |d' :— | d' .,d' :d' .,d' |d' :s | d' .,d' :d' .,d' |d' :s
d :d .,d |d :— | d .,d :d .,d |d :d | d .,d :d .,d |d :d

f | CHORUS.
r' .,d' :t .,l |s :t .,r' |d' :— |— : | s :d' |m' :d'
f .,f :f .,f |f :f .,f |m :— |— : | m :m |s :m
SWINGING 'NEATH THE OLD AP - PLE TREE. | Swing - ing, swing - ing
SWINGING 'NEATH THE OLD AP - PLE TREE.
SWINGING 'NEATH THE OLD AP - PLE TREE.
s .,l :t .,d' |r' :r' .,t |d' :— |— : | d' :— |s :—
| Swing - ing,
s .,s :s .,s |s :s .,s |d :— |— : | d :— |d :—

| *p* | | *p*
s :d' |m' :d' | r' .,d' :t .,l |s :t .,r' |d' :l .,d' |s :— | s :d'
m :m |s :m | f .,f :f .,f |f :f .,f |m :f .,f |m :— | m :m
Swing - ing, swing - ing, | *Lull - ing care to rest 'neath the old ap - ple tree;* | Swing - ing,
d' :— |s :— | t :r' |t :t |d' :d' .,l |d' :— | d' :—
Swing - ing, | *Swing - ing 'neath the old ap - ple tree;* | Swing -
d :— |d :— | s :s |s :s |d :d .,d |d :— | d :—

| | *f*
|m' :d' | s :d' |m' :d' | r' .,d' :t .,l |s :t .,r' |d' :— |— :
|s :m | m :m |s :m | f .,f :f .,f |f :f .,f |m :— |— :
swing - ing, | Swing - ing, swing - ing, | SWINGING 'NEATH THE OLD AP - PLE TREE.
|s :— | d' :— |s :— | s .,l :t .,d' |r' :r' .,t |d' :— |— :
ing, | Swing - ing, | SWINGING 'NEATH THE OLD AP - PLE TREE.
|d :— | d :— |d :— | s .,s :s .,s |s :s .,s |d :— |— :

TWILIGHT IS STEALING.

A. S. Kieffer. B. C. Unseld.

172. Key G. M. 72.

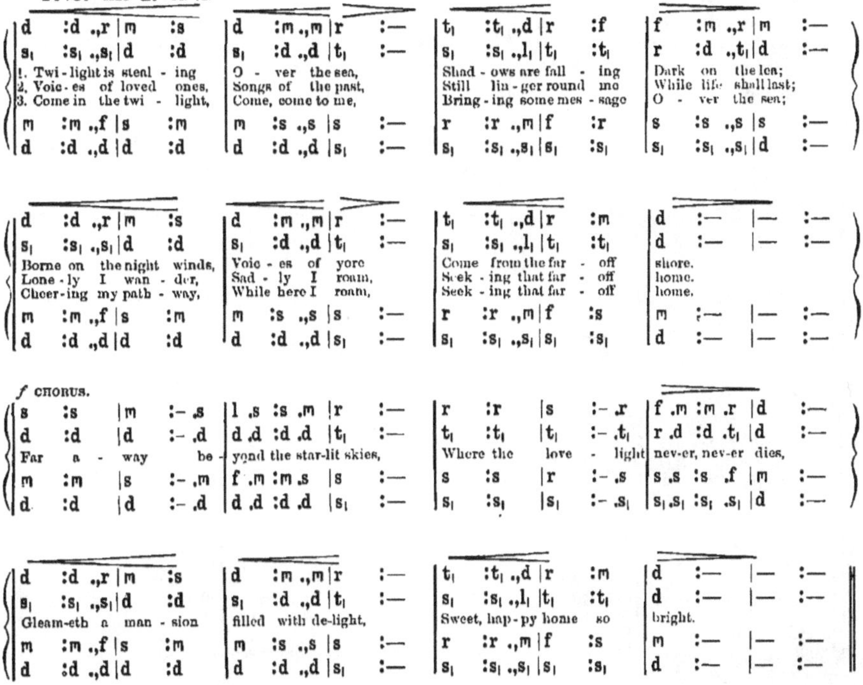

| d :d .,r | m :s | d :m .,m | r :— | t_1 :t_1 .,d | r :f | f :m .,r | m :— |

| s_1 :s_1 .,s_1 | d :d | s_1 :d .,d | t_1 :— | s_1 :s_1 .,l_1 | t_1 :t_1 | r :d .,t_1 | d :— |

1. Twi - light is steal - ing O - ver the sea, Shad - ows are fall - ing Dark on the lea;
2. Voic - es of loved ones, Songs of the past, Still lin - ger round me While life shall last;
3. Come in the twi - light, Come, come to me, Bring - ing some mes - sage O - ver the sea;

| m :m .,f | s :m | m :s .,s | s :— | r :r .,m | f :r | s :s .,s | s :— |

| d :d .,d | d :d | d :d .,d | s_1 :— | s_1 :s_1 .,s_1 | s_1 :s_1 | s_1 :s_1 .,s_1 | d :— |

| d :d .,r | m :s | d :m .,m | r :— | t_1 :t_1 .,d | r :m | d :— | — :— |

| s_1 :s_1 .,s_1 | d :d | s_1 :d .,d | t_1 :— | s_1 :s_1 .,l_1 | t_1 :t_1 | d :— | — :— |

Borne on the night winds, Voic - es of yore Come from the far - off shore.
Lone - ly I wan - der, Sad - ly I roam, Seek - ing that far - off home.
Cheer - ing my path - way, While here I roam, Seek - ing that far - off home.

| m :m .,f | s :m | m :s .,s | s :— | r :r .,m | f :s | m :— | — :— |

| d :d .,d | d :d | d :d .,d | s_1 :— | s_1 :s_1 .,s_1 | s_1 :s_1 | d :— | — :— |

f CHORUS.

| s :s | m :— .s | l .s :s .m | r :— | r :r | s :— .r | f .m :m .r | d :— |

| d :d | d :— .d | d .d :d .d | t_1 :— | t_1 :t_1 | t_1 :— .t_1 | r .d :d .t_1 | d :— |

Far a - way be - yond the star-lit skies, Where the love - light nev-er, nev-er dies,

| m :m | s :— .m | f .m :m .s | s :— | s :s | r :— .s | s .s :s .f | m :— |

| d :d | d :— .d | d .d :d .d | s_1 :— | s_1 :s_1 | s_1 :— .s_1 | s_1 .s_1 :s_1 .s_1 | d :— |

| d :d .,r | m :s | d :m .,m | r :— | t_1 :t_1 .,d | r :m | d :— | — :— ||

| s_1 :s_1 .,s_1 | d :d | s_1 :d .,d | t_1 :— | s_1 :s_1 .,l_1 | t_1 :t_1 | d :— | — :— ||

Gleam-eth a man - sion filled with de-light, Sweet, hap - py home so bright.

| m :m .,f | s :m | m :s .,s | s :— | r :r .,m | f :s | m :— | — :— ||

| d :d .,d | d :d | d :d .,d | s_1 :— | s_1 :s_1 .,s_1 | s_1 :s_1 | d :— | — :— ||

173. Key G. Round for three parts. T. F. S.

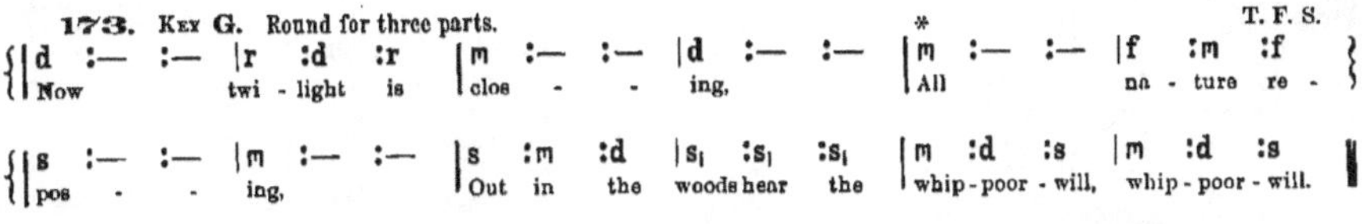

| d :— :— | r :d :r | m :— :— | d :— :— | * m :— :— | f :m :f |

Now twi - light is clos - - ing, All na - ture re -

| s :— :— | m :— :— | s :m :d | s_1 :s_1 :s_1 | m :d :s | m :d :s ||

pos - - ing, Out in the woods hear the whip - poor - will, whip - poor - will.

LOUD THROUGH THE WORLD PROCLAIM.

f **174.** KEY C. M. 104. C. HUNTING.

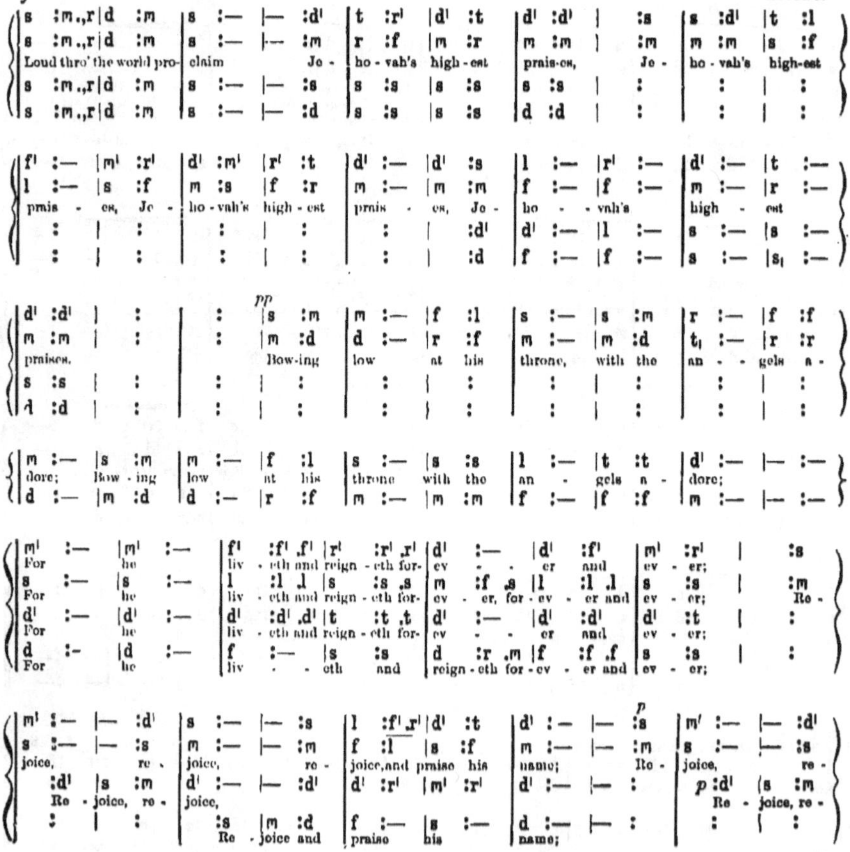

|s :m.,r|d :m |s :— |— :d' |t :r' |d' :t |d' :d' | :s |s :d' |t :l
|s :m.,r|d :m |s :— |— :m |r :f |m :r |m :m | :m |m :m |s :f
Loud thro' the world pro- claim Jo - ho - vah's high - est prais-es, Jo - ho - vah's high-est
|s :m.,r|d :m |s :— |— :s |s :s |s :s |s :s | : | : | :
|s :m.,r|d :m |s :— |— :d |s :s |s :s |d :d | : | : | :

|f' :— |m' :r' |d' :m' |r' :t |d' :— |d' :s |l :— |r' :— |d' :— |t :—
|l :— |s :f |m :s |f :r |m :— |m :m |f :— |f :— |m :— |r :—
prais - es, Jo - ho - vah's high - est prais - es, Jo - ho - - vah's high - est
| : | : | : | : | : | :d' |d' :— |l :— |s :— |s :—
| : | : | : | : | : | :d |f :— |f :— |s :— |s_1 :—

pp

|d' :d' | : | : |s :m |m :— |f :l |s :— |s :m |r :— |f :f
|m :m | : | : |m :d |d :— |r :f |m :— |m :d |t_1 :— |r :r
praises. Bow-ing low at his throne, with the an - - gels a -
|s :s | : | : | : | : | : | : | : | : | :
|d :d | : | : | : | : | : | : | : | : | :

|m :— |s :m |m :— |f :l |s :— |s :s |l :— |t :t |d' :— |— :—
dore; Bow - ing low at his throne with the an - gels a - dore;
|d :— |m :d |d :— |r :f |m :— |m :m |f :— |f :f |m :— |— :—

|m' :— |m' :— |f' :f' .f' |r' :r' .r' |d' :— |d' :f' |m' :r' | :s
For he liv - eth and reign - eth for- ev - - er and ev - er;
|s :— |s :— |l :l .l |s :s .s |m :f .s |l :l .l |s :s | :m
For he liv - eth and reign - eth for- ev - er, for - ev - er and ev - er; Re -
|d' :— |d' :— |d' :d' .d' |t :t .t |d' :— |d' :d' |d' :t | :
For he liv - eth and reign - eth for- ev - - er and ev - er;
|d :— |d :— |f :— |s :s |d :r .m |f :f .f |s :s | :
For he liv - - eth and reign - eth for - ev - er and ev - er;

p (at "Re-")

|m' :— |— :d' |s :— |— :s |l :f'.r' |d' :t |d' :— |— :s |m' :— |— :d'
|s :— |— :s |m :— |— :m |f :l |s :f |m :— |— :m |s :— |— :s
joice, re - joice, re - joice, and praise his name; Re - joice, re -
 :d' |s :m |d' :— |— :d' |d' :r' |m' :r' |d' :— |— : *p* :d' |s :m
Re - joice, re - joice, Re - joice, re -
 : | : | :s |m :d |f :— |s :— |d :— |— : | : | :
Re - joice and praise his name;

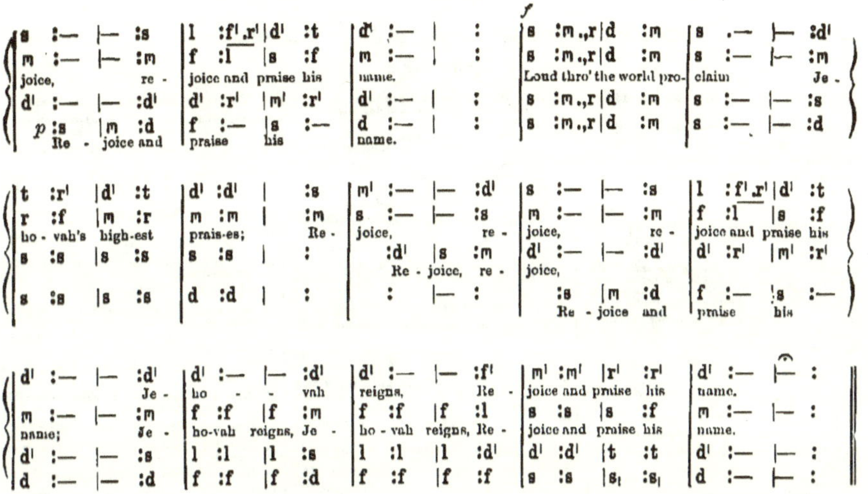

```
s  :—  |—  :s    |l  :f'.r'|d'  :t   |d'  :—  |   :   |s  :m.,r|d  :m  |s  .—  |—  :d'
m  :—  |—  :m    |f  :l    |s   :f   |m   :—  |   :   |s  :m.,r|d  :m  |s  :—  |—  :m
joice,       re -|joice and praise his|name.            |Loud thro' the world pro-|claim      Je -
d' :—  |—  :d'   |d' :r'   |m'  :r'  |d'  :—  |   :   |s  :m.,r|d  :m  |s  :—  |—  :s
p :s   |m  :d    |f  :—    |s   :—   |d   :—  |   :   |s  :m.,r|d  :m  |s  :—  |—  :d
  Re - joice and |praise    his      |name.
```

(*f* over the fourth measure group)

```
t  :r' |d'  :t   |d' :d'  |   :s   |m'  :—  |—  :d'  |s  :—  |—  :s   |l  :f'.r'|d'  :t
r  :f  |m   :r   |m  :m   |   :m   |s   :—  |—  :s   |m  :—  |—  :m   |f  :l    |s   :f
ho - vah's high-est|prais-es;   Re -|joice,        re -|joice,       re -|joice and praise his
s  :s  |s   :s   |s  :s   |   :    |    :d' |s  :m   |d' :—  |—  :d'  |d' :r'   |m'  :r'
                                    |Re - joice,  re -|joice,
s  :s  |s   :s   |d  :d   |   :    |    :   |—  :    |   :s  |m  :d   |f  :—    |s   :—
                                                     |Re - joice and |praise    his
```

```
d' :—  |—  :d'   |d' :—  |—  :d'  |d' :—  |—  :f'  |m' :m' |r'  :r'  |d' :—  |—  :   ||
           Je -  |ho   -   -  vah |reigns,      Re -|joice and praise his|name.
m  :—  |—  :m    |f  :f  |f  :m   |f  :f  |f  :l   |s  :s  |s   :f   |m  :—  |—  :   ||
name;       Je - |ho-vah reigns, Je -|ho - vah reigns, Re -|joice and praise his|name.
d' :—  |—  :s    |l  :l  |l  :s   |l  :l  |l  :d'  |d' :d' |t   :t   |d' :—  |—  :   ||
d  :—  |—  :d    |f  :f  |f  :d   |f  :f  |f  :f   |s  :s  |s,  :s,  |d  :—  |—  :   ||
```

Modifications of Mental Effect. Thus far we have studied the mental effect of tones when sung slowly. All these effects are greatly modified by pitch, by harmony, by quality of tone, but chiefly by speed of movement. Highness in pitch favors the brightness and keenness of effect, makes *ray* more rousing, and *te* more piercing. Lowness in pitch favors the depressing emotions, makes *fah* more desolate, and *lah* more sad. Quick movement makes the strong tones of the scale (d m s) more bold, and the emotional tones (r f l t) gay and lively. Let the pupils sing any exercise containing *fah* and *lah* very slowly indeed, and notice how their mental effects are brought out. Then let them sing the same piece as quickly as they can, keeping the time and observing the change. *Fah* and *lah* are now gay and abandoned instead of weeping and desolate in their effect, and the other tones undergo a similar modification. The tune Manoah will afford a very good illustration. Let it be sung first very slowly and then very quickly. Let the pupils try in the same way other tunes which are deemed most characteristic.

KEY G.

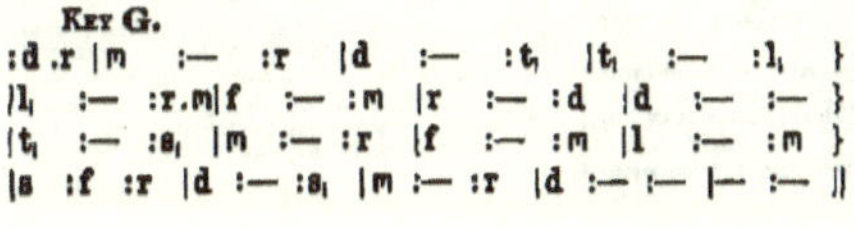

```
:d .r |m   :—  :r    |d   :—  :t,  |t,  :—  :l,  }
|l,   :—  :r.m|f   :—  :m  |r   :—  :d  |d   :—  :—  }
|t,   :—  :s, |m   :—  :r  |f   :—  :m  |l   :—  :m  }
|s  :f  :r  |d  :—  :s, |m  :—  :r  |d  :—  :—  |—  :—  ||
```

"Elementary Rhythms" required for the time exercise of the Elementary Certificate, should be carefully taught by the teacher and diligently practiced by the pupils at home.

Modulator Voluntaries, Ear Exercises, *Pointing and Writing from Memory* are still to be practiced at every lesson. The exercises becoming more and more difficult as the pupils gain facility. The voluntaries will now include *laa-ing* as well as *solfa-ing*, to the teacher's pointing. A few two-part Ear Exercises, as in "Hints for Ear Exercises," can now be wisely introduced, but only to quick and observant classes. To others, each "part" of the exercise will serve as a separate exercise.

Examinations for the Certificate may begin six weeks before the close of the term. All the requirements need not be done at one interview; as soon as a pupil is prepared in any one requirement, he may be examined in that, but all the requirements must be done within six weeks, or else the examination begins again. The examination may be conducted before the whole class, or in private, as suits the convenience of the teacher and pupils.

For instructions in *Voice Training, Breathing, Harmony*, etc., belonging to this step, the teacher will consult the Standard Course.

QUESTIONS FOR WRITTEN OR ORAL EXAMINATION.

DOCTRINE.

1. What two new tones have you learned in this step?
2. Between what two tones does *Fah* come?
3. Between what two tones does *Lah* come?
4. What is the relative position of *Fah* to *Doh*?
5. What is the relative position of *Lah* to *Doh*?
6. What is the mental effect of *Fah*? Of *Lah*?
7. What is the manual sign for *Fah*? For *Lah*?
8. What chord is formed of the tones **f l d**?
9. What is the series of tones, **d r m f s l t d'**, called?
10. Which is the fifth tone of the scale? The third? The sixth? (The teacher will supply additional questions, and also questions on the mental effects and hand-signs.)
11. Each tone of the scale differs from the others, in what?
12. What is meant by "pitch?"
13. What is the eighth tone above or below any given tone called?
14. How is the octave above any tone indicated in the notation?
15. How is the octave below indicated?
16. How is the second octave indicated?
17. Which are the strong, bold tones of the scale?
18. Which are the leaning tones?
19. Which two tones have the strongest leaning or leading tendency?
20. To what tone does **t** lead?
21. To what tone does **f** lead?
22. What is the most important, the strongest, the governing tone of the scale called?
23. What is a family of tones, consisting of a key-tone and six related tones, called?
24. When the tones of a key are arranged in successive order, ascending or descending, what do they make?
25. Must the scale always be sung at the same pitch or may it be sung at different pitches?
26. What is the name of that scale from which all the others are reckoned?
27. What is the name of the pitch that is taken as the key-tone of the Standard Scale?
28. Name the pitches of the Standard Scale?
29. What pitch is *Soh*? *Ray*? *Lah*? (The teacher will supply similar questions.)
30. In the absence of a musical instrument, how may the correct pitch of the Standard Scale be obtained?
31. From what is a scale or key named?
32. How are the different keys indicated in the notation?
33. What is the difference of pitch between the voices of men and the voices of women?
34. What is the name of the pitch that stands about the middle of the usual vocal compass?
35. Is middle **C** a high or a low tone in a man's voice?
36. Is it a high or a low tone in a woman's voice?
37. What are the high voices of women called?
38. What is the usual compass of the Soprano?
39. What are the low voices of women called?
40. What is the usual compass of the Contralto?
41. What are the high voices of men called?
42. What is the usual compass of the Tenor?
43. What are the low voices of men called?
44. What is the usual compass of the Bass?
45. From what octave of the Standard Scale is the pitch of the key-note of any key taken?
46. How is this tone and the six tones above it marked?
47. In the Key **G** the unmarked **G** of the Standard Scale is *doh*, what is the unmarked **A**? The unmarked **E**?
48. How would that *lah* be marked?
49. With what octave marks are the Bass and Tenor parts written?
50. How is the exact rate of movement of a tune regulated?
51. What does M. 60 indicate?
52. How is the rate of very quick, six-pulse measure marked?
53. What is the time-name of a silence on the first half of a pulse? On the second half?
54. How are half-pulse silences indicated in the notation?
55. What is the time-name of a pulse divided into two quarters and a half?
56. How are they indicated in the notation?
57. What is the time-name of a half and two quarters?
58. How are they indicated in the notation?
59. What is the time-name of a pulse divided into a three-quarter-pulse tone and a quarter?
60. How are they indicated in the notation?
61. By what, chiefly, is the mental effect of tones modified?
62. How does a quick movement effect the strong tones of the scale? The emotional tones?

PRACTICE.

63. Sing from memory the pitch of **d'** of the Standard Scale, and sing down the scale.
64. Strike, from the tuning-fork, the pitch of **d'** of the Standard Scale, and sing down the scale, as above.
65. Pitch, from the tuning fork, Key D—G—A—F.
66. Sing to *laa* the *Fah* to any *Doh* the teacher gives.
67. Ditto Fah_{1}. Ditto *Lah*. Ditto Lah_{1}. Ditto any of the tones of the scale the teacher may choose.
68. Taatai, with accent, a four-pulse measure, at the rate of M. 60 from memory. At the rate of M. 120.
69. Taatai, with accent, *eight* four-pulse measures, sustaining the rate of M. 60. The rate of M. 120.
70. Taatai, from memory, any one of the Exs. 155 to 158 and 163 to 167, chosen by the teacher, the first measure being named.
71. Taatai on one tone any one of the Exs. 165, 168, 169, chosen by the teacher.
72. Taatai, in tune, any one of the Exs. 165, 168, 169, chosen by the teacher.
73. Follow the examiner's pointing in a new voluntary containing all the tones of the scale, but no difficulties of time greater than the *second* step.
74. Point and Solfa on the modulator, from memory, any one of the following four Exercises, 115, 116, 118, 119, chosen by the examiner.
75. Write, from memory, any other of these four Exercises, chosen by the examiner.
76. Tell which is *lah*; which is *fah*, as directed on page 34, question 31.
77. Tell what tone of all the scale is sung to *laa*, as on page 34, question 32.
78. Taatai any rhythm of two four-pulse measures belonging to this step, which the examiner shall *laa* to you, see page 34, question 33.
79. Taatai in tune, any rhythm of two four-pulse measures belonging to this step, which the examiner Solfas to you. See page 34, question 34.

FOURTH STEP.

The Intervals of the Scale. Transition to the First Sharp and the First Flat Keys; its process and mental effect. The tones Fe and Ta. Chromatic effect Cadence, Passing and Extended Transition. Pitching Tunes. Thirds of a Pulse. Beating Time. Syncopation.

The Intervals of the Scale. In the art of singing, this subject is not now deemed so important as it once was, for attention is now directed immediately to the character and mental effect of a tone in the scale, rather than to its distance from any other tone. In an elementary class the subject need not be dwelt upon—merely the main facts briefly presented. The teacher or student who wishes an exhaustive treatment of the matter, is referred to Musical Theory, Book I, by John Curwen.

The Tonic Sol-fa statement of the scale-intervals is as follows:

t to d......Little Step......5 Kommas.
l to t .....Greater Step....9 Kommas.
s to l......Smaller Step....8 Kommas.
f to s .....Greater Step ...9 Kommas.
m to f.....Little Step......5 Kommas.
r to m.....Smaller Step....8 Kommas.
d to r......Greater Step....9 Kommas.

Thus the scale contains Three Great Steps, Two Small Steps and Two Little Steps. The difference between a Greater and a Smaller Step is called a Komma; a Greater Step consisting of nine Kommas; a Smaller Step, eight Kommas, and a Little Step, five Kommas. Ordinarily, no distinction is made between the Greater and Smaller Steps, they are simply called Steps, and the Little Step is commonly called a Half-Step.

Intervals are also named Seconds, Thirds, Fourths, Fifths, Sixths, Sevenths, Octaves, and so on. The interval from any tone to the next in the scale is called a Second; from any tone to the third tone is called a Third; to the fourth tone a Fourth, and so on. A Second that is equal to a Step is called a Major Second; a Second that is equal to a Little Step is called a Minor Second. A third that is equal to two Steps is called a Major third—as from d to m—f to l—or s to t A Third that is equal to one full Step and one Little Step (a Step and a Half) is called a Minor Third—as from r to f—m to s—l to d'—or t to r'.

Fah and *Te* are separated by a peculiar interval, called the Tri-tone—equal to three full Steps—it is the only one found in the Scale. Thus f and t become the most marked characteristic tones of the scale. From their mental effects t may be called the *sharp* tone of the scale, and f the *flat* tone. We shall presently see how the whole aspect of the scale changes when f is omitted and a new t put in its place, or when t is omitted and a new f is taken instead.

Transition is the "passing over" of the music from one key into another. (Heretofore this has been called modulation—but in the Tonic Sol-fa system "modulation" has a different meaning.) Sometimes, in the course of a tune, the music seems to have elected a new governing or key-tone tone; and the tones gather, for a time, around this new key-tone in the same relationship and order as around the first. For this purpose one or more new tones are commonly required, and the tones, which do not change their absolute pitch, change, nevertheless, their "mental effect" with the change of key-relationship. To those who have studied the mental effect of each tone, the study of "transition" becomes very interesting. At the call of some single new tone, characteristically heard as it enters the music, the other tones are seen to acknowledge their new ruler, and, suddenly assuming the new offices he requires, to minister in their places around him.

The musical *fact*, thus didactically stated, may be set before the minds of pupils in some such way as the following: First bring up the scale in review, questioning the class as to the mental effects of the tones, the intervals, and the two most marked characteristic tones of the scale. The teacher may then say:

Listen to me while I sing a tune, and notice whether I stay in the same key all through the tune, or whether I go out of it at any point.

Teacher sings the following example to *laa*.

I. KEY **C.**

```
{|d    :m    |s    :m     |l    :l    |s    :—    }
{|s    :s    |d'   :t .l  |s    :f    |m    :—    ||
```

Did I stay in the one key all the time, or did I go out of it at any point?

Listen again, and raise your hands when you feel the key has changed.

Teacher now sings, still to *laa*, example II.

II. KEY **C.**

```
{|d    :m    |s    :m     |l    :l    |s    :—    }
{|s    :s    |d'   :t .l  |s    :fe   |s    :—    ||
```

When the teacher strikes the tone *fe* the pupils will, without doubt, hold up their hands—if they do not, then both examples must be repeated.

You feel that the music has "passed over" into a new key. This change of key during the progress of a tune is called Transition.

It may be well now to repeat the two examples to *laa*, pupils imitating.

Let us now learn what has caused this transition, or change of key. You may sing (solfa-ing) as I point.

The teacher points on the modulator the example I above.

Did you make a transition then, or stay in the same key?

Try it again, as I point

This time he changes second phrase, thus:

III. Key C.

```
{|d   :m   |s   :m    |1   :1   |s   :—   }
{|s   :s   |d'  :t .1 |s   :f   |s   :—   ||
```

Did you make a transition then, or stay in the same key?

Listen to me.

Teacher sings example II to *laa*, pointing as he sings; and at *fe* he *points* to *fah*, on the modulator, but *sings fe*.

Did I sing *fah*, then, or a new tone?

Was the new tone higher or lower than *fah?*

Was it higher or lower than *soh?*

The new tone is a Little Step below *soh*, and is called *fe;* it is to *soh* exactly what *te* is to *doh*. Now sing as I point, listen to the mental effect of *soh*, and tell me whether it still sounds like *soh*.

Pupils sol-fa, to the teacher's pointing, example II, page 65.

What did the last *soh* sound like? What did the *fe* sound like?

Yes; *soh* has changed into *doh*, *fe* is a new *te*, *lah* is changed into *ray*, *te* into *me*, and so on.

The teacher may illustrate this further if he thinks best.

You see that the transition is caused by omitting *fah*, the *flat* tone of the old key, and taking *fe*, the *sharp* tone of a new key, in its place. *Fe* thus becomes the *distinguishing* tone of the new key. The new key is called the "Soh Key," or (on account of the *sharp* effect of the distinguishing tone), the First *Sharp* Key. The new key is shown on the modulator on the right of the old key. You see the new *doh* is placed opposite the old *soh ;* the new *ray* opposite the old *lah ;* the new *me* opposite the old *te*, and so on.

The teacher will now pattern and point on the modulator example II, going into the side column, as indicated in example IV, following.

IV. Key C.

```
{|d   :m   |s   :m    |1   :1   |s   :—   }
 G.t.
{|ˢd  :d   |f   :m .r |d   :t₁  |d   :—   ||
```

Now for another experiment. Instead of putting a *sharp* tone under *soh*, in place of *fah*, let us put a *flat* tone under *doh*, in place of *te*, and see what the effect will be.

Teacher sings, and points on the modulator, example V, which the pupils may sing after him.

V. Key C.

```
{|d   :m   |s   :m    |1   :1    |s   :—   }
{|s   :s   |d'  :s .1 |t   :1 .s |f   :—   ||
```

Have we made a transition or not?

Has the mental effect of any of the tones changed?

Listen again, and in place of *te* we will put a new tone called *ta**; now notice the mental effect of *fah*.

Teacher repeats example V, singing *ta* in the place of *te*—pupils imitating.

Fah has become *doh*, *soh* has become *ray*, *lah* has become *me*, *ta* is a new *fah*, and so on. We have made a transition into a new key, but a *different* new key. The *distinguishing* tone of this new key is *ta*. It is called the "Fah Key," or (on account of the *flat* effect of its distinguishing tone), the First *Flat* Key. The Fah Key is represented on the modulator on the left of the old, or Doh Key.

Teacher will now pattern and point example V, going into the side column, as indicated in example VI.

VI. Key C.

```
{|d   :m   |s   :m    |1   :1    |s   :—   }
 f.F.
{|ˢr  :r   |s   :r .m |f   :m .r |d   :—   ||
```

It will be interesting now to review examples I, II, IV, V and VI.

Adjacent Keys in Transition. Such transitions as have just been studied are called transitions of one remove, because only one change is made in the pitch tones used. When s becomes d the music is said to go into the *first sharp key*, or key of the Dominant. When f becomes d the music is said to go into the *first flat key*, or key of the Sub-Dominant. Eighty per cent. of all the transitions of music are to one or the other of these two keys, and that to the Dominant is the one most used. The relation of these two adjacent keys should be very clearly understood by the pupil, and he should be led to notice how the pitch tones change their mental effect, as described in the following table:

Piercing	t	*becomes*	Calm	m.
Sorrowful	l	"	Rousing	r.
Grand	s	"	Strong	d.
Desolate	f	*is changed for*	Piercing	t.
Calm	m	*becomes*	Sorrowful	l.
Rousing	r	"	Grand	s.
Strong	d	"	Desolate	f.

* For pronunciation, see Chromatic Effects, page 67.

s	d'	f
	t	m
f—ta		
m	l	r
r	s	d
		fe—t,
d	f	
t,	m	l,
l,	r	s,
s,	d	t,

Returning Transition. As a rule, all tunes go back again to their principal key, but the returning transition is not always taken in so marked a manner as the departing transition, because the principal key has already a hold on the mind, and the ear easily accepts the slightest hint of a return to it. Commonly, also, it is in the departing transition that the composer wishes to produce his most marked effect, and in which he therefore makes his chords decisive, and his distinguishing tones emphatic. Let it be carefully noticed, that the return to the orignal key is the same thing in its nature, as going to the first flat key so that a study of the mutual relation of these two keys is the ground work of all studies in transition. The pupils should be taught to draw a diagram of a principal key, with its first sharp key on the right, and its first flat key, on the left, observing carefully the shorter distances between m f and t d', and to learn, by rote, the relations of their notes. Thus, let him say aloud, reading from the middle column to the right, "d f, r s, m l, fe t, s d," and so on; and from the middle column to the left, "d s, r l, m t, and so on. It may be interesting to mention, that in passing to the first sharp key, the old l requires to be raised a komma to make it into a new r; and in passing to the first flat key the old r is lowered a komma, to make a new l. These changes need not trouble the learner, his voice will naturally make them without any special effort.

Notation of Transition. Tonic Sol-faists always prefer that their notes should correspond with the mental effect of the tones they represent. We therefore adopt the plan of giving to some tone, closely preceding the distinguishing tone, *a double name.* We call it by its name in the old key as well as by that which it assumes in the new, pronouncing the old name slightly, and the new name emphatically, thus: *S' Doh, L' Ray, T'' Me,* etc. These are called *bridge-tones;* they are indicated in the notation by *double notes,* called *bridge-notes,* thus: sd, lr, tm, etc.; the small note on the left giving the name of the tone in the old key, and the large note its name in the new key. But when the transition is very brief, less than two measures long, it is more convenient not to alter the names of the tones, but to write the new t as *fe,* and the new f as *ta.* The notation of transition by means of bridge-notes is called the "perfect" notation, because it represents the tones according to the new character and mental effect which they have assumed. The notation by accidentals," as *fe* and *ta,* is called the "imperfect" notation.

The Signature of the New Key is placed over every transition, when written in the "perfect" way. If it is a *sharp* key (*e. i.* to the *right* on the modulator) the new distinguishing tone is placed on the *right* of the key-name, thus, **G.** t. If it is a *flat* key (*e. i.* to the *left* on the modulator) the new distinguishing tone is placed to the *left,* thus, f. **F**; and so on. By this the singer knows that he has a new t or a new f to expect. More distant removes would have their two or three distinguishing notes similarly placed, for which see Sixth Step.

Mental Effects of Transition. The most marked effects of transition arise from the distinguishing tones which are used. Transition to the first sharp key naturally expresses excitement and elevation; that to the first flat key depression and seriousness.

Manual Signs. It is not advisable to use manual signs in teaching transition, because they are apt to distract attention from the modulator, with its beautiful "trinity of keys." The greatest effort should be made to fix the three keys of the modulator in the mind's eye. But if, on occasion, it is wished to indicate transition by manual signs, the teacher may, to indicate transition *to the right* on the modulator, use his *left* hand (which will be to the pupil's right), thus: When with the right hand he reaches a bridge-tone, let him place his left hand close beside it, making the sign proper to the new key, then withdrawing his right hand, let him proceed to signal the music with his left. He can use the reverse process in the flat transition.

Cadence Transition. The most frequent transitions are those which occur in a cadence, that is, at the close of a musical line. When these transitions do not extend more than a measure and a half, they are called Cadence Transitions, and are commonly written in the "imperfect way," that is, by using *fe* or *ta.* Cadence transitions are most frequently made by *fe.* In singing, emphasize this *fe* and the first f that follows it.

Passing Transition is one which is not in a cadence and does not extend more than two or three pulses. The commonest form of the transition to the first flat key, is that in which it makes a *passing* harmonic ornament in the middle of a line, or near the beginning. It is written in the "imperfect" manner.

Extended Transition is that which is carried beyond a cadence. The first sharp key is much used in this way in hymn tunes, often occupying the second or third lines, and sometimes the greater part of both.

Missed Transitions. If one "part" is silent while another changes key *twice*—when the silent "part" enters again, it is necessary, for the sake of the solitary singer, to give *both* bridge-notes, thus, rsd. But the chorus singer must *disregard* these marks and tune himself from the other parts. Such bridge-notes are commonly enclosed in brackets.

Chromatic Effects. The tones *fe* and *ta* are frequently introduced in such a way as *not* to produce transition. When thus used they are called *chromatic tones,* and are used to *color* or ornament the music. Chromatic tones may also be introduced between any two tones of the scale which form the interval of a step. These tones are named from the scale-tone below, by changing the vowel into "e," as *doh, de, ray, re,* etc.; or, from the scale-tone above, by changing the vowel into "a," as *te, ta, lah, la.* The customary pronunciation of this vowel in America is "ay," as in "say;" in England it is pronounced "aw."

Such exercises as the following should be carefully taught by *pattern,* from the modulator. Let them be first sol-faed, and afterward sung to *laa.* In fact, all the early transitions, and all the more difficult transitions, following later, should be well taught from the modulator. If this is not done, transition will become a confusion instead of a beauty and a pleasure to the learner.

In the following exercises the two methods of representing transition are shown. The small notes under the middle phrase showing the "imperfect" method of notation. Sing each exercise first by the "perfect" notation, and then by the "imperfect" method.

175. KEY D. — A.t. — f.D.

```
|d :m |s :m |f :l |s :— |sd :d |t, :d |m :r |d :— |ds :l |s :m |f :r |d :— ||
                        |s  :s |fe :s |t :l |s :— |
```

176. KEY C. — G.t. — f.C.

```
|m :r |d :m |s :f |m :— |ml, :t, |d :m |r :r |d :— |ds :s |l :l |s :f |m :— ||
                        |m   :fe |s :t |l :l |s :— |
```

177. KEY F. — C.t. — f.F.

```
|d :r |m :d |f :m |r :— |rs :l |s :d' |d' :t  |d' :— |d's :f |m :f |m :r |d :— ||
                        |r  :m |r :s  |s  :fe |s  :— |
```

178. KEY C. — G.t. — f.C.

```
|s :f |m :s |d' :t |l :— |lr :m |f  :r |d :t, |ds :— |s :m |f :r |d :t, |d :— ||
                         |l  :t |d' :l |s :fe |s  :— |
```

179. KEY G. — D.t. — f.G.

```
|m :f |s :m |d :r |t, :— |t,m :f |m  :d  |r  :t,  |ds, :— |s, :f, |m, :s, |l, :t, |d :— ||
                         |t,  :d |t, :l, |s, :fe, |s,  :  |
```

180. KEY F. — C.f. — f.F.

```
|m :f |s :m |f :r |d :— |df :m  |f :l |s :t  |d's :— |m :f |m :r |l, :t, |d :— ||
                        |d  :t, |d :m |r :fe |s      |
```

181. KEY C. — G.t. — f.C.

```
:s |s :m |f :s |l :— |— :lr |r :m |r :t,  |ds :— |— :m |f :m |m :r |d :— |— ||
                        :l  |l :t |l :fe  |s  :— |—
```

182. KEY D. — A.t. — f.D.

```
:d |m :r |d :m |s :f |m :ml, |s, :d |t,  :d |m :r |ds :f |m :m |f :m |r :r |d ||
                        :m   |r  :s |fe  :s |t :l |s
```

Extended transition to the first flat key seldom occurs, so that it is not necessary to give more than one or two examples of it.

183. KEY C. — f.F. — C.t.

```
|s :f |m :s |d' :t |l :— |lm :f  |m :r |d :t, |d :— |df :f |m :s |l :t |d' :— ||
                         |l  :ta |l :s |f :m  |f :  |
```

184. KEY G. — f.C. — G.t.

```
|m :r |d :t, |d :l, |s, :— |sr :m  |f   :r  |d  :r  |m  :— |ml, :l, |s, :d |d :t, |d :— ||
                           |s, :l, |ta, :s, |f, :s, |l, :— |
```

185. KEY D. A.t. f.D.

d' :— |s :f |m :— |(m)l, :— |s, :d |d :t, |d :— |(d)s :— |s :f |m :— |l :— |s :d' |d' :t |d' :— ||

m :— |d :t, |d :— |(d)f, :— |s, :s, |s, :f, |m, :— |(m)t, :— |d :r |d :— |d :— |d :r |m :f |m :— ||

s :— |s :s |s :— |(s)d :— |d :m |m :r |d :— |(d)s :— |s :s |s :— |f :— |s :l |s :s |s :— ||

d :— |m :r |d :— |(d)f, :— |m, :d, |s, :s, |d, :— |(d)s, :— |l, :t, |d :— |f :— |m :f |s :s, |d :— ||

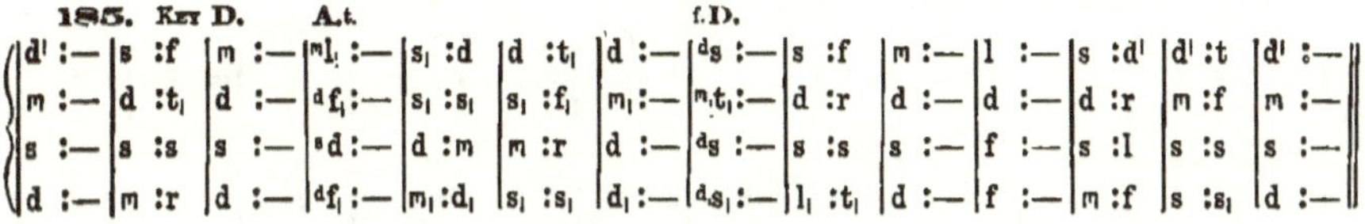

THE BRIGHT NEW YEAR.

186. KEY F. *Joyously.* HUBERT P. MAIN.

m :m |m :m |s :f |f .m :r |f :f |f :f |l :s .f |m :—

d :d |d :d |m :r |r .d :t, |r :t, |r :r |f :m .r |d :—

1. Ver - nal spring and ro - sy sum - mer, Gold - en au - tumn all are past;
2. Slid - ing, skat - ing, laugh-ing, shout-ing, Down the rug - ged hill we go,
3. Tho' the for - est shades are si - lent, And the birds have flown a - way;

s :s |s :s |s :s |s :s |s :s |s .l :t |s :t |d' :s

d :d |d :d |s, :s, |s, :s, |s, :r |t, :s, |t, :s, |d :—

C.t.

(m)l :l |l :l |s :d' |d' .r' :m' |l :f' .r' |d' :d' |t .d' :r' |d' :—

(d)f :f |f :f |s :m |m .f :s |f :f |m :m |f .m :s .f |m :—

O'er the face of na - ture frown-ing, Lone - ly win - ter comes at last;
Hark! the sleigh-bells gai - ly peal - ing, O'er the white and down - y snow;
We can war - ble sweet-est mu - sic, We can sing as light as they:

(s)d' :d' |d' :d' |d' :s |d' :d' |d' :l |s :s |r' .d' :t |d' :—

(d)f :f |f :f |m :d |d :d |f :f |s :s |s, :s, |d :—

f.F.

(d)s :r |r :r |l :s |s .f :m |s :r |r .m :f |m :l |s :— |m :m |f :f

(m)t, :t, |t, :t, |d :d |m .r :d |t, :t, |t, .d :r |d :f |m :— |d :d |t, :t,

Yet she brings us many a pleas-ure, Many a scene of fes - tive cheer, Now with joy our
Can we think the win - ter drear - y, When such mer - ry tones we hear? Now the cup of
Hap-py sea - son, hap - py greet - ing, Friends and kindred far and near; Take our best and

(d)s :s |s :s |f :m |s :s |s :s |s :s |s :d' |d' :— |s :s |s :s

(d)s, :s, |s, :s, |d :d |d :d |s, :s, |s, :s, |d :d |d :— |d :d |r :r

s :d' |d' .t :l |s .l :s .l |s :— .m |r :s |m :— |s .l :s .l |s :— .m |r :s |d :— ||

d :m |l .s :f |m .f :m .f |m :— .d |t, :t, |d :— |d :t, |d :— .d |t, :t, |d :— ||

hearts are glow-ing, While we hail the bright New Year, While we hail the bright New Year.
pleas-ure spar-kles, While we hail the bright New Year, While we hail the bright New Year.
kind-est wish - es, While we hail the bright New Year, While we hail the bright New Year.

d' :s |l .t :d' |d' :d' |d' :— .s |s :s |s :— |m :f |m :— .s |s :f |m :— ||

m :d |f :f |d :d |d :— .d |s, :s, |d :— |d :s, |d :— .d |s, :s, |d :— ||

Bridge-tones approached by the interval of a Second.

187. KEY F. C.t. f.F.

|d :m |r :f |m :r |d :— |t,m :f |s :s |l :t |d' :— |d's :m |r :f |m :r |d :— ‖

188. KEY F. C.t. f.F.

|m :f |s :m |d :r |m :— |rs :s |d' :t |d' :l |s :— |lm :r |m :s |f :r |d :— ‖

189. KEY F. C.t. f.F.

|s :f |m :s |f :m |r :— |ml :t |d' :l |s :f |m :— |fd :t, |d :r |m :f |m :— ‖

Bridge-tones approached by leaps of a Third, Fourth and Fifth.

190. KEY D. A.t. f.D.

|m :r |d :m |s :f |m :— |sd :t, |d :s, |l, :t, |d :— |l,m :f |m :r |d :t, |d :— ‖

191. KEY C. G.t. f.C.

|d' :s |m :f |s :l |s :— |ml, :t, |d :d |m :r |d :— |mt :t |d' :s |f :s |m :— ‖

192. KEY G. D.t. f.G.

|m :r |d :t, |d :l, |s, :— |df :m |f :r |d :t, |d :— |fd :m |r :f |m :r |d :— ‖

193. KEY G. D.t. f.G.

|m :d |s, :m, |s, :f, |m, :— |l,r :d |t, :d |r :f |m :— |lm :m |f :m |r :t, |d :— ‖

194. KEY G. D.t. f.G.

|d :t, |d :l, |s, :f, |m, :— |t,m :f |m :d |r :t, |d :— |sr :t, |d :f |m :r |d :— ‖

GRACIOUS PROMISE.

195. KEY D. A.t. B. C. U.

s :m .f	s :d'	l :t	d' :—	tm :m .f	s :f	m :r	d :—
d :d .t,	d :m	f :f	m :—	rs, :l,	s, :l,	s, :f,	m, :—
1. Wait, my soul, up -		on the Lord,		To his gra - cious		prom-ise flee;	
2. If the sor - rows		of thy case		Seem pe - cul - iar		still to thee;	
m :s	d' :s	l :s	s :—	sd :d	d :d	d :t,	d :—
d :d .r	m :d	f :r	d :—	sd :l,	m, :f,	s, :s,	d, :—

f.D.

| ᵈs :m .f | s :m | r :m | f :— | m :m .f | s :f | m :r | d :— ‖
| ᶠd :d .t₁ | d :d | d :d | t₁ :— | d :d .t₁ | d :r | d :t₁ | d :— ‖

Lay - ing hold up - on his word, "As thy days thy strength shall be."
God has prom - ised need - ful grace, "As thy days thy strength shall be."

| ˡm :s | d' :s | l :s | s :— | s :s | s :l | s :f | m :— ‖
| ᶠd :d .r | m :d | f :m | r :— | d :d .r | m :f | s :s₁ | d :— ‖

NEW HOPE.

T. J. Cook.

196 Key A. — E.t. — f.A.

| s₁ :m₁ .f₁ | s₁ :d | d .l₁ :l₁ .d | s₁ :— | ᵗm :m .f | s :m | s .f :m .r | ᵈs₁ :— |
| m₁ :d₁ .r₁ | m₁ :s₁ | l₁ .f₁ :f₁ | m₁ :— | ˢd :d .t₁ | d :d | t₁ :d .t₁ | ᵈs₁ :— |

1. Sweet peace of conscience, heaven-ly guest, Come, fix thy man - sion in my breast;
2. Come, smiling hope, and joy sin - cere, Come, make your constant dwell - ing here;

| s₁ :s₁ .s₁ | d :d | d :d | d :— | ʳs :s .s | s :s | s :s .f | ᵐt₁ :— |
| d₁ :d₁ .d₁ | d₁ :m₁ | f₁ :f₁ .l₁ | d :— | ˢd :d .r | m :d | s₁ :s₁ | ᵈs₁ :— |

| s₁ :l₁ .t₁ | d :r | m .s :f .m | m :r .r | d :t₁ .l₁ | s₁ :d .r | d :t₁ | d :— ‖
| f₁ :f₁ .f₁ | m₁ :s₁ | s₁ :s₁ | s₁ :— .f₁ | m₁ :s₁ .f₁ | m₁ :s₁ .l₁ | s₁ :s₁ .f₁ | m₁ :— ‖

Dis - pel my doubts, my fears con - trol, And heal the an - guish of my soul.
Still let your pres - ence cheer my heart, Nor sin com - pel you to de - part.

| t₁ :d .r | d :t₁ | d :t₁ .d | d :t₁ .t₁ | d :d | d :d .f | m :r | d :— ‖
| s₁ :s₁ .s₁ | l₁ :s₁ | d₁ .m₁ :r₁ .d₁ | s₁ :— .s₁ | l₁ :f₁ | d₁ :m₁ .f₁ | s₁ :s₁ | d₁ :— ‖

197. Key D. Chromatic Fe.

| d :m | s :— | s :fe | s :— | s :fe | s :f | m :r | d :— ‖

198. Key G.

| m :d | s₁ :fe₁ | s₁ :l₁ | s₁ :— | m :d | s :fe | s :f | m :— ‖

199 Key F.

| d :m | r :m | f :fe | s :— | m :f | fe :s | f :r | d :— ‖

200. Key D.

| m :s | l :s | s :fe | f :— | m :s | l :s | fe :f | m :— ‖

201. Key C.

| s :fe :s | m :f :fe | s :l :s | m :— :— | s :fe :s | d' :t :d' | s :fe :f | m :— :— ‖

202 KEY C. Passing Transition to the first flat key. CHROMATIC TA.

| d' :s | l :ta | l :l | s :— | s :l | ta :l | l :t | d' :— ‖

203. KEY C.

| m :s | d' :ta | l :d' | s :— | s :ta | l :f | m :r | m :— ‖

204. KEY A.

| m :d | s_1 :ta_1 | l_1 :t_1 | d :— | d :ta_1 | l_1 :r | d :t_1 | d :— ‖

205. KEY D.

| s :m | d :ta_1 | l_1 :t_1 | d :— | d :m | s :ta | l :t | d' :— ‖

206. KEY A.

| s_1 :m | r :d | t_1 :ta_1 | l_1 :— | l_1 :ta_1 | t_1 :d | m :r | d :— ‖

207. KEY C.

| s :f | m :l | s :fe | s :— | d' :ta | l :r' | d' :t | d' :— ‖

208. KEY C.

| s .s :fe .f | m :r | r .m :f .s | m :— | d' .d' :t .ta |
Soh, soh, fe, fah, me, ray, That's the way it goes. Now we'll try to -

| l :s | fe .s :f .s | m :— .s | fe .s :f .s | m :— ‖
geth - er, Fe, soh, fah, soh, me; Yes, that's the way it goes.

209. KEY D. FE and TA as bridge-tones.

| d :m | s :m or | {f :l / r :m} | {s :— / f :—} | A.t. $^{fe}t_1$:d | m :r | d :t_1 | d :— | f.D. ^{ta_1}f :m | r :f | m :r | d :— ‖

210. KEY F.

| m :r | d :m or | {s :f / f :m} | {m :— / r :—} | C.t. ^{fe}t :t or | {d' :t / d' :l} | {d' :l / s :f} | {s :— / m :—} | f.F. ^{ta}f :m | f :r | s :f | m :— ‖

VIRTUE WOULD GLORIOUSLY.

211. Key C.

: | : | : | : | : | : | d' :— | t :s
Vir - - - tue would
s :— | m :d | l :l | l :s | f :m .f | s :f | m :fe | s :s
Vir - - - tue would glo - ri - ous - ly and for - ev - er shine By her own

m' :m' | m' :r' | d' :t .d' | r' :d' | t :s | d' :— | l :— .l | l :l
glo - ri - ous ly and for - ev - er, ov - er shine By her ra - diant
s :s | d' :t | l :s | f :fe | s :— | d :— | f :f | f :r
ra - diant light, By her own ra - diant light, Though sun and moon and

r' :— | — :d' | t :d' | r' : | : | : | d' :— | t :s
light, her ra - diant light, Though moon and
r :r | m :fe | s :l | t : | d' :— | t :s | m' :— | :r'
stars were in the deep sea sunk, Though moon and stars, Though

m' :— | :d' | f' :— | m' :— | r' :— | — :r' | d' :— | — :
stars were in the deep sea sunk.
d' :s | d' :ta | l :t | d' :— | — .:d' | t :t | d' :— | — :
moon and stars were in the deep, the deep sea sunk.

GENTLY EVENING BENDETH.

212. Key A♭. C. H. Rink.

Sweetly.

m :m | r :r | d :— | s, :— | l, :t, | d :m | r :— | — :
d :d | t, :s, | s, :— | m, :— | f, :f, | s, :d | t, :— | — :
1. Gen - tly even - ing bend - - - eth, O - ver vale and hill,
2. Save the wood - brook's gush - - - ing, All things si - lent rest;
3. And no even - ing bring - - - eth, To its life re - lease;
4. Rest-less thus life flow - - - eth, Striv - eth in my breast;
d, :m, | s, :f, | m, :— | d, :— | f, :r, | m, :d, | s, :— | — :

m :m | f :m | r :— | s :— | d :f | m :r | d :— | — :
d :d | r :d | t, :— | d :ta, | l, :r | d :s, | m, :— | — :
Soft - ly peace de - scend - eth, And the world is still.
Hea. its rest - less rush - ing, On t'ward o - - cean's breast.
And no sweet bell ring - eth, O'er its wave - lets peace.
God a - - lone be - stow - eth Tran - quil even - ing rest.
d :l, | r, :m, .f, | s, :f, | m, :— | f, :r, | s, :s, | d, :— | — :

ANYWHERE.

213. KEY E♭. B. O. UNSELD.

|m :m |s :m |m :r |r :— |f :f |s :r |m :— |— :
|d :d |m :d |d :t, |t, :— |r :r |t, :t, |d :— |— :
1. A - ny lit - tle cor - ner, Lord, In thy vine - yard wide;
2. Where we pitch our night - ly tent, Sure - ly mat - ters not;
3. All a - long the wil - der - ness, Let us keep our sight;
|s :s |s :s |s :s |s :— |s :s |s :s |s :— |— :
|d :d |d :d |s, :s, |s, :— |s, :s, |s, :s, |d :— |— :

|s :s |l :s |s :m |r :— |r :s |t :l |s :— |— : |s :s |l :d'
|m :m |f :m |m :d |t, :— |t, :r |r :d |t, :— |— : |d :d |d :d
Where thou bid'st me work for thee, There I would a - bide; Mir - a - cle of
If the day for thee is spent, Bless-ed is the spot; Quickly we our
On the mov - ing pil - lar fixed, Con - stant day and night; Then the heart will
|d' :d' |d' :d' |d' :s |s :— |s :s |s :fe |s :— |— : |m :m |f :l
|d :d |d :d |d :d |s, :— |s, :t, |r :r |s, :— |— : |d :d |f :f

|d' :l |s :— |s :s |l :d' |d' :l |s :m |s :m |r :— |m :r |d :—
|d :d |d :— |d :d |d :d |d :d |d :— |m :d |t, :— |t, :t, |d :—
sav - ing grace, That thou giv - est me a place A - ny - where, A - ny - where.
tent may fold, Cheerful march thro' storm and cold, With thy care, With thy care.
make its home, Will-ing, led by thee, to roam A - ny - where, A - ny - where.
|l :f |m :— |m :m |f :l |l :f |m :s |s :s |s :— |s :f |m :—
|f :f |d :— |d :d |f :f |f :f |d :— |d :d |s, :— |s, :s, |d :—

THE LOVELY LAND.

214. KEY E♭. R. LOWRY, by per.

:s |d' :t |d' :s |l :l |l .t :d' |s :s .f |m :r |d :— |—
:m |m :f |s :m |d :d |d :d |m :m .r |d :t, |d :— |—
1. There is a land of pure de - light, Where saints im - mor - tal reign;
2. There ev - er - last - ing spring a - bides, And nev - er fad - ing flowers;
3. Sweet fields a - mong the swell - ing flood Stand dressed in liv - ing green;
:s |s :s |s :s |f :f |f .s :l |d' :s |s :f |m :— |—
:d |d :r |m :d |f :f |f :f |s :s |s, :s, |d :— |—

:s |d' :t |d' :s |l :l |l .t :d' |s :s .f |m :r |d :— |— :
:m |m :f |s :m |d :d |d :d |m :m .r |d :t, |d :— |— :
In - fin - ite day ex - cludes the night, And pleas - ures ban - ish pain;
Death, like a nar - row sea, di - vides This heaven-ly land from ours;
So to the Jews old Ca - naan stood, While Jor - dan rolled be - tween;
:s |s :s |s :s |f :f |f .s :l |d' :s |s :f |m :— |— :
:d |d :r |m :d |f :f |f :f |s :s |s, :s, |d :— |— :

s :- .m |l :s |m :r |d :r |m :d' .,d' |t .l :s .fe |s :— |—
m :- .d |f :m |d :t, |d :t, |d :m .,m |r :r |r :— |—
Oh! the land, the love - ly land, The land o - ver Jor - dan's foam;
s :- .s |d' :d' .s |s :f |m :s |s :s .,s |s :t .l |t :— |—
d :- .d |d :d |s, :s, |d :s, |d :d .,d |r :r |s, :— |—

:s .s |d' :t |d' :s .,s |l .l :l .l |l .t :d' |s :s .,f |m :r |d :— |—
:m .m |m :f |s :m .,m |d .d :d .d |d :d |m :m .,r |d :t, |d :— |—
On the gold - en strand, Wait the happy, happy band, To wel - come the ransomed home.
:d' .d' |s :s |s :s .,d' |d' .d' :d' .d' |d' .t :d' |s :s .,s |s :f |m :— |—
:d .d |d :r |m :d .,d |f .f :f .f |f :f |s :s .,s |s, :s, |d :— |—

MAY IS HERE.

215. Key A.

s, .,s, :m :- .r |d .m, :l, :s, |s, .,s, :l, :t, |d .,r :m :d |s, .,s, :m :- .r
m, .,m, :s, :- .f, |m, .m, :f, :m, |s, .,s, :fe, :f, |m, .,f, :s, :m, |m, .,m, :s, :- .f,
1. May is here, the world re-joic - es, Earth puts on her smiles to greet her, Grove and field lift
2. Birds, thro' ev - ery thicket call - ing, Wake the woods to sounds of glad - ness, Hark! the long - drawn
3. Earth to heav'n lifts up her voic - es, Sky, and fields, and woods, and riv - er, With their heart our
d .,d :d :- .d |d .d :d :d |t, .,t, :d :r |d .,d :d :d |d .,d :d :- .d
d, .,d, :d, :- .d, |d, .d, :d, :d, |s, .,s, :s, :s, |d .,d :d :d |d, .,d, :d, :- .d,

d .,m, :l, :s, |s, .,s, :l, :t, |d .,r :m :d |l .,s :r :— |f .,m :d :—
m, .,m, :f, :m, |s, .,s, :fe, :f, |m, .,f, :s, :m, |t, .,t, :t, :— |d .,d :d :—
up their voic - es, Leaf and flow'rs come forth to meet her. Happy May, blithesome May,
notes are fall - ing, Sad, but pleas - ant in their sad - ness. Happy May, blithesome May, &c.
heart re-joic - es, For his gifts we praise the Giv - er. Happy May, blithesome May, &c.
d .,d :d :d |t, .,t, :d :r |d .,d :d :d |r .,r :f :— |d .,d :m :—
d, .,d, :d, :d, |s, .,s, :s, :s, |d .,d :d :d |s, .,s, :s, :— |d .,d :d :—

m .,r :l, :t, |d .,r :m :f |l .,s :r :— |f .,m :d :— |m .,r :l, :t, |d .,m :d :—
s, .,f, :f, :f, |m, .,f, :s, :— |t, .,t, :t, :— |d .,d :d :— |s, .,f, :f, :f, |m, .,s, :m, :—
Winter's reign has passed away; Happy May, blithesome May, Winter's reign has passed away.
s .,s :r :r |d .,d :d :r |r .,r :f :— |d .,d :m :— |s .,s :r :r |d .,d :d :—
s, .,s, :s, :s, |d .,d :d :— |s, .,s, :s, :— |d .,d :d :— |s, .,s, :s, :s, |d, .,d, :d, :—

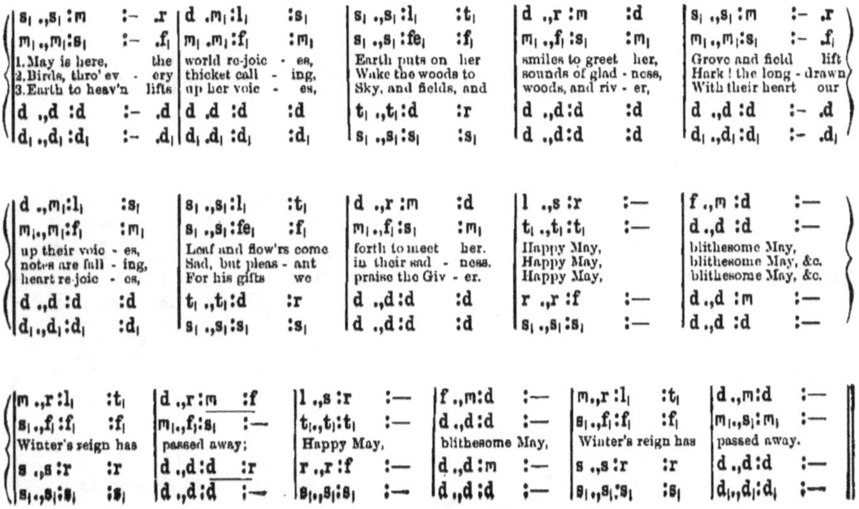

ONWARD, CHRISTIAN SOLDIERS.

216. KEY F. M. 120. A. S. SULLIVAN, Mus. Doc.

s :s |s :s |s :-.l |s :— |r :r |d :r |m :— |— :— |d :m |s :d'

m :m |m :m |f :- |f :— |t_1 :t_1 |l_1 :t_1 |d :— |— :— |d :d |d :d

1. Onward, Chris-tian sol - - diers, March-ing as to war, With the cross of

2. Onward, then, ye faith - - ful, Join our hap - py throng, Blend with ours your

d :m |s :d' |d' :— |t :— |s :s |s :s |s :— |— :— |s :s |s :m

d :d |d :d |r :— |s_1 :— |s :f |m :r |d :— |— :— |m :m |m :m

d' :— |t :— |l :l |m :fe |s :— |— : |r :r |s :r |m :-.f |m :—

r :— |r :— |d :d |d :d |t_1 :— |— : |t_1 :t_1 |r :t_1 |d :-.r |d :—

Je - - - sus Go - ing on be - fore; Christ, the Roy - al Mas - - tor,

voic - - - es In the tri - umph song; Glo - ry, laud and hon - - or

s :-.l |s :— |fe :fe |s :l |s :— |— : |s :s |s :s |s :— |s :—

r :- |r :— |r :r |r_1 :r_1 |s_1 :— |— : |s_1 :s_1 |t_1 :s_1 |d :— |d :—

s :s |d' :s |l :— |— :— |l :s |f :s |l :s |f :s |l :s |f :m

d :d |d :d |d :— |— :— |d :d |d :d |d :— |d :— |d :d |r :d

Leads a - gainst the foe; For - ward in - to bat - - tle, See his ban - ners

Un - to Christ the King; This, through count-less a - - - ges, Men and an - gels

m :m |s :m |f :— |— :— |f :m |f :m |f :m |f :m |f :m |r :r

d :d |m :d |f :— |— :— |f :d |l_1 :d |f :d |l_1 :d |f_1 :f_1 |f_1 :f_1

r :— |— : |d :d |d :d |d :t_1.l_1 |t_1 :d |r :r |r :d.r

t_1 :— |— : |s_1 :s_1 |s_1 :s_1 |s_1 :— |s_1 :— |s_1 :s_1 |s_1 :s_1

go. On - ward, Chris - tian sol - - - - diers, March-ing as to

sing. On - ward, Chris - tian sol - - - - diers, March-ing as to

s :— |— : |m :m |m :m |f :— |f :— |f :f |f :f

s_1 :— |— : |d :s_1 |d :s_1 |r :s_1 |r :s_1 |t_1 :s_1 |t_1 :s_1

m :— |— : |s :s |d' :t |d' :— |s :— |f :m |r :-.d |d :— |— :

s_1 :— |— : |m :m |f :f |m :— |d :— |d :d |t_1 :-.d |d :— |— :

war, With the cross of Je - - - sus Go - ing on be- fore.

war, With the cross of Je - - - sus Go - ing on be- fore.

m :— |— : |d' :d' |s :s |s :— |s :— |l :s |f :-.m |m :— |— :

d :— |— : |d :d |r :r |m :— |m_1 :— |f_1 :f_1 |s_1 :-.s_1 |d :— |— :

FATHER OF MERCIES.

217. KEY E. BERNARD SCHMIDT.

```
pp                          p                            B.t. cres.
|s :— |s :s  |s :— |l :—  |d :-.d |t_ :d  |r :— |d :  |sd :— |d :r    |m :— |f :l_
|d :— |d :t_ |d :— |d :—  |d :-.s_|s_ :s_ |t_ :— |d :  |df_ :— |s_ :s_ |s_ :l_ |l_ :f_
 Fa - ther of  mer - cies,  When the day is  dawn - ing.  Then will I      joy my
|m :— |s :f  |m :— |f :—  |m :-.m |r :m   |f :— |m :  |ml_ :— |d :t_   |d :— |r :—
|d :— |m :r  |d :— |f_ :— |s_ :-.s_|s_ :s_|s_ :— |d :  |df_ :— |m_ :s_  |d :l_ |f_ :—
```

```
             f.E.           pp                                   
|s_ :— |t_ :— |ds :— | :f   |m :— |s :f  |m :— |m :—  |r :-.r |d :d    |d :— |t_ :s
|m_ :— |s_ :— |s.r :— | :r  |d :— |d :—  |d :— |l_ :— |t_ :-.t_ |d :l_ |s_ :— |s_ :t_
 vows   to     thee.   Like  in  -  cense  waft - ed    on the breath of  morn - ing My
|r :d  |r :—  |mt :— | :s   |s :— |ta :l |s :— |fe :— |s :-.s |m :r    |m :— |r :f
|s_ :— |s_ :— |d.s_ :— | :t_ |d :— |d :— |d :— |d :—  |t_ :-.t_ |l_ :fe_ |s_ :— |s_ :r
```

```
cres.                                                 f.A.
|s :— |s :—  |s :— |— :f  |m :— |r :—  |d :— |— :—  |ds_ :— |s_ :s_  |l_ :— |s_ :—
|d :— |m :—  |m :— |— :r  |d :— |t_ :— |d :— |— :—  |l.m_ :— |m_ :m_ |f_ :— |m_ :—
 heart - felt  praise   to   heaven  shall  be.        Yes,  thou art   near  me,
|m :— |d' :— |ta :— |— :l |s :— |s :f  |m :— |— :—  |  :  |  :     |  :  |  :
|d :— |d :—  |m :— |— :f  |s :— |s_ :— |d :— |— :—  |  :  |  :     |  :  |  :
```

```
                               E.t.
|m :d |l_ :t_   |l_ :- |s_ :-   |  :  |  :    |  :  |  :    |  :  |  :    |  :  |(r) :s  |s :l |t :d'
|s_ :m_ |f_ :f_ |f_ :- |m_ :-   |rs_ :- |s_ :s_ |l_ :- |s_ : |m :d |l_ :t_ |d :- | :m   |m :- |m :m
 Sleep - ing or  wak - ing,      Still doth thy  care   un -   changed re -  main.   If   ev - er I
|  :  |  :      |  :- |  :(t_)  |m :- |m :m   |f :- |m :-   |s :m |f :-   |m :- | :d'   |d' :- |s :s
|  :  |  :      |  :- |  :      |  :  |  :    |  :  |  :    |  :  |  :    |  :  |(s. :d  |d :- |m :m
```

```
                                                 p              dim.                          pp
|d' :- |t :l   |s :l |t :d'  |d' :- |t :l   |s :- |m :-  |s :- |m :-  |d :- |r :-   |d :- |- :-
|f :- |f :f    |m :- |m :-   |f :- |f :r    |m :- |d :-  |r :- |d :-  |d :- |t_ :-  |d :- |- :-
 wan - der, thy  ways  for -   sak - ing, O   lead  me     gen - tly    back  a -    gain.
|s :- |s :r    |m :- |s :-   |s :- |s :f    |m :- |s :-  |s :- |d :-  |m :- |f :-   |m :- |- :-
|r :- |r :t_   |d :- |m :-   |r :- |r :t_   |d :- |d :-  |t_ :- |d :- |l_ :- |s_ :- |d :- |- :-
```

HURRAH FOR THE SLEIGH-BELLS!

FANNY J. CROSBY. T. F. SEWARD.

218. KEY G.

.s₁ | m .m ,f :m .r | r .d :s₁ | l₁ .l₁ ,d :t₁ .t₁ ,r | d .s :s .s₁
.m₁ | s₁ .s₁ ,l₁ :s₁ .f₁ | f₁ .m₁ :m₁ | f₁ .f₁ ,f₁ :f₁ .f₁ ,f₁ | m₁ .s₁ :s₁ .m₁

1. Hur - rah for the sleigh-bells! here we go, Jing, jingle, jing, jingle, jing, jing, jing; A - way o'er the white and drift - ing snow, Jing, jingle, jing, jingle, jing.

2. Oh! now is the time for mirth and glee, Jing, jingle, jing, jingle, jing, jing, jing; And yon - der an - oth - er sleigh we see, Jing, jingle, jing, jingle, jing.

3. We'll sing with the bells in cho - rus sweet, Jing, jingle, jing, jingle, jing, jing, jing; We'll sing till we reach the vil - lage street, Jing, jingle, jing, jingle, jing.

D.t. SOLO.

1. The stars are beam - ing bright, The night is cold and clear, While down the rug - ged hill we glide, And sing with mer - ry cheer.

2. Rein up the steeds just here, With - in this ru - ral dell, They want to join us, let them come, We know the par - ty well.

3. Oh! hap - py sleigh - ing time, We hail it with de - light! And who would mind the win - ter's cold, On such a joy - ous night.

Inst., or may be sung with voices to laa.

f.G. CHORUS.

Hur - rah for the sleigh-bells! here we go, Jing, jingle, jing, jingle, jing, jing, jing, A -

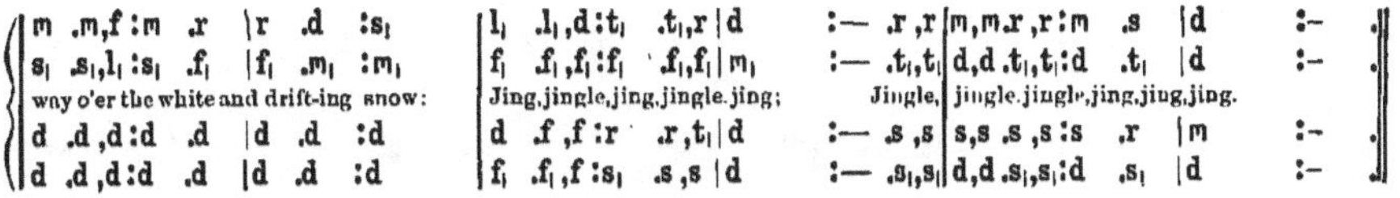

m .m,f :m .r |r .d :s_1 | l_1 .l_1,d :t_1 .t_1,r |d :— .r,r |m,m.r,r :m .s |d :—

s_1 .s_1,l_1 :s_1 .f_1 |f_1 .m_1 :m_1 | f_1 .f_1,f_1 :f_1 .f_1,f_1 |m_1 :— .t_1,t_1 |d,d.t_1,t_1 :d .t_1 |d :—

way o'er the white and drift-ing snow: Jing, jingle, jing, jingle, jing; Jingle, jingle, jingle, jing, jing, jing.

d .d,d :d .d |d .d :d | d .f,f :r .r,t_1 |d :— .s,s |s,s .s,s :s .r |m :—

d .d,d :d .d |d .d :d | f_1 .f_1,f :s_1 .s,s |d :— .s_1,s_1 |d,d .s_1,s_1 :d .s_1 |d :—

CHIME AGAIN.

210. Key A♭. H. R. Bishop.

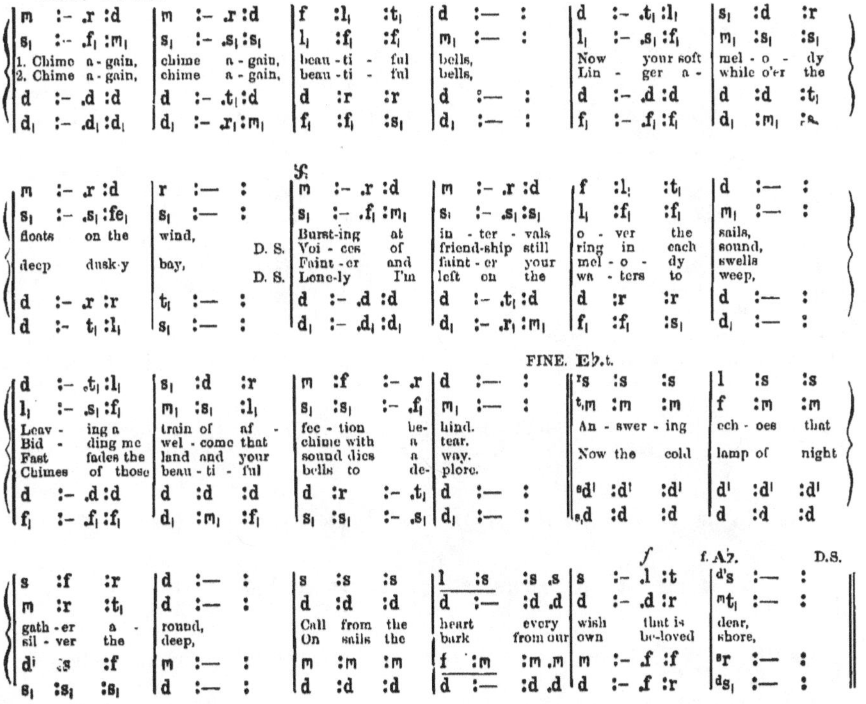

m :— .r :d |m :— .r :d |f :l_1 :t_1 |d :— : |d :— .t_1 :l_1 |s_1 :d :r

s_1 :— .f_1 :m_1 |s_1 :— .s_1 :s_1 |l_1 :f_1 :f_1 |m_1 :— : |l_1 :— .s_1 :f_1 |m_1 :s_1 :s_1

1. Chime a-gain, chime a-gain, beau-ti-ful bells, Now your soft mel-o-dy

2. Chime a-gain, chime a-gain, beau-ti-ful bells, Lin-ger a-while o'er the

d :— .d :d |d :— .t_1 :d |d :r :r |d :— : |d :— .d :d |d :d :t_1

d_1 :— .d_1 :d_1 |d_1 :— .r_1 :m_1 |f_1 :f_1 :s_1 |d_1 :— : |f_1 :— .f_1 :f_1 |d_1 :m_1 :s_1

m :— .r :d |r :— : |𝄋 m :— .r :d |m :— .r :d |f :l_1 :t_1 |d :— :

s_1 :— .s_1 :fe_1 |s_1 :— : |s_1 :— .f_1 :m_1 |s_1 :— .s_1 :s_1 |l_1 :f_1 :f_1 |m_1 :— :

floats on the wind, D. S. Burst-ing at in-ter-vals o-ver the sails,

Voi-ces of friend-ship still ring in each sound,

deep dusk-y bay, D. S. Faint-er and faint-er your mel-o-dy swells

Lone-ly I'm left on the wa-ters to weep,

d :— .r :r |t_1 :— : |d :— .d :d |d :— .t_1 :d |d :r :r |d :— :

d :— t_1 :l_1 |s_1 :— : |d_1 :— .d_1 :d_1 |d_1 :— .r_1 :m_1 |f_1 :f_1 :s_1 |d_1 :— :

FINE. E♭.t.

d :— .t_1 :l_1 |s_1 :d :r |m :f :— .r |d :— : ‖^{r}s :s :s |l :s :s

l_1 :— .s_1 :f_1 |m_1 :s_1 :l_1 |s_1 :s_1 :— .f_1 |m_1 :— : ‖^{t}m :m :m |f :m :m

Leav-ing a train of af-fec-tion be-hind. An-swer-ing ech-oes that

Bid-ding me wel-come that chime with a tear.

Fast fades the land and your sound dies a-way. Now the cold lamp of night

Chimes of those beau-ti-ful bells to de-plore.

d :— .d :d |d :d :d |d :r :— .t_1 |d :— : ‖$^{s}d^1$:d^1 :d^1 |d^1 :d^1 :d^1

f_1 :— .f_1 :f_1 |d_1 :m_1 :f_1 |s_1 :s_1 :— .s_1 |d_1 :— : ‖$_{s}d$:d :d |d :d :d

f f. A♭. D.S.

s :f :r |d :— : |s :s :s |l :s :s .s |s :— .l :t |$^{d^1}s$:— :

m :r :t_1 |d :— : |d :d :d |d :— :d .d |d :— .d :r |$^{m}t_1$:— :

gath-er a-round, Call from the heart every wish that is dear,

sil-ver the deep, On sails the bark from our own be-loved shore,

d^1 :s :f |m :— : |m :m :m |f :m :m .m |m :— .f :f |^{s}r :— :

s_1 :s_1 :s_1 |d :— : |d :d :d |d :— :d .d |d :— .f :r |$^{d}s_1$:— :

220. KEY D. CHROMATIC TONES.

|d :t₁ |d :— |r :de |r :— |m :re |m :d |f :— |— : |s :fe |s :—

|l :se |l :— |t :le |t :s |d' :— |— : |d' :t |d' :— |t :le |t :—

|l :se |l :d' |s :— |— : |f :m |f :— |m :re |m :— |r :de |r :m |d :— |— :

221. KEY G.

|m :re :m |d :t₁ :d |s₁ :fe₁ :s₁ |l₁ :— :— |r :de :r |f :m :f |t₁ :le₁ :t₁ |d :— :—

|l₁ :se₁ :l₁ |r :de :r |f :m :f |r :— :— |s :fe :s |m :r :d |t₁ :le₁ :t₁ |d :— :—

222. KEY C. *Staccato.* Round in two parts. T. F. S.

|d' :d' |t .le :t |l :l |s .fe :s |f :f |m .re :m |r :s |d :—
Trip, trip, fairies light, Dancing all the night, 'Neath the stars so bright, Here and there.

*|d :d |r .de :r |f :f |m .re :m |l :l |s .fe :s |t :t |d' :—
La la la la la, La la la la la, La la la la la, La la la.

223. KEY F. Round in three parts. T. F. S.

|m :m |re :— |m :m |re :— |m :s |f :r |d :r |m :— *|s :s |fe :— |s :s |fe :—
Summer flow'rs, past and gone, Show an-oth - er year is done; Autumn winds, sighing low,

|s :m |r :f |m :r |d :— |s₁ :d |l₁ :d |s₁ :d |l₁ :d |s₁ :d |l₁ :f₁ |s₁ :t₁ |d :—
Tell us how the time doth flow; Spring and summer, autumn, win-ter, Teach a les - son we should know.

224. KEY D.

|d :d |t₁ :d |r :r |de :r |m :m |re :m |f :— |— :— |s :s |fe :s

|l :l |se :l |t :t |le :t |d' :— |— :— |t :t |d' :t |l :l |ta :l

|s :s |la :s |f :— |— :— |m :m |f :m |r :r |ma :r |d :d |ra :ra |d :— |— :—

225. KEY D.

|d :t, |d :de |r :de |r :re |m :re |m :m |f :— |— : |s :fe |s :se

|l :se |l :le |[illegible] :le |t :t |d' :— |— : |t :d' |t :ta |l :ta |l :la

|s :la |s :sa |f :— |— : |m :f |m :ma |r :ma |r :ra |d :ra |d :t, |d :— |— : ||

226. KEY G. Round in two parts.

|d :de |r :t, |d :ta, |l, :t, |d :de |r :re |m :r |d :—
Sum - mer days are now de - clin - ing, With their pre - cious gold - en hours;

*
|m :s |f :r |m :s |f :r |m :m |f :fe |s :f |m :— ||
Dim - ly see the sun is shin - ing Thro' the fad - ing groves and bowers.

227. KEY C. Round in two parts.

|d' :— |t :ta |l :la |s :fe |s :— |fe :f |m : | :

*
|m :d |r :m |f :— |m :re |m :— |ma :r |d :r .m |f .s :l .t ||

NOW THE WINTRY STORMS ARE O'ER.

228. KEY C. T. F. SEWARD.

|m :re :m |s :— :d' |d' :t :d' |l :— :— |r :de :r |f :— :l |s :fe :s |m :— :—
|d :— :d |m :— :m |f :— :f |f :— :— |t, :le, :t, |r :— :f |m :re :m |d :— :—
1. Now the win - try storms are o'er, Spring un - locks her ver - dant store;
2. Now re - spon - sive through the grove, Soft - ly tuned to Spring and love;
|s :fe :s |d' :— :s |l :se :l |d' :— :— |s :— :s |s :— :t |d' :— :d' |s :— :—
|d :— :d |d :— :d |f :— :f |f :— :— |s :— :s |s :— :s |d :— :d |d :— :—

|m :re :m |s :— :d' |d' :t :d' |l :— :— |t :le :t |m' :— :r' |d' :— :d' |d' :— :—
|d :— :d |m :— :m |f :— :f |f :— :— |r :de :r |s :— :f |m :— :f |m :— :—
Smil - ing pleas - ure crowns the day, Sweet - ly breathes the May, the May
Ech - o with her sport - ive lay, Sweet - ly sings of May, sweet May
|s :fe :s |d' :— :ta |l :se :l |d' :— :— |s :— :s |s :— :s |s :— :l |s :— :—
|d :— :d |d :— :d |f :— :f |f :— :— |s :— :s |s, :— :s, |d :— :d |d :— :— ||

RISE, CYNTHIA, RISE.

220. Key E♭. M. 100 twice. HOOK.

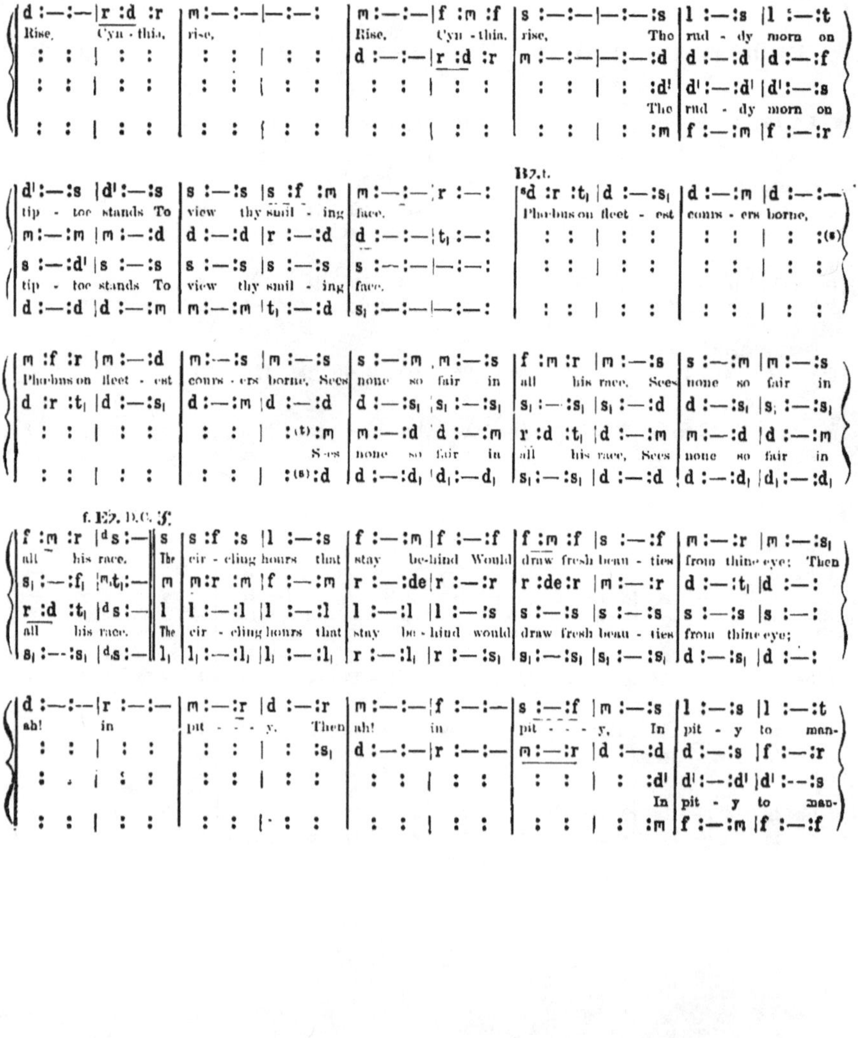

d :— :— | r :d :r	m :— :— | — :— :	m :— :— | f :m :f	s :— :— | — :— :s	l :— :s | l :— :t
Rise, Cyn - thia,	rise,	Rise, Cyn - thia,	rise, The	rud - dy morn on
: : | : :	: : | : :	d :— :— | r :d :r	m :— :— | — :— :d	d :— :d | d :— :f
: : | : :	: : | : :	: : | : :	: : | : :d'	d' :— :d' | d' :— :s
			The	rud - dy morn on
: : | : :	: : | : :	: : | : :	: : | : :m	f :— :m | f :— :r

B♭. t.

d' :— :s | d' :— :s	s :— :s | s :f :m	m :— :— | r :— :	ˢd :r :t₁ | d :— :s₁	d :— :m | d :— :—
tip - toe stands To	view thy smil - ing	face.	Phœbus on fleet - est	cours - ers borne,
m :— :m | m :— :d	d :— :d | r :— :d	d :— :— | t₁ :— :	: : | : :	: : | : :(s)
s :— :d' | s :— :s	s :— :s | s :— :s	s :— :— | — :— :	: : | : :	: : | : :
tip - toe stands To	view thy smil - ing	face.		
d :— :d | d :— :m	m :— :m | t₁ :— :d	s₁ :— :— | — :— :	: : | : :	: : | : :

m :f :r | m :— :d	m :— :s | m :— :s	s :— :m | m :— :s	f :m :r | m :— :s	s :— :m | m :— :s
Phœbus on fleet - est	cours - ers borne, Sees	none so fair in	all his race, Sees	none so fair in
d :r :t₁ | d :— :s₁	d :— :m | d :— :d	d :— :s₁ | s₁ :— :s₁	s₁ :— :s₁ | s₁ :— :d	d :— :s₁ | s₁ :— :s₁
: : | : :	: : | :(t) :m	m :— :d | d :— :m	r :d :t₁ | d :— :m	m :— :d | d :— :m
	Sees	none so fair in	all his race, Sees	none so fair in
: : | : :	: : | :(s) :d	d :— :d₁ | d₁ :— :d₁	s₁ :— :s₁ | d :— :d	d :— :d₁ | d₁ :— :d₁

f. E♭. D.C. *f*

f :m :r | ᵈs :— ‖ s	s :f :s | l :— :s	f :— :m | f :— :f	f :m :f | s :— :f	m :— :r | m :— :s₁
all his race. The	cir - cling hours that	stay be-hind Would	draw fresh beau - ties	from thine eye; Then
s₁ :— :f₁ | ᵐt₁ :— ‖ m	m :r :m | f :— :m	r :— :de | r :— :r	r :de :r | m :— :r	d :— :t₁ | d :— :
r :d :t₁ | ᵈs :— ‖ l	l :— :l | l :— :l	l :— :l | l :— :s	s :— :s | s :— :s	s :— :s | s :— :
all his race. The	cir - cling hours that	stay be - hind would	draw fresh beau - ties	from thine eye;
s₁ :— :s₁ | ᵈs :— ‖ l₁	l₁ :— :l₁ | l₁ :— :l₁	r :— :l₁ | r :— :s₁	s₁ :— :s₁ | s₁ :— :s₁	d :— :s₁ | d :— :

d :— :— | r :— :—	m :— :r | d :— :r	m :— :— | f :— :—	s :— :f | m :— :s	l :— :s | l :— :t
ah! in	pit - - y. Then	ah! in	pit - - - y, In	pit - y to man-
: : | : :	: : | : :s₁	d :— :— | r :— :—	m :— :r | d :— :d	d :— :s | f :— :r
: : | : :	: : | : :	: : | : :	: : | : :d'	d' :— :d' | d' :— :s
			In	pit - y to man-
: : | : :	: : | : :	: : | : :	: : | : :m	f :— :m | f :— :f

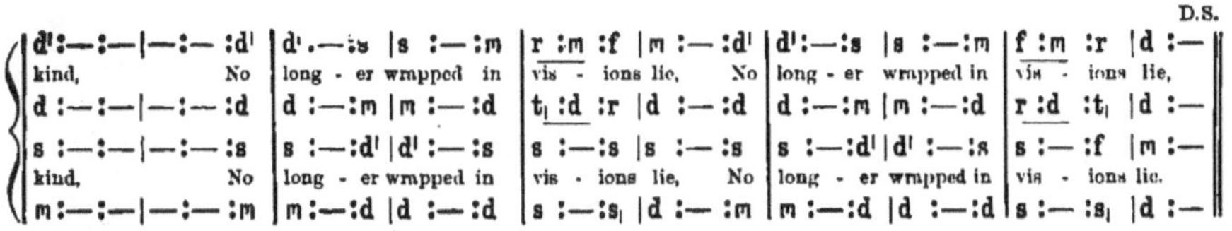

D.S.

d':—:—|—:— :d' | d' .—:s |s :—:m | r :m :f |m :—:d' | d':—:s |s :—:m | f :m :r |d :— ||
kind, No | long - er wrapped in | vis - ions lie, No | long - er wrapped in | vis - ions lie,
d :—:—|—:— :d | d :—:m |m :—:d | t, :d :r |d :—:d | d :—:m |m :—:d | r :d :t, |d :— ||

s :—:—|—:— :s | s :—:d' |d' :—:s | s :—:s |s :—:s | s :—:d' |d' :—:s | s :—:f |m :— ||
kind, No | long - er wrapped in | vis - ions lie, No | long - er wrapped in | vis - ions lie.
m :—:—|—:— :m | m :—:d |d :—:d | s :—:s, |d :— :m | m :—:d |d :—:d | s :—:s, |d :— ||

WITH THE ROSY LIGHT.

230. Key C. M. 120. T. F. Seward.

:m .f |s :d' |r' :m' |f' :l |— :l .l |l .s :s .l |t :d' .r' |m'.d' :d'.r' |m' :m .f
:d .r |m :m |f :s |l :f |— :f .f |f .f :f .f |f :m .f |s .m :m .f |s :d .r
2. With the ros - y light of morn-ing, Where the merry birds awake, And the laughing waters flow, We will
3. By the wood-land streams we'll wan - der, Till the merry bird has gone To its quiet leaf-y nest, And the
:d' .d' |d' :d' |d' :d' |d' :d' |— :d' .d |t .t :t .d' |r' :d' .d' |d'.d' :d'.d' |d' :d' .d'
:d .d |d :d |d :d |f :f |— :f .f |s .s :s .s |s :d .d |d .d :d .d |d :d .d

FINE. G.t.

s :d' |r' :m' |f' :l |— :l .l |l .s :s .l |t :d' .r' |d' :— || :^{t}m .m
m :m |f :s |l :f |— :f .f |f .f :f .f |f :m .f |m :— || :^{s}d .d
haste with joy and glad - ness, Singing gayly as we go, as we go. We will
gold - en sun - beams dy - ing, Gently linger in the west, in the west. Then the
d' :d' |d' :d' |d' :d' |— :d' .d' |t .t :t .d' |r' :s .s |s :— || :^{r}s .s
d :d |d :d |f :f |— :f .f |s .s :s .s |s :s .s |d :— || :^{s}d .d

f .r :r .m |f :s .f |m :s, .d |m :f .m |r .t, :t, .d |r :m .r |d :d .d |d :m .m
r .t, :t, .d |r :m .r |d :s, .s, |s, :s, .s, |s, .s, :s, .s, |s, :s, .s, |s, :m, .f, |s, :d .d
carol to the breeze, Where the old for - est trees Wave their branches in the ray Of the bright king of day, And the
fairies tripping light, To the fields say good-night, With a footstep glad and free We will bound o'er the lea In our
s .s :s .s |s :s .s |s :m .m |s :s .s |f .r :r .m |f :s .f |m :d .r |m :s :s
s, .s, :s, .s, |s, :s, .s, |d :d .d |d :d .d |s, .s, :s, .s, |s, :s, .s, |d, :d, .d, |d, :d :d

f.C. D.C.

f .r :r .m |f :s .f |m :s, .d |m :f .m |r .t, :t, .d |r :m .r |^{d}s :— |
r .t, :t, .d |r :m .r |d :s, .s, |s, :s, .s, |s, .s, :s, .s, |s, :s, .s, |^{s}r :— |
music from the dell, Where the young lil - ies dwell, Shall be echoed far a - way, far a - way.
cheerful homes so dear, We will sing sweet and clear, Till the welkin shall resound with our glee.
s .s :s .s |s :s .s |s :m .m |s :s .s |f .r :r :m |f :s .f |^{m}t :— |
s, .s, :s, .s, |s, :s, .s, |d :d .d |d :d .d |s, .s, :s, :s, |s, :s, .s, |^{d}s, :— |

REST, WEARY PILGRIM.

231. KEY B♭. S. S. C., or T. T. B., or S. C. B. From DONIZETTI.

May be sung in key G, by S. C. T., Tenor singing the lowest part an octave higher than written.

p

| m :— | m :m | re :— | m :— | d :— | d :r | m :— | d : | m :— | m :m |

| s, :— | s, :s, | fe, :— | s, :— | l, :— | la, :la, | s, :— | s, : | d :— | r :r |

1. Rest, wea - ry Pil - grim! from toil re - pos - ing. Night's dark-'ning

2. Rest, wea - ry Pil - grim! till morn ing's break - ing. And birds a -

| d, :— | d, :d, | d, :— | d, :— | f, :— | f, :f, | d, :— | m, : | s, :— | se, :se, |

| m :— | f : | r :— | m :r | d :— | d : | *cres.* r :— | r :m | d :— | d : |

| d :— | r : | t, :— | d :t, | d :— | d : | t, :— | t, :t, | l, :— | l, : |

shad - ows round thee are clos - ing; Drear is the path - way

round thee blithe songs are wak - ing; Hark! thro' the for - est

| l, :— | r, : | s, :— | s, :s, | m, :— | m, : | s, :— | s, :se, | l, :— | l, : |

| m :— | m :f | r :— | r : | m :— | re :m | *f* s :— | f :m | r :— | m :r | d :— | d : |

| d :— | d :r | t, :— | t, : | d :— | d :d | m :— | r :de | r :l, | d :t, | d :— | s, : |

frown - ing be- fore thee! No stars on high to guide and watch o'er thee!

chill winds are blow - ing! Here, there is friend - ship and kind wel-come glow - ing!

| l, :— | l, :r, | s, :— | s, : | s, :— | fe, :s, | ta, :— | l, :s, | f, :— | s, :f, | m, :— | m, : |

p

| d :— | d :r | m :— | d : | *pp* d :— | d :r | m :— | — :— | d :— | — :— | — :— | — : ||

| l, :— | l, :l, | s, :— | s, : | la, :— | la, :la, | s, :— | — :— | m, :— | — :— | — :— | — : ||

Rest, wea-ry Pil - grim! Rest, wea-ry Pil - - grim!

| f, :— | f, :f, | d, :— | m, : | f, :— | f, :f, | d, :— | — :— | d, :— | — :— | — :— | — : ||

Pitching Tunes. In the third step the pupil was taught to pitch the key tone of a tune by singing down the Standard Scale, stepwise, to the tone required. A shorter way may now be taught. In pitching key G the pupil need not run down to G stepwise, but will fall upon it at once from C'. In pitching key F he will take C' as s, and fall to the key-tone, thus, C'—s m d. Key E may be pitched by falling to m, thus, C'—d' s m md. Key A is pitched by falling to l, thus, C'—d' l—ld. Key D, thus, C'—d r'—r d'. The key may be pitched a little-step higher (sharper), or a little-step lower (flatter), than any tone of the Standard Scale. The tones thus required are named "C sharp," "D sharp," "E flat," "D flat," etc., and the sign ♯ is used for "sharp," and ♭ for "flat." A sharp bears no relation to the tone below it, and after which, for convenience, it is named, but its relation is to the tone above it. It is to the tone above it the same that t is to d, or *fe* to s. In order to strike it correctly, sing the tone above, and then smoothly descend a little-step to it. A flat bears no relation to the tone above it, and after which it is named. Its relation is to the tone below it, to which it is the same as f to m, or *ta* to l. To pitch it correctly, in the cases of G♭, A♭ and D♭, we should sing the tone below, and then rise to it a little-step. In the key B♭ take C' as s, and sing s f—fd. In Key E♭ take C' as l, thus, C'—l t d'.

See *Manual for Teachers School Series*, page 30, for plan for pitching keys.

232. Key G. THE MILLER.

ZOLLNER.

.s₁	d .,s₁ :m₁ .f₁	s₁ .,l₁ :s₁ .d	m .,r :d .r	m .,f :m .d
.	:	: .d	d .,s₁ :m₁ .f₁	s₁ .,l₁ :s₁ .d
1. To	wan - der is the	mil - lers's joy, To	wan - der is the	mil - ler's joy, To
2. We've	learnt it from the	flow - ing stream, We've	learnt it from the	flow - ing stream, The
3. We	see this al - so	in the wheels, We	see this al - so	in the wheels, The
4. Oh!	wan - d'ring ev - er	is my joy, Oh!	wan - d'ring ev - er	is my joy, Oh!
.	:	:	:	: .m
.	:	:	:	: .d

m :r	d : .s₁	r .r :m ,r .de,r	t₁ .r :s₁ .s₁
d :t₁	d : .s₁	t₁ .t₁ :t₁ .t₁	s₁ .s₁ :s₁ .s₁
wan - - - - -	der. The	mil - lers all do	love to roam, To
flow - - ing	stream. It	neith - er rests by	day nor night. Its
bus - - y	wheels, Which	do not turn a -	lone by day, But
wan - der - -	ing. Fare -	well my par - ents,	friends and home, Let
s :f	m : .s	f .s :f .s	f .s :f .s
s₁ :s₁	d₁ : .s₁	s₁ .s₁ :s₁ .s₁	s₁ .s₁ :s₁ .s₁

r .r :m ,r .de,r	t₁ .r :s₁ .s₁	l₁ .t₁ :d .r	m .,r :d .m
t₁ .t₁ :t₁ .t₁	s₁ .s₁ :s₁ .s₁	l₁ .t₁ :d .r	m .,r :d .d
leave their vil - lage,	house and home, To	leave their vil - lage,	house and home, To
course it fol - lows	with de - light, Its	course it fol - lows	with de - light, The
keep it up all	night so gay, But	keep it up all	night so gay, The
me un - to the	wide world roam, Let	me un - to the	wide world roam, And
f .s :f .s	f .s :f .s₁	l₁ .t₁ :d .r	m .,r :d .d
s₁ .s₁ :s₁ .s₁	s₁ .s₁ :s₁ .s₁	l₁ .t₁ :d .r	m .,r :d .d

s :t₁	s :t₁	s :t₁	d :–
t₁ :s₁	t₁ :s₁	t₁ :s₁	s₁ :–
wan - - der,	wan - - der,	wan - - - - -	der.
flow - - ing,	flow - - ing,	flow - - ing	stream.
bus - - y,	bus - - y,	bus - - y	wheels.
wan - - der,	wan - - der,	wan - - - - -	der.
r :s	r :s	r :f	m :–
s₁ :s₁	s₁ :s₁	s₁ :s₁	d₁ :–

233. Key C. Round in four parts.

T. F. S.

s .fe :s	s .fe :s	m .re :m	m .re :m
Soh, fe, soh,	soh, fe, soh,	me, re, me,	me re, me.

d' .l :s .m	d' .l :s .m	d .d ,d :m .s	d' :
Now be - ware, and	sing with care, And	keep ev - ery voice in	tune.

MURMURING BROOKLET.

MARY C. SEWARD. R. SCHUMANN.

222:3-4. KEY B♭. Repeat *pp* D. C. 𝄋 F. t.

```
s, :d :t, |l, :r :d | t, :l, :t, |d :- :m | s, :d :t, |l, :r :d | t, :l, :t, |d :- :- || t m :- :- |f :- :-
Murm'ring brook-let | gent-ly flow-ing, | Wind-ing free the | fields a-mong. || Loo...
m, :- :- |f, :- :- | - :- :- |m, :- :- | m, :- :- |f, :- :- | - :- :- |m, :- :- || r s, :d :t, |l, :r :d
Loo... | ... | Loo... | ... || Sweet and pure as
s, :- :- |l, :- :- | s, :- :- |- :- :- | s, :- :- |l, :- :- | s, :- :- |- :- :- || s d :- :- |l :- :-
Loo... | ... | Loo... | ... || Loo...
d, :- :- |f, :- :- | s, :- :- |d, :- :- | d, :- :- |f, :- :- | s, :- :- |d, :- :- || s d :- :- |f, :- :-
```

Repeat *pp.* D. S. f B♭.

```
- :- :r |d :- :- | m :- :- |f :- :- | - :- :r |d :- :- || d s, :d :t, |l, :r :d | t, :l, :t, |d :- :m
... | Loo... | ... || Glad and gay its | work ful-fil-ling
t, :l, :t, |d :- :m | s, :d :t, |l, :r :d | t, :l, :t, |d :- :- || l m, :- :- |f, :- :- | - :- :- |m, :- :-
bub-bling fountain, | Sing-ing soft its | rip-pling song. || Loo... | ...
s :- :- |- :- :- | s :- :- |l :- :- | s :- :- |- :- :- || d s, :- :- |l, :- :- | s, :- :- |- :- :-
... | Loo... | ... || Loo... | ...
s, :s :f |m :r :d | d :- :- |f, :- :- | s, :s :f |m :r :d || f d, :- :- |f, :- :- | s, :- :- |d, :- :-
```

f. E♭.

```
s, :d :t, |l, :r :d | t, :l, :t, |d :- :d s, | d :m :l |s :m :d | t, :d :l, |s, :l, :t, | d :m :l |s :m :d
Car-ing not for | cloud or sun. 'Tis | roll-ing, rush-ing, | on-ward push-ing, | Ceas-ing not when
m, :- :- |f, :- :- | - :- :- |m, :- :d s, | d :m :l |s :m :d | t, :d :l, |s, :l, :t, | d :m :l |s :m :d
Loo... | ...
s, :- :- |l, :- :- | s, :- :- |- :- :d s, | d :m :l |s :m :d | t, :d :l, |s, :l, :t, | d :m :l |s :m :d
Loo... | ...'Tis | roll-ing, rush-ing, | on-ward push-ing, | Ceas-ing not when
d, :- :- |f, :- :- | s, :- :- |d, :- :d s, | d :m :l |s :m :d | t, :d :l, |s, :l, :t, | d :m :l |s :m :d
```

```
t, :d :l, |s, :- :s, | d :m :l |s :m :d | t, :d :l, |s, :l, :t, | d :m :l |s :m :d | t, :d :l, |s, :- :s
once be-gun; 'Tis | whirl-ing, twirl-ing, | wind-ing, turn-ing, | Rest-ing not till | work is done.
t, :d :l, |s, :- :s, | d :m :l |s :m :d | t, :d :l, |s, :l, :t, | d :m :l |s :m :d | t, :d :l, |s, :- :s
t, :d :l, |s, :- :s, | d :m :l |s :m :d | t, :d :l, |s, :l, :t, | d :m :l |s :m :d | t, :d :l, |s, :- :s
once be-gun; 'Tis | whirl-ing, twirl-ing, | wind-ing, turn-ing, | Rest-ing not till | work is done.
t, :d :l, |s, :- :s, | d :m :l |s :m :d | t, :d :l, |s, :l, :t, | d :m :l |s :m :d | t, :d :l, |s, :- :s
```

```
s :d' :t |l :r' :d' | t :l :t |d' :— :m' | s :d' :t |l :r' :d' | t :l :t |d' :— :—
Mur-m'ring brook-let | gent-ly flow-ing, | Wind-ing free the | fields a-mong;
m :— :— |f :— :— | — :— :— |m :— :— | m :— :— |f :— :— | — :— :— |m :— :—
Loo... | ... | Loo... | ...
d :— :— |l :— :— | s :— :— |— :— :— | s :— :— |l :— :— | s :— :— |— :— :—
Loo... | ... | Loo... | ...
d :— :— |f, :— :— | s, :— :— |d :— :— | d :— :— |f, :— :— | s, :— :— |d :— :—
```

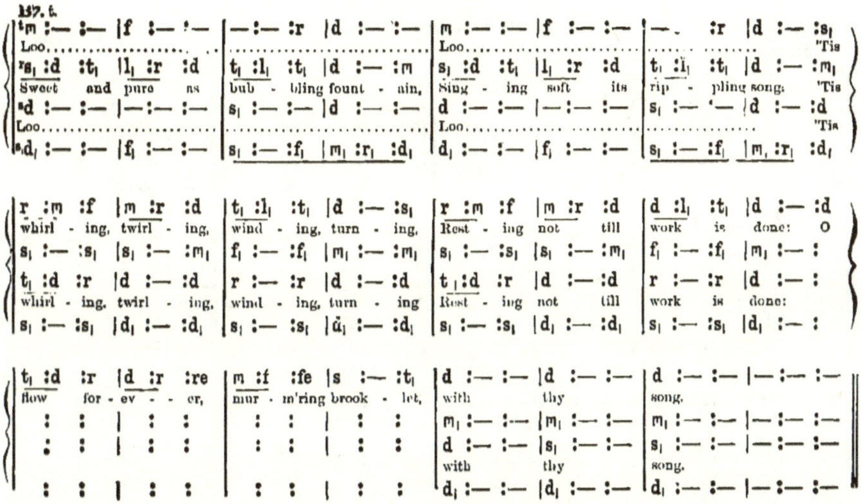

137. t.

m :— :— |f :— :— |— :— :r |d :— :— |m :— :— |f :— :— |— :— :r |d :— :s,

Loo.. Loo.. 'Tis

s, :d :t, |l, :r :d |t, :l, :t, |d :— :m |s, :d :t, |l, :r :d |t, :l, :t, |d :— :m,

Sweet and pure as bub - bling fount - ain, Sing - ing soft its rip - pling song: 'Tis

d :— :— |— :— :— |s, :— :— |d :— :— |d :— :— |— :— :— |s, :— :— |d :— :d

Loo.. Loo.. 'Tis

d, :— :— |f, :— :— |s, :— :f, |m, :r, :d, |d, :— :— |f, :— :— |s, :— :f, |m, :r, :d,

r :m :f |m :r :d |t, :l, :t, |d :— :s, |r :m :f |m :r :d |d :l, :t, |d :— :d

whirl - ing, twirl - ing, wind - ing, turn - ing, Rest - ing not till work is done: O

s, :— :s, |s, :— :m, |f, :— :f, |m, :— :m, |s, :— :s, |s, :— :m, |f, :— :f, |m, :— :

t, :d :r |d :— :d |r :— :r |d :— :d |t, :d :r |d :— :d |r :— :r |d :— :

whirl - ing, twirl - ing, wind - ing, turn - ing Rest - ing not till work is done:

s, :— :s, |d, :— :d, |s, :— :s, |d, :— :d, |s, :— :s, |d, :— :d, |s, :— :s, |d, :— :

t, :d :r |d :r :re |m :f :fe |s :— :t, |d :— :— |d :— :— |d :— :— |— :— :—

flow for - ev - - er, mur - m'ring brook - let, with thy song.

: : | : : | : : | : : |m, :— :— |m, :— :— |m, :— :— |— :— :—

: : | : : | : : | : : |d :— :— |s, :— :— |s, :— :— |— :— :—

with thy song.

: : | : : | : : | : : |d, :— :— |d, :— :— |d, :— :— |— :— :—

OH, WIPE AWAY THAT TEAR.

235. Key C. M. 108.

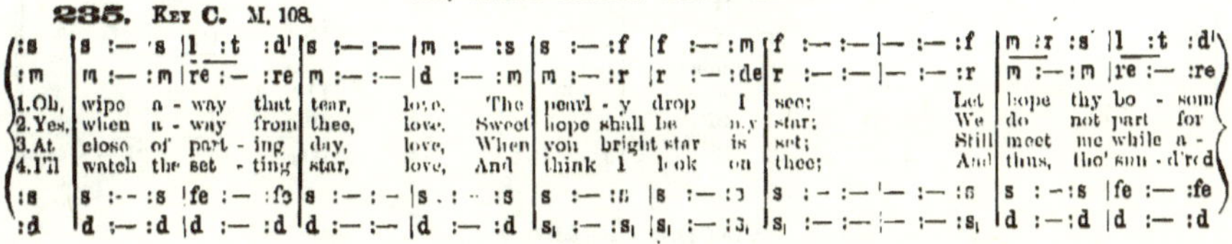

:s |s :— :s |l :t :d' |s :— :— |m :— :s |s :— :f |f :— :m |f :— :— |— :— :f |m :r :s |l :t :d'

:m |m :— :m |re :— :re |m :— :— |d :— :m |m :— :r |r :— :de |r :— :— |— :— :r |m :— :m |re :— :re

1. Oh, wipe a - way that tear, love, The pearl - y drop I see: Let hope thy bo - som

2. Yes, when a - way from thee, love, Sweet hope shall be my star: We do not part for

3. At close of part - ing day, love, When yon bright star is set; Still meet me while a -

4. I'll watch the set - ting star, love, And think I look on thee; And thus, tho' sun - der'd

:s |s :— :s |fe :— :fe |s :— :— |s :— :s |s :— :s |s :— :s |s :— :— |— :— :s |s :— :s |fe :— :fe

:d |d :— :d |d :— :d |d :— :— |d :— :d |s, :— :s, |s, :— :s, |s, :— :— |— :— :s, |d :— :d |d :— :d

OUT IN THE SHADY BOWERS.

T. F. S.

236. Key A♭. T. F. Seward.

s, :fe, :s,	t, .l, :l, .se, :l,	r :de :r	f .m :m .re :m
m, :re, :m,	f, .f, :f, .f, :f,	f, :m, :f,	l, .s, :s, .fe, :s,
1. Out in the	shad-y greenwood bowers,	Balm - y the	air with fragrant flowers,
2. On mos - sy	banks where blossoms creep,	From ev - ery	side the fresh buds peep,
d :d :d	d .d :d .d :d	t, :le, :t,	d .d :d .d :d
d :d :d	f, .f, :f, .f, :f,	s, :s, :s,	d, .d, :d, .d, :d,

FINE.

s, :fe, :s,	t, .l, :l, .se, :l,	s, :l, :t,	d :— :—
m, :re, :m,	f, .f, :f, .f, :f,	f, :f, :f,	m, :— :—
Swift flee the	happy summer hours	On wings a -	way.
Sun - beams and	flow'rs their revels keep,	And songs re -	sound
d :d :d	d .d :d .d :d	t, :d :r	d :— :—
d :d :d	f, .f, :f, .f, :f,	s, :s, :s,	d :— :—

E♭. t.

^{r}s :fe :s	s .d' :d' .s :l	f :r :l	l .s :s .m :s
^{t}m :re :m	m .m :m .m :f	r :r :t	f .m :m .d :m
Birds fill the	air with sweetest song,	Soft - ly the	brooklet flows a - long,
Un - der the	leaf-y for - est bough	Where zeph - yrs	whisper soft and low,
^{s}d' :d' :d'	d' .s :s .d' :d'	t :t :t	d' .d' :d' .d' :d'
^{s}d :d :d	d .d :d .d :f	s :s :s	d .d :d .d :d

f. A♭. D.C.

s :fe :s	s .d' :d' .s :l	f :r :s	^{d}s, :— :—
m :re :m	m .m :m .m :f	r :t, :t,	^{d}s, :m, :f,
There pass our	hours, a hap - py throng,	Day af - ter	day.
Spend we the	hours as swift they go,	While joys a -	bound.
d' :d' :d'	d' .s :s .d' :d'	t :s :f	^{m}t, :d :r
d :d :d	d .d :d .d :f	s :s :s,	^{d}s, :— :—

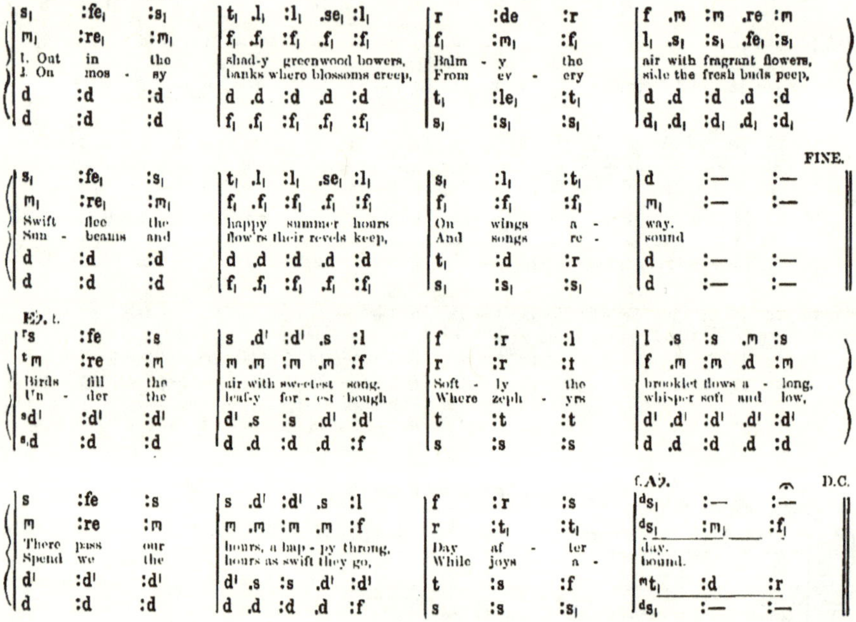

SINGING CHEERILY.

237. Key B♭. Words and Music by W. F. Sherwin.

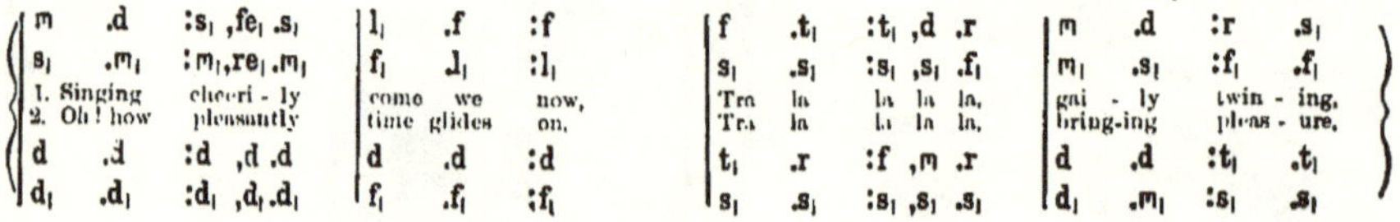

m .d :s, ,fe, .s,	l, .f :f	f .t, :t, ,d .r	m .d :r .s,
s, .m, :m, ,re, .m,	f, .l, :l,	s, .s, :s, ,s, .f,	m, .s, :f, .f,
1. Singing cheeri - ly	come we now,	Tra la la la la,	gai - ly twin - ing,
2. Oh! how pleasantly	time glides on,	Tra la la la la,	bring-ing pleas - ure,
d .d :d ,d .d	d .d :d	t, .r :f ,m .r	d .d :t, .t,
d, .d, :d, ,d, .d,	f, .f, :f,	s, .s, :s, ,s, .s,	d, .m, :s, .s,

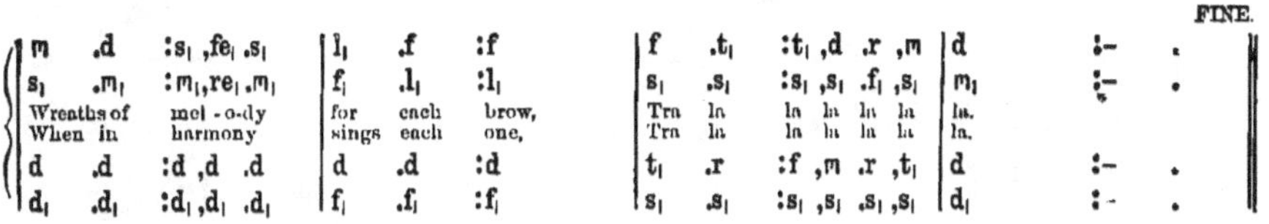

FINE.

m .d :s₁ ,fe₁ .s₁	l₁ .f :f	f .t₁ :t₁ ,d .r ,m	d :– .
s₁ .m₁ :m₁,re₁ .m₁	f₁ .l₁ :l₁	s₁ .s₁ :s₁ ,s₁ .f₁ ,s₁	m₁ :– .
Wreaths of mel - o-dy	for each brow,	Tra la la la la la	la.
When in harmony	sings each one,	Tra la la la la la	la.
d .d :d ,d .d	d .d :d	t₁ .r :f ,m .r ,t₁	d :– .
d₁ .d₁ :d₁ ,d₁ .d₁	f₁ .f₁ :f₁	s₁ .s₁ :s₁ ,s₁ .s₁ ,s₁	d₁ :– .

F.t.

df .r :r ,m .f ,l	s .d' :d' .,s	t .l :s ,fe .s	l .s :m ,f .s
fet₁ .t₁ :t₁ ,d .r ,f	m .m :m .,m	s .f :m ,re .m	f .m :d ,r .m
Eyes that sparkle with a	pure de - light, So	bright-ly gleam-ing.	On us beam-ing,
All life's trials are a -	while for - got, Its	troubled dream ing,	I - - dle scheming,
lr .s :s ,s .s ,s₁	s .s :s .,s	s .s :s .s	s .s :s .s
rs₁ .s₁ :s₁ ,s₁ .s₁ ,s₁	d .d :d .,d	s₁ .s₁ :s₁ .s₁	d .d :d .d

f. B♭. D. C.

f .r :r ,m .f ,l	s .d' :d' .,s	t ,l .s ,f :m .r	ds₁ :f
r .t₁ :t₁ ,d .r ,f	m .m :m .,m	r ,f .m ,r :d .t₁	ds₁ :s₁
Bring with beauty in their	glance to night, A	cheery welcome to our	song. So—
Care and wea-ri-ness can	harm us not, If	we can sing a mer - ry	glee. Then—
s .s :s ,s .s ,s	s .s :s .,s	s ,s .s ,s :s .f	mt₁ :t₁
s₁ .s₁ :s₁ ,s₁ .s₁ ,s₁	d .d :d .,d	s₁ ,s₁ .s₁ ,s₁ :s₁ .s₁	ds₁ :s₁

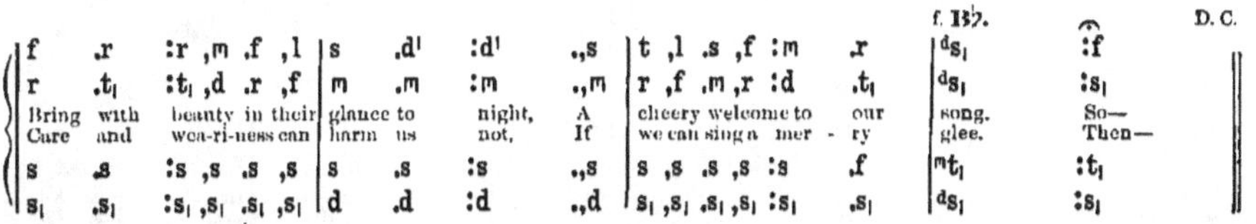

HOW SWEET TO GO STRAYING.

238. KEY B♭. T. F. SEWARD.

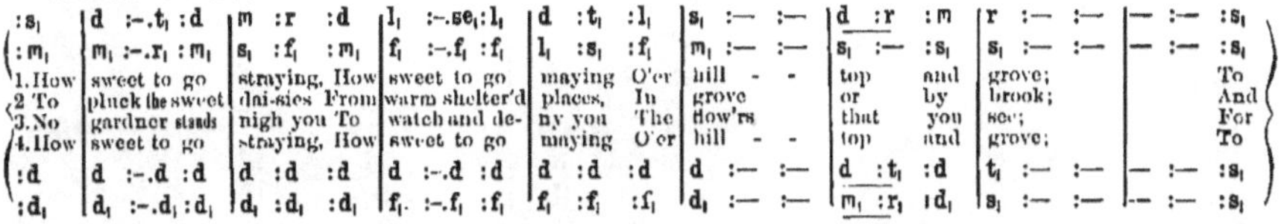

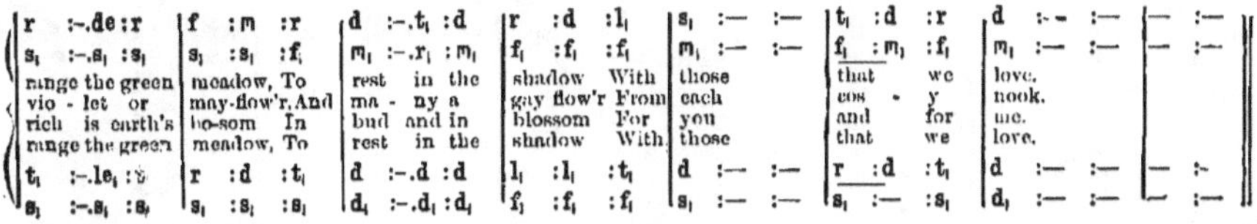

:s₁	d :–.t₁ :d	m :r :d	l₁ :–.se₁ :l₁	d :t₁ :l₁	s₁ :– :–	d :r :m	r :– :–	– :– :s₁
:m₁	m₁ :–.r₁ :m₁	s₁ :f₁ :m₁	f₁ :–.f₁ :f₁	l₁ :s₁ :f₁	m₁ :– :–	s₁ :– :s₁	s₁ :– :–	– :– :s₁
1. How	sweet to go	straying, How	sweet to go	maying O'er	hill - -	top and	grove;	To
2. To	pluck the sweet	dai-sies From	warm shelter'd	places, In	grove	or by	brook;	And
3. No	gardner stands	nigh you To	watch and de-	ny you The	flow'rs	that you	see;	For
4. How	sweet to go	straying, How	sweet to go	maying O'er	hill - -	top and	grove;	To
:d	d :–.d :d	d :d :d	d :–.d :d	d :d :d	d :– :–	d :t₁ :d	t₁ :– :–	– :– :s₁
:d₁	d₁ :–.d₁ :d₁	d₁ :d₁ :d₁	f₁ :–.f₁ :f₁	f₁ :f₁ :f₁	d₁ :– :–	m₁ :r₁ :d₁	s₁ :– :–	– :– :s₁

r :–.de :r	f :m :r	d :–.t₁ :d	r :d :l₁	s₁ :– :–	t₁ :d :r	d :– :–	– :–
s₁ :–.s₁ :s₁	s₁ :s₁ :f₁	m₁ :–.r₁ :m₁	f₁ :f₁ :f₁	m₁ :– :–	f₁ :m₁ :f₁	m₁ :– :–	– :–
range the green	meadow, To	rest in the	shadow With	those	that we	love.	
vio - let or	may-flow'r, And	ma - ny a	gay flow'r From	each	cos - y	nook.	
rich is earth's	bo-som In	bud and in	blossom For	you	and for	me.	
range the green	meadow, To	rest in the	shadow With	those	that we	love.	
t₁ :–.le₁ :s	r :d :t₁	d :–.d :d	l₁ :l₁ :t₁	d :– :–	r :d :t₁	d :– :–	– :–
s₁ :–.s₁ :s₁	s₁ :s₁ :s₁	d₁ :–.d₁ :d₁	f₁ :f₁ :f₁	s₁ :– :–	s₁ :– :s₁	d₁ :– :–	– :–

SWEET EVENING HOUR.

T. F. SEWARD. Arr. from KULLAK, by THEO. F. SEWARD.

230. KEY B♭.

:	:	:	: .s,	s, :l, .d	s, :- .m
			O	sweet ev'n -ing	hour, O
:	:	:	: .m,	m, :f, .r,	m, :- .s,
s, :—	s, :—	s, :—	s, :—	s, :—	s, :-
Sweet	ev'n - - -	ing	hour,	Sweet	ev'n - - -
d, :—	d, :—	d, :—	d, :—	d, :—	d, :—

r .t, :d .l,	t, :s, .s,	s, :l, .d	s, :- .m	r .t, :s, .l,
calm and qui - et	ev'n - - ing. How	gen - - tle thy	power; 1. From	care each heart re -
f, .s, :m, .f,	r, :f, .f,	m, :f, .r,	m, :- .s,	s, .s, :s, .s,
s, :—	s, :—	s, :—	s, :- .d	r .r :m .m
ing	hour,	Sweet	hour; 2. From	care each heart re -
d, :—	d, :—	d, :—	d, :- .d	t, .t, :d .d

t, :s, .s,	f :m .d	t, :d	s, .s, :s, .s,	l, :s, .s,
s, :s, .s,	s, :s, .s,	s, :s,	f, .f, :f, .f,	f, :f, .s,
liev - - ing. The	birds to their	nests with	cheerful songs re -	tir - - - ing. All
liev - - ing. The	stars, one by	one, in	heav'ns blue vault ap	pear - - ing. The
r :t, .t,	t, :d .m	f :m .d	t, .t, :t, .t,	d :t, .t,
s, :s, .s,	s, :s, .s,	s, :s,	s, .s, :s, .s,	s, :s, .s,

f :m .d	t, :d	r .r :r .r	r :m .r	r :m .r
s, :s, .s,	s, :s,	s, .s, :fe, .fe,	s, :s,	fe, :fe,
na - - ture's glad	voic - es	come with sound in -	spir - - ing.	Come till
light zeph - yrs	play where	ros - es are in -	twin - - ing.	Fra - grance
t, :d .m	f :m	r .r :d :d	t, :d .t,	d :d
s, :s, .s,	s, :d	t, .t, :l, :l,	s, :s,	l, :l,

r :d	t, :l,	s, :- .s,	s, :l, .d	s, :- .m
all is	hushed to	rest. O	sweet ev'n - ing	hour, O
s, :s,	f, :f,	f, :- .f,	m, :f, .r,	m, :- .s
t, :m	r :d	t, :- .	s, :—	s, :—
fling - - ing	ev - - ery - -	where.	Sweet	ev'n - - - -
s, :s,	s, :s,	s, :- .	d, :—	d, :—

| r .t_1 :d .l_1 | t_1 :s_1 .s_1 | s_1 :l_1 .d | s_1 :– .m | r :m_1 .t_1 |
calm and qui - et | ev'n - - ing, How | gen - - tle thy | power, O | sweet ev'n - ing
| f_1 .s_1 :m_1 .f_1 | r_1 :f_1 .f_1 | m_1 :f_1 .r_1 | m_1 :– .s_1 | f_1 :f_1 .f_1 |
| s_1 :— | s_1 :— | s_1 :— | s_1 :– .d | t_1 :d .r |
ing | hour, | Sweet | hour, O | sweet ev'n - ing
| d_1 :— | d_1 :— | d_1 :— | d_1 :– .d_1 | s_1 :s_1 .s_1 |

| d :– .s_1 | s_1 :l_1 .d | s_1 :— | s_1 :— | s_1 :— ||
hour, Sweet | ev'n - ing | hour; | Sweet | hour.
| m_1 :– .s_1 | s_1 :fe_1 | s_1 :— | f_1 :— | m_1 :— ||
| d :– .m | m :re | m :– .m | r :l_1 .t_1 | d :— ||
hour, Sweet | ev'n - - ing | hour; O | sweet ev'n - ing | hour.
| d_1 :– .d_1 | d_1 :d_1 | d_1 :– | s_1 :— | d_1 :— ||

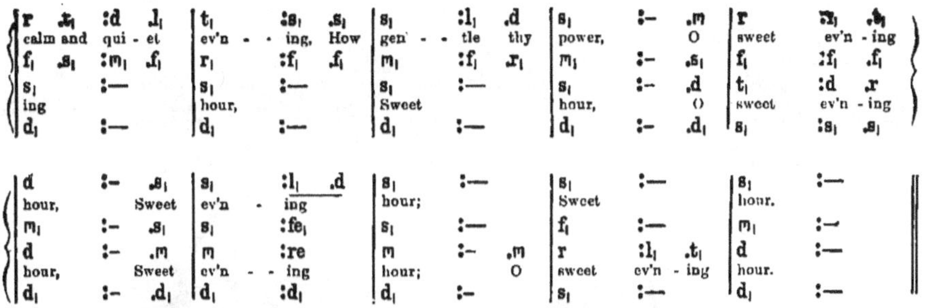

IN THE VINEYARD.

Eliza M. Sherman. B. C. Unseld, by per.

240. Key F.

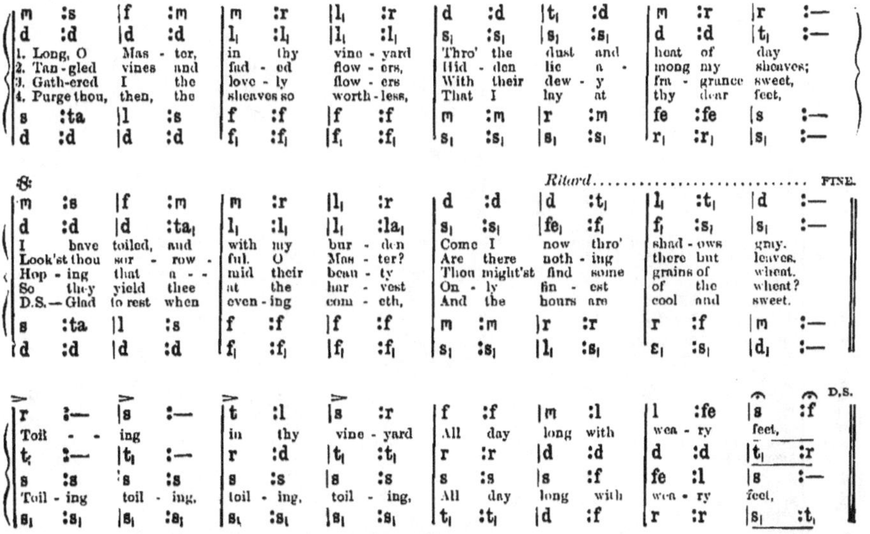

| m :s | f :m | m :r | l_1 :r | d :d | t_1 :d | m :r | r :— |
| d :d | d :d | l_1 :l_1 | l_1 :l_1 | s_1 :s_1 | s_1 :s_1 | d :d | t_1 :— |
1. Long, O Mas - ter, in thy vine - yard Thro' the dust and heat of day
2. Tan-gled vines and fad - ed flow - ers, Hid - den lie a - mong my sheaves;
3. Gath-ered I the love - ly flow - ers With their dew - y fra - grance sweet,
4. Purge thou, then, the sheaves so worth - less, That I lay at thy dear feet,
| s :ta | l :s | f :f | f :f | m :m | r :m | fe :fe | s :— |
| d :d | d :d | f_1 :f_1 | f_1 :f_1 | s_1 :s_1 | s_1 :s_1 | r_1 :r_1 | s_1 :— |

𝄋 *Ritard.* FINE.

| m :s | f :m | m :r | l_1 :r | d :d | d :t_1 | l_1 :t_1 | d :— ||
| d :d | d :ta_1 | l_1 :l_1 | l_1 :la_1 | s_1 :s_1 | fe_1 :f_1 | f_1 :s_1 | s_1 :— ||
I have toiled, and with my bur - den Come I now thro' shad - ows gray.
Look'st thou sor - row - ful, O Mas - ter? Are there noth - ing there but leaves.
Hop - ing that a - - mid their beau - ty Thou might'st find some grains of wheat.
So they yield thee at the har - vest On - ly fin - est of the wheat?
D.S.—Glad to rest when even - ing com - eth, And the hours are cool and sweet.
| s :ta | l :s | f :f | f :f | m :m | r :r | r :f | m :— ||
| d :d | d :d | f_1 :f_1 | f_1 :f_1 | s_1 :s_1 | l_1 :s_1 | s_1 :s_1 | d_1 :— ||

D.S.

| r :— | s :— | t :l | s :r | f :f | m :l | l :fe | s :f ||
Toil - - ing | in thy vine - yard | All day long with | wea - ry feet,
| t_1 :— | t_1 :— | r :d | t_1 :t_1 | r :r | d :d | d :d | t_1 :r ||
| s :s | s :s | s :s | s :s | s :s | s :f | fe :l | s :— ||
Toil - ing toil - ing, toil - ing, toil - ing, All day long with wea - ry feet,
| s_1 :s_1 | s_1 :s_1 | s_1 :s_1 | s_1 :s_1 | t_1 :t_1 | d :f | r :r | s_1 :t_1 ||

Beating Time. It was recommended in the first step (see note, page 11) not to allow pupils to beat time until they have gained a sense of time. If the teacher wishes, he may now teach beating time according to the following diagrams. The beating should be done by one hand (palm downwards), chiefly by the motion of the wrist, and with but little motion of the arm. The hand should pass swiftly and decidedly from one *point* of the beating to the next, and it should be held steadily at each point as long as the pulse lasts. The direction of the motion is from the thinner to thicker end of each line. The thicker end shows the "point of rest" for each pulse.

NOTE.—It is better to beat the second pulse of three pulse measure to the right, than (as some do) towards the left, because it thus corresponds with the medium beat of the four-pulse measure, and the second pulse of three-pulse measure is *like* a medium pulse. It is commonly treated (both rhythmically and harmonically) as a continuation of the *first* pulse. Similar reasons show a propriety in the mode of beating a six-pulse measure; but when this measure moves *very* quickly, it is beaten like a two pulse measure, giving a beat on each accented pulse.

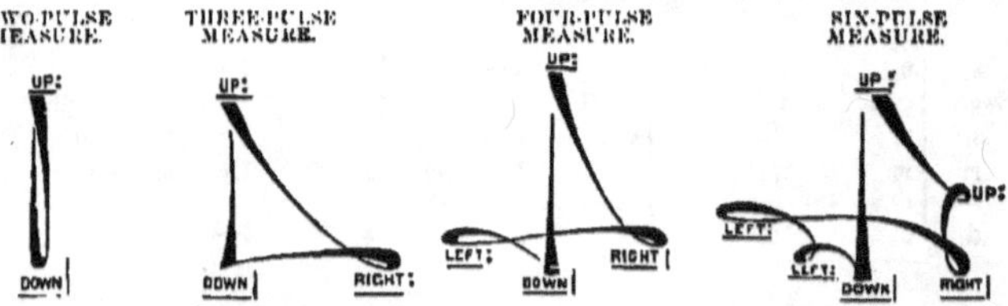

The Silent Quarter-pulse is indicated, like the other silences, by a vacant space among the pulse divisions. It is named *sa* on the accented, and *se* on the unaccented part of a pulse.

241. KEYS C, G.

TAA TAI TAA fe fe	TAA TAI TAA se fe	TAA se fe TAA se fe	TAA TAI TAA
l .l :l .l ,l	l .l :l . ,l	l . ,l :l . ,l	l .l :l
s .s :s .m ,t	s .s :s . ,s	l . ,s :s . ,s	l .t :d^1
m .r :d .r ,m	f .m :r . ,r	m . ,d :r . ,t_1	d .r :d

HURRAH!

242. KEY A. D.C.

,d	d .s_1 :s_1 ,d	d .l_1 :l_1 . ,f	m . ,d :r . ,t_1	d :– .
,m_1	m_1 .m_1 :m_1 .m_1	l_1 .f_1 :f_1 . ,l_1	s_1 . ,m_1 :f_1 . ,r_1	m_1 :– .
1. We	shout with joy this	hap - py day, Hur-	rah! hur-rah! hur-	rah!
With	song we drive dull	care a - way, Hur-	rah! hur-rah! hur-	rah!
2. Here	Free - dom's star is	ris - ing high, Hur-	rah! hur-rah! hur-	rah!
It	shines in splen - dor	in the sky, Hur-	rah! hur-rah! hur-	rah!
3. Here	sci - ence fair, and	learn - ing bright, Hur-	rah! hur-rah! hur-	rah!
Have	shed a pure and	bril - liant light, Hur-	rah! hur-rah! hur-	rah!
,d	d .d :d .d	d .d :d . ,d	d . ,d :t_1 . ,r	d :– .
,d_1	d_1 .d_1 :d_1 .d_1	f_1 .f_1 :f_1 . ,f_1	s_1 . ,s_1 :s_1 . ,s_1	d_1 :– .

,d	t_1 .,d :r .t_1	d .,r :m .d	t_1 .,d :r .t_1	d .,r :m .
,m_1	r_1 .,m_1 :f_1 .r_1	m_1 .,f_1 :s_1 .m_1	r_1 .,m_1 :f_1 .r_1	m_1 .,f_1 :s_1 .
We	love the land that	gave us birth, The	dear - est land of	all the earth;
And	Free - dom's voice will	ev - er - more In	tri - umph ring from	shore to shore;
And	knowl - edge, truth and	lib - er - ty, Our	watch - words ev - er -	more shall be.
,d	r .,d :t_1 .r	d .,d :d .d	r .,d :t_1 .r	d .,d :d ,
,d_1	s_1 .,s_1 :s_1 .s_1	d_1 .,d_1 :d_1 .d_1	s_1 .,s_1 :s_1 .s_1	d_1 .,d_1 :d_1 ,

CHORUS.

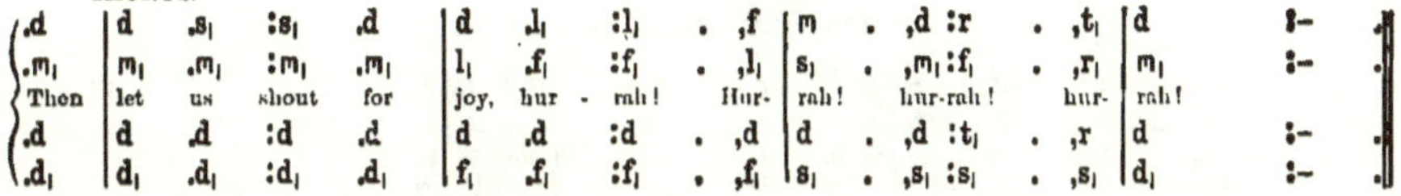

,d	d ,s, :s, ,d	d ,l, :l, . ,f	m . ,d :r . ,t,	d :-
,m,	m, ,m, :m, ,m,	l, ,f, :f, . ,l,	s, . ,m, :f, . ,r,	m, :-
Then	let us shout for	joy, hur - rah! Hur-	rah! hur-rah! hur-	rah!
,d	d ,d :d ,d	d ,d :d . ,d	d . ,d :t, . ,r	d :-
,d,	d, ,d, :d, ,d,	f, ,f, :f, . ,f,	s, . ,s, :s, . ,s,	d, :-

Thirds of a pulse are indicated by commas turned to the right, thus,—: , , | The first third of a pulse is named TAA, the second third TAI, the third third TEE; and the silences and continuations are named in the same manner as before.

243. KEYS C, G.

TAA TAI TEE TAA	TAA TAI TEE TAA	TAA TAA	TAA TAI TEE TAA
l ,l ,l :l	l ,l ,l :l	l :l	l ,l ,l :l
s ,l ,t :d'	d' ,t ,l :s	s :d'	t ,d' ,r' :d'
d ,r ,m :r	r ,m ,f :m	m :d	s, ,l, ,t, :d

244. KEYS A, F.

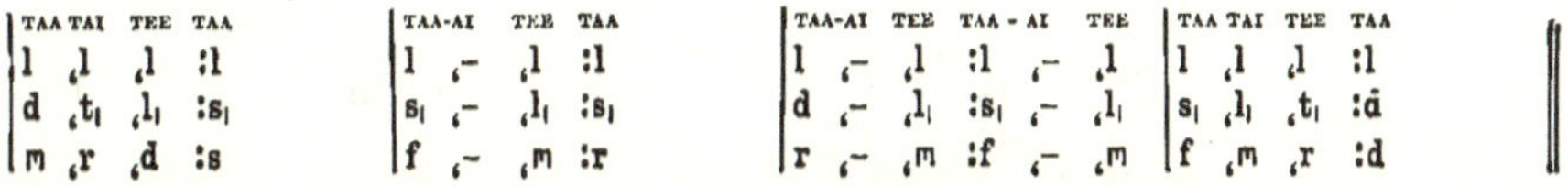

TAA TAI TEE TAA	TAA-AI TEE TAA	TAA-AI TEE TAA - AI TEE	TAA TAI TEE TAA
l ,l ,l :l	l ,- ,l :l	l ,- ,l :l ,- ,l	l ,l ,l :l
d ,t, ,l, :s,	s, ,- ,l, :s,	d ,- ,l, :s, ,- ,l,	s, ,l, ,t, :d
m ,r ,d :s	f ,- ,m :r	r ,- ,m :f ,- ,m	f ,m ,r :d

245. KEY G, D.

TAA TAI TAA	TAA TAI TEE TAA	TAA TAI TEE	
l .l :l	l ,l ,l :l	l ,l ,l :l ,l ,l	l .l :l
d .t, :d	t, ,d ,r :d	d ,r ,m :f ,m ,r	d .t, :d
s .f :m	f ,s ,f :m	s ,l ,s :f ,s ,f	m .r :d

246. KEY C. Round in three parts.

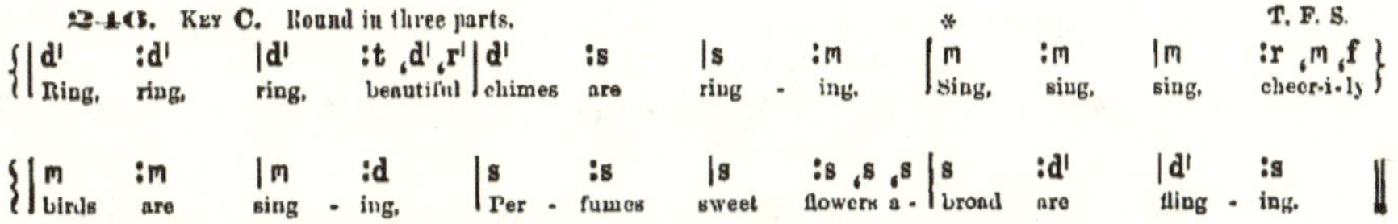

d' :d'	d' :t ,d' ,r'	d' :s	s :m	* m :m	m :r ,m ,f
Ring, ring,	ring, beautiful	chimes are	ring - ing.	Sing, sing,	sing, cheer-i-ly

T. F. S.

m :m	m :d	s :s	s :s ,s ,s	s :d'	d' :s
birds are	sing - ing.	Per - fumes	sweet flowers a -	broad are	fling - ing.

247 KEY C. Round for two parts.

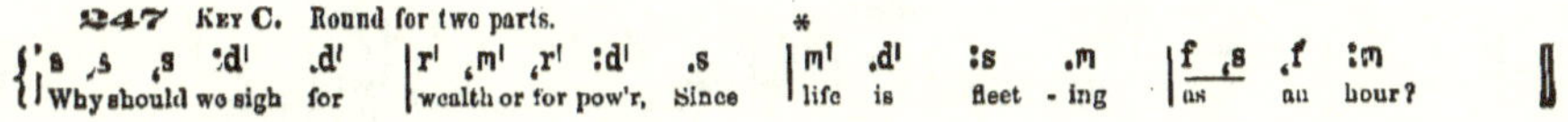

s ,s ,s :d' .d'	r' ,m' ,r' :d' .s	* m' .d' :s .m	f ,s ,f :m
Why should we sigh for	wealth or for pow'r, Since	life is fleet - ing	as an hour?

MERRILY SINGS THE LARK.

248. Key B♭.

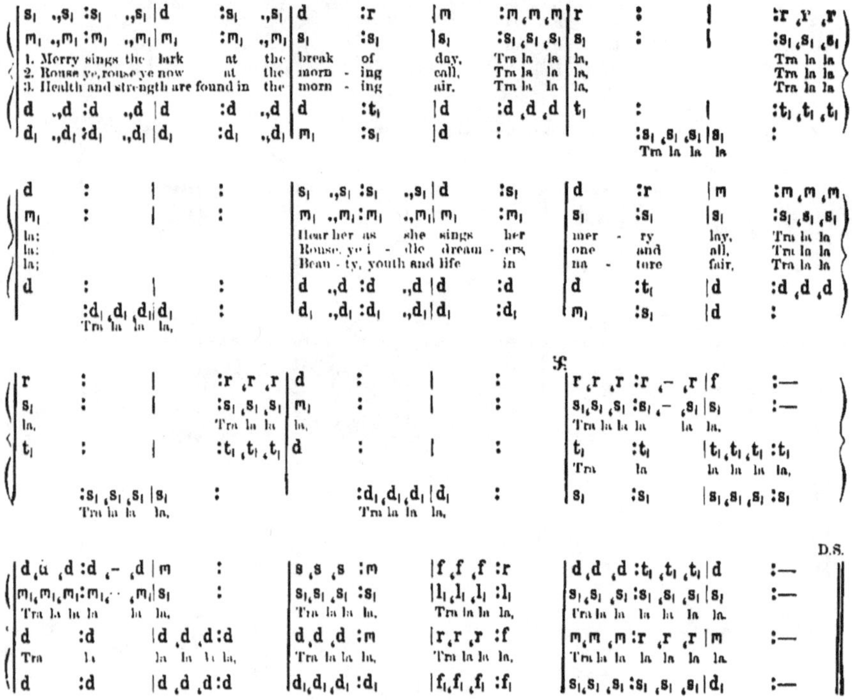

|s, .,s, :s, .,s, |d :s, .,s, |d :r |m :m.m.m |r : | :r.r.r
|m, .,m, :m, .,m, |m, :m, .,m, |s, :s, |s, :s,.s,.s, |s, : | :s,.s,.s,
1. Merry sings the lark at the break of day, Tra la la la, Tra la la
2. Rouse ye, rouse ye now at the morn - ing call, Tra la la la, Tra la la
3. Health and strength are found in the morn - ing air, Tra la la la, Tra la la
|d .,d :d .,d |d :d .,d |d :t, |d :d.d.d |t, : | :t,.t,.t,
|d, .,d, :d, .,d, |d, :d, .,d, |m, :s, |d : | :s,.s,.s, |s, :
Tra la la la

|d : | : |s, .,s, :s, .,s, |d :s, |d :r |m :m.m.m
|m, : | : |m, .,m, :m, .,m, |m, :m, |s, :s, |s, :s,.s,.s,
la; Hear her as she sings her mer - ry lay, Tra la la
la; Rouse, ye i - dle dream - ers one and all, Tra la la
la; Beau - ty, youth and life in na - ture fair, Tra la la
|d : | : |d .,d :d .,d |d :d |d :t, |d :d.d.d
| :d,.d,.d, |d, : |d, .,d, :d, .,d, |d, :d, |m, :s, |d :
Tra la la la,

|r : | :r.r.r |d : | : 𝄋 |r.r.r :r .– .r |f :—
|s, : | :s,.s,.s, |m, : | : |s,.s,.s, :s, .– .s, |s, :—
la, Tra la la la, Tra la la la la la.
|t, : | :t,.t,.t, |d : | : |t, :t, |t,.t,.t, :t,
Tra la la la la la,
| :s,.s,.s, |s, : | :d,.d,.d, |d, : |s, :s, |s,.s,.s, :s,
Tra la la la, Tra la la la,

|d.d.d :d .– .d |m : |s.s.s :m |f.f.f :r |d.d.d :t,.t,.t, |d :— D.S.
|m,.m,.m, :m, .– .m, |s, : |s,.s,.s, :s, |l,.l,.l, :l, |s,.s,.s, :s,.s,.s, |s, :—
Tra la la la la la. Tra la la la. Tra la la la. Tra la la la la la la.
|d :d |d.d.d :d |d.d.d :m |r.r.r :f |m.m.m :r.r.r |m :—
Tra la la la la la, Tra la la la. Tra la la la. Tra la la la la la la.
|d :d |d.d.d :d |d,.d,.d, :d, |f,.f,.f, :f, |s,.s,.s, :s,.s,.s, |d, :— ||

249. Key D. Round for four parts.

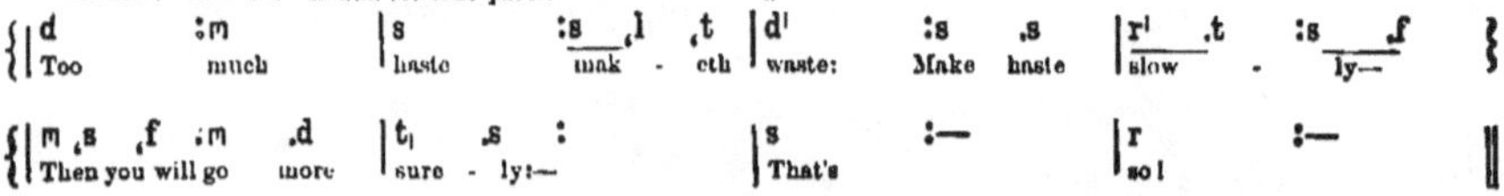

|d :m |s :s .l .t |*d' :s .s |r' .t :s .f
Too much haste mak - eth waste: Make haste slow - ly—
|m .s .f :m .d |t, .s : |s :— |r :— ||
Then you will go more sure - ly:— That's so!

Syncopation is the anticipation of accent. It requires an accent to be struck before its regularly recurring time, changing a *weak* pulse or a weak part of a pulse into a *strong* one, and the immediately *following* strong pulse or part of a pulse into a *weak* one. It must be boldly struck, and the strong accent on the immediately following pulse must be omitted.

250.

| l :l | — :l | l :l | — :l | l :l | — :l | — :l | l :l ‖
| TAA TAA | -AA TAA | TAA TAA | -AA TAA | TAA TAA | -AA TAA | -AA TAA | TAA TAA |

251.

| l l :- .l | l l :- .l | l .l :l .l | l . :l . ‖
| TAA TAI - AA TAI | TAA TAI - AA TAI | TAA TAI TAA TAI | TAA *SAI* TAA *SAI* |

252. KEY C. Round in two parts. T. F. S.

| s :s | — :s | l :l | — :l | t :t | — :t | d' :d' | d' : |
Come now, oh, come now, Or we shall be late, I fear.

| *m : | m : | f : | f : | s : | s : | d : | : ‖
Yes, we're com - ing right a - - long.

253. KEY C. Round in two parts.

| d :— | r :— | m :— | f :— | r :— | m :— | f :— | m :— |
No, no, no, no, no, no, no, no!

| * :d' | — :t | — :ta | — :l | — :r' | — :d' | — :t | d' :— ‖
Yes, yes, yes, yes, yes, yes, yes, yes!

254. KEY C. Round in two parts.

| d' .d' :- .t | l .l :- .s | f .m :r .f | m : |
Come now, O come now, Or we shall be too late;

| *m .m :m | f .f :f .m | r .d' :- .t | d' : ‖
No, no, no, no, no, no, And you, too, must wait.

255. KEY F. Round in three parts.

| m :m .,f | s :d | m :r .,d | r :- .d | m :s .l | s :m .d |
Call John the boat - man, call him a - gain, For loud roars the tem - pest and

| s, :m .,r | d : | * .d :d .d | d :- .d | d :t, .l, | s, :- .t, |
fast falls the rain. John is a - sleep, he sleeps ver - y sound, His

| d .d .d | d :d .d | m :s .,f | m :s | — .d .,r | m .m : .d |
oars are at rest, and his boat is a - ground, Loud roars the riv - er, so

| s .s :- .l | t : .s ,s | s .s :m .f | s : .m | s .s :s, .,s, | d : ‖
rap-id and deep; But the louder you call John, the sounder he will sleep.

HEAR THE WARBLING NOTES.

T. F. S.
256. KEY G. M. 100. T. F. SEWARD.

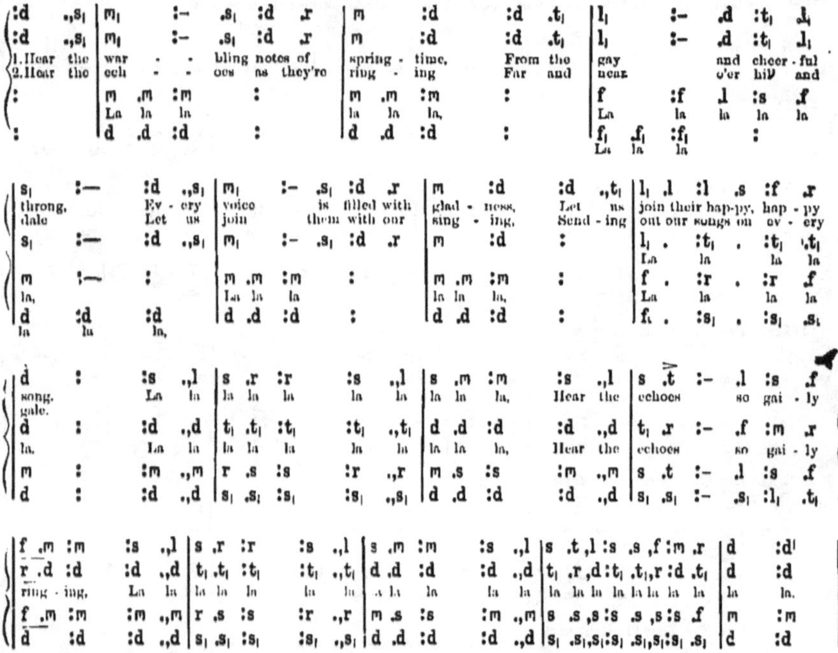

:d .,s1 | m1 :– .s1 :d .r | m :d :d .t1 | l1 :– .d :t1 .l1
:d .,s1 | m1 :– .s1 :d .r | m :d :d .t1 | l1 :– .d :t1 .l1
1. Hear the | war - - bling notes of | spring - time, From the | gay and cheer - ful
2. Hear the | ech - - oes as they're | ring - ing Far and | near o'er hill and
: | m .m :m : | m .m :m : | f :f .l :s .f
La la la | la la la, | La la la la la
: | d .d :d : | d .d :d : | f1 .f1 :f1 :
La la la

s1 :— :d .,s1 | m1 :– .s1 :d .r | m :d :d .,t1 | l1 .l :l .s :f .r
throng. Ev - ery | voice is filled with | glad - ness, Let us | join their hap-py, hap - py
dale Let us | join them with our | sing - ing, Send - ing | out our songs on ev - ery
s1 :— :d .,s1 | m1 :– .s1 :d .r | m :d : | l1 . :t1 . :t1 .t1
La la la la
m :— : | m .m :m : | m .m :m : | f . :r . :r .f
la, | La la la | la la la, | La la la la
d :d :d | d .d :d : | d .d :d : | f1 . :s1 . :s1 .s1
la la la,

d : :s .,l | s .r :r :s .,l | s .m :m :s .,l | s .t :– .l :s .f
song. La la | la la la la la | la la la, Hear the | echoes so gai - ly
gale.
d : :d .,d | t1 .t1 :t1 :t1 .,t1 | d .d :d :d .,d | t1 .r :– .f :m .r
la. La la | la la la la la | la la la, Hear the | echoes so gai - ly
m : :m .,m | r .s :s :r .,r | m .s :s :m .,m | s .t :– .l :s .f
d : :d .,d | s1 .s1 :s1 :s1 .,s1 | d .d :d :d .,d | s1 .s1 :– .s1 :l1 .t1

f .m :m :s .,l | s .r :r :s .,l | s .m :m :s .,l | s .t ,l :s .s ,f :m .r | d :d'
r .d :d :d .,d | t1 .t1 :t1 :t1 .,t1 | d .d :d :d .,d | t1 .r ,d :t1 .t1 ,r :d .t1 | d :d
ring - ing, La la | la la la la la | la la la la la | la la la la la la la la | la la.
f .m :m :m .,m | r .s :s :r .,r | m .s :s :m .,m | s .s ,s :s .s ,s :s .f | m :m
d :d :d .,d | s1 .s1 :s1 :s1 .,s1 | d .d :d :d .,d | s1 .s1 ,s1 :s1 .s1 ,s1 :s1 .s1 | d :d

COME, LET US ALL BE MERRY.

257. KEY E. M. 80. Arranged, and new words.

.d ,r | m .m :m .s | s .f : .r ,m | f .s :l .t | d' .s : .m ,f | s .s :s .l
.d ,r | m .m :m .s | s .f : .r ,m | f .s :l .t | d' .s : .d | m .m :m .f
1. Come, | let us all be | mer-ry, For | grieving is a | fol - ly; All | care and trou-ble
2. A - | way with all the | tra - ces Of | sad - ness, gloom and | sor - row; If | we must wear long
3. So | when the clouds are | low'ring, Then | let us laugh the | stronger, For | thus all care o'er-
.d ,r | m .m :m .s | s .f : .r ,m | f .s :l .t | d' .s : .s | d' .d' :d' .d'
.d ,r | m .m :m .s | s .f : .r ,m | f .s :l .t | d' .s : .d | d .d :d .d

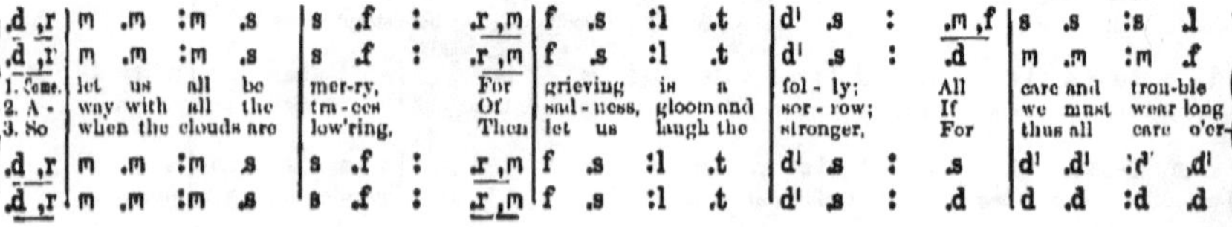

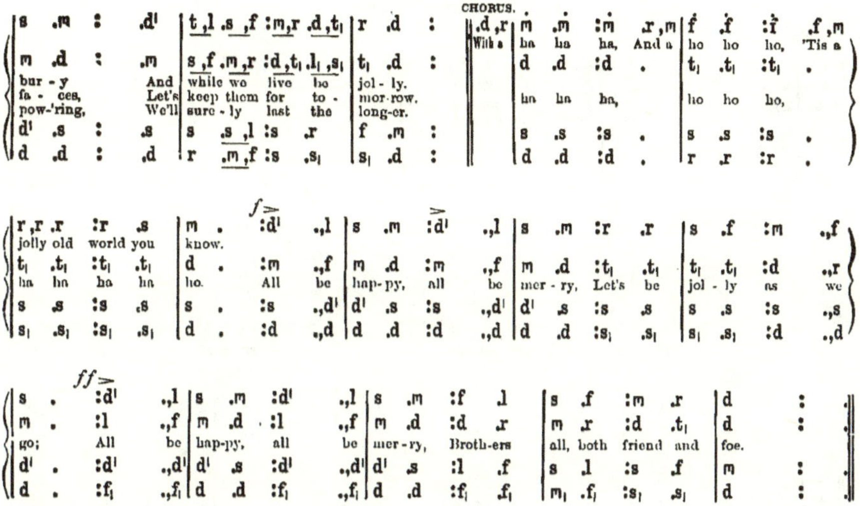

				CHORUS.		
s .m : .d^1	t ,l .s ,f :m,r .d ,t_1	r .d :		.d ,r	$\dot{m}$.$\dot{m}$:$\dot{m}$ .r ,m	$\dot{f}$.$\dot{f}$:$\dot{f}$ .f ,m
				With a	ha ha ha, And a	ho ho ho, 'Tis a
m .d : .m	s ,f .m ,r :d ,t_1 .l_1 ,s_1	t_1 .d :			d .d :d .	t_1 .t_1 :t_1 .
bur - y And	while we live be	jol - ly.				
fa - ces, Let's	keep them for to -	mor-row.			ha ha ha,	ho ho ho,
pow-'ring, We'll	sure - ly last the	long-er.				
d^1 .s : .s	s .s ,l :s .r	f .m :			s .s :s .	s .s :s .
d .d : .d	r .m ,f :s .s_1	s_1 .d :			d .d :d .	r .r :r .

	f >	>		
r ,r .r :r .s	m . :d^1 .,l	s .m :d^1 .,l	s .m :r .r	s .f :m .,f
jolly old world you	know.			
t_1 .t_1 :t_1 .t_1	d . :m .,f	m .d :m .,f	m .d :t_1 .t_1	t_1 .t_1 :d .,r
ha ha ha ha	ho. All be	hap-py, all be	mer - ry, Let's be	jol - ly as we
s .s :s .s	s . :s .,d^1	d^1 .s :s .,d^1	d^1 .s :s .s	s .s :s .,s
s_1 .s_1 :s_1 .s_1	d . :d .,d	d .d :d .,d	d .d :s_1 .s_1	s_1 .s_1 :d .,d

ff >				
s . :d^1 .,l	s .m :d^1 .,l	s .m :f .l	s .f :m .r	d :
m . :l .,f	m .d :l .,f	m .d :d .r	m .r :d .t_1	d :
go; All be	hap-py, all be	mer - ry, Broth-ers	all, both friend and	foe.
d^1 . :d^1 .,d^1	d^1 .s :d^1 .,d^1	d^1 .s :l .f	s .l :s .f	m :
d . :f_1 .,f_1	d .d :f_1 .,f_1	d .d :f_1 .f_1	m_1 .f_1 :s_1 .s_1	d :

Expression.—The following table shows the names of the different degrees of power; the abbreviations and marks by which they are known, and their definitions. The teacher will explain these topics, as may be required, at convenient points in his course of lessons. *See Manual for Teachers School Series* for method of presenting the subject.

NAME.	PRONOUNCED.	MARKED.	MEANING.
PIANISSIMO	Pe-ah-*nissimo*	*pp*	Very Soft.
PIANO	Pe-*ah*-no	*p*	Soft.
MEZZO	*Met*-zo	*m*	Medium.
FORTE	*Four*-tay	*f*	Loud.
FORTISSIMO	Four-*tissimo*	*ff*	Very Loud.
CRESCENDO	Cre-*shen*-do	*cres.* or <	Increase.
DIMINUENDO	Dim-in-oo-*en*-do	*dim.* or >	Diminish.
SWELL		< >	Increase and diminish.
SFORZANDO	Sfort-*zan*-do	*sf.* or *fz.* or >	Explosive.
LEGATO	Lay-*gah*-to	——	Smooth, Connected.
STACCATO	Stock-*kah*-to	' ' '	Short, Detached.

MOVEMENT WORDS.

LARGO		Very slow.
ADAGIO	A-*daj*-o	Very slow.
LARGHETTO		Slow.
ANDANTE	An-*dahn*-tay	Slow.
ANDANTINO	An-dahn-*tee*-no	Moderately slow.
MODERATO	Mo-day-*rah*-to	Moderately, medium.
ALLEGRETTO		Moderately fast.
ALLEGRO	Al-*lay*-gro	Fast.
RITARDANDO		Gradually slower.
ACCELERANDO	At-chel-e-*rahn*-do	Gradually faster.
A TEMPO	Ah *taim*-po	In Time.

The Hold 𝄐, indicates that the tone is to be prolonged at option of the leader.

Da Capo, or D. C., means repeat from the beginning.

Dal Segno, or D. S., means repeat from the 𝄋

Fine indicates the place to end after a D. C. or D. S.

NUTTING SONG.

258. KEY C. B. C. UNSELD.

:s | d' :— :d' | t :— :r' | d' :— :l | s :— :m | f :— :f | l :— :s | s :— :— | m :— :m.f

:s | m :— :m | r :— :f | m :— :f | m :— :d | r :— :r | f :— :f | m :— :— | d :— :l.r

1. Who has no sun - shine in his heart May call the au - tumn so - ber, But
2. The yel - low moon is clear and bright, The si - lent up - land light - ing, The
3. Hur - rah! the nuts are drop - ping ripe In all the for - est bow - ers, We'll

:s | s :— :s | s :— :s | s :— :d' | d' :— :d' | t :— :t | t :— :t | d' :— :— | s :— :s

:s | d :— :d | s :— :s | d :— :d | d :— :d | s :— :s | s, :— :s, | d :— :— | d :— :d

| s :— :d' | t :— :r' | d' :— :l | s :— :d' | t :— :t | r' :d' :l | s :— :— | s :— :s

| m :— :m | r :— :f | m :— :f | m :— :m | r :— :r | r :— :r | r :— :— | r :— :r

boys with puls - es leap - ing wild, Should love the brown Oc - to - ber. A -
mead - ow grass is crisp and white, The frosts are keen and bit - ing. A
climb as high as squir - rels go, We'll shake them down in show - ers. When

| s :— :s | s :— :s | s :— :d' | d' :— :s | s :— :s | fe :l :d' | t :— :— | t :— :t

| d :— :d | s :— :s | d :— :d | d :— :d | r :— :r | r :— :r | s :— :— | s :— :s

| t :— :d' | r' :— :t | d' :— :l | s :— :s | t :— :d' | r' :— :t | d' :— :— | m' :— :m'

| r :— :m | f :— :f | m :— :f | m :— :m | r :— :m | f :— :f | m :— :— | s :— :s

long the glade, and on the hill, The rud - dy oaks are glow - ing, And
shin - ing moon, a frost - y sky, A gust - y morn to fol - low, To
heads are gray, and eyes are dim, We'll call the au - tumn so - ber, But

| r' :— :d' | t :— :r' | d' :— :d' | d' :— :d' | r' :— :d' | t :— :r' | d' :— :— | d' :— :d'

| s :— :s | s, :— :s, | d :— :d | d :— :d | s :— :s | s, :— :s, | d :— :— | d :— :d

| r' :— :r' | d' :— :d' | t :— :t | l :— :l | s :— :d' | t :— :r' | d' :— :— | d' :— :—

| f :— :f | m :— :m | r :— :r | d :— :d | m :— :m | r :— :f | m :— :— | m :— :—

mer - ry winds are out by night, Thro' all the for - ests blow - ing.
drive the with - ered leaves a - bout, And heap them in the hol - low.
now, with life in ev - ery limb, We love the brown Oc - to - ber.

| t :— :t | l :— :l | se :— :se | l :— :l | d' :— :d' | s :— :s | s :— :— | s :— :—

| s :— :s | l :— :l | m :— :m | f :— :f | s :— :s | s, :— :s, | d :— :— | d :— :—

𝄋 CHORUS.

| d' :— :— | l :— :— | d' :— :— | — :— :d' | t :— :d' | r' :— :t | d' :— :r' | m' :— :—

| f :— :— | f :— :— | f :— :— | — :— :f | r :— :m | f :— :f | m :— :f | s :— :—

Ho! ho! ho! The gold - en au - tumn bright with glee,

| l :— :— | d' :— :— | l :— :— | — :— :l | s :— :s | s :— :s | s :— :s | s :— :—

| f :— :— | f :— :— | f :— :— | — :— :f | s :— :s | s, :— :s, | d :— :d | d :— :—

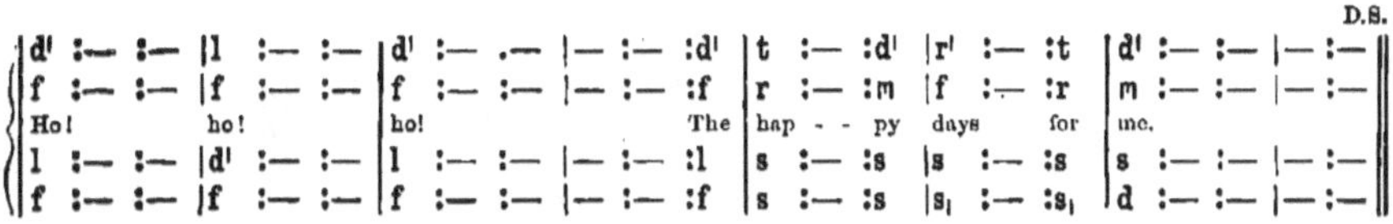

D.S.

|d' :— :— |l :— :— |d' :— :— |— :— :d' |t :— :d' |r' :— :t |d' :— :— |— :— ||

|f :— :— |f :— :— |f :— :— |— :— :f |r :— :m |f :— :r |m :— :— |— :— ||

Ho! ho! | ho! The | hap - - py days for | me.

|l :— :— |d' :— :— |l :— :— |— :— :l |s :— :s |s :— :s |s :— :— |— :— ||

|f :— :— |f :— :— |f :— :— |— :— :f |s :— :s |s, :— :s, |d :— :— |— :— ||

CHRISTMAS CAROL.

259. Key A♭. T. F. Seward.

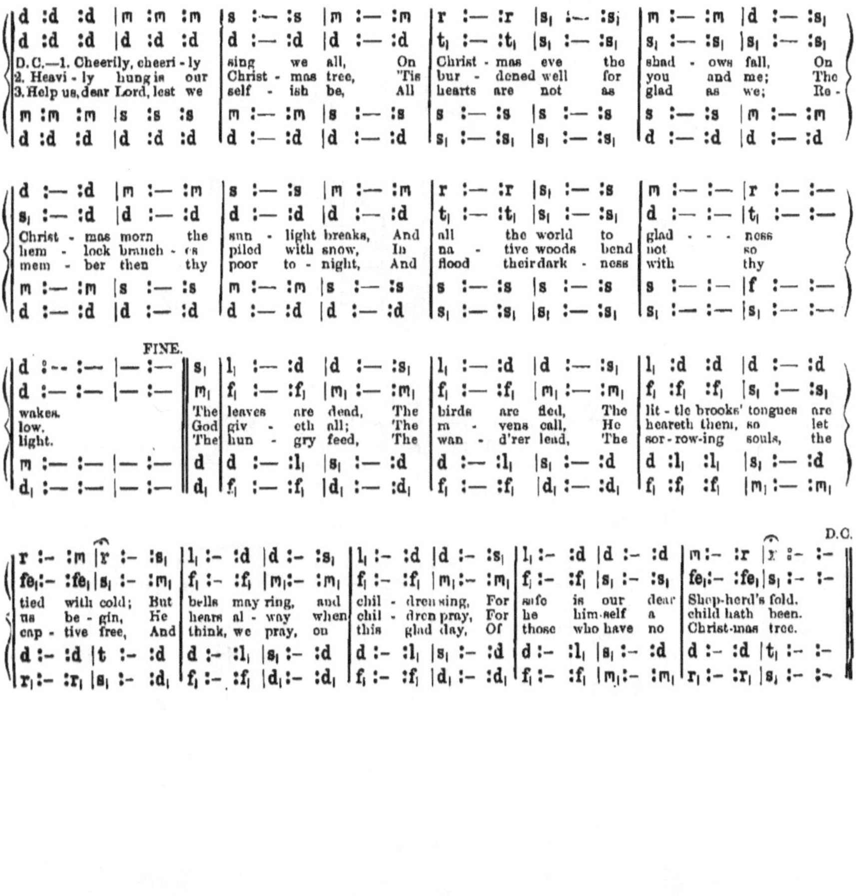

|d :d :d |m :m :m |s :— :s |m :— :m |r :— :r |s, :— :s, |m :— :m |d :— :s, |

|d :d :d |d :d :d |d :— :d |d :— :d |t, :— :t, |s, :— :s, |s, :— :s, |s, :— :s, |

D. C.—1. Cheerily, cheeri - ly | sing we all, On | Christ - mas eve the | shad - ows fall, On

2. Heavi - ly hung is our | Christ - mas tree, 'Tis | bur - dened well for | you and me; The

3. Help us, dear Lord, lest we | self - ish be, All | hearts are not as | glad as we; Re -

|m :m :m |s :s :s |m :— :m |s :— :s |s :— :s |s :— :s |s :— :s |m :— :m |

|d :d :d |d :d :d |d :— :d |d :— :d |s, :— :s, |s, :— :s, |d :— :d |d :— :d |

|d :— :d |m :— :m |s :— :s |m :— :m |r :— :r |s, :— :s |m :— :— |r :— :— |

|s, :— :d |d :— :d |d :— :d |d :— :d |t, :— :t, |s, :— :s, |d :— :— |t, :— :— |

Christ - mas morn the | sun - light breaks, And | all the world to | glad - - - ness

hem - lock branch - es | piled with snow, In | na - tive woods bend | not so

mem - ber then thy | poor to - night, And | flood their dark - ness | with thy

|m :— :m |s :— :s |m :— :m |s :— :s |s :— :s |s :— :s |s :— :— |f :— :— |

|d :— :d |d :— :d |d :— :d |d :— :d |s, :— :s, |s, :— :s, |s, :— :— |s, :— :— |

FINE.

|d :— :— |— :— ||s, |l, :— :d |d :— :s, |l, :— :d |d :— :s, |l, :d :d |d :— :d |

|d :— :— |— :— ||m, |f, :— :f, |m, :— :m, |f, :— :f, |m, :— :m, |f, :f, :f, |s, :— :s, |

wakes. || The | leaves are dead, The | birds are fled, The | lit - tle brooks' tongues are

low. || God | giv - eth all; The | ra - vens call, He | heareth them, so let

light. || The | hun - gry feed, The | wan - d'rer lead, The | sor - row-ing souls, the

|m :— :— |— :— ||d |d :— :l, |s, :— :d |d :— :l, |s, :— :d |d :l, :l, |s, :— :d |

|d, :— :— |— :— ||d, |f, :— :f, |d, :— :d, |f, :— :f, |d, :— :d, |f, :f, :f, |m, :— :m, |

D.C.

|r :— :m |r :— :s, |l, :— :d |d :— :s, |l, :— :d |d :— :s, |l, :— :d |d :— :d |m :— :r |r :— :— ||

|fe, :— :fe, |s, :— :m, |f, :— :f, |m, :— :m, |f, :— :f, |m, :— :m, |f, :— :f, |s, :— :s, |fe, :— :fe, |s, :— :— ||

tied with cold; But | bells may ring, and | chil - dren sing, For | safe is our dear | Shep-herd's fold.

us be - gin, He | hears al - way when | chil - dren pray, For | he him-self a | child hath been.

cap - tive free, And | think, we pray, on | this glad day, Of | those who have no | Christ-mas tree.

|d :— :d |t :— :d |d :— :l, |s, :— :d |d :— :l, |s, :— :d |d :— :l, |s, :— :d |d :— :d |t, :— :— ||

|r, :— :r, |s, :— :d, |f, :— :f, |d, :— :d, |f, :— :f, |d, :— :d, |f, :— :f, |m, :— :m, |r, :— :r, |s, :— :— ||

COME UNTO ME.

260. KEY A♭. T. F. SEWARD.

p
d :— |d :d |d :— |— :— |m :— |f :f |m :— |— :d |l, :t, |d :f
s, :— |l, :l, |s, :— |— :— |s, :— |l, :l, |s, :— |— :s, |f, :s, |— :s,
Come un - to me, Come un - to me, all ye that
m :— |f :f |m :— |— :— |d :— |d :d |d :— |— :d |d :r |d :t,
d, :— |d, :d, |d, :— |— :— |d, :— |d, :d, |d, :— |— :m, |f, :— |m, :r,

m :m |d :m |r :— |d :l, |s, :s, | : |s, :m |r :d |l, :— |d :—
s, :s, |s, :s, |s, :— |fe, :— |s, :s, | : |m, :s, |s, :s, |f, :— |re, :—
la - bor and are heav - y la - den; Come un - to me, and
d :d |m :d |t, :— |l, :d |t, :t, | : |d :— |t, :d |d :— |d :—
d, :d, |d, :d, |r, :— |r, :— |s, :s, | : |d, :— |r, :m, |f, :— |fe, :—

p
d :d |r :t, |d :— |— :— | : | : |s :s |f :f |m :— |d :d
Take my yoke up - on you and
m, :m, |f, :f, |m, :— |— :— | : | : |t, :t, |l, :s, |s, :— |s, :s,
I will give you rest.
d :d |t, :r |d :— |— :— |m :— |d :— |r :— |d :r |d :— |d :d
Take my yoke up - on you and
s, :s, |s, :s, |d, :— |— :— |d :— |m, :— |s, :— |l, :t, |d :— |m, :m,

d :— |l, :— |s, :— |— :s, |p l, :— |l, :— |t, :— |d :— |f :f |m :— |r :— |— :r
learn of me; For I am meek and low-ly of heart, And
l, :— |f, :— |m, :— |— :m, |f, :— |f, :— |s, :— |s, :— |s, :s, |s, :— |s, :— |— :s,
d :— |d :— |d :— |— : |d :d |d :d |r :— |d :d |t, :— |d :— |t, :— |— :t,
learn of me; Take my yoke up- on you and learn of me; And
f, :— |l, :— |d :— |— : |f, :f, |f, :f, |f, :— |m, :m, |r, :— |d, :— |s, :— |— :s,

p
m :m |d :— |pp s, :— |s, :— |s, :— |s, :— |s, :— |m :m |m :d |f :m |s :f |m :r
s, :s, |m, :— |m, :— |m, :— |r, :m, |f, :r, |m, :— |s, :s, |s, :m, |l, :s, |ta, :l, |s, :l,
ye shall find rest un - to your souls, For my yoke is eas - y and my
d :d |d :— |d :— |d :— |t, :d |r :t, |d :— |d :d |d :— |d :— |m :f |s :l
d, :d, |d, :— |d, :— |m, :— |s, :— |s, :— |d, :— |d, :d, |d, :— |d, :— |de, :r, |m, :f,

rit. pp

| d :m | r :— | d :— | — :— | d :— | r .:-.r | m :— | — :— | f :m | r :-.d | d :— | — :— ||

| s_1 :s_1 | s_1 :— | s_1 :— | — :— | m_1 :s_1 | s_1 :-.s_1 | s_1 :— | — :— | f_1 :s_1 | f_1 :-.m_1 | m_1 :— | — :— ||

burden is light. Come un - to me, Come un - to me.

| m :s | f :— | m :— | — :— | d :— | t_1 :-.t_1 | d :— | — :— | d :— | t_1 :-.d | d :— | — :— ||

| s_1 :s_1 | s_1 :— | d_1 :— | — :— | d_1 :m_1 | s_1 :-.s_1 | d :— | — :— | l_1 :d | s_1 :-.d_1 | d_1 :— | — :— ||

EVERY DAY HATH TOIL AND TROUBLE.

201. KEY A♭. M. 120. BEETHOVEN.

| m :m | f :s | s :f | m :r | d :d | r :m | m :— | r :

| s_1 :s_1 | s_1 :s_1 | s_1 :l_1 .t_1 | d :s_1 | s_1 :s_1 | s_1 :s_1 | s_1 :— | — :

1. Ev - ery day hath toil and troub - le, Ev - ery heart hath care;
2. Pa - tient - ly en - dur - ing ev - er Let thy spir - it be
3. La - bor! wait! though mid - night shad - ows Gath - er round thee here,

| d :d | r :m | m :r | d :t_1 | d :d | t_1 :d | d :— | t_1 :

| d :d | d :d | s_1 :s_1 | s_1 :f_1 | m_1 :m_1 | r_1 :d_1 | s_1 :— | — :

| m :m | f :s | s :f | m :r | d :d | r :m | r :— | d :

| s_1 :s_1 | s_1 :s_1 | s_1 :l_1 .t_1 | d :s_1 | s_1 :s_1 | s_1 :s_1 | f_1 :— | m_1 :

Meek - ly bear thine own full bur - den, And thy broth - er's share..........
Bound, by links that can - not sev - er, To hu - man - i - ty............
And the storm a - bove thee low - 'ring, Fills the heart with fear...........

| d :d | r :m | m :r | d :t_1 | d :d | t_1 :d | t_1 :— | d :

| d :d | d :d | s_1 :s_1 | s_1 :f_1 | m_1 :m_1 | r_1 :d_1 | s_1 :— | d_1 :

| r :r | m :d | r :m .f | m :d | r :m .f | m :r | d :r | s_1 :—

| s_1 :s_1 | s_1 :s_1 | s_1 :s_1 | s_1 :s_1 | s_1 :s_1 | s_1 :se_1 | l_1 .s_1 :fe_1 | s_1 :—

Fear not, shrink not, though the bur - den Heav - y to thy heart may prove;
La - bor! wait! thy crown is read - y When thy wea - ry task is done;
Wait in hope, the morn - ing dawn - eth, When the gloom - y night is gone;

| t_1 :t_1 | d :m | t_1 :d .r | d :m | t_1 :d .r | d :m | m :r .d | t_1 :—

| s_1 :s_1 | d :d | s_1 :s_1 | d :d | s_1 :s_1 | d :t_1 | l_1 :r_1 | s_1 :—

| m :m | f :s | s :f | m :r | d :d | r :m | r :— | d : ||

| s_1 :d | t_1 :ta_1 | l_1 :l_1 | l_1 :l_1 | s_1 :s_1 | f_1 :m_1 | f_1 :— | m_1 : ||

God shall fill thy mouth with glad - ness, And thy heart with love............
Count not lost the fleet - ing mo - ments, Life has but be - gun............
And a peace - ful rest a - waits thee, When thy work is done...........

| d :m | r :de | r :r | s :f | m :m | r :d | t_1 :— | d : ||

| d_1 :d_1 | r_1 :m_1 | f_1 :f_1 | f_1 :f_1 | s_1 :s_1 | s_1 :s_1 | s_1 :— | d_1 : ||

THE SWEET VOICE.

GRACE J. FRANCES. HUBERT P. MAIN, by per.

202. KEY D♭. A♭. t.

```
:s  |s  :m  :f  |s  :d' :d' |d' :-  :-  |t  :-  :l  |s  :r  :m  |f  :m  :r  |m  :-  :-  |-  :-  :m l,
:d  |d  :d  :r  |m  :m  :m  |f  :-  :-  |f  :-  :f  |f  :t, :d  |t, :t, :t, |d  :-  :-  |-  :-  :d f,
1. I    dreamed that afar I had   wan - - dered, And   stood on a des-ert a-   lone;   A
2. The  cares of my life in a     mo - - ment Were     lost in a thrill of de- light;  The
3. That voice in my heart I will  cher - - ish, And    when I am sad and op-   pressed, Its
:m  |m  :s  :s  |d' :s  :ta |l  :-  :-  |d' :-  :d' |t  :f  :m  |r  :s  :s  |s  :-  :-  |-  :-  :s d
:d  |d  :d  :d  |d  :d  :d  |f, :-  :-  |f, :-  :f, |s, :s, :s, |s, :s, :s, |d  :-  :-  |-  :-  :d f,
```

f. D♭.

```
|s, :d  :r  |m  :f  :m  |m  :-  :-  |r  :-  :l, |d  :-  :d  |t, :l, :t, |d s :-  :-  |-  :-  :m
|s, :s, :s, |s, :s, :s, |f, :-  :-  |f, :-  :f, |m, :-  :m, |f, :f, :f, |m t, :-  :-  |-  :-  :d
 voice o'er my spir-it came   steal - - ing: How    soft its mag-ic-al     tone.
 desert transformed to a      gar - - den, Where    all was love-ly and    bright.   Sweet
 e-cho, per-haps, in my       slum - - ber Will     calm my sor-row to     rest.
|d  :d  :t, |d  :r  :d  |l, :-  :-  |l, :-  :d  |d  :-  :d  |r  :r  :r  |d s :-  :-  |-  :-  :s
|m, :m, :r, |d, :t2 :d, |f, :-  :-  |f, :-  :f, |s, :-  :s, |s, :s, :s, |d s, :-  :-  |-  :-  :d
```

```
|r  :-  :-  |-  :-  :f  |m  :-  :-  |-  :-  :   |s  :-  :-  |-  :d' :m  |s  :-  :-  |-  :-  :
 voice,             sweet voice,                 Dear          lov-ing    voice!
|t, :-  :t, |t, :-  :r  |d  :-  :m  |m  :-  :   |d  :-  :-  |-  :m  :d  |d  :-  :-  |-  :-  :
 voice, sweet voice, sweet voice, sweet voice,   Dear          lov-ing    voice!
|s  :-  :s  |s  :-  :s  |s  :-  :s  |s  :-  :   |m  :-  :-  |-  :s  :s  |m  :-  :-  |-  :-  :
|s, :-  :-  |-  :-  :s, |d  :-  :-  |-  :-  :   |d  :-  :-  |-  :d  :d  |d  :-  :-  |-  :-  :
```

```
|l  :-  :-  |l  :t  :d' |m' :-  :d' |s  :-  :-  |r  :m  :f  |m  :-  :r  |d  :-  :-  |-  :-  :s
|d  :-  :-  |f  :f  :f  |m  :-  :m  |d  :-  :-  |d  :d  :d  |t, :-  :t, |d  :-  :-  |-  :-  :
 Where, where is the       bliss it gave?         Why is the vis - ion    o'er?           Sweet
|f  :-  :-  |l  :se :l  |s  :-  :s  |m  :-  :-  |l  :s  :l  |s  :-  :f  |m  :-  :-  |-  :-  :
|f, :-  :-  |f, :f, :f, |d  :-  :d  |d  :-  :-  |f  :m  :r  |s, :-  :s, |d  :-  :-  |-  :-  :
```

```
|r  :-  :-  |-  :-  :s  |m  :-  :-  |-  :-  :s  |t  :-  :l  |s  :r  :f  |m  :d' :l  |s  :-  :-
 voice,             Sweet voice,            That  made my in - - most    soul re-joice.
|   :t, :t, |t, :-  :   |   :d  :d  |d  :-  :d  |t, :-  :t, |t, :-  :r  |d  :m  :re |m  :-  :-
   sil-ver voice,          sil-ver voice, That    made my in - - most    soul re-joice.
|   :s  :s  |s  :-  :   |   :m  :m  |m  :-  :m  |r  :-  :r  |r  :s  :s  |s  :-  :fe |s  :-  :-
|   :s, :s, |s, :-  :   |   :d  :d  |d  :-  :d  |s, :-  :s, |s, :-  :s, |d  :-  :d  |d  :-  :-
```

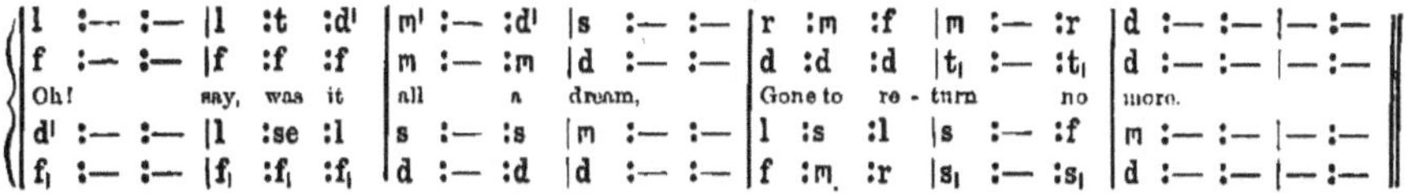

| l :— :— | l :t :d' | m' :— :d' | s :— :— | r :m :f | m :— :r | d :— :— | — :— ||
| f :— :— | f :f :f | m :— :m | d :— :— | d :d :d | t, :— :t, | d :— :— | — :— ||
Oh! say, was it all a dream, Gone to re - turn no more.
| d' :— :— | l :se :l | s :— :s | m :— :— | l :s :l | s :— :f | m :— :— | — :— ||
| f, :— :— | f, :f, :f, | d :— :d | d :— :— | f :m :r | s, :— :s, | d :— :— | — :— ||

SABBATH EVENING.

263. KEY B♭. B. C. UNSELD.

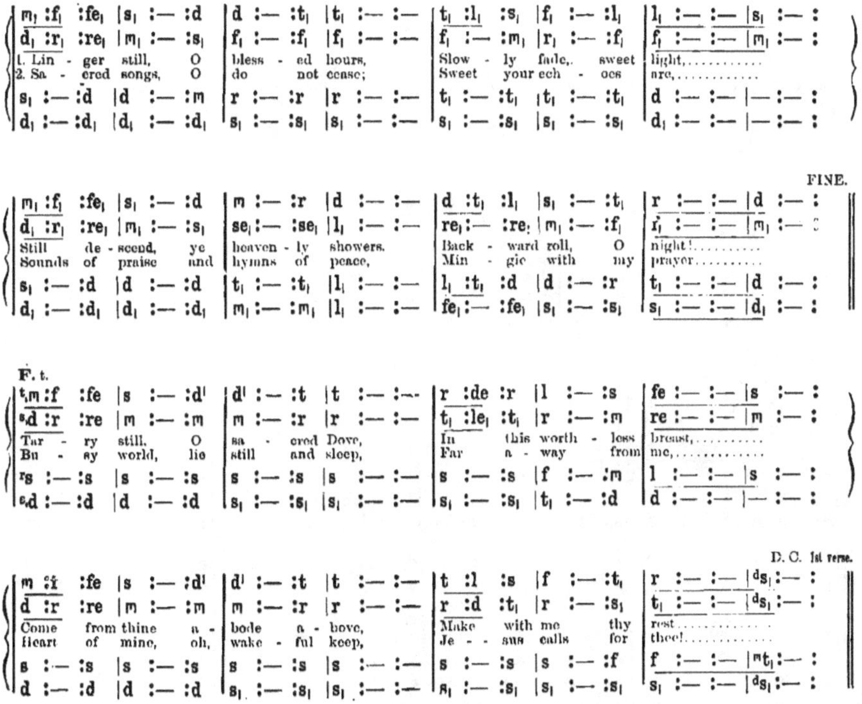

| m, :f, :fe, | s, :— :d | d :— :t, | t, :— :— | t, :l, :s, | f, :— :l, | l, :— :— | s, :— :
| d, :r, :re, | m, :— :s, | f, :— :f, | f, :— :— | f, :— :m, | r, :— :f, | f, :— :— | m, :— :
1. Lin - ger still, O bless - ed hours, Slow - ly fade, sweet light,...........
2. Sa - cred songs, O do not cease; Sweet your ech - oes are,............
| s, :— :d | d :— :m | r :— :r | r :— :— | t, :— :t, | t, :— :t, | d :— :— | — :— :
| d, :— :d, | d, :— :d, | s, :— :s, | s, :— :— | s, :— :s, | s, :— :s, | d, :— :— | — :— :

FINE.

| m, :f, :fe, | s, :— :d | m :— :r | d :— :— | d :t, :l, | s, :— :t, | r :— :— | d :— :
| d, :r, :re, | m, :— :s, | se, :— :se, | l, :— :— | re, :— :re, | m, :— :f, | r, :— :— | m, :— :
Still de - scend, ye heaven - ly showers. Back - ward roll, O night!..........
Sounds of praise and hymns of peace, Min - gle with my prayer.........
| s, :— :d | d :— :d | t, :— :t, | l, :— :— | l, :t, :d | d :— :r | t, :— :— | d :— :
| d, :— :d, | d, :— :d, | m, :— :m, | l, :— :— | fe, :— :fe, | s, :— :s, | s, :— :— | d, :— :

F. t.

| ^t m :f :fe | s :— :d' | d' :— :t | t :— :— | r :de :r | l :— :s | fe :— :— | s :— :
| ^s d :r :re | m :— :m | m :— :r | r :— :— | t, :le, :t, | r :— :m | re :— :— | m :— :
Tar - ry still, O sa - cred Dove, In this worth - less breast,..........
Bu - sy world, lie still and sleep, Far a - way from me,.............
| ^r s :— :s | s :— :s | s :— :s | s :— :— | s :— :s | f :— :m | l :— :— | s :— :
| ^s d :— :d | d :— :d | s, :— :s, | s, :— :— | s, :— :s, | t, :— :d | d :— :— | — :— :

D. C. 1st verse.

| m :f :fe | s :— :d' | d' :— :t | t :— :— | t :l :s | f :— :t, | r :— :— | ^d s, :— :
| d :r :re | m :— :m | m :— :r | r :— :— | r :d :t, | r :— :s, | t, :— :— | ^d s, :— :
Come from thine a - bode a - bove, Make with me thy rest.............
Heart of mine, oh, wake - ful keep, Je - - sus calls for thee!............
| s :— :s | s :— :s | s :— :s | s :— :— | s :— :s | s :— :f | f :— :— | ^m t, :— :
| d :— :d | d :— :d | s, :— :s, | s, :— :— | s, :— :s, | s, :— :s, | s, :— :— | ^d s, :— :

HOPE WILL BANISH SORROW.

George Bennett. — Hubert Main, by per.

204. Key A♭.

1. Once a-gain we're doom'd to part, Deem not 'tis for-ev-er; Love, if root-ed in the heart, Time nor tide can sev-er; 'Tis the sad a-dieus that chill, Make the parting sadder still, Say "we'll meet to-mor-row," Hope will banish sor-row.
2. When I'm far a-way from thee, O'er the o-cean sail-ing, You will of-ten muse of me, Tears and sighs pre-vail-ing; But ne'er think of me with fear, Check at once the ris-ing tear, Sing "we'll meet to-mor-row," Hope will banish sor-row.
3. Faith and trust in heav'n we have, God is ev-er near-est; He can still the storm-y wave, Hear me safe-ly, dear-est; Then fare-well my na-tive shore, Clasp me to thy heart once more, Sing "we'll meet to-mor-row," Hope will banish sor-row.

Rall.

LANGDON. C. M.

205. Key F. — T. F. Seward.

1. Fa-ther! I long, I faint, to see The place of thine a-bode; I'd leave thine earth-ly courts, and flee Up to thy seat, my God!
2. There all the heaven-ly hosts are seen, In shin-ing ranks they move, And drink im-mor-tal vig-or in, With won-der and with love.
3. Fa-ther! I long, I faint, to see The place of thine a-bode; I'd leave thine earth-ly courts, and be For-ev-er with my God.

H. H. HAYDEN.

200. EVENING ON THE LAKE.

KEY C. M. 108. M. L. BARTLETT, by per.

:s .d' |t :l |s :s .f |m :l |s :l .t |d' :s |l .s :f .m
:m |s :f |m :d |d :— .t, |d :f |m :m |f .m :r .d
1. Now bright - ly on the yield - ing wave, The moon's soft rays are
2. The eve - ning bree - zes gent - ly blow, A sweet re - fresh - ment
3. We gai - ly dip the gleam - ing oar, And on - ward now are
:s |s :l .t |d' :l .la |s :f |m :l .la |s :d' |d' :s
:d |d :d |d :d |d :d |d :d |d :d |d :t, .d

|m :— |r :s .d' |t :l |s :s .f |m :l |s :d'
|d :— |t, :d .m |s :f |m :d |d :— .t, |d :m
glanc - - ing; The spark - ling wa - ter seems to move, As
bring - - ing, As on - ward blithe - some - ly we go, Our
dash - - ing, While faint and faint - er grows the shore On
|s :— |s :s |s :l .t |d' :l .la |s :f |m :s
|s :— |s :m .d |d :d |d :d |d :d |d :d

|t .l :s .l |t :l |l :— |s :s |s .r' :t .l |s :s
|r :r |r :m .fe |fe :— |s :s |f :f |f :f
if with joy 'twere danc - - ing, And we are full of
mer - ry cho - - rus sing - - ing. Our wa - t'ry path - way
which the waves are plash - - ing. We bid each thought of
|s .d' :t .d' |r' :d' |d' :— |t :t |t :r' .d' |t :t
|r :r |r :r |r :— |s :s |s :s |s :s

|s .m' :d' .l |s :s |l .t :d' |d' :r' |m' :— |— :s
|m :f |m :m |f :s |m :l |se :— |— :f
an - swering glee, With hap - py hearts we sing, And
gleams with light, The hour is full of joy, All
sor - row flee, Care to the winds we fling, And
|d' :l .d' |d' :d' |d' :d' |d' :l |t :— |— :t
|d :d |d :d |f :m |l :f |m :— |— :r

|s .m' :m' .r' |r' .d' :s .se |l .r' :r' .d' |t :s |l .t :d' .r' |m' :r' |d' :— |—
|m .s :se |m :d |f :fe |s :m |f :s .l |s :f |m :— |—
far a - cross the wa - ters free, Our mer - ry notes shall ring.
na - ture smiles on us to - night, No trou - ble shall an - noy.
far a - cross the wa - ters free, Our mer - ry notes shall ring.
|d' :t |d' :d' |d' :r' |r' :d' |d' .r' :d' |d' :t |d' :— |—
|d :m |l :m |f :r |s :d |f .r :m .f |s :s |d :— |—

SLEEP, BELOVED.

Mary C. Seward.

Theo. F. Seward.

267. Key G.

pp — *Inst.*

| m :re .m :f .m | s :— :f .m | r :de .r :m .r | d :m_1 .f_1 :fe_1 .s_1 |

| d :— :d | d :m .d :d | t_1 :— :t_1 | d :d_1 .r_1 :re_1 .m_1 |

1. Fall - - - ing | shad - - - ows | length - - en | now;

2. Blos - - - soms | fold their | pet - - - als | round,

| s :fe .s :l .s | m :s .m :l .s | f :m .f :s .f | m : : |

| d :— :d | d :— :d | s_1 :— :s_1 | d_1 : : |

| m :re .m :f .m | s :— :m | r :— :r | r :— :— |

| d :— :d | d :m .d :s_1 .d | t_1 :l_1 .t_1 :d .l_1 | t_1 :— :— |

Dark and | still the | wood - - - lands | lie;

Clouds are | sleep - - - ing | in the | sky;

| s :fe .s :l .s | m :s .m :d .m | s :fe .s :l .fe | s :— :— |

| d :— :d | d :— :d | r :— :r | s_1 :— :— |

---

pp

| r :d .t_1 :l_1 .s_1 | s_1 :— .d :f .m | r :d .t_1 :l_1 .s_1 | s :— :— .f |

| f_1 .s_1 :f_1 .s_1 :f_1 .s_1 | s_1 :— :d | f_1 .s_1 :f_1 .s_1 :f_1 .s_1 | s_1 .t_1 :d .r :m .r |

Birds a - - | sleep on | leaf - - - - y | bough,

Soft - - - ly | hushed comes | eve - - - - ry | sound,

| t_1 :r :f | m .s :m .s :l .s | t_1 :r :f | m .r :m .f :s |

| s_1 :— :s_1 | d_1 :— :d_1 | s_1 :— :s_1 | d :— :— |

| m :re .m :f .m | s :— .l :f .r | d :t_1 .d :r .re | m :— :d |

| d :— :d | ta_1 :— :l_1 | s_1 :— :t_1 .l_1 | s_1 :— :d |

Hushed the | zeph - er's | faint - - - est | sigh, Then

Bliss - ful | dreams are | hov - - - 'ring | nigh, Then

| s :fe .s :l .s | m :de :r .f | m :r .m :f .fe | s :— :m .s |

| d :— :d | d :m_1 :f_1 | s_1 :— :s_1 | d_1 .m_1 :s_1 .d :s_1 .m_1 |

Rit. pp

| m :re .m :f .s | l :— .s :f .r | d :t_1 .d :r .m | d :— :— |

| d :— :d | l_1 :— .ta_1 :l_1 | s_1 :— :t_1 | d .l_1 :s_1 .f_1 :m_1 |

sleep be - - | lov - - - ed, | lul - - - la - - | by.

sleep be - - | lov - - - ed, | lul - - - la - - | by.

| s :fe .s :s | f .de :r .de :r .f | m :r .m :f .s | m .f :m .r :d |

| d_1 :— :r_1 .m_1 | f_1 .m_1 :r_1 .m_1 :f_1 | s_1 :— :s_1 | d_1 :— :— |

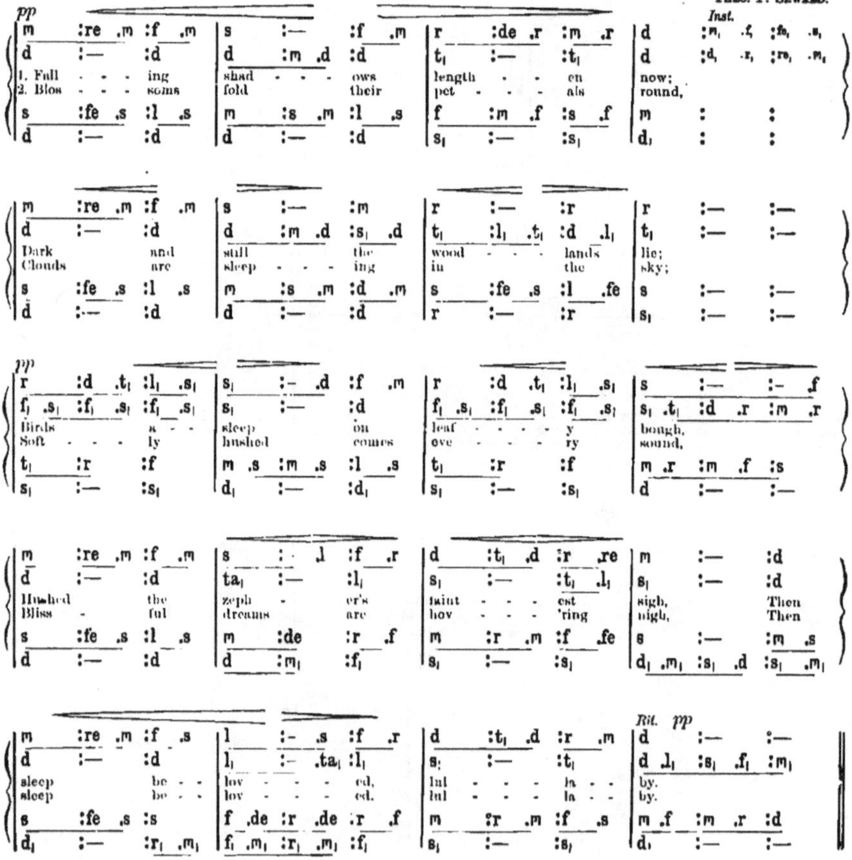

ELEMENTARY RHYTHMS.

FOR PUPILS PREPARING FOR THE FIRST AND SECOND GRADE CERTIFICATES.

These Rhythms must be done at the rate indicated by the metronome mark. The pupil must *laa* or *taatai* one complete measure and any portion of a measure which is required, as an introduction to the Exercise—the Exercise itself being taken up without pause or slackening of speed, at the right moment. The exercise must be taatai'd on one tone. For amusement, it may be taatai'd in tune.

The keys are fixed so as to bring the tones within the reach of all voices. The Rhythm may often be learned slower than marked, and when familiar the pupils will take pleasure in largely increasing the speed. J. C.

They are to be taught by pattern. Three or four may be practised at each lesson until the whole are learned. The pupil is expected to practice them at home until they are thoroughly familiar, so that any one taken by lot can be correctly done.

For the First Grade Certificate, Requirement 2 is, "*Taatai* once, and then *laa* on one tone in perfectly correct time, any of the rhythms (Nos. 1, 3, 4, 5, 7, 9 or 11 which the Examiner may select. [Two attempts allowed; a different test to be given for the second trial.]"

For the Second Grade Certificate, the College (see p. 3) will supply to the Examiner the test to be used. It will not contain any difficulties beyond those in "Elementary Rhythms."

TAATAI.

1. Key F. M. 100. *Bugle Call.* "Fall in."

{| s_1 .d :d | s_1 .d :d | s .m :s .m | d .d :d | s_1 .d :d | s_1 .d :d | s .m :s .m | d .d :d ‖

2. Key F. M. 100. *Bugle Call,* "Close."

{ :m | d :s_1 .m | d .d :s_1 .m | d :s_1 .m | d .d :s_1 .m | d :— | m ‖

3. Key A. M. 100. *Bugle Call,* "Fatigue."

{ :s_1 | d :m .s_1 | d :m .s_1 | d .s_1 :m .s_1 | d .s_1 :m .s_1 | d :m .s_1 | d :m .s_1 | d .s_1 :m .s_1 | d ‖

4. Key F. M. 100. *Bugle Call,* "Guard."

{| s .m :d .s_1 | d .m :s_1 | s .m :d .s_1 | d :— | s .m :d .s_1 | d .m :s_1 | s .m :d .s_1 | d :— ‖

5. Key A. M. 100. *Bugle Call,* "Advance."

{ :s_1 | d .d :d .s_1 | d .d :d .s_1 | d .s_1 :d .s_1 | d .d :d | s_1 :— | s_1 :— | s_1 :— | — ‖

6. Key A. M. 144. *Bugle Call,* "Extend."

{| m :— | d :— | m .d :m .d | s_1 :— | m :— | d :— | m .d :m .d | s_1 :— ‖

7. Key E. M. 100. *Bayly,* "In happier hours."

{| d :d .r :m .f | s :— :l | s :f .m :f .s | m :d :d }

{| d :d .r :m .f | s :s :l | s :f .m :f .s | m :— :— ‖

9. Key E. M. 100. *Hymn Tune,* "Simeon."

|s :s .f |m :- .f |m :r |d :- .d |f :- .m |l :- .s |t_1 :d |r :- .r

|m :r .d |f :m .r |s :l |s :- .s |s :- .l |s .f :m .f |m :r |d :--

SAA.

10. Key D. M. 100. (The pupils to take each part alternately). J. R. Thomas, "Picnic."

|m .f :r .m |d :s |m .f :r .m |d :s |s .f :m .f |s :d^1 |l .s :f .m |r :—
|d :d |d :t_1 |d :d |d :t_1 |d :d |m :d |t_1 :d |s_1 :—

| :s | :s | :s | :s |f .s :l .t |d^1 :m |r :s |d :—
|r : |m : |r : |m : |f :r |m :d |d :t_1 |d :—

11. Key C. M. 72. **Tafatefe.** *Bugle Call,* "Walk and Drive." Altered.

|d ,d .d ,d :d .d |m .d :d |m ,m .m ,m :m .m |s .m :m |d^1 ,d^1 .d^1 ,d^1 :d^1 .d^1

|s ,s .s ,s :s .m |d ,d .d ,d :m .s |m .d :d |d :d |m .d :d |m :m

|s .m :m |d^1 ,d^1 .d^1 ,d^1 :d^1 |s ,s .s ,s :s |d ,d .d ,d :m .s |m .d :d

12. Key D. M. 72. **TAAtefe.** *Bugle Call,* "Lay up or Litter down."

|d .d ,d :d .d |d .s_1 :d .s_1 |m .m ,m :m .m |m .d :m .d

|s .s ,s :s .s |d^1 .s :d^1 .s |d .d ,d :d .d |d :

13. Key F. M. 100. **tafaTAI.** *Bugle Call,* "Defaulters."

:s_1 .s_1 |d ,s_1 .m :d ,s_1 .m |s .s ,s :s .s_1 |d ,s_1 .m :d ,s_1 .m |d

14. KEY G. M. 100. **TAA-efe.** *Bugle Call,* "Salute for the Guard."

| d :d .,d | s_1 :s_1 .,s_1 | d :d .,d | d : | d .d :m .d | m .s :m .d | s_1 :s_1 .,s_1 | s_1 : ||

15. KEY C. M. 100. *Bugle Call,* "Officers."

:s .,s | d^1 :s .,s :s .,s | m :s :s | d^1 :s .,s :s .,s | s :–

:s | d^1 :s .,s :s .,s | m :s :m | d :d .d :d .d | d :— ||

16. KEY F. M. 100. *Bugle Call,* "Orders."

:s_1 .,s_1 | d :— | m :s_1 .,s_1 | d :— | m :s_1 .,s_1 | d :s_1 .,s_1 | m :s_1 .,s_1 | d :— | m

:s_1 | d .,s_1 :m .,s_1 | d .,s_1 :m .,s_1 | d .,s_1 :m .,s_1 | d :m | s :— | — :m .,d | s_1 :– .d | m ||

17. KEY C. M. 100. *Hymn Tune,* "Truro."

| d :m .,f | s :– .s | l :t | d^1 :– .s | d^1 :s | f .m :r .d | f :m | r : ||

18. KEY F. M. 100. *Bugle Call,* "General Salute."

:s_1 | d :d .,d | d .m :s .m | d :d .,d | d :s_1 .,d | m :d .,m | s :s_1 .,s_1 | s_1 :s_1 .,s_1 | s_1

:s_1 | d :d .,d | d .m :s .m | d :d .,d | d :s_1 .,d | m :d .,m | s :s_1 | d :d .,d | d ||

19. KEY F. M. 100. **-AA-efe.** *Bugle Call,* "Asembly."

| s :— | – .,m :d .s_1 | d :— | – .,s_1 :d .s_1 | d .,s_1 :d .s_1 | d .,s_1 :d .s_1

| d :m | – :— | s :— | – .,m :d .s_1 | d :— | — : ||

20. KEY F. M 100. *Hymn Tune,* "Serenity."

:d | t_1 .,d :r :s | s :— :fe | s :— :d .,t_1 | l_1 :– .t_1 :d .r | m :— :r | d :– – ||

21. KEY F. M 100. *Hymn Tune,* "Arlington."

:d | m .m :m :r | d .,d :d :r | m .s :f :m | m :r

:f | m .,m :m :l | s .,s :s :d^1 | r .f :m :r | d :— ||

22. KEY F. M. 100. *Barnell*, "Hark ! sweet echo."

{ | s :- .m :f .l | s .,m :d .d :d | l :- .s :f .m | r .,t_1 :s_1 .s_1 :s_1 ‖

23. KEY F. M. 72. *Mazzinghi*, "Tom Starboard."

{ :s | m .,f :r .,m :d .s_1 | d : :r | m .,f :s .,m :l,s .f,m | r : }

{ :s | m .,f :r .,m :d .s_1 | l_1 : :t_1 | d .r :m .s,f:m .r | d : ‖

24. KEY F. M. 72. "Home, sweet Home."

{ :d | m .,f :f .,s | s .,m :m | f .,m :f .,r | m :- .d,d | m .,f :f .,s | s :m .s | f .,m :f .r | d ‖

25. KEY C. M. 60. J. R. THOMAS, "Picnic."

{ | s ,f .m ,f :s .l | s .m^1 :d^1 | r^1 .,d^1 :t ,l .s ,f | m :— }

{ | s ,f .m ,f :s .l | s .m^1 :d^1 | t .d^1,t :l .t ,l | s : ‖

26. KEY F. M. 100. *Hymn Tune*, "Prestwich."

{ :s .f | m :— :r.m | f :— :m | m :r :d | d :t_1 :t_1 | d :-.r :m | m.r :d :t_1 | d :— :— | : ‖

Modulator Voluntaries now include transition of one remove. These should not be made too difficult by wide and unexpected leaps on to the distinguishing tone; nor too easy by always approaching the distinguishing tone stepwise. While the effects of transition are in process of being learnt, these exercises may be *sol-fa-ed*, but the teacher cannot now be *content* with sol-fa-ing. Every exercise should also be sung to *laa*.

Sight-laa-ing. The laa-voluntaries are really sight-singing exercises, if the teacher does not get into self-repeating habits of pointing. See p. 17. But, at their best, they give no practice in reading *time* at sight. Therefore the absolute necessity of sight-laa-ing from new music from the book or the black-board.

Memorizing the three keys. The pupils should now know from memory, not only what is above any one note on the modulator and what below it, but what is on its right and what on its left. The one key no longer stands alone on the mind's modulator. It has an elder brother on the right and a younger on the left, and each of its tones bears cousinship to the other two families, and may be called to enter them. Therefore, at all the later lessons of this step, exercises should be given in committing to memory this relationship, p. 67. The pupils must learn to say these relations, collectively and each one for himself, *without* the modulator.

Memory Patterns. It is difficult to indicate divisions of time by the motions of the pointer on the modulator with sufficient nicety to *guide* the singers in following a voluntary, and it is important to exercise the memory of tune and rhythm. For these reasons our teachers give *long patterns*—extending to two or more sections—including some of the more delicate rhythms. These patterns are given laa-ing, but pointing on the modulator. The pupils imitate them, *without* the teacher's pointing, first sol-fa-ing and then laa-ing.

Memory Singing. The practice of singing whole pieces to words, from memory—in obedience to the order "Close books: eyes on the baton"—is a very enjoyable one. The singer enjoys the exercise of subordination to his conductor, along with a sense of companionship in that subordination, and delights in the effects which are thus produced. This practice is very needful at the present stage in order to *form a habit*, in the singer, of *looking up* from his book. This should now be his normal position. But, as from necessity, the learner's eyes have hitherto been much engaged with his book, he will have to make a conscious effort to form "the habit of looking up." Occasional "Memory Singing" will make him feel the use and pleasure of this.

Ear Exercises (which will now include *fe* and *ta*, and new difficulties of time), *Dictation, Pointing and Writing from Memory*, should still be practised. Writing from memory does not at all take the place of pointing from memory. There have been pupils who could write from memory, but could not point the same tunes on the modulator. It is important to establish in the memory that pictorial view of key-relationship which the modulator gives, especially now that the study of Transition is added to that of the scale.

QUESTIONS FOR WRITTEN OR ORAL EXAMINATION.

DOCTRINE.

1. How many greater steps are there in the scale, and between which tones do they occur?
2. How many smaller steps are there and where do they occur?
3. How many little steps are there, and where are they?
4. What is the difference between a greater and a smaller step called?
5. How many kommas has a greater step? A smaller step? A little step?
6. By what other names are intervals called?
7. What is the interval from any tone to the next in the scale called?
8. What is the interval from any tone to the third tone from it called?
9. What is a Second called that is equal to one full step?
10. What is a Second called that is equal to a little step (half-step)?
11. What kind of a Third is equal to two steps?
12. What kind of a Third is equal to one full step and one little step?
13. What is the interval from *fah* to *te* called?
14. Which are the two most marked characteristic tones of the scale?
15. From their mental effects, what are *fah* and *te* called?
16. What is a change of key during the course of a tune called?
17. Which is the sharp distinguishing tone, and what is its mental effect?
18. Which is the flat distinguishing tone, and what is its mental effect?
19. On which side of the modulator is the first sharp key? On which side is the first flat key?
20. In going to the first sharp key what does the *soh* of the old key become in the new? What does the old *lah* become? What does the old *te* become? (The teacher will supply additional questions.)
21. In going to the first flat key what tone of the old key becomes *doh* in the new? What tone becomes *ray*? (The teacher will supply additional questions.)
22. What is that tone called on which the change is made from one key to another?
23. How are bridge-tones indicated in the notation?
24. What is the meaning of the little notes placed on the right or left of the key signature in transition?
25. What are the general mental effects of transition to the first sharp key? To the first flat key?
26. What is a Cadence Transition? Is it written in the "perfect" or "imperfect" way?
27. What is a Passing Transition? How written?
28. What is Extended Transition? How written?
29. What is the name for a silent quarter-pulse on the strong part of a pulse? On the weak part? How is it indicated in the notation?
30. What is the name of a pulse divided into thirds? How indicated in the notation?
31. What is syncopation?
32. What is its effect upon a weak pulse, or weak part of a pulse?
33. What is its effect upon the next following strong pulse?

PRACTICE.

34. Teacher singing to figures, Exercise 175, let the pupil tell to what figure the distinguishing tone of the first sharp key was sung. The same with 176.
35. In the same manner let the pupil name the distinguishing tone of the first flat key, in Exercises 183 and 184.
36. Teacher singing to figures, No. 265 (each line beginning with 1); let the pupil name by its figure, first, the distinguishing tone of the departing transition; and, second, that of the returning transition.
37. Pitch, without a tuning fork, the keys B, B flat, E, E flat and A flat. The pupil has not satisfied this requirement, if, when tested, he is found to be wrong so much as a step.
38. Taatai from memory any one of the Exercises 241, 243, 252, 254, the first pulse being named.
39. Beat a number of two-pulse measures describing the motions of the hand. The same with four-pulse measure. The same with six-pulse measure.
40. Follow the examiner's pointing in a new voluntary containing transition, both to the first sharp and first flat keys, and singing to *laa*.
41. Point and sol-fa on the modulator, from memory, any one of the pieces on pages 73 to 76, chosen by the examiner.
42. Write, from memory, any other of these pieces chosen by the examiner.
43. Sing to *laa* at first sight, any exercise not more difficult than these pieces.
44. Tell which is *fe* and which is *ta*, as directed, page 34, question 31.
45. Tell what tone (*fe* or *ta*) is *laa*, as directed, page 34, question 32.
46. Taatai any rhythm of two or three four-pulse measures, belonging to this step, which the examiner shall *laa* to you. See page 34, question 33.
47. Taatai in tune, any rhythm of two or three four-pulse measures, belonging to this step, which the examiner shall *sol-fa* to you.

INDEX.—Part I.

For Index to Part II, see page 224.

PART 2

THE

TONIC SOL-FA MUSIC READER

REVISED AND IMPROVED.

A COURSE OF INSTRUCTION AND PRACTICE IN THE

TONIC SOL-FA METHOD OF TEACHING SINGING,

WITH A

CHOICE COLLECTION OF MUSIC SUITABLE FOR DAY SCHOOLS AND SINGING SCHOOLS.

BY THEODORE F. SEWARD AND B. C. UNSELD.

APPROVED BY JOHN CURWEN.

The Biglow & Main Co., Publishers,

135 FIFTH AVENUE, NEW YORK. LAKESIDE BUILDING, CHICAGO.

FOR SALE BY BOOKSELLERS AND MUSIC DEALERS GENERALLY.

PREFACE TO PART II.

The second part of the Tonic Sol-fa Music Reader may be regarded as somewhat unique among books of its class. In the number of the subjects treated, the condensed yet thorough method of their presentation, and the variety of exercises, illustrations and pleasing musical selections, it cannot but prove of great value alike to teachers and to students. Its characteristic features may be classified as follows:

1. The advanced musical work of the fifth and sixth steps clearly elucidated and carefully developed through suitable exercises.
2. A choice set of choruses and part-songs of a corresponding grade.
3. A voice-training department, with helpful suggestions to the teacher and progressive exercises for the pupils.
4. A staff notation department in which the relation of Tonic Sol-fa training to the staff is fully explained and illustrated.

Every great reform, whether it be religious, educational or political, is sure to be misunderstood at first. The great mistake of teachers and the public with regard to Tonic Sol-fa has been in its relation to the staff. It has been supposed to be an enemy of the staff, intended to rival and supplant it. It is no more antagonistic to the staff than arithmetic is to algebra, or a dictionary to Shakespeare. It affords a most important, and, to the average human being, an *indispensable* preparation for the staff. As most of the singing people in America do not yet avail themselves of this preparation, they are very imperfect readers of the staff, while in England thousands are able to join the best vocal societies who are not even known as Tonic Sol-faists.

Yet it should also be understood that Tonic Sol-fa is a complete system in itself. It treats every musical truth philosophically, it symbolizes it educationally, and its literature embraces nearly all the classical vocal music that is printed in the staff notation—English glees, German glees, masses, cantatas and oratorios, from Handel's *Messiah* to Gounod's *Redemption*. Thus it gives music to the masses of the people who have not time to learn the staff. In addition to the thousands of staff readers it has created in England, there are many other thousands who sing oratorios from the Tonic Sol-fa notation.

No greater mistake can be made by teachers or learners than to suppose that the benefits of Tonic Sol-fa can be gained by using its methods and devices without employing the notation. The prevalence of this error is doing vast injury to the musical interests of this country. The use of the notation has placed England far in advance of America in its popular musical culture.

The educational value of the Tonic Sol-fa notation is shown by the fact that the staff department of this book is much more comprehensive than the instruction of ordinary staff books, explaining principles for reading difficult music; modulations, transitions, analysis of the minor, etc., which in staff books usually receive no attention whatever.

THEODORE F. SEWARD.
BENJAMIN C. UNSELD.

Requirements for the Third Grade or Intermediate Certificate.

Questions and answers, to prepare for the Third Grade Musical Theory are supplied by the College at 2 Cents per Copy, plus postage.

Examiners.—Those who hold the Fourth Grade, or a higher certificate, with Theory, and who have been appointed to examine by the College of Music.

Before examination, Candidates must satisfy the Examiner that they hold the Second Grade Certificate.

1. *Memory.*—(a) Bring the names of three tunes, each containing either the sharp fourth (*fe*), the flat seventh (*ta*), or the leading note of the minor mode (*se*), and half-pulse notes, and write from memory in time and tune one of these tunes, chosen by lot.

Written or printed copies of the above tunes should be given to the Examiner for comparison with the Written Exercises.

The memory copies are required to be exact as respects: name, key, time, tune, etc.

2. *Time.*—*Taatai* at first sight and then *laa* in perfectly correct time, a rhythmic test including any of the following time forms; viz.: triplets, half-pulse silences, and syncopations. [Two attempts allowed; a different test to be given for the second trial.]

Candidates may *laa* instead of *taatai-ing* the test.

3. *Modulator.*—(a) Sing *laa* to the Examiner's pointing on the modulator a voluntary including transitions of one remove. (b) *Sol-fa* a voluntary including easy transitions of two and three removes, and phrases in the minor mode.

Candidates may *laa* instead of *sol-faing* 3b.

4. *Tune.*—Pitch the key-tone by means of a given C and sing the required tests which shall contain no division of time less than half-pulses: (a) *Sol-fa* once, then *laa* a test including transition of one remove. (b) *Laa* once, then sing to words a test without transition. (c) *Sol-fa* once, then *laa* a test in the minor mode which may contain the tones *ba* and *se*.

Candidates may sing to *laa* instead of *sol-faing* 4 a and 4 c.

5. *Ear Test.*—Write the Sol-fa notes of any two simple phrases of five tones each, the Examiner telling the pitch of the key-tone, sounding the Doh chord, and singing the tune to *laa* or playing it not more than twice. [Two attempts allowed: a different test to be given for the second trial.]

The College will supply to the Examiner the tests to be used in Nos. 2, 4, and 5.

NOTE.—The registration fee for this Certificate is 30 cents, which is exclusive of Examiner's fee. Registration fee stamp may be purchased from the Examiner.

Persons holding the Third Grade or Intermediate Certificate are Members of The American Tonic Sol-fa Association, but only the members who subscribe the amount of the annual dues, one dollar, shall be entitled to voting privileges, the Official Journal, the College Calendar, and the other prints and pamphlets that may be issued by this organization.

FIFTH STEP.

The Modes, Major and Minor. The Modern Minor. Modulation and Transitional Modulation.

The Modes.—Thus far in our studies *Doh* has been the key-tone, or point of repose. Any tone of the Scale may be made to predominate in a tune so as to bear the character of a key-tone and to give something of its own peculiar mental effects to the music. A mode of using the common Scale which makes *Ray* the most prominent tone is called the *Ray Mode*. A Mode which makes *Lah* predominant is called the *Lah Mode*. Tunes in the *Ray* and *Lah Modes* have a sad, plaintive effect. Tunes in the *Doh Mode* are more or less bright and joyous. The *Doh Mode* on account of its Major Third is called the *Major Mode*. The *Ray* and *Lah Modes* having Minor Thirds are called *Minor Modes*. A Major Mode is distinguished by the Major Third; a Minor Mode by the Minor Third.

The Modern Minor.—Of the Minor Modes the *Lah Mode* is the one most used at the present day. To give *Lah* the importance of a Key-tone, modern harmony requires it to have a *leading* tone (*se*), bearing the same relation to *Lah* that *te* has to *doh*. The introduction of *se* creates an unpleasant melodic interval between *fah* and *se*, to avoid which, Melody occasionally requires a new tone a step below *se*, called *ba*, having the same relation to *se* that *lah* has to *te*. In a *downward* melody *soh* is sometimes used instead of *se*. The *Lah Mode* thus modified by these new tones is called the *Modern Minor*. The essential Seventh of the Modern Minor, that required by Harmony, is *se*; the occasional Seventh, that required by Melody, is *Soh*. The essential Sixth, that required by Harmony, is *fah*; the occasional Sixth, that required by Melody, is *ba*.

Modulation.—A change of mode, during the progress of a tune, is called *Modulation*. A change from the major to the minor mode of the same key is called a Modulation to the Relative Minor. A change from the minor to the major mode of the same key is called a Modulation to the Relative Major. The mental effect of a modulation into the Minor mode is that of passing into shadow and gloom. Modulation into the Major mode has the effect of sunshine and cheerfulness.

The term "modulation" commonly means change of *key*, but in the Tonic Sol-fa method change of *key* is called transition, change of *mode*, modulation.

Transitional Modulation.—A change of both key and mode, during the course of a tune, is called *Transitional Modulation*. The commonest form of this change is that from the Major mode to the Relative Minor of the First Flat key. Another, though less frequent Transitional Modulation, is that to the Relative Minor of the First Sharp key.

RAY MODE.	DOH MODE.	LAH MODE.	MODERN with SE.	MINOR. with BA.
Ray'	r'	r'	r'	r'
Doh'	**DOH'**	d'	d'	d'
Te	*TE*	t	t	t
Lah	*LAH*	*Lah*	*Lah*	*Lah*
			Se	*Se*
Soh	**SOH**	*Soh*		
				Ba
Fah	*FAH*	*Fah*	*Fah*	
Me	**ME**	*Me*	*Me*	*Me*
Ray	*RAY*	*Ray*	*Ray*	*Ray*
d	**DOH**	*Doh*	*Doh*	*Doh*
t,	t,	*Te,*	*Te,*	*Te,*
l,	l,	*Lah,*	*Lah,*	*Lah,*

208. KEY C. *Ray is D.* RAY MODE.

{ :r |f :r |l :f |m :r |l :l |d' :l |t :r' |l }
Their | blood a - - | bout Je - - | ru - sa - - | lem, Like | wa - ter | they have | shed;

{ :l |d' :s |l :f |m :r |l :d' |t :s |l :m |r ‖
And | there was | none to | bu - ry | them, When | they were | slain and | dead.

209. KEY G. *Ray is A.* RAY MODE.

{ :l |r :— |f :r |m :— |r :— |l, :r |d :r |m :d |t, :l, }
1.'Tis | sweet | to re - | mem - | ber | cher-ished scenes | of | child-hood, Oh, | how
2.But | now | all are | past, | and | dear ones | have gone | with them, Oh, | how

{ |r :— |f :r |m :— |r :l, |l, :r |r :d |r :— |— ‖
pure | is the | fount - | ain of | hap - pi - | ness they | bring.
sweet, | yet how | sad, | are the | pen - sive | thoughts they | bring. .

270. KEY B♭. *Lah is A.* LAH MODE.. **This may be sung in the *Modern Minor* by singing se for every s.**

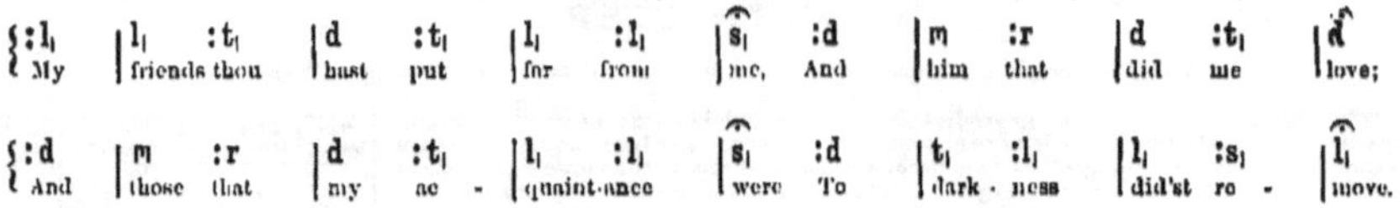

:l_1 | l_1 :t_1 | d :t_1 | l_1 :l_1 | s_1 :d | m :r | d :t_1 | d
My | friends thou | hast put | far from | me, And | him that | did me | love;

:d | m :r | d :t_1 | l_1 :l_1 | s_1 :d | t_1 :l_1 | l_1 :s_1 | l_1
And | those that | my ac - | quaint-ance | were To | dark - ness | did'st re - | move.

271. KEY E♭. *Lah is C.* LAH MODE. T. F. S.

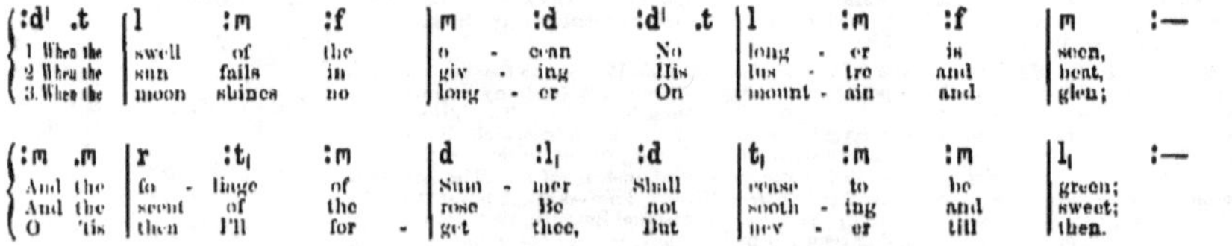

:d' .t | l :m :f | m :d :d' .t | l :m :f | m :—
1 When the | swell of the | o - cean No | long - er is | seen,
2 When the | sun fails in | giv - ing His | lus - tre and | heat,
3 When the | moon shines no | long - er On | mount - ain and | glen;

:m .m | r :t_1 :m | d :l_1 :d | t_1 :m :m | l_1 :—
And the | fo - liage of | Sum - mer Shall | cease to be | green;
And the | scent of the | rose Be not | sooth - ing and | sweet;
O 'tis | then I'll for - | get thee, But | nev - er till | then.

272. KEY C. *Lah is A.* MODERN MINOR.

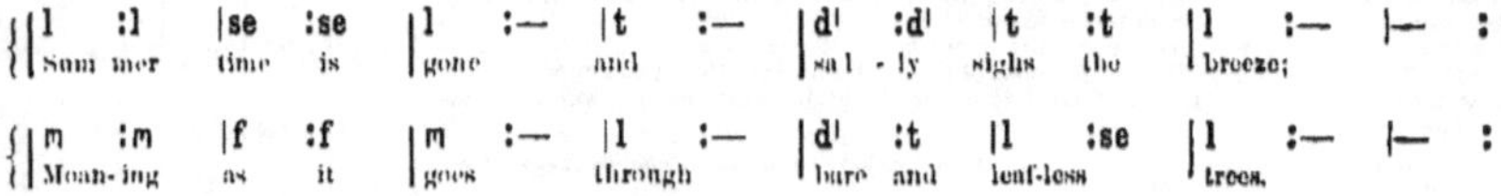

| l :l | se :se | l :— | t :— | d' :d' | t :t | l :— | — :
| Sum mer | time is | gone | and | sal - ly | sighs the | breeze;

| m :m | f :f | m :— | l :— | d' :t | l :se | l :— | — :
| Moan- ing | as it | goes | through | bare and | leaf-less | trees.

273. KEY G. *Lah is E.* T. F. S.

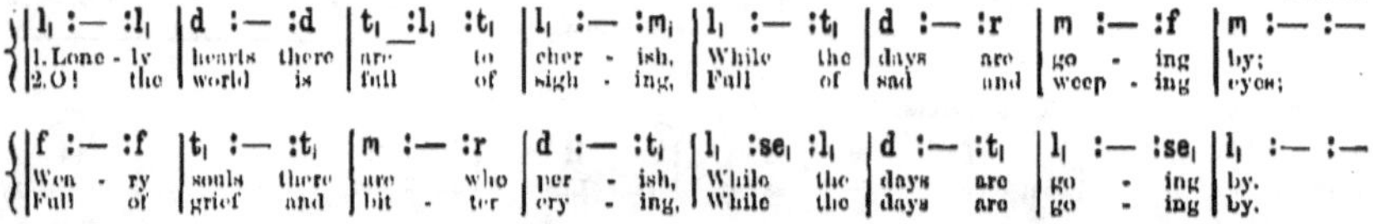

| l_1 :— :l_1 | d :— :d | t_1 _l_1 :t_1 | l_1 :— :m_1 | l_1 :— :t_1 | d :— :r | m :— :f | m :— :—
| 1. Lone - ly | hearts there | are to | cher - ish, | While the | days are | go - ing | by;
| 2. O ! the | world is | full of | sigh - ing, | Fall of | sad and | weep - ing | eyes;

| f :— :f | t_1 :— :t_1 | m :— :r | d :— :t_1 | l_1 :se_1 :l_1 | d :— :t_1 | l_1 :— :se_1 | l_1 :— :—
| Wea - ry | souls there | are who | per - ish, | While the | days are | go - ing | by.
| Full of | grief and | bit - ter | cry - ing, | While the | days are | go - ing | by.

274. KEY F. *Lah is D.* Round in four parts.

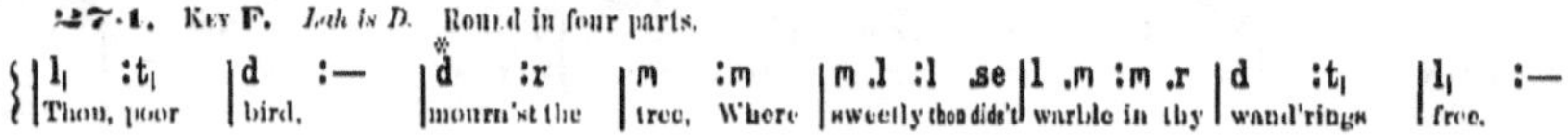

| l_1 :t_1 | d :— | *d :r | m :m | m .l :l .se | l .m :m .r | d :t_1 | l_1 :—
| Thou, poor | bird, | mourn'st the | tree, Where | sweetly thou did'st | warble in thy | wand'rings | free.

275. KEY C. *Lah is A.*

1st Division. *2d Division.*

276. KEY F. *Lah is D.* Round in two parts.

l_1 :l_1	t_1 :t_1	d :d	r :—	m :m	f :f	se :se	l :—

l :l	se :se	f :f	m :—	r :r	d :d	t_1 :t_1	l_1 :— ‖

277. KEY C. *Lah is A.*

d^1 :–	t :l	se :–	l :–	l :f	m :m	m :– ‖
m :–	m :m	m :–	m :–	f :r	d :t_1	d :– ‖
:—	t :d^1	t :–	l :–	l :l	l :se	l :– ‖
:–	se :l	m :–	d :–	r :r	m :m	l_1 :– ‖

278. KEY G. *Lah is E.*

d :–	d :r	m :–	m :–	r :d	t_1 :t_1	l_1 :– ‖
l_1 :–	l_1 :l_1	se_1 :–	l_1 :–	se :l_1	l_1 :se_1	l_1 :– ‖
m :–	d :l_1	t_1 :–	d :–	r :m	m :r	d :– ‖
l_1 :–	l_1 :f_1	m_1 :–	d :–	t_1 :l_1	m_1 :m_1	l_1 :– ‖

279. KEY F. *Lah is D.* Round in two parts.

l_1 :l_1	t_1 :t_1	d :d	r :—	m :m	ba :ba	se :se	l :—

l :l	s :s	f :f	m :—	r :r	d :d	t_1 :t_1	l_1 :— ‖

280. KEY C. *Lah is A.*

l :l	s :s	f :f	m :m	f :m	r :d	t_1 :l_1	m :—
Say, my	heart, why	art thou	swell - ing?	Why so	heav - y,	sad and	weak?

m :m	ba :se	l :se	l :t	d^1 :t	l :m	ba :se	l :— ‖
Tears from	out thy	depths are	well - ing,	Say, what	would thy	fol - ly	seek?

281. KEY G. *Lah is E.* Round for two parts.

d :m	d :l_1	t_1 :r	d :—	l_1 :se_1	l_1 :l_1	l_1 .se_1 :ba_1.se_1	l_1 :— ‖
Hark! with -	out the	storm is	loud,	See, a -	bove the	black - en'd	cloud.

282. KEY E♭. *Lah is C.* Round for four parts.

:l	se :l	t :m	m :ba.se	l :l_1	t_1 :d	r :d .r	m :r	d :
In	dark-ness	and in	lone - li -	ness The	watch-man	on his	way must	press;

>m :—	>m :—	>m :—	— :d .r	m :l	se.ba :m .r	d :t_1	l_1 ‖
Twelve	o' -	- clock!	Hear the	hol - low	sound in the	emp - ty	street.

283. KEY A♭. *Lah is F.* Round for four parts.

m_1 :m_1	l_1 :l_1	t_1 :t_1	d :—	m :m .r	d :l_1	se_1 :ba_1.se_1	l_1 :— ‖
Gone is	Au - tumn's	kind - ly	glow,	Now the	blasts of	win - ter	blow.

If the teacher prefers, the Minor Mode may be introduced in imitation exercises of Major with Relative Minor. This will show the shadowy, dependent character of the Minor. The Minor Mode is so much an artificial imitation of the Major that, perhaps, the easiest way of teaching it is by comparing the Minor with its Relative Major. Let the Major be considered as a substance and the Minor as its shadow.

284. KEY G. *Major.* *Relative Minor.*

| d :d | r :r | m :r | d :— | l_1 :l_1 | t_1 :t_1 | d :t_1 | l_1 :— ||

285. KEY E♭. *Major.* *Relative Minor.*

| d :r | m :d | s .f :m .r | d :— | l_1 :t_1 | d :l_1 | m .r :d .t_1 | l_1 :— ||

286. KEY A. *Major.*

| d :d | t_1 :t_1 | d :r | m :— | m :f | m :r | d :t_1 | d :— |

Relative Minor, with Se.

| l_1 :l_1 | se_1 :se_1 | l_1 :t_1 | d :— | d :r | d :t_1 | l_1 :se_1 | l_1 :— ||

287. KEY G. *Major.* *Relative Minor.*

| d :t_1 | d :r | m .r :d .t_1 | d :d | l_1 :se_1 | l_1 :t_1 | d .t_1 :l_1 .se_1 | l_1 :l_1 ||

288. KEY F. *Major.*

| m :r | d :— | r :d | t_1 :— | r :d | t_1 :r | d :t_1 | d :— |

Relative Minor.

| d :t_1 | l_1 :— | t_1 :l_1 | se_1 :— | t_1 :l_1 | se_1 :t_1 | l_1 :se_1 | l_1 :— ||

289. KEY C. *Major.* *Relative Minor.*

| d^1 :s | d^1 :d^1 | t .d^1 :r^1 .t | d^1 :— | l :m | l :l | se .l :t .se | l :— ||

290. KEY C. *Major.* *Relative Minor, with Ba.*

| d^1 :d^1 | t :t | l :t | d^1 :— | l :l | se :se | ba :se | l :— ||

291. KEY A♭. *Major.* *Relative Minor.*

| m :r | d :s_1 | d .t_1 :l_1 .t_1 | d :— | d :t_1 | l_1 :m_1 | l_1 .se_1 :ba_1 .se_1 | l_1 :— ||

292. KEY C. *Major.* *Relative Minor.*

:s | d^1 :t | d^1 :s | l :t | d^1 :m | l :se | l :m | ba :se | l ||

293. KEY B♭. *Major.* *Relative Minor.*

| d :s_1 | l_1 .t_1 :d .r | m :r | d :— | l_1 :m_1 | ba_1 .se_1 :l_1 .t_1 | d :t_1 | l_1 :— ||

AVELIN.

204. KEY D. *Lah is B.* MODERN MINOR.

|m :m |f :f |m :m |m :— |m :m |l :l |l :se |l :—
|d :d |r :r |d :t, |d :— |d :d |m :f |m :r |d :—
1.Ho - ly Spir - it! pi - ty me, Pierced with grief for griev - ing Thee;
2.Oh, be mer - ci - ful to me, Now in bit - ter - ness for Thee;
|l :l |l :l |l :se |l :— |l :se |l :l .t |d' :t |l :—
|l, :l, |r :r |m :m |l, :— |l, :t, |d :r |m :m |l, :—

|m :m |f :f |m :l |se :— |se :se |l :l .t |d' :t |l :—
|d :d |r :r |m :m |m :— |m :m |m :f |m :r |d :—
Pres - ent, though I mourn a - part, List - en to a wail - ing heart.
Fath - er! par - don thro' Thy Son, Sins a - gainst the Spir - it done.
|l :l |l :l |l :d' |t :— |t :t |l :l |l :se |l :—
|l, :l, |r :r |d :l, |m :— |m :r |d :r |m :m |l, :—

THE SAD LEAVES ARE DYING.

205. KEY B♭. *Lah is G.* CHESTER G. ALLEN.

:m, |d :— |t, :l, |t, :— |m, :m, |m :— |r :d |t, :— |— :t, |d :— |t, :l,
:m, |l, :— |l, :l, |se, :— |m, :m, |m, :— |m, :m, |m, :— |— :m, |m, :— |m, :m,
1.The sad leaves are dy - ing, the sweet birds have down, My play - mates of
2.My fond hopes are dy - ing, my loved ones have down, The friends of my
:d |m :— |r :d |t, :— |se, :r |d :— |t, :l, |se, :— |— :t, |m :— |r :d
:l, |l, :— |l, :l, |m, :— |m, :se, |l, :— |se, :l, |m, :— |— :se, |l, :— |l, :l,

FREEDOM SPREADS HER DOWNY WINGS.

206. KEY C. *Lah is A.* Extended modulation to Relative Major. Cossack Melody.

l .,l :l .l	l .d' :t .l	se .,se :se .,se	se .t :l .se	l .,l :l .l
m .,m :m .m	m .m :m	m .,m :m .,m	m .m :m	m .,m :m .m
1. Free-dom spreads her	down-y wings,	O - ver all cre-	a - ted things,	Glo - ry to the
2. Happiest spot on	which the sun,	E'er with ge - nial	rays hath shown!	Let us band from
3. Hearts a - live with	pa - triot fire,	Let her fame your	deeds in - spire;	Weave the strain and
d' .,d' :d' .d'	d' .l :r' .d'	t .,t :t .,t	t .r' :d' .t	d' .,d' :d' .d'
l .,l :l .l	l .l :se .l	m .,m :m .,m	m .m :m	l .,l :l .l

l .d' :t .l	t .f' :m' .,se	l :- .	d' .,d' :d' .d'	d' .m' :r' .d'
m .m :m	f .l :se .,m	m :- .	m .,m :m .m	m .s :f .m
King of kings,	Bend to Him the	knee.	Kneel be-fore His	ra-diant throne.
sire to son	All that makes her	great.	Sound the clar - ion	peals of fame,
wake the lyre,	Where your al - tars	stand;	Far as rolls the	swelling sea,
d' .l :r' .d'	r' .r' :t .,r'	d' :- .	s .,s :s .s	s .d' :t .d'
l .l :se .l	r .r :m .,m	l :- .	d .,d :d .d	d .d :d

t .,t :t .t	t .r' :d' .t	l .,l :l .l	l .d' :t .l	t .f' :m' .,se	l :—
f .,f :f .f	f .f :s .f	m .,m :m .m	m .m :m	f .l :se .,m	m :—
Bow to Him and	Him a - lone,	He the on - ly	King we own,	And He made us	free.
Breathe Columbia's	hal-lowed name,	From our fathers	freedom came,	'Tis our birth right	here.
Send the song of	lib - er - ty,	Hon - or thee the	brave, the free,	And our na - tive	land.
r' .,r' :r' .r'	r' .t :m' .r'	d' .,d' :d' .d'	d' .l :r' .d'	r' .r' :t .,r'	d' :—
s .,s :s .s	s .s :s .se	l .,l :l .l	l .l :se .l	r .r :m .,m	l, :—

HARK! THE PEALING.

207. KEY G. *Lah is E.*

d :d	l, :t,	d :d	l, :t,	d :d	t, :—	l, :l,	s, .—
l, :l,	l, :l,	l, :l,	l, :l,	l, :l,	se, :—	l, :f,	m, :—
1. Hark! the	peal - ing,	soft - ly	steal - ing,	Eve - ning	bell,	eve - ning	bell;
2. Wel-come	is the	sil - v'ry	mu - sic,	Sil - v'ry	bell,	sil - v'ry	bell;
m :m	d :r	m :m	d :r	m :m	m :r	d :d	d :—
l, :l,	l, :l,	l, :l,	l, :l,	l, :l,	m, :—	f, :f,	d, :—

m :m	d :r	m :m	d :r	m :r	d :t,	l, :—	— :
s, :s,	m, :f,	s, :s,	d :d	d :t,	l, :se,	l, :—	— :
Clear-ly	ech - o,	sweet-ly	ech - o,	Gen - tly	down the	dell,	
Sweet-ly	tell - ing,	gen - tly	tell - ing	Of the	day's fare -	well.	
d :d	d :d	d :d	m :f	s :f	m :r	d :—	— :
d, :d,	d, :d,	d, :d,	d, :d,	d, :r,	m, :m,	l, :—	— :

LITTLE BY LITTLE.

208. KEY C. *Lah is A.* T. F. SEWARD.

| l :l .l \|d' :d' \| t :t .t \|r' :— \| d' :d' .d' \|m'.r' :d' .t \| l :se .se \|l :— |
| d :d .d \|m :m \| m :m .m \|m :— \| m :m .m \|m :m .f \| m :r .r \|d :— |
| 1. Lit - tle by lit - tle, sure - ly and slow, Make we our fu - ture of bliss and of woe; |
| 2. Lit - tle by lit - tle creep - eth the tide, Soon like a tor - rent it sweeps far and wide; |
| l :l .l \|l :l \| se :se .se \|t :— \| l :l .l \|d' .t :l .r' \| d' :t .t \|l :— |
| l, :l, .l, \|l, :l, \| m :m .m \|m :— \| l :l .l \|l :l .r \| m :m .m \|l, :— |

| s :s .f \|m.s :d' \| s :s .f \|m :— \| m :m.m \|m.r :d \| m :— \|m :m \| l :— \|— : |
| r :r .r \|d .m:m \| r :r .r \|d :— \| r :r .r \|d .t, :l, \| t, :— \|d :r \| d :— \|— : |
| Ev - er be climb-ing up to the light, Else we must downward go in - to the night. |
| Guard each begin-ing, turn to the light, Else we must downward go in - to the night. |
| t :t .t \|d' :d' \| t :t .t \|d' :— \| se :se.se\|l .l :l \| se :— \|l :t \| l :— \|— : |
| s :s .s \|d :d \| s :s .s \|d :— \| t, :t, .t, \|l, .l, :l, \| m :— \|m :m \| l, :— \|— : |

NIGHT! LOVELY NIGHT!

T. F. SEWARD. Arr. from MENDELSSOHN.

209. KEY B♭. *Lah is G.* T. F. SEWARD.

| m :t, .,d \|l, : .l, \| t, .d :r .f \|m :l . \| m :t, .,d \|l, :se, .l, \| t, :m, \|l, : |
| m, :f, .,f, \|m, : .m, \| f, .f, :f, .l, \|l, :m, . \| m, :f, .,f, \|m, :m, .m \| m, :m, \|m, : |
| 1. Night, lovely night I sing thy wondrous beauty; Stars shining bright Over field and flow'r; |
| 2. Brightly the moon O'er hill and valley shin - ing Robes ev - ery tree With its sil - very light; |
| d :r .,r \|d : .d \| r .r :r .r \|d :d . \| d :r .,r \|d :r .d \| t, :m \|d : |
| l, :l, .,l, \|l, : .l, \| l, .l, :l, .l, \|l, :l, . \| l, :l, .,l, \|l, :t, .l, \| se, :m, \|l, : |

FINE.

| m :t, .,d \|l, : .l, \| t, .d :r .f \|m :l . \| m :t, .,d \|l, :se, .l, \| t, :m, \|l, : . |
| m, :f, .,f, \|m, : .m, \| f, .f, :f, .l, \|l, :m, . \| m, :f, .,f, \|m, :m, .m, \| m, :m, \|m : . |
| Perfumes so rare From blossoms sweet ascending, Fill all the air, Like a fra - grant bower. |
| Soon, ah! too soon Her pearly rays declin - ing, Leave in its dark - ness The si - lent night. |
| d :r .,r \|d : .d \| r .r :r .r \|d :d . \| d :r .,r \|d :r .d \| t, :m \|d : . |
| l, :l, .,l, \|l, : .l, \| l, .l, :l, .l, \|l, :l, . \| l, :l, .,l, \|l, :t, .l, \| se, :m, \|l, : . |

D.C.

| .d \| r .m :f .r \|m.r :d .d \| r .m :f .r \|m.r :d .m \| r .d :t, .r \|d .t, :l, .d \| t, .l, :se, .t, \|m :— |
| .l, \| t, .d :r .t, \|d .d :d .d \| t, .d :r .t, \|d .d :d . \| : \| : \| : \|se, :— |
| No glare of day can equal thee, Thou dark and silent mystery; What marvels are beneath thee hid, O thou mysterious night! |
| .m \| s .s :s .s \|s .f :m .m \| s .s :s .s \|s .f :m .s \| f .m :r .f \|m .r :d .m \| r .d :t, .t, \|t, :— |
| .l, \| s, .s, :s, .s, \|s, .s, :s, .s, \| s, .s, :s, .s, \|s, .s, :s, . \| : \| : \| : \|m, :— |

WHEN THE LEAVES ARE FALLING FAST.

MARIE MASON. T. F. SEWARD.

300. KEY G. *Lah is E.* *Tenderly and softly.* M. 96.

1. When the leaves are fall - ing fast, 'Mid the for - est shad - ows, When the Sum-mer days are past, Drear - y are the meadows; Sor - row creeps up - on the heart, Joy we feel too soon depart; Then the ten-der tear-drops start, Tears a - mid the shadows.
2. Soft - ly comes the thought of home, Home we prized so dear - ly; On - ly once in life shall e - ver come, That dear word so near - ly. Home where sun-shine comes un-sought, Home where kindness lives unbought, Home where first the moth - er taught Les - sons loved so dear - ly.
3. As the years are pass - ing on, Swift - ly, swift - ly pass - ing, Mem - 'ry brings the bless - ings gone, All our path - way trac - ing. Tears may fall, and hearts grow sore, Joys de - part - ed come no more, Till we gain the far - ther shore, O'er the riv - er pass-ing.

ASTON. S. M.

CHARLES WESLEY. JOHN HEYWOOD.

301. KEY B♭. *Lah is G.*

1. A charge to keep I have, A God to glo - ri - fy, A nev - er - dy - ing soul to save, And fit it for the sky;
2. To serve the pres - ent age, My call - ing to ful - fil: O may it all my pow - ers en - gage To do my mas - ter's will.
3. Help me to watch and pray, And on Thy - self re - ly, As - sured, if I my trust be - tray, I shall for ev - er die.

T. F. S.

WHY WAILETH THE WIND?

302. Key B♭. *Lah is G.* T. F. Seward, by per.

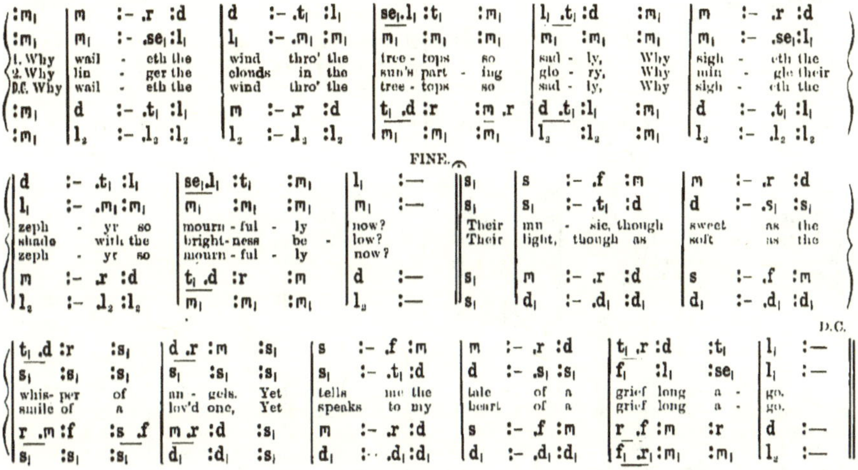

:m, | m :- .r :d | d :- .t, :l, | se,.l, :t, :m, | l, .t, :d :m, | m :- .r :d
:m, | m, :- .se, :l, | l, :- .m, :m, | m, :m, :m, | m, :m, :m, | m, :- .se, :l,
1. Why | wail - eth the | wind thro' the | tree - tops so | sad - ly, Why | sigh - eth the
2. Why | lin - ger the | clouds in the | sun's part - ing | glo - ry, Why | min - gle their
D.C. Why | wail - eth the | wind thro' the | tree - tops so | sad - ly, Why | sigh - eth the
:m, | d :- .t, :l, | m :- .r :d | t, .d :r :m .r | d .t, :l, :m, | d :- .t, :l,
:m, | l,, :- .l,, :l,, | l,, :- .l,, :l,, | m, :m, :m, | l,, :l,, :m, | l,, :- .l,, :l,,

FINE.

d :- .t, :l, | se,.l, :t, :m, | l, :— || s, | s :- .f :m | m :- .r :d
l, :- .m, :m, | m, :m, :m, | m, :— || s, | s, :- .t, :d | d :- .s, :s,
zeph - yr so | mourn - ful - ly | now? || Their | mu - sic, though | sweet as the
shade with the | bright-ness be - | low? || Their | light, though as | soft as the
zeph - yr so | mourn - ful - ly | now?
m :- .r :d | t, .d :r :m | d :— || s, | m :- .r :d | s :- .f :m
l,, :- .l,, :l,, | m, :m, :m, | l,, :— || s, | d, :- .d, :d, | d, :- .d, :d,

D.C.

t, .d :r :s, | d .r :m :s, | s :- .f :m | m :- .r :d | t, .r :d :t, | l, :—
s, :s, :s, | s, :s, :s, | s, :- .t, :d | d :- .s, :s, | f, :l, :se, | l, :—
whis- per of | an - gels. Yet | tells me the | tale of a | grief long a - | go.
smile of a | lov'd one, Yet | speaks to my | heart of a | grief long a - | go.
r .m :f :s .f | m .r :d :s, | m :- .r :d | s :- .f :m | r .f :m :r | d :—
s, :s, :s, | d, :d, :s, | d, :- .d, :d, | d, :- .d, :d, | f, .r, :m, :m, | l,, :—

ENNERDALE.

303. Key F. Passing Modulation to Relative Minor. C. Steggall.

:s | m :d | l, :r | t, :— | — :d | l, .t, :d | f :m .r | m :— | —
:t, | d :s, | f, :l, | s, :— | — :s, | f, :s, | l, :t, | d :— | —
1. Come, | we that | love the | Lord, | And | let our | joys be | known;
2. Let | those re - | fuse to | sing | That | nev - er | know our | God;
3. Then | let our | songs a - | bound, | And | ev - ery | tear be | dry;
:s | s :m | d :f | r :— | — :m | d :m | l :s | s :— | —
:s, | d :m, | f, :r, | s, :— | — :m, | f, :m, | r, :s, | d, :— | —

:m | m :- .r | d :m | l :f | r :s | d .r :m | r :r | d :— | —
:l, | se, :l, .t, | d :t, | l, :r | t, :d | l, :d | d :t, | d :— | —
Join | in a | song of | sweet ac - | cord, And | thus sur - | round the | throne.
But | fav' - rites | of the | heavenly | King May | speak their | joys a - | broad.
We're | march - ing | thro' Im - | manuel's | ground To | fair - er | worlds on | high.
:d | m :m | m :m | f :l | s :s | m :s | s :- .f | m :— | —
:l,, | m, :ba, .se, | l, :s, | f, :r, | s, :m, | l, :m, .f, | s, :s, | d, :— | —

SAD MEMORIES.

CARRIE COVINGTON.

304. KEY D.

MARY C. SEWARD, by per.

Fai - ry - like,	fai - ry - like,				
s :-.f :m	s :-.f :m	t :t :r^1	d^1 :— :s	f :f :f	l :f :r
:m.r :d	:m.r :d	f :f :f	m :— :m	d :d :d	d :d :d
1. Fairy - like,	fairy - like,	o - ver my	spir - it,	Steal-eth re -	membrance of
2. Grace-fully,	grace-fully,	down in yon	mead - ow,	Bend-eth the	wil - low - bough
:s.s :s	:s.s :s	s :s :s	s :— :d^1	l :l :l	f :l :f
:d.d :d	:d.d :d	s_1 :s_1 :s_1	d :— :d	d :d :d	d :d :d

		Ten - der - ly,	ten - der - ly,		
m :r :d	s :— :—	s :-.f :m	s :-.f :m	t :t :r^1	d^1 :s :m
d :d :d	t_1 :— :—	:m.r :d	:m.r :d	f :f :f	m :m :d
hap - pi - er	hours;	Ten-der-ly,	ten-der-ly,	e'en as the	fragrance, Of
o - ver each	grave;	Blighted and	withered lie	all the fair	flowers, All
s :f :m	r :— :—	:s.s :s	:s.s :s	s :s :s	s :d^1 :s
d :d :d	s_1 :— :—	:d.d :d	:d.d :d	s_1 :s_1 :s_1	d :d :d

				Beau - ti - ful,	beau - ti - ful,
r :m :f	s :m :d	m :— :r	d :— :—	m :-.r :d	m :-.r :d
d :d :d	d :d :d	d :— :t_1	d :— :—	:d.t_1 :l_1	:d.t_1 :l_1
sweet scent - ed,	fad - ed, au -	tum nal	flowers;	Beauti-ful,	beauti-ful,
that I most	cherished but	could not	save.	Des-o-late,	des-o-late,
l :s :f	m :s :m	s :— :f	m :— :—	:l.l :l	:l.l :l
f_1 :s_1 :l_1	s_1 :s_1 :s_1	s_1 :— :s_1	d :— :—	:l_1.l_1 :l_1	:l_1.l_1 :l_1

						Si - lent - ly,
m :l :d^1	t :m :—	m :-.m :m	d^1 :t :l	s :fe :l	s :— :—	s :-.f :m
d :d :m	r :r :—	d :-.d :d	m :r :m	r :r :r	r :— :—	:m.r :d
all were my	loved ones,	Pur - er than	lil - ies my	blossoms now	sleep;	Si-lent-ly,
now is the	hearth-stone,	Drear are the	halls which re -	ech-oed with	glee;	Weari-ly,
l :l :l	se :t :—	d^1 :-.d^1 :d^1	d^1 :r^1 :d^1	t :l :d^1	t :— :—	:s.s :s
l_1 :l_1 :l_1	m :m :—	l_1 :-.l_1 :l_1	l_1 :t_1 :d	r :r :r	s_1 :— :—	:d.d :d

si - lent-ly,						
s :-.f :m	t :t :r^1	d^1 :s :m	r :m :f	s :m :d	m :— :r	d :— :—
:m.r :d	f :f :f	m :m :d	d :d :d	d :d :d	d :— :t_1	d :— :—
si-lently,	like fall - ing	snow-flakes. They	left me in	sor-row a -	lone to	weep.
weari-ly,	passeth the	lone hours Of	wait-ing be -	lov-ed to	come to	thee.
:s.s :s	s :s :s	s :d^1 :s	l :s :f	m :s :m	s :— :f	m :— :—
:d.d :d	s_1 :s_1 :s_1	d :d :d	f_1 :s_1 :l_1	s_1 :s_1 :s_1	s_1 :— :s_1	d :— :—

HOME RETURNING.

305. KEY D. *With strong accent.* Extended modulation to Relative Minor. T. F. SEWARD.

d .,m :s :l	s .,f :r' :—	r .,m :f :l	s .,m :d' :—	d .,m :s :l
d .,d :m :f	m .,r :f :—	t, .,d :r :f	m .,d :m :—	d .,d :m :f
1. Home return - ing	from a-far,	Heart with joy up -	lift-ed high.	Yonder see the
2. Other lands have	treasure vast,	Home alone has	love to share,	Now for-get - ting
m .,s :d' :d'	s .,s :s :—	s .,s :s :t	d' .,d' :s :—	m .,s :d' :d'
d .,d :d :d	s .,s :s :—	s, .,s, :s, :s,	d .,d :d :—	d .,d :d :d

			p	
s .,f :r' :—	r' .,d' :t :s	l .,t :d' :—	m .,re :m :l	t .,d' :l :—
m .,r :f :—	f .,m :r :t,	d .,r :m :—	d .,d :d :d	r .,m :d :—
guiding star,	O what pleas - ure	draweth nigh;	Long I've wandered	sad and lone,
all the past,	In the joy that	waits me there;	Ma-ny years have	pass'd a-way,
s .,s :s :—	s .,s :s :s	s .,s :s :—	l .,l :l :l	se .,se :l :—
s .,s :s :—	s .,s :s :s	s .,s :d :—	l, .,l, :l, :l,	m .,m :l, :—

				cres.
m .,re :m :l	d' .,l :t :—	m .,re :m :l	t .,d' :l :—	l .,se :l :d'
d .,d :d :d	m .,m :m :—	d .,d :d :d	r .,m :d :—	f .,f :f :f
Home and dear ones	far a - way,	From my heart all	hope hath flown,	Welc me now this
Weary years they've	seen to me,	Waiting for this	happy day,	Home be lov - ed
l .,l :l :l	l .,l :se :—	l .,l :l :l	se .,se :l :—	d' .,t :d' :l
l, .,l, :l, :l,	l, .,d :m :—	l, .,l, :l, :l,	m .,m :l :—	f .,f :f :f

f				
t .,l :m' :—	m' .,r' :d' :s	s .,f :r' :—	r' .,d' :t :r	l .,s :m :—
re .,re :m :—	s .,f :m :m	m .,r :f :—	f .,m :r :t,	t, .,t, :d :—
hap-py day;	Home return - ing,	from a-far,	Hearts with joy up -	lift ed high,
now I see;	Home, &c.			
l .,l :se :—	d' .,d' :d' :d'	s .,s :s :—	s .,s :s :s	s .,s :s :—
f .,f :m :—	d .,d :d :d	s .,s :s :—	s, .,s, :s, :s,	s, .,s, :d :—

m' .,r' :d' :s	s .,f :r' :—	r' .,d' :t :s	l .,t :d' :—
s .,f :m :m	m .,r :f :—	f .,m :r :t,	d .,r :m :—
Yonder see the	guiding star,	O what pleas - ure	draweth nigh.
d' .,d' :d' :d'	s .,s :s :—	s .,s :s :s	s .,s :s :—
d .,d :d :d	s .,s :s :—	s .,s :s :s	s .,s :d :—

HURRAH! WELCOME THE DAY.

306. Key D♭. *With spirit.* M. 112, twice. (Cadence modulation to Relative Minor.) Hubert P. Main, by per.

```
:s |s :— :— |m :d :m |s :— :— |— :— :d' |d' :s :m |s :— :f |m :— :— |— :— :s
:s |s :— :— |m :d :m |s :— :— |— :— :m  |m :m :d  |m :— :r |d :— :— |— :— :s
1. Hur-rah!  welcome the  day,     Tra  la la la  la  la  la!    A-
2. Hur-rah!  mer-ry are   we,      Tra  la la la  la  la  la!    The
3. A- way,   hunters, a-  way!     Tra  la la la  la  la  la!    We'll
:s |s :— :— |m :d :m |s :— :— |— :— :s  |s :s :s  |s :— :s |s :— :— |— :— :s
:s |s :— :— |m :d :m |s :— :— |— :— :d  |d :d :d  |s, :— :s, |d :— :— |— :— :s

                                 A♭.t.                                   f.D♭.
|s :— :— |m :d :m |s :— :— |— :— :ᵐl, |s, :d :m |m :— :r |d :— :— |— :— :ᵈs
|s :— :— |m :d :m |s :— :— |— :— :ᵈf, |m, :m, :s, |s, :— :f, |m, :— :— |— :— :ˡm
way,  Let us a-  way!   Tra  la la la  la  la  la!   We'll
stag  yon-der we see,   Tra  la la la  la  la  la!   Then
soon  cap-ture the prey, Tra la la la  la  la  la!   Then
|s :— :— |m :d :m |s :— :— |— :— :ˢd |d :d :d |t, :— :t, |d :— :— |— :— :ᵈs
|s :— :— |m :d :m |s :— :— |— :— :ᵈf, |s, :s, :s, |s, :— :s, |d, :— :— |— :— :ᵈs

                 cres.           †                                †
|l :— :s |l :— :t |d' :— :r' |m' :— :s |l :— :s |l :— :t |d' :— :— |s :— :s
|f :— :f |f :— :f |m :— :m |m :— :m |f :— :f |f :— :f |m :— :— |m :— :m
climb to yon-der rock-y steep.  Our  Al-pine song re-peat-ing.  While
gai-ly on while  spear and lance In  morn-ing's light are gleam-ing; No
gath-er'd safe with friends at home, Our Al-pine song re-peat-ing; The
|t :— :t |s :— :s |s :— :s |s :— :d' |t :— :t |s :— :s |s :— :— |d' :— :d'
|s :— :s |s, :— :s, |d :— :d |d :— :d |s :— :s |s, :— :s, |d :— :— |d :— :d

                           † rall.
|l :— :s |l :— :t |d' :— :r' |m' :— :m |r :— :l |t :d' :t |l :— |— :— :—
|f :— :f |f :— :f |m :— :m |m :— :r |d :— :d |r :m :r |d :— |— :— :—
far and clear the  bu-gle's note With  joy our ear shall greet.
faint-ing heart nor flag-ging steed, Till ro-sy eve shall beam.
gen-tle tones we  dear-ly love,  With  joy our ear will greet.
|t :— :t |s :— :s |s :— :s |s :— :se |l :— :l |se :— :se |l :— |— :— :—
|s :— :s |s, :— :s, |d :— :d |d :— :t, |l, :— :l, |m :— :m |l, :— |— :— :—

CHORUS.
:s |s :— :— |m :d :m |s :— :— |— :— :d' |d' :s :m |s :— :f |m :— :— |— :—
:s |s :— :— |m :d :m |s :— :— |— :— :m  |m :m :d  |m :— :r |d :— :— |— :—
Hur-rah!  wel-come the  day,     Tra  la la la  la  la  la.
:s |s :— :— |m :d :m |s :— :— |— :— :s  |s :s :s  |s :— :s |s :— :— |— :—
:s |s :— :— |m :d :m |s :— :— |— :— :d  |d :d :d  |s, :— :s, |d :— :— |— :—
```

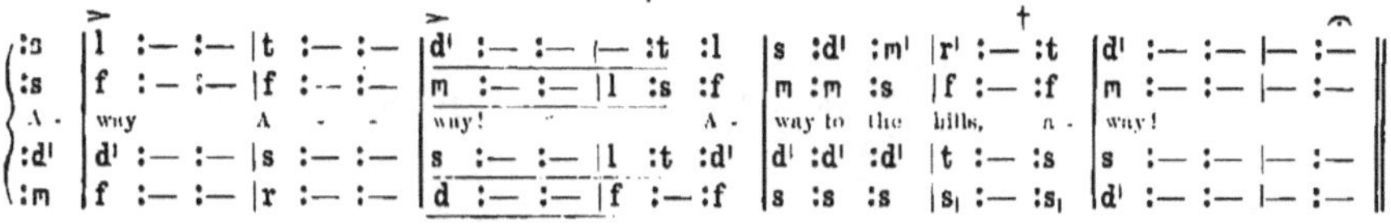

:s |l :— :— |t :— :— |d' :— :— |— :t :l |s :d' :m' |r' :— :t |d' :— :— |— :—
:s |f :— :— |f :— :— |m :— :— |l :s :f |m :m :s |f :— :f |m :— :— |— :—
A - way A - - way! A - way to the hills, a - way!
:d' |d' :— :— |s :— :— |s :— :— |l :t :d' |d' :d' :d' |t :— :s |s :— :— |— :—
:m |f :— :— |r :— :— |d :— :— |f :— :f |s :s :s |s_1 :— :s_1 |d' :— :— |— :—

THE SONG OF THE OLD BELL.

307. Key B♭. *With steady movement.*

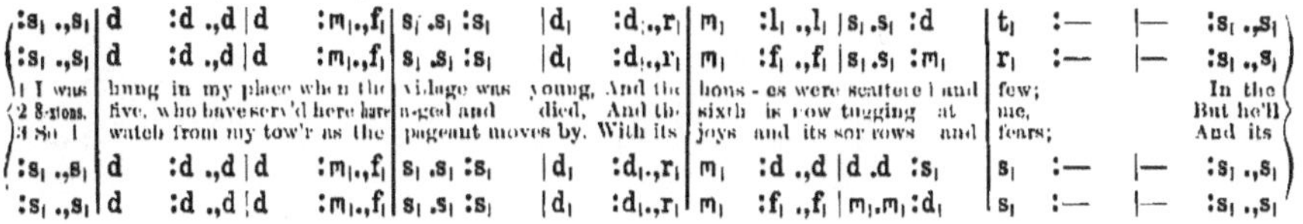

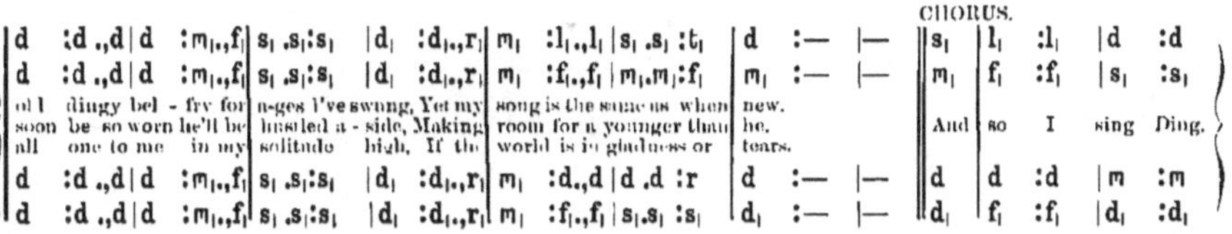

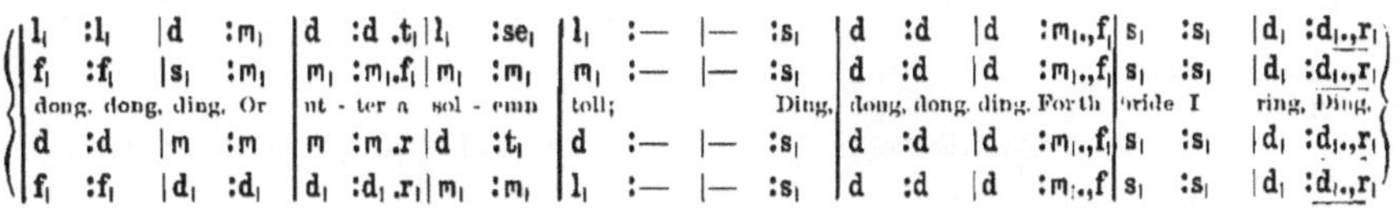

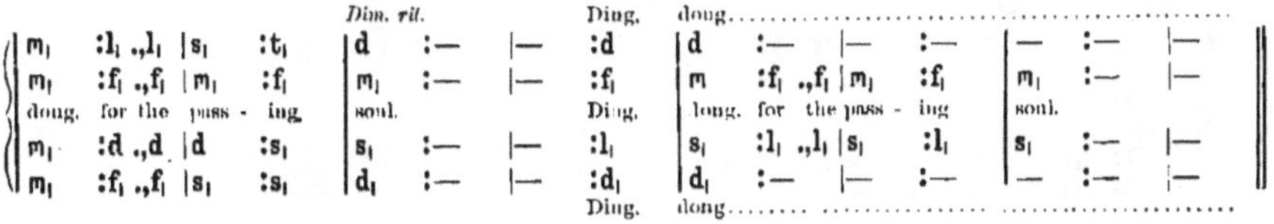

:s_1 .,s_1 |d :d .,d |d :m_1 .,f_1 |s_1 .s_1 :s_1 |d_1 :d_1 .,r_1 |m_1 :l_1 .,l_1 |s_1 .s_1 :d |t_1 :— |— :s_1 .,s_1
:s_1 .,s_1 |d :d .,d |d :m_1 .,f_1 |s_1 .s_1 :s_1 |d_1 :d_1 .,r_1 |m_1 :f_1 .,f_1 |s_1 .s_1 :m_1 |r_1 :— |— :s_1 .,s_1
1 I was hung in my place when the village was young, And the hous - es were scatter'd and few; In the
2 Sexton five, who have serv'd here have aged and died, And the sixth is now tugging at me, But he'll
3 So I watch from my tow'r as the pageant moves by, With its joys and its sor rows and fears; And its
:s_1 .,s_1 |d :d .,d |d :m_1 .,f_1 |s_1 .s_1 :s_1 |d_1 :d_1 .,r_1 |m_1 :d .,d |d .d :s_1 |s_1 :— |— :s_1 .,s_1
:s_1 .,s_1 |d :d .,d |d :m_1 .,f_1 |s_1 .s_1 :s_1 |d_1 :d_1 .,r_1 |m_1 :f_1 .,f_1 |m_1 .m_1 :d_1 |s_1 :— |— :s_1 .,s_1

|d :d .,d |d :m_1 .,f_1 |s_1 .s_1 :s_1 |d_1 :d_1 .,r_1 |m_1 :l_1 .,l_1 |s_1 .s_1 :t_1 |d :— |— ‖ CHORUS. :s_1 |l_1 :l_1 |d :d
|d :d .,d |d :m_1 .,f_1 |s_1 .s_1 :s_1 |d_1 :d_1 .,r_1 |m_1 :f_1 .,f_1 |m_1 .m_1 :f_1 |m_1 :— |— ‖ :m_1 |f_1 :f_1 |s_1 :s_1
old dingy bel - fry for a-ges I've swung, Yet my song is the same as when new.
soon be so worn he'll be hustled a - side, Making room for a younger than he.
all one to me in my solitude high, If the world is in gladness or tears.
And so I sing Ding,
|d :d .,d |d :m_1 .,f_1 |s_1 .s_1 :s_1 |d_1 :d_1 .,r_1 |m_1 :d .,d |d .d :r |d :— |— ‖ :d |d :d |m :m
|d :d .,d |d :m_1 .,f_1 |s_1 .s_1 :s_1 |d_1 :d_1 .,r_1 |m_1 :f_1 .,f_1 |s_1 .s_1 :s_1 |d_1 :— |— ‖ :d_1 |f_1 :f_1 |d_1 :d_1

|l_1 :l_1 |d :m_1 |d :d .t_1 |l_1 :se_1 |l_1 :— |— :s_1 |d :d |d :m_1 .,f_1 |s_1 :s_1 |d_1 :d_1 .,r_1
|f_1 :f_1 |s_1 :m_1 |m_1 :m_1 .f_1 |m_1 :m_1 |m_1 :— |— :s_1 |d :d |d :m_1 .,f_1 |s_1 :s_1 |d_1 :d_1 .,r_1
dong, dong, ding, Or ut - ter a sol - emn toll; Ding, dong, dong, ding, Forth bride I ring, Ding,
|d :d |m :m |m :m .r |d :t_1 |d :— |— :s_1 |d :d |d :m_1 .,f_1 |s_1 :s_1 |d_1 :d_1 .,r_1
|f_1 :f_1 |d_1 :d_1 |d_1 :d_1 .r_1 |m_1 :m_1 |l_1 :— |— :s_1 |d :d |d :m_1 .,f_1 |s_1 :s_1 |d_1 :d_1 .,r_1

Dim. rit. Ding, dong...
|m_1 :l_1 .,l_1 |s_1 :t_1 |d :— |— :d |d :— |— :— |— :— |—
|m_1 :f_1 .,f_1 |m_1 :f_1 |m_1 :— |— :f_1 |m :f_1 .,f_1 |m_1 :f_1 |m_1 :— |—
dong, for the pass - ing soul. Ding, dong, for the pass - ing soul.
|m_1 :d .,d |d :s_1 |s_1 :— |— :l_1 |s_1 :l_1 .,l_1 |s_1 :l_1 |s_1 :— |—
|m_1 :f_1 .,f_1 |s_1 :s_1 |d_1 :— |— :d_1 |d_1 :— |— :— |— :— |—
Ding, dong..

Transitional Modulation.

308. KEY F. (*First Sharp minor.*) **C.t.** *Lah is A.* f.F.

|m :r |d :m |s :f |m :— |ml, :se, |l, :l,.t, |d :t, |l, :— |l,m :m |f :m.r |d :t, |d :—
|m :re |m :m.fe |s :fe |m :—

309. KEY F. (*First Flat minor.*) f.B♭. *Lah is G.* F.t.

|m :r |d :m |s :f |m :— |rl, :se, |l, :l,.t, |d :t, |l, :— |t,m :m |f :m.r |d :t, |d :—
|r :de |r :r.m |f :m |m :—

310. KEY G. (*First Flat minor.*) f.C. *Lah is A.*

|d :s, |l, :s, |d :r |m :— |rl :t |d' :t |l :se |l :—
|r :m |f :m |r :de |r :—

G.t.

|lr :r |m :r |d :t, |d :s, |l, :t, |d :f |m :r |d :—

311. KEY G. (*First Sharp minor.*) D.t. *Lah is B.*

|d :s, |l, :s, |d :r |m :— |ml :t |d' :t |l :se |l :—
|m :fe |s :fe |m :re |m :—

f.G.

|sr :r |m :r |d :t, |d :s, |l, :t, |d :f |m :r |d :—

312. KEY G. (*First Flat minor.*)

|d :— :d |s, :— :d |t, :l, :t, |d :— : |d :— :m |s :— :m |f :m :r |d :— :

f.C. *Lah is A.*

|rl :— :t |d' :— :l |se :ba :se |l :— : |r :— :m |r :— :d |t, :l, :t, |d :— :
|r :— :m |f :— :r |de :t, :de |r :— :

313. KEY G. (*First Sharp minor.*)

|d :— :d |s, :— :d |t, :l, :t, |d :— : |d :— :m |s :— :m |f :m :r |d :— :

D.t. *Lah is B.* f.G.

|ml :— :t |d' :— :l |se :ba :se |l :— : |sr :— :m |r :— :d |t, :l, :t, |d :— :
|m :— :fe |s :— :m |re :de :re |m :— :

GRACE CHURCH.

314. Key G. Extended Transitional Modulation to First Flat minor. Pleyel, arr.

|m :— :r |d :— :t, |d :— :r |m :— :— |s :— :f |m :— :r |d :— :t, |d :— :— |
|d :— :l, |s, :— :f, |m, :fe, :s, |s, :— :— |d :— :t, |d :— :l, |s, :— :s, |s, :— :— |
1. Depth of mer - cy! can there be Mer - cy still re - served for me?
2. I have long with - stood His grace, Long pro - voked Him to His face;
3. Now in - cline me to re - pent! Let me now my fall la - ment!
|s :— :f |m :— :r |d :— :t, |d :— :— |s :— :s |s :— :f |m :— :r |m :— :— |
|d :— :f, |s, :— :s, |l, :— :s, |d :— :— |m :— :r |d :— :f, |s, :— :s, |d :— :— |

f C. *Lah is A.* G.t.

|(r)l :— :t |d' :— :t |l :— :se |l :— :— |(d')f :— :m |l :— :s |f :m :r |d :— :— ||
|(l)m :— :r |m :— :f |m :— :r |d :— :— |(r)s, :— :d |d :— :d |r :d :t, |d :— :— ||
Can my God His wrath for - bear? Me, the chief of sin - ners spare?
Would not heark - en to His calls; Grieved Him by a thous - and falls.
Now my foul re - volt de - plore! Weep, be - lieve, and sin no more.
|(r)l :— :se |l :m' :r' |d' :— :t |l :— :— |(l)r :— :s |f :— :s |l :s :f |m :— :— ||
|(f,)d :— :t, |l, :— :r |m :— :m |l :— :— |(fe)t, :— :d |f, :— :m, |f, :s, :s, |d, :— :— ||

O PARADISE!

315. Key E♭. Extended Transitional Modulation to First Sharp minor. Joseph Barnby.

:m |f :-.m |m :m |s :-.f |f :m |r :d |r :f |m :— |— :(m)l, |l, :-.l, |se, :l, |
:d |d :-.d |d :d |d :-.d |d :d |t, :d |d :t, |d :— |— :(l)r, |m, :-.m, |m, :m, |
1. O Par - a - dise! O Par - a-dise! Who doth not crave for rest? Who would not seek the
2. O Par - a - dise! O Par - a-dise! We're look - ing, wait - ing here; We long to be where
:s |l :-.s |s :d' |t :-.l |l :s |f :m |l :s |s :— |— :(f)t, |d :-.d |t, :d |
:d |d :-.d |d :d |d :-.d |d :d |s, :l, |f, :s, |d :— |— :(d)f, |m, :-.m, |m, :l, |

f.E♭. Where loy - al hearts and true, B♭.t.

|t, :-.t, |l, :d |d :l, |t, :r |(d)s :— |— :s |d' :s |t :l |s :— |— :(s)d |t, :r |
|m, :-.m, |m, :fe, |s, :m, |f, :f, |(m)t, :— |— :t, |d :— |t, :d |r :t, |d :(s)d, |f, :f, |
hap - py land Where they that loved, are blest? Where loy - al hearts and true Stand ev - er
Je - sus is, To feel, and see Him near.
|r :-.r |d :r |m :d |r :t, |(d)s :— |— :s |s :— |f :— |f :f |m :(m)l, |l, :l, |
|se, :-.se, |l, :l, |s, :s, |s, :s, |(d)s :— |— :f |m :— |r :d |t, :s, |d :(t)m, |r, :t, |

f.E♭.

|d :t, |(d)s :— |s :— |d' :m |t :l |s :m |d :f |r :— |— :r |d :— |— ||
|m, :m, |(m)t, :— |t, :— |d :d |d :d |t, :t, |d :d |d :— |t, :— |d :— |— ||
in the light, All rapt-ure through and thro'. In Gods's most ho - ly sight.
|se, :r |(d)s :— |f :— |m :s |s :f |r :s |m :f |s :r |f :— |m :— |— ||
|m, :m, |(l)m :— |r :— |d :d |f, :f, |s, :s, |l, :r |s, :— |s, :— |d :— |— ||

EVENTIDE.

316. KEY E♭. Cadence Transitional Modulation to First Flat minor. W. H. MONK.

|m :— |m :r |d :— |s :— |l :s |s :f |m :— |— :— |m :— |f :s
|d :— |t, :t, |d :— |d :— |d :t, |d :r |d :— |— :— |d :— |d :d

1. A - - bide with me! fast falls the e - ven - tide; The dark - ness
2. Swift to its close ebbs out life's lit - tle day; Earth's joys grow
3. I need Thy pres - ence ev - ery pass - ing hour; What but Thy

|s :— |s :f |m :— |d :— |d :s |s :s |s :— |— :— |s :— |f :m
|d :— |s, :s, |l, :— |m, :— |f, :s, |l, :t, |d :— |— :— |d :t, |l, :s,

|l :— |s :— |f :r |m :fe |s :— |— :— |m :— |m :r |d :— |s :—
|d :— |d :— |d :r |d :d |t, :— |— :— |d :— |t, :t, |d :— |d :—

deep - - ens; Lord, with me a - bide! When oth - er help - - ers
dim, its glo - ries pass a - way; Change and de - cay in
grace can foil the tempt-er's power? Who, like Thy - self, my

|f :— |m :— |l :s |s :d |r :— |— :— |m :f |s :f |m :— |d' :t
|f, :— |d :— |r :t, |d :l, |s, :— |— :— |d :— |s, :s, |l, :— |m, :—

|s :f |f :m |r :— |— :— |r :— |m :f |m :r |d :f |m :— |r :— |d :— |— :—
|d :d |de :de |r :— |— :— |t, :— |d :t, |d :t, |d :r |d :— |t, :— |d :— |— :—

fail, and com-forts flee, Help of the helpless, O a - bide with me!
all a - round I see; O Thou Who chang - est not, a - bide with me.
guide and stay can be? Through cloud and sunshine, Lord, a - bide with me.

|l :l |l :s |f :— |— :— |s :— |s :s |s :f |m :l |s :— |— :f |m :— |— :—
|f, :-.s, |l, :l, |r :— |— :— |f :— |m :r |d :s, |l, :f, |s, :— |s, :— |d :— |— :—

ST. CECILIA.

317. KEY E. Passing Transitional Modulation to First Flat minor. R. R. CHOPE.

:m |s :f |m :f |r :— |m :m |d' :t |l :l |s :— |—
:d |d :t, |d :d |d :t, |d :d |d :r |m :r .d |t, :— |—

1. The year is swift - ly wan - - ing; The sum - mer days are past;
2. The ev - er - chang - ing seas - - ons In si - lence come and go;
3. Be - hold the bend - ing orch - - ards With boun-teous fruit are crowned;

:s |s :s |s :l |s :— |s :s |s .fe :s |s :fe |s :— |—
:d |m :r |d :f, |s, :— |d :d |l, :t, |d :r |s, :— |—

:m |f :m |r :d |t, :— |d :r |m :f |r :t, |d :— |—
:de |r :de |r :l, |s, :— |d :s, |s, :f, |l, :s, |s, :— |—

And life, brief life is speed - - ing; The end is near - ing fast.
But Thou e - - ter - nal Fa - - ther, No time nor change canst know.
Lord, in our hearts more rich - - ly Let heaven-ly fruits a - - bound.

:s |f :s |l :f |r :f |m :r |d :d |f :r .f |m :— |—
:l, |r :m |f :r |s, :— |l, :t, |d :l, |f, :s, |d :— |—

IN THE HOUR OF TRIAL.

318. Key F. J. B. Dykes.

d :d |r :m	f :— |m :—	m :m |r :d	t_1 :— |— :—	d :d |r :m
s_1 :d |d :d	d :— |d :—	d :t_1 |l_1 :s_1	s_1 :— |— :—	s_1 :d |d :d
1.In the hour of	tri - al,	Je - sus pray for	me;	Lest, by base de -
2.If with sore af -	flic - tion	Thou in love chas -	tise,	Pour Thy ben - e -
3.When my lamp low	burn - ing	Sinks in mor - tal	pain;	Earth to earth re -
m :m |f :s	l :— |s :—	s :s |f :m	r :— |— :—	m :m |f :s
d :d |d :d	d :— |d :—	m_1 :m_1 |f_1 :d	s_1 :— |— :—	d :d |d :d

f :— |m :—	m :m |re :re	m :— |— :—	s :s |s :m	f :— |r :—
d :l_1 |d :—	d :d |t_1 :t_1	t_1 :— |— :—	m :r |de :de	r :d |t_1 :—
ni - al,	I de - part from	Thee.	When thou seest me	wav - er,
dic - tion	On the sac - ri -	fice.	Free- ly on Thine	al - tar
turn - ing,	Dust to dust a -	gain;	On Thy truth re -	ly - ing,
l :f |s :—	fe :fe |fe :l	s :— |— :—	t :t |l :l	l :— |s :f
d :— |d :—	l_1 :l_1 |t_1 :t_1	m :— |— :—	m :m |l_1 :l_1	r :— |s_1 :—

m :m |r :d	t_1 :— |— :—	d :d |r :m	f :— |m :—	m :d |r :-.d	d :— |— :—
d :d |l_1 :l_1	s_1 :— |— :—	s_1 :s_1 |s_1 :d	d :— |d :—	d :d |d :t_1	d :— |— :—
With a look re -	call;	Nor for fear or	fa - vor	Suf-fer me to	fall.
I will lay my	will,	And tho' flesh may	fal - ter,	Bless and praise Thee	still.
In that hour of	strife,	Je - sus, take me,	dy - ing,	To e - ter - nal	life.
m :s |f :m	r :— |— :—	m :m |f :s	l :— |s :—	s :m |r :f	m :— |— :—
d :d |f_1 :f_1	s_1 :— |— :—	d :d |t_1 :ta_1	l_1 :f_1 |d :—	s_1 :s_1 |s_1 :s_1	d :— |— :—

BATTISHILL.

319. Key G. Cadence Transitional modulation to First Flat minor.

s :m |r :d	r :r |m :—	f :m |l :s	f :m |r :—
d :d |t_1 :d	d :t_1 |d :—	d :d |d :d	t_1 :d |t_1 :—
1.Children of the	heaven-ly King,	As we jour - ney,	let us sing:
2.We are trav' - ling	home to God,	In the way our	fa - thers trod;
3.Lord! o - be - dient -	ly we'll go,	Glad - ly leav - ing	all be - low:
m :s |s :m	s :s |s :—	f :s |f :m	f :s |s :—
d :d |s_1 :l_1	s_1 :s_1 |d :—	l_1 :d |f_1 :d_1	r_1 :m_1.f_1 |s_1 :—

s :m |r :d	r :m |f :—	l :s |t_1 :d	m :r |d :—
d :d |t_1 :d	l_1 :de |r :—	t_1 :d |s_1 :m_1	s_1 :- .f_1 |m_1 :—
Sing our Sav - iour's	wor - thy praise,	Glo-rious in His	works and ways.
They are hap - py	now, and we	Soon their hap - pi -	ness shall see.
On - ly Thou our	lead - er be,	And we still will	fol - low Thee.
s :s |s :m	l :s |f :—	r :m |r :d	d :t_1 |d :—
m_1 :d |s_1 :l_1	f_1 :m_1 |r_1 :—	f_1 :m_1 |s_1 :l_1	s_1 :s_1 |d_1 :—

DEXTER SMITH. **BROKEN THREADS.** WM. MASON, Mus. Doc., by per.

320. KEY E♭. B♭. t. *Lah is G.*

| d :d | d .t, :l, .t, | d :d | r :— | ᵐl, :l, | l, .se, :ba, .se, | l, :l, | t, :—
| s, :s, | s, :s, | s, :s, | s, :— | ˢd, :f, | m, :m, | m, :m, | m, :—
1. As the shut - tle swift - ly flies Back and forth be - fore our eyes,
2. Weav-ing ev - - er day by day, As the shut - tles brisk - ly play,
3. Weav-ing in life's bus - y loom, Ming-ling sun - shine with the gloom,
4. Bro - ken threads in life a - bound, In each sta - tion they are found;
| m :m | r :r | m :m | f :— | ᵐl, :r | t, :t, | d :d | r :—
| d :s, | r :s, | d :s, | d .t, :l, .t, | ᵈf, :r, | m, :m, | l, :m, | l, .se, :ba, .se,

f. E♭.

| d :d | d .r :m .f | m :r | d :— | ᵗᵃf :f | f .m :r .d | r :r | s :— | f :f | f .m :r .d
| m, :ta, | l, :l, | s, :f, | m, :— | ˢr :t, | d :s, | d .t, :l, .t, | d :r .m | r :r | d :s,
Blend-ing with its fing-ers light, Warp and woof, till they u - nite In a fa - bric
Bro-ken threads how oft an - noy, And our pre - cious time em - ploy; Warning us by
Warp and woof of deeds we blend, Till life's fa - bric has an end; Bro-ken threads we
May Faith's kind and friend-ly hand, Helps us to ad - just the strand; That, when life's last
| d :r .m | f :d | d .t, :l, .t, | d :— | ᵈs :s | s :s | s :s | s :— | s :l .t | d' :s .d'
| l, :s, | f, :f, | s, :s, | d, :— | ᵐt, :s, | d :m | s :f | f .m :r .d | t, :s, | d :m

| r :r | s :l .t | d' :— .t | l .s :f .m | m .r :m .f | s :l .t | d' :— .t | l .s :f .m | m :r | d :— ‖
| s, :s, | s, :f | m .d :r .m | f .m :r .d | d .t, :d .r | m :f | m .d :r .m | f .m :r .d | d :t, | d :— ‖
good and strong. Let us hear the weav-er's song, Let us hear the weav-er's song.
warp re - proof, We must watch the warp and woof, We must watch the warp and woof.
oft - en bind, Bur - den-ing the no - ble mind, Bur - den-ing the no - ble mind.
tide shall ebb, There shall be a per - fect web, There shall be a per - fect web.
| d' .t :l .t | d' :s | s .m :f .s | l :l | s :s | s :— | s .m :f .s | f :l | s :f | m :— ‖
| s :f | m :r | d : .d | f :f | s :f | m :r | d :— .d | f, :f, | s, :s, | d :— ‖

FERNIEHURST. S. M.

321. KEY F. Cadence Transitional modulation to First Sharp minor.

:d | r :m | f :f | m :— | — :m | m :m | s :fe | m :— | —
:d | d :d | d :r | d :— | — :m | r :d | t, :l, | s, :— | —
1. Not what these hands have done Can save this guilt - y soul;
2. Not what I feel or do Can give me peace with God;
3. Thy work, a - lone, O Christ, Can ease this weight of sin;
:m | f :s | l :t | d' :— | — :s | se :l | m :m .re | m :— | —
:d | d :d | d :d | d :— | — :d | t, :l, | t, :t, | m :— | —

:m | r :t, | d :l | s :f | m :m | m :r | d :r | d :— | — ‖
:t, | t, :s, | s, :d | r :t, | d :ta, | l, :l, | d :t, | d :— | — ‖
Not what this toil - ing flesh has borne, Can make my spir - it whole.
Not all my pray'rs, and sighs, and tears, Can bear my aw - ful load.
Thy blood a - lone, O Lamb of God, Can give me peace with - in.
:s | s :f | m :m | s :s | s :s | s :f | m :f | m :— | — ‖
:m | f :r | m :l, | t, :r | d :de | r :r | s, :s, | d :— | — ‖

THE HOMELAND.

322. KEY E♭. A. S. SULLIVAN.

:d |m :m |l :l |s :— |s :f |m :d |d :t, |d :— |— :d |m :m |l :l
:d |d :d |d :d |t, :— |t, :r |d :s, |s, :s, |s, :— |— :d |d :d |d :d
1. The Homeland! O the Home - land! The land of souls free - born! No gloomy night is
2. My Lord is in the Home - land, With an-gels bright and fair; No sin-ful thing nor
3. For loved ones in the Home - land, Are wait-ing [illegible] to come Where nei-ther death nor
:m |s :s |f :m |r :— |r :s |s :m |l :f |m :— |— :m |s :s |f :m
:d |d :d |f, :f, |s, :— |s, :t, |d :d |s, :s, |d :— |— :d |d :d |f, :f,

B♭ t.

s :— |s :f |(m)l, :t, |l, :se |l, :— |— :l, |d :-.d |d :d |t, :— |m, :t,
t, :— |t, :r |(d)f, :f, |m, :m, |m, :— |— :m, |f, :-.f, |m, :re, |m, :— |m, :se,
known there, But aye the fade - less morn; I'm sigh - ing for that coun - try, My
e - vil Can ev - er en - ter there; The mu - sic of the ran - somed Is
sor - row In - vade their ho - ly home: O dear, dear na - tive coun - try! O
r :— |r :s |(s)d :r |d :t, |d :— |— :d |l, :-.l, |l, :l, |t, :— |t, :m
s, :— |s, :t, |(d)f, :r, |m, :m, |l, :— |— :l, |l, :-.l, |l, :l, |se, :— |se, :m,

f. E♭.

d :-.d |r :m |d :— |— :(d)s |s :s |t :l.s |d' :— |s :f |m :d |d :r |d :— ||
l, :-.l, |f, :f, |m, :— |— :(m)t, |d :d |f :f.f |m :d |ta, :l, |s, :s, |l, :t, |d :— |—
heart is ach - ing here; There is no pain in the Home - land To which I'm drawing near.
ring - ing in my ears, And when I think of the Home - land My eyes are wet with tears.
rest and peace a - bove! Christ bring us all to the Home - land Of His e - tern - al love.
m :-.m |t, :t, |d :— |— :(s)r |m :s |s :s.s |s :— |d :d |d :m |f :f |m :— |—
l, :-.l, |s, :s, |d, :— |— :(ta)f, |m, :m |r :r.r |d :— |m, :f, |s, :s, |s, :s, |d :— |—

PETROX.

323. KEY E♭. "Passing" Transitional Modulation to First Flat minor. W. BOYD.

m :s |f :m |r :— |d :— |r :m |f :l |d :— |t, :—
m :r |d :d |t, :— |l, :— |l, :de |r :l, |s, :— |s, :—
1. Lord, Thy word a - bid - eth, And our foot - steps guid - eth:
2. When our foes are near us, Then Thy word doth cheer us,
3. O, that we dis - cern - ing Its most ho - ly learn - ing,
d' :t |l :s |f :— |m :— |l :s |f :r |m :— |r :—
d :d |d :d |s, :— |l, :— |f :m |r :f, |s, :— |s, :—

r :m |f :l |s :— |m :— |r :d |f :m |r :— |d :—
l, :de |r :r |r :— |d :— |t, :d |d :d |t, :— |d :—
Who its truth be - liev - eth Light and joy re - ceiv - eth.
Word of con - so - la - tion, Mes - sage of sal - va - tion.
Lord, may love and fear Thee, Ev - er - more be near Thee.
f :s |f :fe |s :— |s :— |f :m |l :s |f :— |m :—
f :m |r :d |t, :— |d :— |s, :l, |f, :d |s, :— |d :—

THE LAST SLEEP.

p **324.** KEY D. Transitional Modulation, sharp and flat. *cres.* J. BARNBY.

| d :— \|d :d | d :— \|— :— | f :- .f \|m :r | r :— \|m : | m :— \|m :m |
| s₁ :— \|s₁ :s₁ | l₁ :— \|— :— | d :- .d \|t₁ :t₁ | t₁ :— \|d : | r :— \|r :r |

1. Sleep thy last sleep, Free from care and sor - - row; Rest, where none
2. Life's dream is past, All its sin, its sad - - ness; Bright - ly at
3. Though we may mourn Those in life the dear - - est, They shall re -

| m :— \|m :m | m :— \|— :— | l :- .l \|s :f | f :— \|m : | se :— \|se :se |
| d :— \|d :d | l₁ :— \|— :— | f₁ :- .f₁ \|s₁ :s₁ | s₁ :— \|d : | t₁ :— \|t₁ :t₁ |

A.t. f.D.

| m :— \|— :— | ˡr :- .r \|d :t₁ | t₁ :— \|d : | ᵈs :— \|s :s | s :— \|— :— |
| d :— \|— :— | ᵐl₁ :- .l₁ \|se₁ :se₁ | se₁ :— \|l₁ : | ᵐ.t₁ :d \|r :m | r :— \|d :— |

weep, Till th'e - ter - nal mor - - row; Though dark waves roll
last Dawns a day of glad - - ness. Un - - der thy sod,
turn, Christ, when Thou ap - pear - - est! Soon shall Thy voice

| l :— \|— :— | ᵈf :- .f \|m :r | r :— \|d : | ˢ.r :m \|f :s | f :— \|m :— |
| l₁ :— \|— :— | ᶠᵉ.t₁ :- .t₁ \|m₁ :m₁ | m₁ :— \|l₁ : | ᵈ.s₁ :— \|s₁ :s₁ | d :— \|— :— |

m *f* *rall.* *lentando.* *p*

| l :- .l \|l :l | l :— \|l :— | t :— \|l :s | d' :— \|d :— | d :- .d \|d :f | r :— \|d :— |
| de :r \|m :f | m :— \|r :— | r :— \|d :t₁ | d :— \|ta₁ :— | l₁ :- .l₁ \|l₁ :l₁ | t₁ :— \|d :— |

O'er the si - lent riv - er, Thy fainting soul Je - sus can de - liv - - er.
Earth re-ceive our treas - ure, To rest in God, Wait - ing all His pleas - ure.
Comfort those now weep - ing, Bid - ding re - joice All in Je - sus sleep - ing.

| m :f \|s :l | s :— \|f :— | f :— \|f :f | m :— \|— :— | f :- .f \|f :r | f :— \|m :— |
| l₁ :l₁ \|l₁ :l₁ | r :— \|r :— | s₁ :— \|s₁ :s₁ | l₁ :— \|s₁ :— | f₁ :- .f₁ \|f₁ :f₁ | s₁ :— \|d :— |

ESTHER.

325. KEY D♭. Transitional Modulation, Sharp Cadence, Flat "passing." J. BARNBY.

| m :r \|m :f | r :- .r \|d :— | s :f \|m :fe | s :fe \|m :— |
| d :t₁ \|d :d | t₁ :- .t₁ \|d :— | r :t₁ \|m :m | m :re \|m :— |

1. Soft - ly now the light of day Fades up - on my sight a - - way;
2. Thou, whose all - per - va - ding eye Naught es - capes, with - out, with - in!
3. Soon, for me, the light of day Shall for ev - er pass a - way!

| s :s \|s :l | s :- .f \|m :— | r :s \|s :d' | t :- .l \|s :— |
| d :s₁ \|d :f₁ | s₁ :- .s₁ \|d :— | t₁ :s₁ \|d :l₁ | t₁ :t₁ \|m :— |

| l :s \|f :l | r' :d' \|t :— | d' :t \|l :f .m | r :- .m \|d :— |
| m :de \|r :r | f :f \|f :— | m :r \|d :l₁ | t₁ :t₁ \|d :— |

Free from care, from la - bor free, Lord! I would com - mune with Thee.
Par - don each in - firm - i - - ty, O - pen fault, and se - cret sin.
Then, from sin and sor - row free, Take me, Lord! to dwell with Thee.

| m :l \|l :f | s :l \|r' :— | d' :se \|l :r .m | f :f \|m :— |
| dᵃ :l₁ \|r :d | t₁ :l₁ \|s₁ :— | l₁ :m \|f :f₁ | s₁ :s₁ \|d :— |

SING YE JEHOVAH'S PRAISES.

326. KEY G. *Allegretto.* T. F. SEWARD, by per.

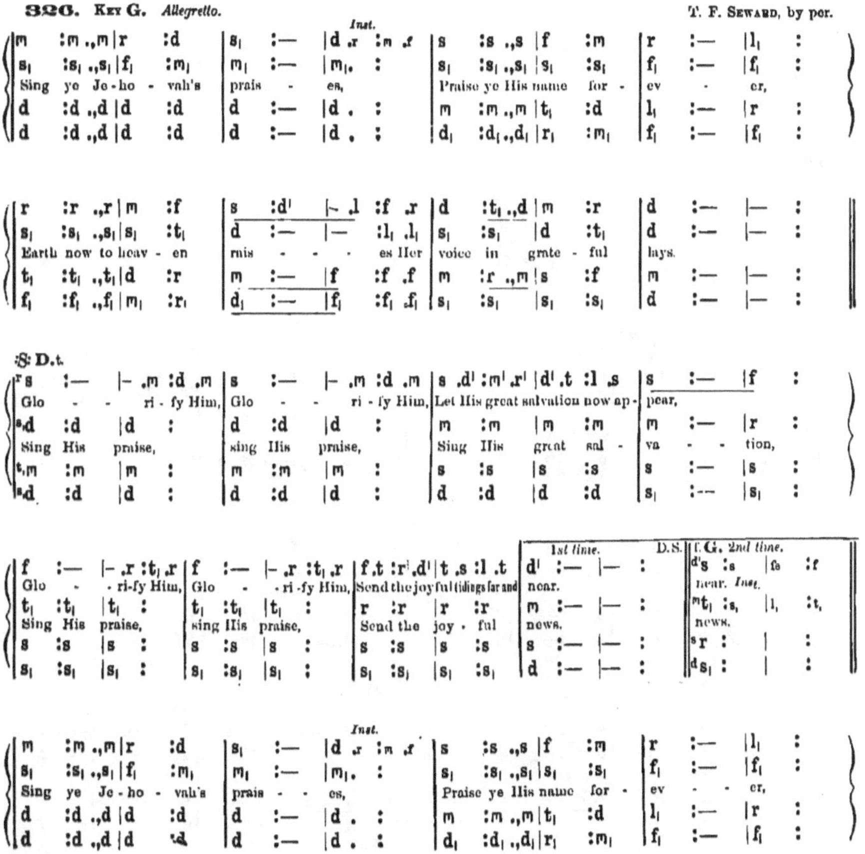

Inst.

|m :m .,m |r :d |s, :— |d .r :m .f |s :s .,s |f :m |r :— |l, :|
|s, :s, .,s, |f, :m, |m, :— |m,. : |s, :s, .,s, |s, :s, |f, :— |f, :|
Sing ye Je - ho - vah's prais - es, Praise ye His name for - ev - er,
|d :d .,d |d :d |d :— |d . : |m :m .,m |t, :d |l, :— |r :|
|d :d .,d |d :d |d :— |d . : |d, :d, .,d, |r, :m, |f, :— |f, :|

|r :r .,r |m :f |s :d' |— .l :f .r |d :t, .,d |m :r |d :— |— :||
|s, :s, .,s, |s, :t, |d :— |— :l, .l, |s, :s, |d :t, |d :— |— :||
Earth now to heav - en rais - - - es Her voice in grate - ful lays.
|t, :t, .,t, |d :r |m :— |f :f .f |m :r .,m |s :f |m :— |— :||
|f, :f, .,f, |m, :r, |d, :— |f, :f, .f, |s, :s, |s, :s, |d :— |— :||

𝄋 D.t.

|^r s :— |— .m :d .m |s :— |— .m :d .m |s .d' :m' .r' |d' .t :l .s |s :— |f :|
Glo - - ri - fy Him, Glo - - ri - fy Him, Let His great salvation now ap - pear,
|^s d :d |d : |d :d |d : |m :m |m :m |m :— |r :|
Sing His praise, sing His praise, Sing His great sal - va - - tion,
|^t m :m |m : |m :m |m : |s :s |s :s |s :— |s :|
|^s d :d |d : |d :d |d : |d :d |d :d |s, :— |s, :|

|f :— |— .r :t, .r |f :— |— .r :t, .r |f .t :r' .d' |t .s :l .t |
Glo - - ri-fy Him, Glo - - ri-fy Him, Send the joyful tidings far and
|t, :t, |t, : |t, :t, |t, : |r :r |r :r |
Sing His praise, sing His praise, Send the joy - ful
|s :s |s : |s :s |s : |s :s |s :s |
|s, :s, |s, : |s, :s, |s, : |s, :s, |s, :s, |

1st time. D.S.
|d' :— |— :|
near.
|m :— |— :|
news.
|s :— |— :|
|d :— |— :|

f. G. *2nd time.*
||^d s :s |fe :f
near. *Inst.*
|^m t, :s, |l, :t,
news.
|^s r : | :
|^d s, : | :

Inst.

|m :m .,m |r :d |s, :— |d .r :m .f |s :s .,s |f :m |r :— |l, :|
|s, :s, .,s, |f, :m, |m, :— |m,. : |s, :s, .,s, |s, :s, |f, :— |f, :|
Sing ye Je - ho - vah's prais - - es, Praise ye His name for - ev - - er,
|d :d .,d |d :d |d :— |d . : |m :m .,m |t, :d |l, :— |r :|
|d :d .,d |d :d |d :— |d . : |d, :d, .,d, |r, :m, |f, :— |f, :|

|r :r .,r |m :f |s :d' |- .l :f .r |d :t₁ .,d |m :r |d :— |— :
|s₁ :s₁ .,s₁ |s₁ :t₁ |d :— |— :l₁ .l₁ |s₁ :s₁ |d :t₁ |d :— |— :
Earth now to heav - en mis - - - es Her voice in grate - ful lays.
|t₁ :t₁ .,t₁ |d :r |m :— |f :f .f |m :r .,m₁ |s :f |m :— |— :
|f₁ :f₁ .,f₁ |m₁ :r₁ |d₁ :— |f₁ :f₁ .f₁ |s₁ :s₁ |s₁ :s₁ |d :— |— :

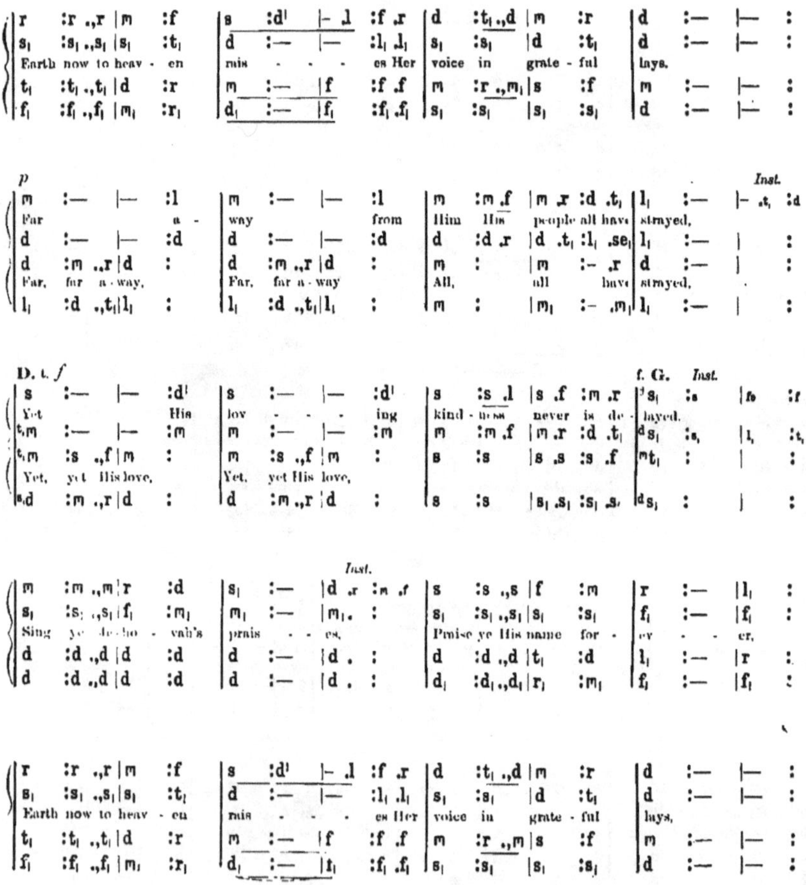

p *Inst.*
|m :— |— :l |m :— |— :l |m :m .f |m .r :d .t₁ |l₁ :— |- .t₁ :d
Far a - way from Him His people all have strayed,
|d :— |— :d |d :— |— :d |d :d .r |d .t₁ :l₁ .se₁ |l₁ :— | :
|d :m .,r |d : |d :m .,r |d : |m : |m :- .r |d :— | :
Far, far a - way, Far, far a - way All, all have strayed,
|l₁ :d .,t₁ |l₁ : |l₁ :d .,t₁ |l₁ : |m : |m₁ :- .m₁ |l₁ :— | :

D. t. *f* f. G. *Inst.*
|s :— |— :d' |s :— |— :d' |s :s .l |s .f :m .r |ᵗs₁ :s |fe :f
Yet His lov - - - - ing kind - ness never is de - layed.
|ᵗm :— |— :m |m :— |— :m |m :m .f |m .r :d .t₁ |ᵈs₁ :s₁ |l₁ :t₁
|ᵗm :s .,f |m : |m :s .,f |m : |s :s |s .s :s .f |ᵐt₁ : | :
Yet, yet His love, Yet, yet His love,
|ˢd :m .,r |d : |d :m .,r |d : |s :s |s₁ .s₁ :s₁ .s₁ |ᵈs₁ : | :

Inst.
|m :m .,m |r :d |s₁ :— |d .r :m .f |s :s .,s |f :m |r :— |l₁ :
|s₁ :s₁ .,s₁ |f₁ :m₁ |m₁ :— |m₁ . : |s₁ :s₁ .,s₁ |s₁ :s₁ |f₁ :— |f₁ :
Sing ye Je - ho - vah's prais - - es, Praise ye His name for - ev - - er,
|d :d .,d |d :d |d :— |d . : |d :d .,d |t₁ :d |l₁ :— |r :
|d :d .,d |d :d |d :— |d . : |d₁ :d₁ .,d₁ |r₁ :m₁ |f₁ :— |f₁ :

|r :r .,r |m :f |s :d' |- .l :f .r |d :t₁ .,d |m :r |d :— |— :
|s₁ :s₁ .,s₁ |s₁ :t₁ |d :— |— :l₁ .l₁ |s₁ :s₁ |d :t₁ |d :— |— :
Earth now to heav - en mis - - - es Her voice in grate - ful lays,
|t₁ :t₁ .,t₁ |d :r |m :— |f :f .f |m :r .,m |s :f |m :— |— :
|f₁ :f₁ .,f₁ |m₁ :r₁ |d₁ :— |f₁ :f₁ .f₁ |s₁ :s₁ |s₁ :s₁ |d :— |— :

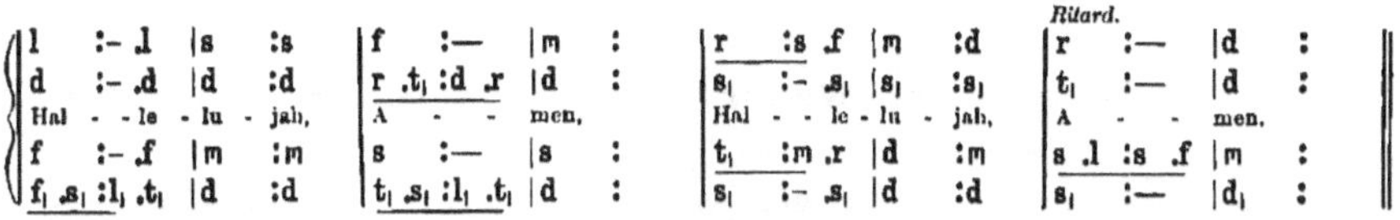

Ritard. (over the last measures)

l :-.l |s :s |f :— |m : |r :s .f |m :d |r :— |d :
d :-.d |d :d |r .t_1 :d .r |d : |s_1 :-.s_1 |s_1 :s_1 |t_1 :— |d :
Hal - - le - lu - jah, A - - men, Hal - - le - lu - jah, A - - men.
f :-.f |m :m |s :— |s : |t_1 :m .r |d :m |s .l :s .f |m :
f_1 .s_1 :l_1 .t_1 |d :d |t_1 .s_1 :l_1 .t_1 |d : |s_1 :-.s_1 |d :d |s_1 :— |d_1 :

THE KING AND THE MILLER.

327. KEY C. *Lah is A* U.

:m |l :— :l |se :— :m |d^1 :— :d^1 |t :— :r^1 |d^1 :— :l |t :— :se |l :— :— |— :—
:m |m :— :m |m :— :m |m :— :m |f :— :f |m :— :d |r :— :r |d :— :— |— :—
1. There dwelt a mil - ler hale and bold, Be - side the riv - - er Dee;
2. "Thou'rt wrong, my friend," said old king Hal, "As wrong as wrong can be;
3. The mil - - ler smiled and doffed his cap— "I earn my bread," quoth he;
4. "Good friend," said Hal, and sighed the while, "Fare- well, and hap - py be;
:m |d^1 :— :d^1 |t :— :se |l :— :l |t :— :l |l :— :l |se :— :t |l :— :— |— :—
:m |l_1 :— :l_1 |t_1 :— :t_1 |d :— :d |r :— :r |m :— :m |m :— :m |l_1 :— :— |— :—

:m |l :— :l |se :— :m |d^1 :— :d^1 |t :— :r^1 |d^1 :— :l |t :— :se |l :— :— |— :—
:m |m :— :m |m :— :m |m :— :m |m :— :m |m :— :d |r :— :r |d :— :— |— :—
He worked and sang from morn till night, No lark more blithe than he;
For could my heart be light as thine, I'd glad - ly change with thee.
"I love my wife, I love my friend, I love my chil - dren three.
But say no more, if thou'dst be true, That no one en - - vies thee;
:m |d^1 :— :d^1 |t :— :se |l :— :l |se :— :t |l :— :l |se :— :t |l :— :— |— :—
:m |l_1 :— :l_1 |m :— :m |d :— :d |m :— :se |l :— :l |m :— :m |l_1 :— :— |— :—

:d^1 .r^1 |m^1 :— :m^1 |m^1 :— :d^1 |r^1 :— :r^1 |r^1 :— :t |d^1 :— :l |r^1 :— :d^1 |d^1 :— :— |t :—
:m .f |s :— :s |s :— :s |s :— :s |s :— :f |m :— :m |f :— :r |m :— :— |r :—
And this the bur - - den of his song For ev - er used to be;
And tell me now, what makes thee sing With voice so loud and free,
I owe no one I can - not pay, I thank the riv - er Dee,
Thy meal - y cap is worth my crown; Thy mill my king - dom's fee,
:s |d^1 :— :d^1 |d^1 :— :d^1 |t :— :t |t :— :r^1 |d^1 :— :d^1 |l :— :l |s :— :— |— :—
:d |d — :d |d :— :m |s :— :s |s :— :s |l :— :l |f :— :fe |s :— :— |— :—

:m |l :— :l |se :-.ba :m |d^1 :— :d^1 |t :— :r^1 |d^1 :-.t :l |t :— :se |l :— :— |— :—
:m |m :— :m |m :— :m |m :— :m |m :— :m |m :-.r :d |r :— :r |d :— :— |— :—
"I en - - vy no one— no, not I! And no one en - - vies me!"
While I am sad, tho' I'm the king, Be - side the riv - - er Dee?
That turns the mill that grinds the corn To feed my babes and me!"
Such men as thou are Eng - land's boast, O mil - ler of the Dee!"
:m |d^1 :— :d^1 |t :-.l :se |l :— :l |se :— :t |l :— :l |se :— :t |l :— :— |— :—
:m |l_1 :— :d |m :— :m |l :— :l |m :— :se |l :— :l |m :— :m |l_1 :— :— |— :—

Questions for Written or Oral Examination.

DOCTRINE.

1. What tone has, thus far, been the key-tone, or point of whose?

2. Must *Doh* always be taken as the key-tone, or may any other tone be made to predominate in a tune?

3. What is meant by the *Ray Mode*?

4. What is meant by the *Lah Mode*?

5. What are the general mental effects of the *Ray* and *Lah Modes*?

6. What is the mental effect of the *Doh Mode*?

7. What is the *Doh Mode* commonly called?

8. What are the *Ray* and *Lah Modes* called?

9. What is the distinguishing interval of the Major Mode? The Minor Mode?

10. Which of the Minor Modes is the most used at the present day?

11. What is required to give *Lah* the importance of a key-tone?

12. What does the introduction of *Se* create?

13. How is this avoided?

14. What is the *Lah Mode* modified by these new tones called?

15. What is the essential Seventh of the Modern Minor? The occasional Seventh?

16. What is the essential Sixth? The occasional Sixth?

17. What is a change of Mode called?

18. What is the change from the Major to the Minor mode of the same key called? From the Minor to the Major?

19. What is the mental effect of a modulation into the Relative Minor? Into the Major?

20. What is a change of both key and mode called?

21. What is the commonest form of this change?

22. What is another, though less frequent Transitional Modulation?

PRACTICE.

23. Draw from memory a modulator illustrating the Minor Mode.

24. Imitate in the Minor Mode any Major phrases sung or played by the Examiner, but none more difficult than Nos 284 to 293.

25. Pitch from the tuning fork the *Lah* of key D G, E♭, A.

26. Follow the Examiner's pointing in a voluntary containing all the tones of the Modern Minor, including also, modulations to the Relative Minor, and Transitional modulations to the First Flat and First Sharp Minor.

27. Point and sol-fa on the modulator any one of the following four exercises, 272, 274, 280, 281, chosen by the Examiner

28. Write from memory any other of these four exercises chosen by the Examiner.

29. Sing at sight, sol-fa or *laa*, any exercises in the Minor Mode not more difficult than those pieces.

SIXTH STEP.

Transitions of more than one remove.

Two Removes.—The transitions used thus far have been transitions of *one remove*—to the First Sharp key or First Flat key—requiring the change of but one tone. But the music often passes into the *Second, Third* and *Fourth* Sharp or Flat keys, requiring the change of two, three and four tones. Transitions to the First Sharp or First Flat keys are called transition of One Remove. Transitions to the Second Sharp or Second Flat keys are called transitions of Two Removes. In two-sharp removes the music is placed one step higher; *fah* and *doh* of the old Key are omitted and two new tones, *me* and *te* are taken instead. Of these two distinguishing tones **t** is the more important because it distinguishes the *second* sharp remove from the first. In the signature this new **t** is placed nearest the key-name; thus—**A.**t.m. In two-flat removes the music is placed one step lower; *te* and *me* of the old key are omitted and *doh* and *fah* of the new key take their places. The new **f** is the more important because it distinguishes the *second* flat remove from the first. In the signature this new **f** is placed nearest the key-name, thus—d.f.**A.** Of the mental effects, transition of two sharp removes is expressive of rising emotion, more intense or more excited feeling. Transition of two flat removes is expressive of falling emotion, more intense seriousness and depression. When the music passes over the first sharp key to the first flat key or *vice versa*—swinging across the modulator—we call this form of two removes "oscillating transition." It is of frequent occurrence and is generally quite easy to sing. This "oscillation" across the original key keeps that key in mind, and lessens the violent effect of the two removes. A transition of two removes from a Principal Key (a principal transition) is seldom used except for imitation and sequence. Such transitions are comparatively easy when the music is exactly imitated in the new key.

Three Removes.—Transitions to the Third Sharp or Third Flat keys are called transitions of Three Removes. Three sharp removes place the new key a Minor Third below, and three flat removes a Minor Third above the old key. In other words, *lah* becomes *doh* and *doh*, becomes *lah*. On account of this relation between the *lah* of one key and the *doh* of the other, transitions of three removes are commonly Transitional *Modulations*. The mental effects are obvious- for a transition of three flat removes and a modulation from major to minor together naturally produce a gloomy depression of feeling; and a transition of three sharp removes and a modulation from minor to major combines to produce a strange kind of excitement. In transitions of three removes three tones of the old key are taken out to give place to the three distinguishing tones of the new key. In three-sharp removes *soh, doh* and *fah* of the old key are displaced by *lah, me* and *te* of the new key. The **t** is the last new tone required and is placed nearest the key-name in the signature, thus—**A.**t.m.l. In three flat removes the *te, me* and *lah* of the old key are displaced by *soh, doh* and *fah* of the new key. The **f** is the last new distinguishing tone and is placed nearest the key-name in the signature, thus—s.d.f.**A.** In Transitional Modulations of three removes the similarity of the upper part of the two modes (**m ba se l** and **s l t d'**) assists the ear in passing over from one key into the other, especially if that form of the minor mode containing *ba* is used. The third flat remove is the more difficult to sing, simply because the minor mode into which it enters is itself artificial and difficult. The third sharp remove is the less difficult, because the major mode into which it enters is more natural to the ear.

Four Removes.—Transitions into the Fourth Sharp or Fourth Flat keys are called transitions of Four Removes. Four flat removes place the new key a Major Third below, and four sharp removes a Major Third above the previous key. In other words, *doh* becomes *me*, or *me* becomes *doh*. In four-flat removes the tones of the old key displaced are *te, me, lah* and *ray*; the distinguishing tones of the new key are *ray, soh, doh* and *fah*. The new **f**, being the last new flat, is placed nearest the key-name in the signature, thus—r.s.d.f.**A.** In four-sharp removes the tones of the old key displaced are *ray, soh, doh* and *fah*; the distinguishing tones of the new key are *ray, lah, me* and *te*. The new **t**, being the last new sharp, is placed nearest the key-name in the signature, thus—**A.**t.m.l.r.

Difficult Removes.—All removes beyond the first are difficult to sing without the aid of instruments. The greater the number of changes, the greater is the difficulty of adjusting the ear and mind to the new relations. Of 32 or more possible transitions and transitional modulations only nine or ten are much used. Transitions of the third, fourth and other removes are not much used except in connection with instrumental accompaniment.

Relation of Keys in a Tune.—Every tune has its *Principal Key* (that is, commencing, and closing, and prevailing key). The other keys are called *Subordinate Keys.* Transitions from and to the Principal Key are called Principal Transitions. Transitions between Subordinate Keys are called Subordinate Transitions. In speaking of Subordinate Keys we have to bear in mind not merely their relation of one, two, or three removes (flat or sharp) from the last key heard, but also their more important relation to the Principal Key. Subordinate Keys may be three or four removes from each other, but only one or two from the Principal Key.

328. KEY C. TWO SHARP REMOVES

| s :f | m :s | d^1 :t | l :— | D.t.m. ^ls :f | m :s | d^1 :t | l :— |

f.G. | ^lm :f | m :r | d :t_1 | d :— | f.C. ^ds :f | m :l | s :t | d^1 :— ||

329. KEY D.

| d :t_1 | d :m | s .f :m .r | d :— | E.t.m. rd :t_1 | d :m | s .f :m .r | d :— |

f.A. | $^ds_1$:l_1 | s_1 :d | d .t_1 :l_1 .t_1 | d :s_1 | f.D. ^lm :f | m :r | s .f :m .r | d :— ||

330. KEY F.

| m :s | d .r :m | f :m | r :— | s :r | m .f :s | G.t.m. ^ls :r | m .f :s |

f.C. | $^fd^1$:s | l .t :d^1 | r^1 :r^1 | d^1 :— | f.F. $^{d^1}s$:m | r .m :f | m :r | d :— ||

MODULATOR, Showing Two Removes.	
r^1	d^1
de^1	t
d^1	*ta*
t	l
l	s
s	f
fe	m
f	*ma*
m	r
r	d
de	t_1
d	*ta_1*
t_1	l_1

331. KEY G.

| s_1 :l_1 .t_1 | d :t_1 .d | m .r :d .t_1 | d :— | A.t.m. $^ls_1$:l_1 .t_1 | d :t_1 .d | m .r :d .t_1 | d :— |

f.D. | ^lm :s | f .m :r | r :f | m .r :d | f.G. $^ds_1$:l_1 .t_1 | d :t_1 .d | m .r :d .t_1 | d :— ||

332. KEY E♭.

| d :m | r :f | m .s :f .m | r :— | F.t.m. rd :m | r :f | m .s :f .m | r :— |

f.B♭. | $^rl_1$:l_1 | t_1 :l_1 .t_1 | d :l_1 | s_1 :— | f.E♭. ^sd :m | r :m .f | s .f :m .r | d :— ||

333. KEY D. TWO FLAT REMOVES. d.t.C.

{| s :l | s .f :m .r | d :r | m :— | ^f s :l | s .f :m .r | d :r | m :— }

G.t. D.t.

{| ^m l, :l, | s, :d | d .t, :d .r | m :— | ^m l :l | s :m | s .f :m .r | d :— ||

334. KEY G. d.f.F.

{| m :r | d :s, | l, .s, :l, .t, | d :— | ^r m :r | d :s, | l, .s, :l, .t, | d :— }

C.t. G.t.

{| ^t, m :f | s :m | f .s :l .t | d' :— | ^t m :f | m :r | d .s, :l, .t, | d :— ||

335. KEY C. *Subordinate, sharp.* f.F.

{| s :m | d' :t | l :d' | s :— | ^s r :m | f :r | d :r | m :— }

G.t.m. f.C.

{| ^m r :m | f :r | d :r | m :— | ^m t :t | d' :s | l :t | d' :— ||

336. KEY C. *Subordinate, flat.* G.t.

{| s :f | m :s | d' :t .| l :— | ^l r :m | f :r | d :t, | d :— }

d.f.F. f.C.

{| ^d r :m | f :r | d :t, | d :— | ^d f :f | m :s | l :t | d' :— ||

337 KEY B♭. F.t. d.f.E♭.

{ :s, | d :t, | d :s, | l, :s, | d :^t, m | s :m | f :r | d :— | — :^d r | s :r | m :f }

F.t.m. f.B♭.

{| f :m | m :^m r | s :r | m :f | f :m | m :^m t, | d :s, | l, :t, | d :— | — ||

338. KEY E♭. F.t.m. G.t.m. A.t.m.

{| r :f | m :r | d :r | m :— | ^m r :f | m :r | d :r | m :— | ^m r :f | m :r | d :r | m :— | ^m r :f | m :r }

d.f.G. d.f.F. d.f.E♭.

{| d :t, | d :— | ^d r :f | m :r | d :t, | d :— | ^d r :f | m :r | d :t, | d :— | ^d r :f | m :r | d :t, | d :— ||

CORONA.

330. Key F. C.t. H. J. Gauntlett.

```
:s, |m :-.m |r :d |s :— |— :s, |f :-.f |m :r |m :— |— :ᵐl |s :l |s :d'
:s, |m :-.m |r :d |s :— |— :s, |f :-.f |m :r |m :— |— :ᵈf |s :r |s :m
1.Thou art gone up on high To mansions in the skies; And round Thy throne un-
2.Thou art gone up on high: But Thou didst first come down, Through earth's most bit - ter
3.Thou art gone up on high: But Thou shalt come a - gain, With all the bright ones
:s, |m :-.m |r :d |s :— |— :s, |f :-.f |m :r |m :— |— :ˢd' |d' :t |d' :d'
:s, |m :-.m |r :d |s :— |— :s, |f :-.f |m :r |m :— |— :ᵈf |m :f |m :d
```

d.f.B♭.

```
|d' :r' |r' :s |m' :-.m' |m' :r' |d' :— |— :ˡt, |m :-.r |d :t, |t, :— |— :t,
|m :fe |s :s |s :-.fe |s :f |m :— |— :ˢl, |se, :-.se, |l, :l, |se, :— |— :m,
ceas-ing - ly The songs of praise a - rise. But we are ling' - ring here With
ag - o - ny To pass un - to Thy crown. And girt with griefs and fears Our
of the sky At - tend - ant in Thy train. O by Thy sav - ing power So
|d' :d' |t :t |d' :-.d' |d' :t |d' :— |— :ᵈr |r :-.t, |m :r |m :— |— :r
|l :l |s :s |d' :-.l |s :s, |d :— |— :ᵐf, |m, :-.m, |m, :f, |m, :— |— :se,
```

F.t.

```
|d :-.t, |l, :s, |ᶠt, :r |t, :s, |m :-.d |f :r |s :— |— :f |m :-.f |m :r |d :— |— ||
|m, :-.m, |m, :m, |ʳs, :r |t, :s, |d :-.d |d :t, |d :— |— :d |d :-.d |d :t, |d :— |— ||
sin and care op - press'd, Lord, send Thy promised Com-fort - er, And lead us to Thy rest.
onward course must be; But on - ly let that path of tears Lead us at last to Thee.
make us live and die, That we may stand, in that dread hour, At Thy right hand on high.
|d :-.r |d :d.t, |ˡr :r |t, :s, |s :-.l |l :s |s :— |— :l |s :-.l |s :f |m :— |— ||
|l, :-.se, |l, :d, |ʳs, :r |t, :s, |d :-.f |r :f |m :— |— :f |s :-.s, |s, :s, |d :— |— ||
```

ELLWOOD.

340. Key C. G. A. Macfarren.

```
|s :m' :d' |s :— :l |s :— :— |m :— : |s :l :t |d' :— :t |l :— :— |— :— :—
|m :s :m |m :— :f |m :— :— |d :— : |d :— :d |d :— :s |f :— :— |— :— :—
1.Je - sus is our Shep - - herd, Wip - ing ev - ery tear;
2.Je - sus is our Shep - - herd, Well we know His voice
3.Je - sus is our Shep - - herd, For the sheep He bled;
|d' :— :d' |d' :— :d' |d' :— :— |s :— : |s :— :s |s :— :d' |d' :— :— |l :— :—
|d :— :d |d :— :d |d :— :— |d :— : |m :— :m |m :— :m |f :— :m |r :— :d
```

G.t.

```
|r' :— :s |s :l :t |d' :— :— |l :— : |ˡm :l :s |f :— :r |d :— :— |— :— :—
|f :— :f |f :— :f |m :— :— |l :— : |ˢd :— :d |t, :— :t, |d :— :— |— :— :—
Fold - ed in His bo - - som, What have we to fear?
How its gen - tlest whis - - per Makes our heart re - joice;
Ev - ery lamb is sprin - - kled With the blood He shed;
|s :— :t |t :d' :r' |d' :— :— |m' :— : |ʳs :f :m |r :— :f |m :— :— |— :— :—
|t, :— :r |s :— :s, |l, :— :— |d :— : |ʳs, :— :s, |s, :— :s, |d :— :— |— :— :—
```

d.f.F. ... G.t.m. ... f.C.

^{d}r :— :r |f :m :r |s :— :— |m :— :— |^{m}r :— :r |f :m :r |^{s}r' :— :— |— :— :—
$^{s}l_1$:— :l_1 |t_1 :— :t_1 |d :— :— |d :— :— |$^{de}t_1$:— :t_1 |t_1 :— :t_1 |^{d}s :— :— |f :— :—
On - ly let us fol - - low Whith - er He doth lead,
Ev - en when He chid - - eth, Ten - der is His tone:
Then on each He set - - teth His own se - - cret sign.—
^{ma}f :— :f |r :— :s |s :— :— |s :— :— |^{l}s :— :s |r :— :s |^{s}r' :— :— |t :— :—
^{d}r :— :r |s_1 :— :f_1 |m_1 :— :— |d :— :— |$^{l}s_1$:— :s_1 |s_1 :— :f_1 |$^{m}t_1$:— :— |s_1 :— :—

s :m' :d' |s :— :l |s :— :— |m :— : |f :s :l |t :— :s |d' :— :— |— :— :—
m :s :m |m :— :f |m :— :— |d :— : |d :r :m |f :— :f |m :— :— |— :— :—
To the thirst - y des - - ert, Or the dew - - y mead.
None but He shall guide us; We are His a - lone.
"They that have My Spir - - - it, Those" saith He, "are Mine."
ta :— :ta |ta :— :l |ta :— :— |ta :— : |l :ta :d' |r' :— :t |d' :— :— |— :— :—
d :— :d |d :— :d |d :— :— |d :— : |f :— :f |r :— :s |d :— :— |— :— :—

CLARK.

341. Key G.

m :s |f :m |r :m |r :d |m :r |l :s |s :fe |s :— |s :l |s :m |d :r |m :m
d :d |d :d |d :d |t_1 :d |s_1 :r |d :r |d :d |t_1 :— |s_1 :fe_1 |s_1 :s_1 |s_1.d:t_1.l_1 |l_1 :se_1
1. Light of those whose dreary dwelling Borders on the shades of death, Come, and by Thy love's re - veal - ing
2. Still we wait for Thine ap-pear-ing; Life and joy Thy beams im-part, Chas-ing all our fears, and cheering
3. Save us in Thy great com-passion, O Thou mild, pa - ci - fic Prince, Give the knowledg of sal - va - tion,
s :ta |l :s |fe :fe |f :m |d :r |m.fe:s |l :l |s :— |m :ma |r :m |m :f |t.d:r
d :d |d :d |l_1 :r_1 |s_1 :d |d :t_1 |l_1 :t_1 |r :r |s_1 :— |d :d |t_1 :d |l_1 :f_1 |m_1 :m_1

D.t.

m :l_1 |l_1 :r |r :m |d :— |^{r}s :s |l :d' |t :r' |r' :d' |s :se |l :t
l_1 :s_1 |f_1 :l_1 |t_1 :t_1 |d :— |^{t}m :s |f :ma |r :f |f :m |d :r |d :m
Dis - si - pate the clouds be - neath. The new heaven and earth's Cre - a - tor, In our deep - est
Ev - ery poor be - night - ed heart. Come, and man - i - fest the fav - or God hath for our
Give the par - don of our sins. By Thine all - re - stor - ing mer - it, Ev - ery burdened
de :de |r :f |f :f |m :— |^{s}d' :d' |d' :l |s :t |t :d' |d' :t |l :se
l_1 :l_1 |r :r_1 |s_1 :s_1 |d :— |^{s}d :m |f :fe |s :s |d :d |m :m |l_1 :m

E.t.m ... d.f.D. ... f.G.

d' :r' |m' :— |^{m}r' :t |s :d' |^{d}r' :t |s :d' |^{d}s :l |s :f |m :r |d :—
m :l |se :— |^{e}f :f |f :m |^{ma}f :f |f :m |$^{ma}ta_1$:ta_1 |ta_1 :l_1 |t_1 :t_1 |d :—
darkness rise, Scatt'ring all the night of nat - ure Pour-ing eye - sight on our eyes.
ransomed race; Come, Thou glo-rious God and Sav - iour, Come, and bring the gos - pel - grace.
soul re - lease, Ev - ery wea - ry, wand'ring spir - it Guide in - to Thy per - fect peace.
l :l |t :— |^{de}t :r' |d' :ta |^{l}t :r' |d' :ta |^{l}m :m |d :f |f :f |m :—
l s:f |m :— |$^{l}s_1$:s_1 |d :d |$^{f}s_1$:s_1 |d :d |$^{f}d_1$:d_1 |f_1 :f_1 |s_1 :s_1 |d :—

WEST HEATH.

342. KEY C. E. J. HOPKINS.

:s |m :s |d' :s |l :- .t |d' :r' |m' :t |d' :l |s :- .f |m
:m |d :t, |d :s |f :- .s |s :s |s :s |s :f |m :r |d
1.Fear not, O lit - tle flock, the foe Who mad - ly seeks your o - ver - throw,
2.Be of good cheer; your cause be - longs To Him who can a - venge your wrongs;
3.A - men, Lord Je - sus, grant our pray'r! Great Cap - tain, now Thine arm make bare;
:s |s :f |s :d' |d' :- .r' |d' :t |d' :r' |d' :d' |d' :t |s
:d |d :r |m :m |f :- .f |m :r |d :s |m :f |s :s, |d

G.t. d.f.F.

:ᵐl, |s, :d |r :m |r :— |d :ᵈr |t, :r |s :t, |d :- .r |m
:ᵈf, |s, :l, |l, :f, |f, :— |m, :ˢl, |s, :fe, |s, :s, |s, :- .t, |d
Dread not his rage or power: What tho' your cour - age some - times faints,
Leave it to Him, our Lord. Tho' hid - den yet from mor - tal eyes,
Fight for us once a - gain! So shall Thy saints and mar - tyrs raise
:ᶠᵉt, |d :m |r :d |t, :— |d :ᵈr |r :d |m :f |m :- .f |s
:ˡr, |m, :l, |f, :r, |s, :— |d, :ᵐfe, |s, :l, |t, :s, |m :- .r |d

G.t.m. f.C.

:ᵐr |t, :r |s :t, |d :- .r |m :ᵈs |d' :d' |r' :m' |r' :— |d'
:ˢᵉfe, |s, :fe, |s, :s, |s, :- .t, |d :ᵈs |s :l |l :f |f :— |m
His seem - ing tri - umph o'er God's saints Lasts but a lit - tle hour.
Sal - va - tion shall for you a - rise: He gird - eth on His sword!
A - might - y cho - rus to Thy praise, World with - out end, A - men.
:ᵐr |r :d |r :f |m :- .f |s :ᵐf |d' :m' |r' :d' |t :— |d'
:ᵗl, |s, :l, |t, :s, |m :- .r |d :ᵗᵃf |m :l |f :r |s :— |d

PRENTISS.

343. KEY E♭.

|m :s :d' |t :- .l :s |l :s :m |r :— :— |m :ba :se |l :- .t :d' |t :t :l
|d :d :d |d :- .m :m |re :m :d |t, :— :— |t, :d :t, .m |m :- .r :d |r :d :d
1.More love to Thee, O Christ More love to Thee! Hear Thou the pray'r I make, On bend - ed
2.Let sor - row do its work Send grief and pain; Sweet are Thy mes - sen-gers, Sweet their re -
3.Then shall my lat - est breath Whisper Thy praise; This be the part - ing cry My heart shall
|s :m :m |s :- .f :m |fe :s :s |s :— :— |se :l :t |l :- .se :l |s :fe :fe
|d :d :d |d :- .d :d |d :d :m |s :— :— |m :m :r |d :- .t, :l, |r :r :r

f.A. B.t.m. f.E♭.

|s :— :— |ʳr :s, :f |m :- .r :d |ᵐr :s, :f |m :- .r :d |ᶠd' :m :r |d :— :—
|t, :— :— |ᵈs, :s, :t, |d :- .t, :d |ˡs, :s, :t, |d :- .t, :d |ᵈs :d :t, |d :— :—
knee; This is my earn - est plea, More love, O Christ, to Thee, More love to Thee!
frain, When they can sing with me, More love, O Christ, to Thee, More love to Thee!
raise, This still its pray'r shall be, More love, O Christ, to Thee, More love to Thee!
|s :— :— |ˢr :r :r |m :- .f :s |ᵐr :r :r |m :- .f :m |ᶠd' :s :f |m :— :—
|s :— :f |ᵐt, :t, :s, |d :- .r :m |ᵈᵉt, :t, :s, |d :- .d :d .ta, |ˡm :s :s, |d :— :—

SAUNDERS.

344. KEY F. C.t. *Lah is A.*

d :— |r :m |m :-.r|r :— |f :— |m :r |d :— |— :— |ᵐl :— |t :d'
s, :— |s, :s, |l :-.l,|l, :— |l, :— |t, :t, |d :— |— :— |ˢd :— |r :m

1. Thine is the pow - er, Lord, Hum - bly we crave, Thou wilt Thy -
2. Thine is the pow - er, Lord, Low - ly we bend; Trust - ing Thy
3. Thine is the pow - er, Lord, Ours is the need; 'Tis in Thy

m :— |f :s |s :-.f|f :— |l :— |s :f |m :— |— :— |ᵐl :— |l :l
d :— |d :d |f, :-.f,|f, :— |s, :— |s, :s, |d :— |— :— |ᵈf :— |m :m

d.f.B♭. *Lah is G.*

d' :-.t |t :— |r' :— |d' :t |l :— |— :— |ˡt, :— |t, :m |m :-.m|m :—
f :-.f |f :— |f :— |m :r |d :— |— :— |ʳm, :— |ba, :se, |l, :-.l,|l, :—

self re - veal, Might - y to save. Thine is the pow - er, Lord,
gra - cious word, Kins - man and Friend. Thine is the pow - er, Lord,
gra - cious word, Dare we to plead. Thine is the pow - er, Lord,

l :-.l |l :— |l :— |se :se |l :— |— :— |ˡt, :— |r :r |d :-.d|d :—
r :-.r |r :— |t, :— |m :m |l :— |— :— |ᶠᵉse, :— |m, :m, |l, :-.l,|l, :—

F.t.

r :d |d :t, |d :— |— :— |ᵗm :— |m :r |d :-.r|m :— |f :— |r :-.d|d :— |— :—
l, :— |se, :se, |l, :— |— :— |ᶠᵉt, :— |t, :t, |d :-.t,|d :— |d :— |t, :-.d|d :— |— :—

Help us to win, Hard are we now be - set, Striv - ing with sin.
Grant us Thy peace; Now, from the temp - ter, Lord, Grant us re - lease.
Are we not Thine? Be Thou our watch and word, Sav - iour Di - vine.

m :— |m :r |d :— |— :— |ʳs :— |m :m |m :-.f|s :— |l :— |ᵗf :-.m|m :— |— :—
m, :— |m, :m, |l, :— |— :— |ʳs, :— |se, :se, |l, :-.l,|s, :— |f, :— |s, :-.d|d :— |— :—

GRACIOUS SPIRIT, HOLY GHOST.

p **345.** KEY E♭. *mf* B♭.t. *Lah is G.* CARYL FLORIO.

d :d |f :-.m |r :m |d :— |ᵐl, :l, |r :-.d |t, :d |l, :—
d :t, |l, :-.d |d :t, |d :— |ᵈf, :f, |f, :-.f, |f, :m, |d, :r,

1. Gra-cious Spir - it, Ho - ly Ghost, Taught by Thee, we cov - et most,
2. Love is kind, and suf - fers long; Love is meek, and thinks no wrong;
3. Faith will van - ish in - to sight; Hope be emp - tied in de - light;

m :m |f :-.s |l :s |m :— |ᵐl, :l, |se, :-.l, |l, :se, |l, :t,
d :d |d :-.d |f, :s, |d :t, |ˡr, :d, |t₂ :-.d, |r, :m, |l, :—

f d.f.A♭. *Lah is F.* *p* E♭.t.

ᵈr :r |f :-.m |r :m |d :— |ᵈf :f |m :r |d :— |— :—
ᵐᵃf, :f, |se, :-.se, |se :se, |l, :s, |ᶠᵉt, :t, |t, :t, |d :— |— :—

Of Thy gifts at Pen - te - cost, Ho - ly, Heav'n - ly Love.
Love than Death it - self more strong: There-fore, give us Love.
Love in Heav'n will shine more bright: There-fore, give us Love.

ᵈr :r |r :-.t, |f :m |m :— |ᵐl :l |s :f |m :— |— :—
ˡt, :t, |m, :-.m, |m, :m, |l, :— |ʳs, :s, |s, :s, |d :— |— :—

346. KEY E♭. *Lah is C.* THREE SHARP REMOVES.

{|l :l |se :se |l :— |m :— |f :f |d :r |m :— |— : }

C.t.l.m.
{|ms :s |d' :r' |m' :— |d' :— |m' :r' |d' :t |d' :— |— : ||

347. KEY C. *Lah is A.*

{|l :-.l |se :l |m :m |f :m |l :-.t |d' :d' |t :l |se :— }

A.t.m.l.
{|ld :-.d |m :r |d :t, |d :s, |l, :-.l, |s, :d |m :r |d :— ||

348. KEY E. THREE FLAT REMOVES.

{|m :r |d :m |s :l |s :m |s :d |t, :d |f :m |r :— }

s.d.f.G. *Lah is E.* E.t.m.l.
{|mad :t, |l, :d |m :f |m :d |ms :m |f :r |d :t, |d :— ||

349. KEY G. From DYKES.

{:s, |s, :d |d :m |s :— |— :d |f :m |m :r |d :— |— }

s.d.f.B♭. *Lah is G.* G.t.l.m.
{:dl, |l, :d |t, :se, |l, :— |— :m |r :d |t, :t, |t,r :— |— }

{:s, |s, :m |r :d |d :f |m :r |d :t,.d |r :-.t, |d :— |— ||

350. KEY G. s.d.f.B♭. *Lah is G.*

{|m :r |d :-.d |f :m |m :r |md :r |m :-.m |f :m |m :— }

G.t.m.l.
{|m :r |d :-.t, |d :r |m :— |ms :-.f |m :r.d |d :t, |d :— ||

MODULATOR, Showing 3 Removes.	
d'	ma'
t	r'
l	d'
se	t
s	*ta*
ba	l
f	*la*
m	s
r	f
de	m
d	*ma*
t,	r
l,	d

LANDSDOWNE.

J. B. DYKES.

351. KEY D. s.d.f.F. *Lah is D.*

```
|s :-.m|s :d' |l :d' |s :— |l .t :d' |r' :s |s :— |— :— |sm :-.d|m :l
|m :-.d|m :m  |f :f  |m :— |f :m    |r.f :m |m :— |r :— |mad :-.l,|d :d
|d' :-.s|d' :d'|d' :d'|d' :— |d' :d' |s :s |s :d' |t :— |d'l :-.m|l :l
|d :-.d|d :d  |f :l  |d' :— |f :d    |t, :d |s :— |— :— |dl, :-.l,|l, :l,
```

1. Ev - ery morn-ing the red sun Ris - es warm and bright; But the eve-ning
2. Ev - ery spring the sweet young flow'rs O - pen fresh and gay, Till the chil - ly
3. Who shall go to that fair land? All who love the right: Ho - ly chil-dren

```
|f :l |m :d.r |m :— |f :— |m :— |— :— ||D.t.m.l. ms :m :f |s :— :d'
|r :r |d :l,.t, |d :— |— :r |d :— |t, :— ||dem :d :r |m :r :m
|l :l |l :l.l |m :l |— :t |l :— |se :— ||ld' :s :-.s |s :f :s
|r :f |l :m.m |m :— |r :— |m :— |— :— ||ld :— :d |d :— :d
```

com - eth on And the dark, cold night: There's a bright land
au-tumn hours Wither them a - way! There's a land we
there shall stand, In their robes of white; For that heaven, so

```
|r' :— :d' |t :— :— |d' :— :t.l |l :s :m |m :— :r |d :— :— ||
|f :— :m |f :— :— |f :m :re |m :— :d |t, :— :t, |d :— :— ||
|s :t :d' |r' :— :— |d' :— :d' |d' :— :s |s :— :f |m :— :— ||
|s :— :s |s :— :se |l :s :fe |s :— :s |s, :— :s, |d :— :— ||
```

far a - way Where 'tis nev - er end - ing day.
have not seen, Where the trees are al - - ways green.
bright and blest, Is our ev - - er - last - - ing rest.

WHEN DAYLIGHT FADES AWAY.

BEETHOVEN.

352. KEY G. D.C.

```
:s, |m :r :d |t, :l, :l, |f :m :r |d :t, :t, |l :s :t, |d :m :s |l :s :t, |d :— ||
:s, |s, :— :s, |s, :f, :s, |l, :— :la, |s, :— :s, |t, :— :s, |s, :d :d |d :— :s, |s, :— ||
:s, |d :t, :d |d :— :de |r :de :r |m :r :r |f :— :f |m :s :s |f :m :r |m :— ||
:s, |d, :r, :m, |f, :— :m, |r, :m, :f, |s, :— :s, |s, :— :s, |d :— :m, |f, :s, :s, |d, :— ||
```

1. When day - light soft - ly fades a - way, In yon - der ma - ny - col - ored west.
And sol - emn night on si - - lent wing, Ap - pears in eb - - on man - tle drest.
2. O, ev - er wel - come sa - cred hour, When shep - herds heard the an - gel strain,
I too by faith can list the song That once re - sound - ed on the plain.

𝄋 s.d.f.B♭. *Lah is G.* G.t.m.l. D.S.

```
:sm |f :m :r |r :d :d |r :d :ta, |ta, :l, :l, |d :t, :l, |ms :m :m |l :s :t, |d :— ||
:dl, |se, :— :se, |m, :— :m, |m, :— :m, |f, :f, :f, |re, :— :.e, |ms, :d :d |t, :— :s, |s, :— ||
:mad |t, :— :t, |l, :— :l, |s, :— :d |d :d :d |l, :t, :d |dem :s :s |f :— :f |m :— ||
:dl, |m, :— :m, |l, :— :l, |d, :— :d, |f, :f, :f, |f, :— :f, |ms, :— :s, |s, :— :s, |d, :— ||
```

'Tis then my thoughts from earth - ly pleasures That ev - er in - suf - fi - cient prove;
Are wont to turn a - way to heaven And dwell up - on Al - might - y love.
O, let my long - ing spir - it ev - er In ho - ly ad - o - ra - tion stray;
To Him who sit - teth in the heavens, When day - light soft - ly fades a - way.

353. KEY B♭. *Lah is G.* ※ **VOX DILECTI.** J. B. DYKES.

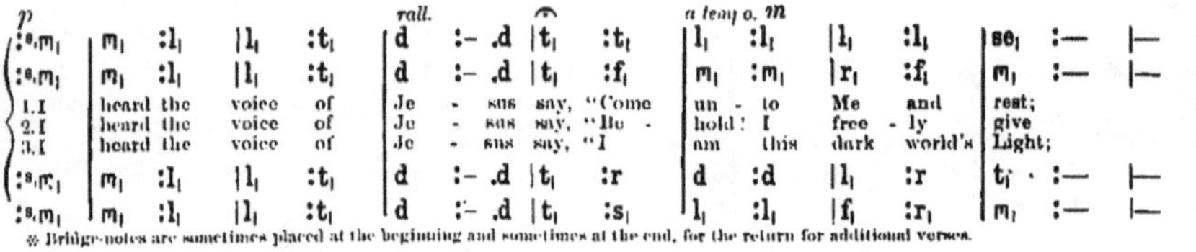

p — *rall.* — *a tempo. m*

:s.m, | m, :l, | l, :t, | d :- .d | t, :t, | l, :l, | l, :l, | se, :— | —
:s.m, | m, :l, | l, :t, | d :- .d | t, :f, | m, :m, | r, :f, | m, :— | —
1. I heard the voice of Je - sus say, "Come un - to Me and rest;
2. I heard the voice of Je - sus say, "Be - hold! I free - ly give
3. I heard the voice of Je - sus say, "I am this dark world's Light;
:s.m, | m, :l, | l, :t, | d :- .d | t, :r | d :d | l, :r | t, :— | —
:s.m, | m, :l, | l, :t, | d :- .d | t, :s, | l, :l, | f, :r, | m, :— | —

※ Bridge-notes are sometimes placed at the beginning and sometimes at the end, for the return for additional verses.

:m, | m, :l, | l, :l, | d :- .r | t, :m | r :d | t, :l, | m, :— | —
:m, | m, :m, | f, :f, | m, :- .m, | m, :t, | r, :m, | f, :fe, | m, :— | —
Lay down, thou wea - ry one, lay down Thy head up - on My breast;"
The liv - ing wa - ter; thirst - y one! Stoop down, and drink and live:"
Look un - to Me; thy morn shall rise, And all thy day be bright:"
:t, | d :d | d :r | d :l, | t, :t, | l, :l, | t, :t, .l, | se, :— | —
:se, | l, :l, | f, :r, | l, :l, | s, :s, | f, :m, | r, :re, | m, :— | —

G. t.m.l.

:ms, | s, :m | r :d | d :l, | s, :s, | d :r .m | f :m .r | r :— | —
:ms, .f, | m, :m, | f, :s, | l, :f, | d, :r, | m, :f, .s, | l, .t, :d | t, :— | —
I came to Je - sus as I was, Wea - ry, and worn, and sad:
I came to Je - sus, and I drank Of that life - giv - ing stream;
I looked to Je - sus, and I found, In Him, my Star, my Sun;
:dm .r | d : .s, | l, .t, :d | d :d .r | m :r | d :d .t, | d .r :m .f | s :— | —
:ms, | d :d, | d, .r, :m, | f, :l, .t, | d :t, | l, :l, .s, | f, :d, | s, :— | —

f — *ff*

:r | s :- .f | m :m | l :- .s | f :r | d :m | s :- .t, | d :— | —
:s, | s, :- .s, | s, :l, | l, :- .l, | l, :l, .t, | d :d | t, :- .s, | s, :— | —
I found in Him a rest - ing-place, And He has made me glad.
My thirst was quenched, my soul re - vived, And now I live in Him.
And, in that light of life, I'll walk Till trav - 'ling days are done.
:t, .d | r :- .r | d :de .r | m :- .m | r :f | m :s | f :- .f | m :— | —
:s, .l, | t, :- .t, | d :l, .t, | de :- .de | r :f, | s, :s, | s, :- .s, | d, :— | —

THE STORM.

f **354.** KEY F. *Lah is D. Maestoso.* BORNHARDT.

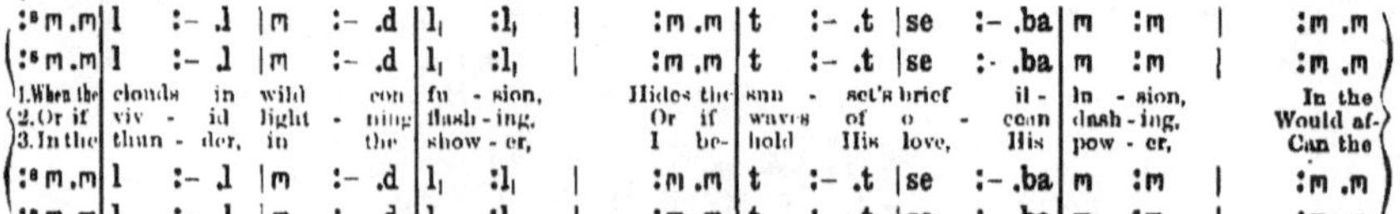

:m .m | l :- .l | m :- .d | l, :l, | :m .m | t :- .t | se :- .ba | m :m | :m .m
:m .m | l :- .l | m :- .d | l, :l, | :m .m | t :- .t | se :- .ba | m :m | :m .m
1. When the clouds in wild con fu - sion, Hides the sun - set's brief il - lu - sion, In the
2. Or if viv - id light - ning flash - ing, Or if waves of o - cean dash - ing, Would af-
3. In the thun - der, in the show - er, I be- hold His love, His pow - er, Can the
:m .m | l :- .l | m :- .d | l, :l, | :m .m | t :- .t | se :- .ba | m :m | :m .m
:m .m | l :- .l | m :- .d | l, :l, | :m .m | t :- .t | se :- .ba | m :m | :m .m

D.t.m.l. *p Andante.*

```
|l  :m  |d  :l,  |m  :-  |-  :m.f |s  :-.s |s.l :t.d' |r' :-.t |s  :s.s  |s  :-.s  |s.l :t.d' |
|l  :m  |d  :l,  |m  :-  |-  :d.r |m  :-.m |m   :m    |f  :-   |f  :f.f  |m  :-.m  |m   :m    |
 ter - ror  of the  night,  Still my  heart is cheer - ful  sing - - ing, Un-to  Hope's strong an-chor
 fright my  stead-fast  soul,  In the  Fa - ther's love a -  bid - - ing  I be-  hold the strife sub -
 true heart  stoop to  fear?  Lo, the  bow of prom - ise  cheer - ing, On the  eve - ning clouds ap -
|l  :m  |d  :l,  |m  :-  |-  :s.s |d' :-.d'|d'  :s    |s  :-   |t  :t.t  |d' :-.d' |d'  :d'   |
|l  :m  |d  :l,  |m  :-  |-  :d.d |d  :-.d |d   :d    |s  :-   |s  :s,.s,|d  :-.d  |d   :d    |

|r' :-.t |s  :s.s  |m' :m' |r' :r' |d' :-  |d' :t.l |s  :d' |t.d':r'.t |d' :-  |-  ||
|f  :-   |f  :s.s  |s  :s  |f  :f  |m  :-  |f  :f   |m  :m  |r.m :f.r  |m  :-  |-  ||
 cling - ing; Or in  storm or dusk - y  night, I a -  wait the cheer - ing  light.
 sid - - ing; Wave and  wind in His con -  trol May not  harm the trust - ing  soul.
 pear - ing! In the  west, now doub - ly  clear, Doth the  beauteous sun ap -  pear.
|t  :-   |r' :t.t  |d' :d' |t  :t  |d' :-  |l  :d'  |d' :s  |s   :s    |s  :-  |-  ||
|s  :-   |s  :s,.s,|d  :d  |s  :s  |l  :-  |f  :f   |s  :s  |s,  :s,   |d  :-  |-  ||
```

DAWSON.

355. Key C. U.

```
|d  :-.d |m  :s  |f  :l  |d' :s  |m' :-.m' |r' :t  |d' :m' |r' :-  |
|d  :-.d |d  :d  |d  :f  |s  :f  |m  :-.s  |s  :s  |s  :fe |s  :f  |
 1.Now, my soul, thy  voice up - rais - ing,  Tell, in sweet and  mourn-ful strain,
 2.Through His heart the  spear is pierc - ing,  Though His foes have  seen Him die;
 3.Je - sus, may these  pre - cious fount - ains  Drink to thirst - ing  souls af - ford;
|m  :-.m |s  :d' |l  :d' |d' :t  |d' :-.d' |t  :r' |d' :d' |t  :-  |
|d  :-.d |d  :m  |f  :f  |m  :r  |d  :-.d  |r  :f  |m  :r  |s  :-  |
```

r.s.d.f. A♭.

```
|m  :-.m  |r  :t,  |d  :l,  |s, :m,  |l, :-.t,  |d  :d  |r  :re  |m  :-  |
|s, :-.s, |s, :f,  |m, :f,  |m, :m,  |f, :-.s,  |s, :m, |l, :l,  |se, :- |
 How the Cru - ci -  fied, en - dur - ing  Grief, and wounds, and  dy - ing pain,
 Blood and wa - ter  thence are stream - ing  In a tide of  mys - ter - y,
 Let them be our  cup and heal - ing  And at length our  full re - ward;
|m  :-.d  |t, :r   |d  :d   |d  :d   |d  :-.d   |d  :d  |d  :t,  |t,  :- |
|d  :-.d  |s, :s,  |l, :f,  |d, :d,  |f, :-.f,  |m, :l, |f, :f,  |m,- :- |
```

C.t.m.l.r.

```
|d' :-.d' |s  :d' |t  :l  |s  :m  |f  :-.f  |m  :d  |m  :r  |d  :-  ||
|m  :-.m  |f  :s  |s  :f  |m  :d  |d  :-.d  |d  :d  |d  :t, |d  :-  ||
 Free - ly of His  love was off - ered,  Sin - less was for  sin - ners slain.
 Wa - ter from our  guilt to cleanse us,  Blood to win us  crowns on high.
 So a ran - somed  world shall ev - er  Praise Thee, its re -  deem - ing Lord.
|s  :-.d' |t  :d  |d' :d' |d' :s  |d' :-.d' |d' :s  |s  :f  |m  :-  ||
|d  :-.d  |r  :m  |f  :f  |d  :d  |l  :-.l  |s  :m  |s  :s, |d  :-  ||
```

THE LIGHT AT HOME.

356. KEY F. *Moderato.* Wm. Mason, Mus. Doc., by per.

:s, | l, :- .t, | d :r | m :l | s :m | d :d | f :m | r :- .d | r :s,
:s, | s, :- .s, | s, :t, | d :d | d :d | d :d | t, :d | t, :- .l, | t, :s,
1. The light at home! how bright it beams, When eve - ning shad - ows round us fall! And
2. When through the dark and storm - y night, The way - ward wan - d'rer home - ward hies, How
3. The light at home! how still and sweet, It peeps from you - der cot - tage door, The
:m | f :- .r | m :s | s :f | m :s | l :s | s :s | s :- .s | s :t,
:d | d :- .d | d :s, | d :d | d :d | f :m | r :d | s, :- .s, | s, :s,

| l, :- .t, | d :r | m :l | s :m | r :- .r | l :fe | s :— | — :r
| s, :- .f, | m, :s, | s, :d | t, :le, | t, :- .t, | d :d | t, :— | — :ta,
from the lat - tice far it gleams, To soothe and com - fort all. When
cheer - ing is that twink-ling light, Which through the gloom he spies! It
wea - ry la - bor - er to greet, When toils of day are o'er! Sad
| d :- .r | d :t, | d :m | m :s | s :- .s | fe :l | s :— | — :s
| s, :- .s, | l, :s, | d :l, | m :de | r :- .r | r :r | s, :— | — :s

r.s.d.f. D7.

| r :- .m | f :l | r' :d' | t :t re' | m' :d' | s :f | f :- .m | m :m | ba :se | l :t
| l, :- .de | r :m | r :r | r :r fe | s :m | m :r | r :- .d | d :d | m :m | m :m
wea - ried with the toils of day, And strife for glo - ry, gold or fame, How sweet to seek the
is the light at home; he feels That lov - ing hearts will meet him there, And soft - ly through his
is the soul that does not know The blessings that its beams im - part, The cheer-ful joys and
| l :- .s | f :m | f :fe | s :la d' | d' :s | l :t | t :- .d' | d' :d' | m' :r' | d' :t
| f :- .m | r :d | t, :l, | s, :f l, | s, :s, | s, :s, | d :- .d | d :d | d' :t | l :s

F.t.m.l.r.

| d' :- .t t :t s | d' :s | f :m | m :- .r | d :l, | l, :- .s, | l, :d | d :— | —
| m : .re | re :re t, | d :d | d :d | t, :- .t, | d :f, | m, :- .m, | m, :l, | s, :— | —
qui - et way, Where lov - ing lips will lisp our name, A - round the light at home.
bo - som steals, The joy and love that ban - ish care, A - round the light at home.
hopes that flow, And light-en up the heav - iest heart, A - round the light at home.
| l :- .l | l :l f | m :s | l :l | s :- .f | m :r | m :- .m | d :f | m :— | —
| fe :- .fe | fe :fe r | d :m, | f, :fe, | s, :- .s, | l, :t, | d :- .d | l, :f, | d, :— | —

APRIL.

357. KEY A. *Allegretto.* H. E. Nichol.

:s, | s, :l, :t, | d :t, :l, | t, :— :— | t, :— :d | r :m :f | f :m :r | m :— :— | — : :s,
:s, | s, :— :s, | s, :— :s, | s, :— :— | s, :— :s, | s, :— :s, | t, :— :t, | d :— :— | — : :s,
1. She comes to us a maid - en, With half a - vert - ed face, (Her) Her
2. She loves to hide her blush - es Be - hind a veil of show'r, (But) But
3. We can - not choose but love her, A maid and still a child; (The) The
:m | m :— :m | m :— :m | f :— :— | f :— :m | r :— :r | s :— :s | s :— :— | — : :m
:d | d :— :d | s, :— :s, | r :— :— | s, :— :l, | t, :— :t, | s, :— :s, | d :— :— | s, :— :—

E.t.

| s_1 :l_1 :t_1 | d :t_1 :l_1 | r :— :— | r :— :^{r}s | se :— :se | se :be :se | l :— :— | d^1 :— :— |
| s_1 :— :s_1 | s_1 :— :s_1 | s_1 :— :— | s_1 :— :^{s}d | r :— :r | r :— :r | d :— :— | ma :— :— |
hands with buds are la - - den, Her form is full of grace, Her
soon her weep - ing blush - es, Grown hap - py in an hour, Grown
stars are bright a - bove her, The ver - y winds are mild, The
| m :— :m | m :— :m | r :— :— | r :— :^{s}d^1 | t :— :t | t :— :t | l :— :— | l :— :— |
| d :— :d | l_1 :— :l_1 | t_1 :— :— | t_1 : :^{t}m_1 | m_1 :— :m_1 | m_1 :— :m_1 | f_1 :— :— | fe_1 :— :— |

r.s.d.f.C. *Lah is A.*

| s :m :s | m :— :r | d :— :— | — : :^{d}m | ba :se :l | l :se :ba | se :— :— | t :— :t |
| m :— :d | t_1 :— :t_1 | d :— :— | — : :^{d}m | m :— :m | m :— :m | m :— :— | m :— :m |
form is full of grace, So ten - der, shy, ca - pri - cious, So
hap - py in an hour, She pours a tide of splen - dor O'er
ver - y winds are mild, She sets our feet to danc - ing, She
| d^1 :— :m | f :— :f | m :— :— | — : :^{m}se | l :t :d^1 | d^1 :t :l | t :— :— | se :— :se |
| s_1 :— :s_1 | s_1 :— :s_1 | d :— :— | — : :^{d}m | m :— :— | m :— :— | m :— :— | m :— :— |
So ten - - der, shy, ca - -
She pours, etc.
She sets, etc.

A.t.m.l. *rall.*

| d^1 :r^1 :m^1 | m^1 :r^1 :d^1 | t :— :r^1 | m^1 :— :d^1 | ^{t}r :— :t_1 | d :— :l_1 | r :— :— | s_1 :— ||
| m :— :m | m :— :m | m :— :m | m :— :m | ^{m}s_1 :— :s_1 | fe_1 :— :fe_1 | f_1 :— :— | — :— ||
dew - y, sweet and fair, so sweet and fair, so sweet and fair.
all the wait - ing earth, o'er all the wait - ing, wait - ing earth.
stirs our hearts to praise, our hearts to praise, our hearts to praise.
| l :t :d^1 | d^1 :t :l | se :— :t | d^1 :— :l | ^{se}t_1 :— :r | l_1 :— :d | d :— :— | t_1 :— ||
| m :— :— | m :— :m | m :— :— | m :— :— | ^{m}s_1 :— :— | s_1 :— :— | s_1 :— :— | — :— ||
pri - - - cious, so dew - - y, sweet and fair.

a tempo.

| :s_1 | s_1 :l_1 :t_1 | d :t_1 :l_1 | t :— :— | t_1 :— :d | r :m :f | f :m :r | m :— :— | — :— :f |
| :s_1 | s_1 :— :s_1 | s_1 :— :s_1 | s_1 :— :— | s_1 :— :s_1 | s_1 :— :s_1 | t_1 :— :t_1 | d :— :— | t_1 :— :t_1 |
Our A - pril is de - li - - cious, What - ev - er guise she wear: Our
Our A - pril, sad and ten - - der, Or gay and full of mirth; Our
Our dar - ling A - pril, glanc - ing A - long the gold - en days: Our
| :f | m :— :m | m :— :m | f :— :— | f :— :m | r :— :r | s :— :s | s :— :— | — :— :s |
| :s_1 | d :— :d | s_1 :— :s_1 | r :— :— | s_1 :— :l_1 | t_1 :— :t_1 | s_1 :— :s_1 | d :— :d_1 | r_1 :— :r_1 |
Our A - pril
Our A - pril, etc.
Our dar - ling, etc.

FAREWELL.

P. DAVID.

f 358. KEY D. *f* A.t.

:s |d' :-.s |m :f |s :-.m |d :d |r :— |f :— |m :— |— :s |d' :-.s |$^{m}l_1$:t_1
:s |d' :-.s |m :f |s :-.m |d :d |d :— |t_1 :— |d :— |— :s |d' :-.s |$^{m}l_1$:t_1
1.Fare-|well! the nev - er - |more has come, *p* the |nev - - er - - |more! Fare - |well! the nev - er -
2.Then |wel - come bold - er |life, wide air, *f* and |larg - - er |scope, Then |wel - come bold - er
3.Fare-|well! yet where-so - |e'er you go, *p* we |breathe a |spell, Fare - |well! yet where-so -
:s |d' :-.s |m :f |s :-.m |d :d |s :— |s :— |s :— |— :s |d' :-.s |$^{m}l_1$:t_1
:s |d' :-.s |m :f |s :-.m |d :d |s_1 :— |s_1 :— |d :— |— :s |d' :-.s |$^{m}l_1$:t_1

f.D. *Animato.*

|d :-.t_1 |l_1 :d |m :— |m :— |l_1 :— |— :^{l}m |f :-.m |f :l |m :-.f |m :m
|d :-.t_1 |l_1 :l_1 |l_1 :— |se_1 :— |m_1 :— |— :^{l}m |r :-.d |r :r |d :-.r |d :d
|more has come, *p* the |nev - er - |more! In |boy - hood's fair - y - |land, I ween, With
|life, wide air, *f* and |larg - er |scope; A |bon - ny wel - come, |bon - ny world, A
|e'er you go, *p* we |breathe a |spell; A |thous - and sprites at |our command, 'Twixt
|d' :-.t_1 |l_1 :d |d :— |t_1 :— |d :— |— :^{l}m |l :-.l |l :f |m :-.l |l :l
|d' :-.t_1 |l_1 :m_1 |m_1 :— |m_1 :— |l_1 :— |— :^{l}m |r :-.l_1 |r :f_1 |l_1 :-.l_1 |l_1 :l_1

F. t.m.l.r.

|f :-.m |f :l |d' :-.t |l :m |r' :— |d' :— |^{t}s :— |— :m |s :— |f :r
|r :-.d |r :r |m :-.r |d :m |m :— |m :— |^{m}d :— |— :d |d :— |t_1 :—
|Fan - cy, boy-hood's |fair - y queen, *f* On |life's great |shore, on |life's great
|bon - ny light on |sails unfurl'd, *f* Oh! |wel - come |hope, oh! |wel - come
|you and us, from |fair - y - land; *p* Brook |no fare - |well, brook |no fare -
|l :-.l |l :f |l :-.m m :d' |t :— |l :— |^{se}m :— |— :s |m :— |r :f
|r :-.m |r :f_1 |l_1 :-.l_1 |l_1 :l_1 |se_1 :— |l_1 :— |$^{t}s_1$:— |— :s_1 |s_1 :— |s_1 :—

r.s.d.f.D.

|^{d}m :— |— :m |t :— |— :m |d' :— |— :m |se :— |— :m |l :— |— :—
|^{d}m :— |— :m |m :— |— :m |m :— |— :m |m :— |— :m |m :— |— :—
| | |r : |— :m |d :— |— :m |t_1 :— |— :m |d :m |— :—
|shore. *f* To |stand and |work, and |dream and |dream, ...
|hope. *p* Then |go, then |go, the |while, the |while. . . . .
|well! *p* Fare - |well, the |good old |days live |on. . . . .
|^{m}se :— |— : |:m |se : |:m |l : |:m |t : |:d' |d' :—
To stand, to stand, and work, and dream, and dream.
Then go, then go, then go, the while, the while,
Fare - well, the good old days live on, live on.
|^{d}m :m |m : |:m |se : |:m |l : | : | | :m |d' :t
| | |:m_1 |se_1 : |:m_1 |l_1 : | | |To stand on
The while our
The good old

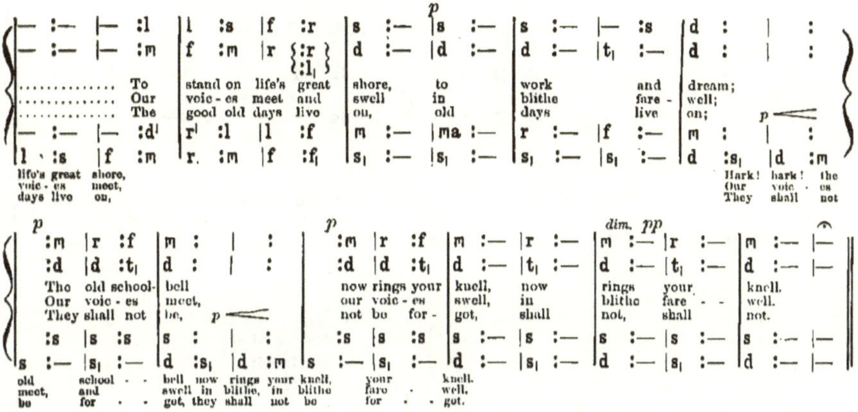

— :—	— :l	l :s	f :r	s :—	s :—	s :—	— :s	d :	:
— :—	— :m	f :m	r :r :l,	d :—	d :—	d :—	t, :—	d :	:
.... To	stand on life's great	shore, to	work and	dream;
.... Our	voic - es meet and	swell in	blithe fare -	well;
.... The	good old days live	on, old	days live	on;
— :—	— :d'	r' :l	l :f	m :—	ma :—	r :—	f :—	m :	:
l :s	f :m	r :m	f :f,	s, :—	s, :—	s, :—	s, :—	d :s,	d :m

life's great shore, / voic - es meet, / days live on, ... Hark! hark! the / Our voic - es / They shall not

p *p* *dim. pp*

:m	r :f	m :	:	:m	r :f	m :—	r :—	m :—	r :—	m :—	—
:d	d :t,	d :	:	:d	d :t,	d :—	t, :—	d :—	t, :—	d :—	—
The old school-	bell	now rings your	knell, now	rings your	knell.
Our voic - es	meet,	our voic - es	swell, in	blithe fare - -	well.
They shall not	be,	not be for -	got, shall	not, shall	not.
:s	s :s	s :	:	:s	s :s	s :—	s :—	s :—	s :—	s :—	—
s :—	s, :—	d :s,	d :m	s :—	s, :—	d :—	s, :—	d :—	s, :—	d :—	—

old school - - / meet, and / be for - - ; bell now rings your knell, / swell in blithe, in blithe / got, they shall not be ; your knell. / fare - well. / for - - got.

MIDNIGHT CRY.

350. KEY C. Sir G. A. MACFARREN.

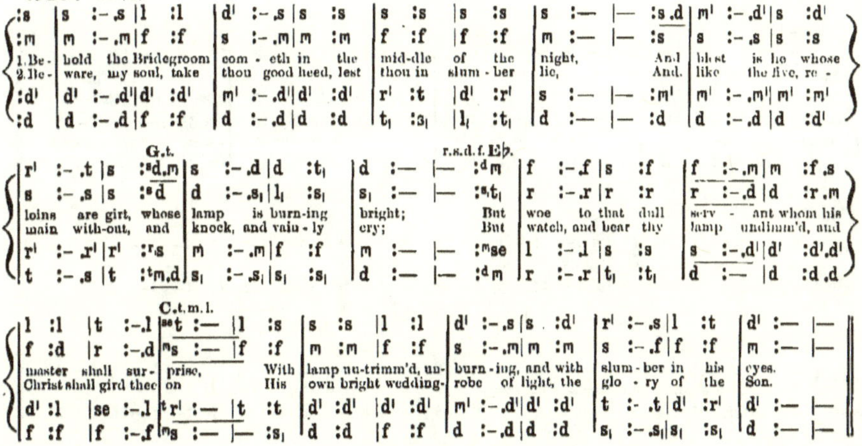

:s	s :-.s	l :l	d' :-.s	s :s	s :s	s :s	s :—	— :s.d	m' :-.d'	s :d'
:m	m :-.m	f :f	s :-.m	m :m	f :f	f :f	m :—	— :s	s :-.s	s :s
1. Be-	hold the Bridegroom	com - eth in the	mid-dle of the	night, And	blest is he whose
2. Be-	ware, my soul, take	thou good heed, lest	thou in slum - ber	lie, And	like the five, re -
:d'	d' :-.d'	d' :d'	m' :-.d'	d' :d'	r' :t	d' :r'	s :—	— :m'	m' :-.m'	m' :m'
:d	d :-.d	f :f	d :-.d	d :d	t, :s,	l, :t,	d :—	— :d	d :-.d	d :d'

G.t. r.s.d.f. E♭.

r' :-.t	s :ˢd.m	s :-.d	d :t,	d :—	— :ᵈm	f :-.f	s :f	f :-.m	m :f.s
s :-.s	s :ˢd	d :-.s,	l, :s,	s, :—	— :ˢt,	r :-.r	r :r	r :-.d	d :r.m
loins are girt, whose	lamp is burn-ing	bright; But	woe to that dull	serv - ant whom his
main with-out, and	knock, and vain - ly	cry; But	watch, and bear thy	lamp undimm'd, and
r' :-.r'	r' :ʳs	m :-.m	f :f	m :—	— :ᵐse	l :-.l	s :s	s :-.d'	d' :d'.d'
t :-.s	t :ᵗm.d	s, :-.s,	s, :s,	d :—	— :ᵈm	r :-.r	t, :t,	d :—	d :d.d

C.t.m.l.

l :l	t :-.l	ˢᵉt :—	l :s	s :s	l :l	d' :-.s	s :d'	r' :-.s	l :t	d' :—	—
f :d	r :-.d	ᵐs :—	f :f	m :m	f :f	s :-.m	m :m	s :-.f	f :f	m :—	—
master shall sur-	prise, With	lamp un-trimm'd, un-	burn - ing, and with	slum - ber in his	eyes.
Christ shall gird thee	on His	own bright wedding-	robe of light, the	glo - ry of the	Son.
d' :l	se :-.l	ᵗr' :—	t :t	d' :d'	d' :d'	m' :-.d'	d' :d'	t :-.t	d' :r'	d' :—	—
f :f	f :-.f	ᵐs :—	— :s,	d :d	f :f	d :-.d	d :d	s, :-.s,	s, :s,	d :—	—

JACK AND JILL.

p **300.** KEY F. *Lah is D.*

SOP.	m :— :m	r :— :f	m :— :m	r :— :f	m :— :l	d' :— :t	t :— :—	l :— :—
	Jack and	Jill went	up the	hill, To	fetch a	pail of	wa -	- ter;
ALTO.	d :— :d	t_1 :— :r	d :— :d	t_1 :— :r	d :— :d	m :— :r	r :— :—	d :— :—

ff FINE.

S. & T.	d' :— :t	l :— :s	f :— :m	r :— :d.r	m :— :r	d :— :t_1	l_1 :— :—	l_1 :— :
	Jack fell	down and	broke his	crown, And	Jill came	tum - bling	af -	- ter.
A. & B.	d :— :t_1	l_1 :— :s_1	f :— :m	r :— :d.r	m :— :r	d :— :t_1	l_1 :— :—	l_1 :— :

𝄋 *p*

d :— :m	r :— :m	d :— :s_1	m_1 :— :s_1	d :— :m	r :— :m	d :— :—	d :— :
Goos - ey,	goos - ey	gan - -	der, Oh,	whith - er	dost thou	wan -	- der?
m_1 :— :s_1	f_1 :— :s_1	m_1 :— :—	m_1 :— :m_1	m_1 :— :s_1	f_1 :— :s_1	m_1 :— :—	m_1 :— :
d :s_1 :s_1	s_1 :s_1 :s_1	s_1 :s_1 :s_1	s_1 :s_1 :s_1	s_1 :— :s_1	s_1 :s_1 :s_1	s_1 :— :—	: :t_1
Hey, did-dle,	did-dle, the	cat and the	fid - dle, The	cow jumped	o - ver the	moon:	The
d_1 :d_1 :d_1	d_1 :d_1 :d_1	d_1 :d_1 :d_1	d_1 :d_1 :d_1	d_1 :— :d_1	d_1 :d_1 :d_1	d_1 :— :—	: :m_1

f A.t.m.l.r   r.s.d.f. F.   D.S.

ᵐd :— :m	r :— :m	d :— :s_1	m_1 :— :s_1	d :— :m	r :— :m	ᵈm :— :—	m :— :
Up	stairs and	down	stairs, And	in my	la - - dy's	cham -	- ber.
ˢᵉm_1 :— :s_1	f_1 :— :s_1	m_1 :— :—	m_1 :— :m_1	m_1 :— :s_1	f_1 :— :s_1	ᵐse_1 :— :—	se_1 :— :
ᵗs_1 :s_1 :s_1	s_1 :— :s_1	s_1 :— :s_1	s_1 :s_1 :s_1	s_1 :s_1 :s_1	s_1 :s_1 :s_1	ˢt_1 :— :—	— :— :
lit - tle	dog laugh'd to	see	such sport, And the	dish ran	a - way with the	spoon.	
d_1 :d_1 :d_1	d_1 :— :d_1	d_1 :— :d_1	d_1 :d_1 :d_1	d_1 :d_1 :d_1	d_1 :d_1 :d_1	ᵈm_1 :— :—	— :— :

p

SOP.	m :— :m	r :— :f	m :— :m	r :— :f	m :— :l	d' :— :t	t :— :—	l :— :—
	Jack and	Jill went	up the	hill, To	fetch a	pail of	wa -	- ter;
ALTO.	d :— :d	t_1 :— :r	d :— :d	t_1 :— :r	d :— :d	m :— :r	r :— :—	d :— :—

ff

S. & T.	d' :— :t	l :— :s	f :— :m	r :— :d.r	m :— :r	d :— :t_1	l_1 :— :—	l_1 :— :
	Jack fell	down and	broke his	crown, And	Jill came	tum - bling	af -	- ter.
A. & B.	d :— :t_1	l_1 :— :s_1	f :— :m	r :— :d.r	m :— :r	d :— :t_1	l_1 :— :—	l_1 :— :

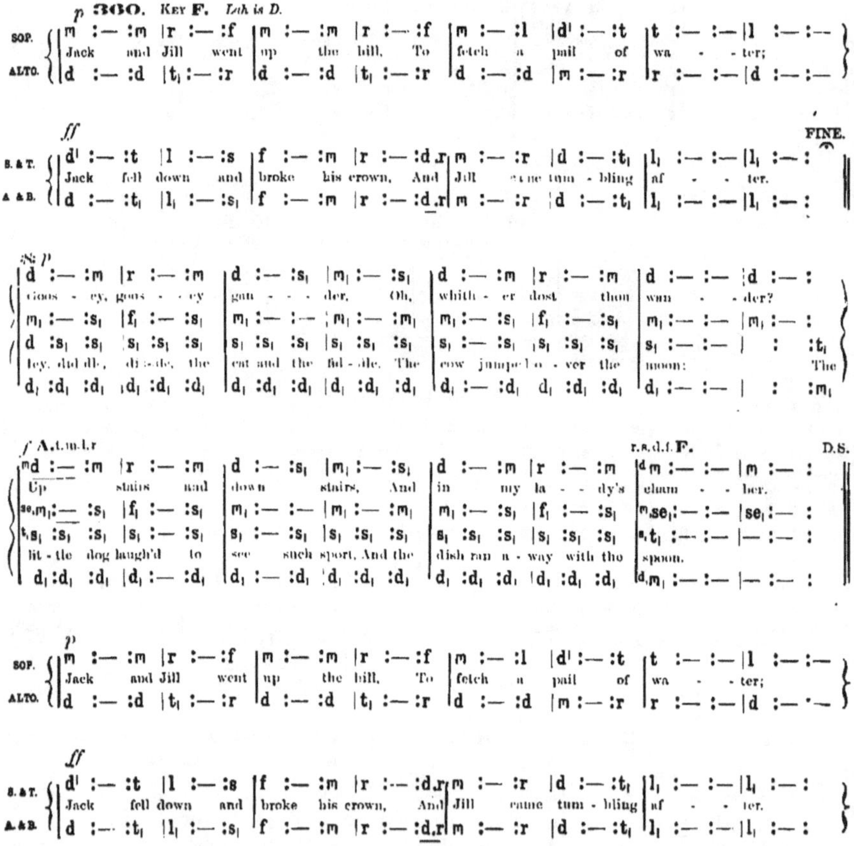

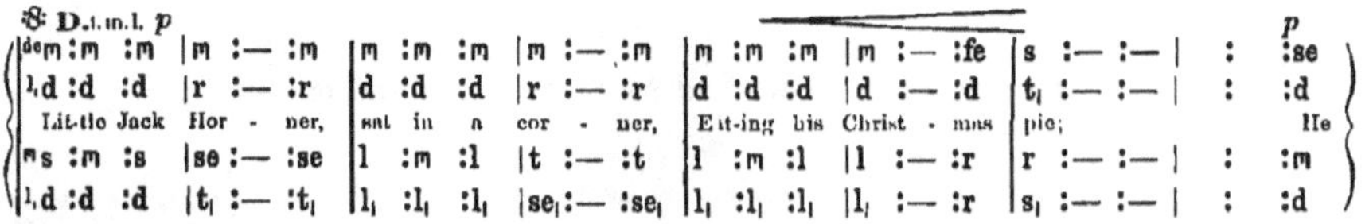

𝄋 D.t.m.l. *p*

ᵈᵉm :m :m	m :— :m	m :m :m	m :— :m	m :m :m	m :— :fe	s :— :—	: :se
ˡ.d :d :d	r :— :r	d :d :d	r :— :r	d :d :d	d :— :d	t_1 :— :—	: :d
Lit-tle Jack Hor - ner,	sat in a cor - ner,	Eat-ing his Christ - mas	pie; He
ᵐs :m :s	se :— :se	l :m :l	t :— :t	l :m :l	l :— :r	r :— :—	: :m
ˡ.d :d :d	t_1 :— :t_1	l_1 :l_1 :l_1	se_1 :— :se_1	l_1 :l_1 :l_1	l_1 :— :r	s_1 :— :—	: :d

ff — *1st time.* D.S. — *2d time.* s.d.f F. D.C.

l :l :l	l :- :l	l :l :l	l :l :l	l :l :l	l :- :t	d' :- :-	: :	ᵈ'l :- :	: :
d :d :d	de :- :de	r :r :r	m :m :m	f :f :f	f :- :f	m :- :-	: :	ᵐde :- :	: :
put in his thumb, and	pulled out a plum, And said	"what a good boy am	I."	I."
f :f :f	s :- :s	f :f :f	s :s :s	f :r :l	s :- :s	s :- :-	: :	ˢm :- :	: :
f :f :f	m :- :m	r :r :r	de :de :de	r :r :r	s :- :s_1	d :- :-	: :	ᵈl_1 :- :	: :

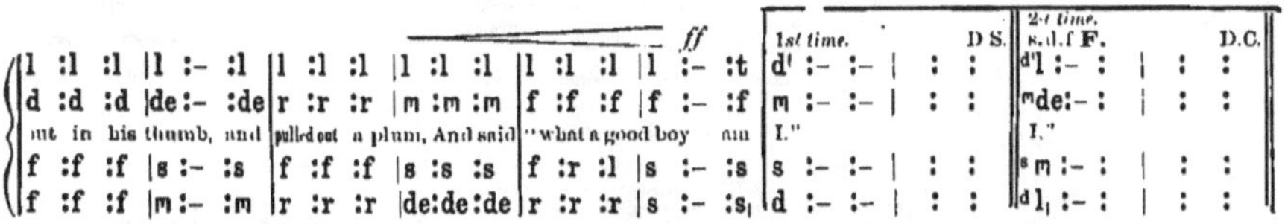

ALL MERRILY SINGING.

From "Faust."

(Note.—The first movement is to be sung as a round in four parts, the Soprano, Alto, Tenor and Base following each other consecutively.)

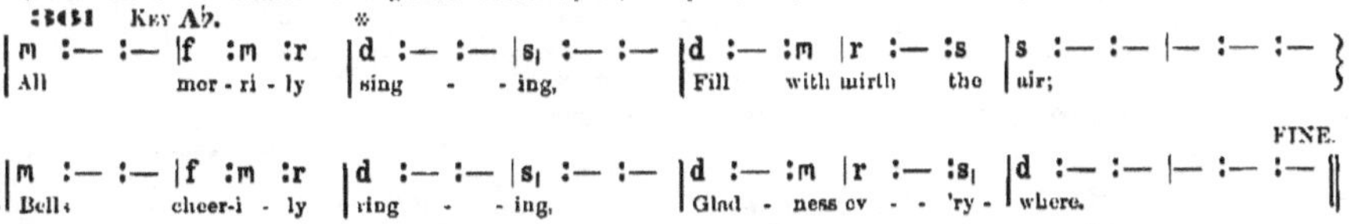

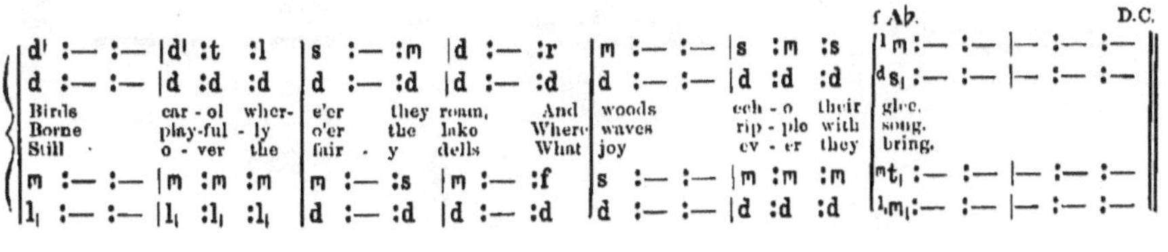

:3431 KEY A♭. ※

| m :— :— | f :m :r | d :— :— | s_1 :— :— | d :— :m | r :— :s | s :— :— | — :— :— |
| All mer - ri - ly | sing - - ing, | Fill with mirth the | air; |

FINE.

| m :— :— | f :m :r | d :— :— | s_1 :— :— | d :— :m | r :— :s_1 | d :— :— | — :— :— ||
| Bells cheer-i - ly | ring - - ing, | Glad - ness ev - - 'ry - | where. |

E♭.t.

ˢ.d' :— :—	d' :t :l	s :— :m	d :— :r	m :— :—	s :m :s	l :— :—	— :— :—
ˢ.d :— :—	d :d :d	d :— :d	d :— :d	d :— :—	d :d :d	d :— :—	— :— :—
1. Far o - ver the	fields they come, With	hearts mer - ry and	free,
2. Glad mel - o - dy	fills the breeze, And	glides gai - ly a -	long,
3. O beau-ti - ful	sil - - ver bells, That	ring, cheer-i - ly	ring,
ᵗm :— :—	m :m :m	m :— :s	m :— :f	s :— :—	m :m :m	m :— :—	— :— :—
ᵐl_1 :— :—	l_1 :l_1 :l_1	d :— :d	d :— :d	d :— :—	d :d :d	l_1 :— :—	— :— :—

f A♭. D.C.

d' :— :—	d' :t :l	s :— :m	d :— :r	m :— :—	s :m :s	ˡm :— :—	— :— :—	
d :— :—	d :d :d	d :— :d	d :— :d	d :— :—	d :d :d	ᵈs_1 :— :—	— :— :—	
Birds car - ol wher-	e'er they roam, And	woods ech - o their	glee.
Borne play-ful - ly	o'er the lake Where	waves rip - ple with	song.
Still o - ver the	fair - y dells What	joy ev - er they	bring.
m :— :—	m :m :m	m :— :s	m :— :f	s :— :—	m :m :m	ᵐt_1 :— :—	— :— :—	
l_1 :— :—	l_1 :l_1 :l_1	d :— :d	d :— :d	d :— :—	d :d :d	ˡm_1 :— :—	— :— :—	

QUESTIONS FOR WRITTEN OR ORAL EXAMINATION.

DOCTRINE.

1. What are transitions to the first sharp or first flat keys called?
2. What are transitions to the second sharp or second flat keys called?
3. What interval, upward or downward, is the music moved in two sharp removes?
4. What tones of the old key are omitted?
5. What new tones are introduced?
6. Which of these is the more important, and why?
7. Where is this new tone placed in the signature?
8. In two flat removes, by what interval, upward or downward, is the music moved?
9. What tones of the old key are omitted?
10. What new tones take their places?
11. Which of these is the more important, and why?
12. Where is this new tone placed in the signature?
13. What is the mental effect of two sharp removes? Of two flat removes?
14. What is oscillating transition?
15. What are transitions to third sharp or third flat keys called?
16. In three sharp removes, by what interval, upward or downward, is the new key moved? In three flat removes?
17. In three sharp removes, what does *Lah* become?
18. In three flat removes, what does *Doh* become?
19. On account of the relation between *Lah* and *Doh* of the two keys, transitions of three removes are commonly what?
20. What is the mental effect of a transitional modulation of three flat removes? Of three sharp removes?
21. In three sharp removes, what tones of the old key are displaced?
22. What new tones take their places?
23. Which of these is the last new sharp, and where is it placed in the signature?
24. In three flat removes, what tones are displaced?
25. What new tones take their places?
26. Which is the last new flat and where is it placed in the signature?
27. In transitions of *four sharp removes*, by what interval, upward or downward, is the new key placed? *In four flat removes?*
28. In four flat removes, what does *Doh* become?
29. In four sharp removes, what does *Me* become?
30. In four flat removes, what tones are displaced?
31. What new tones take their places?
32. Which of these is the last new flat, and where is it placed in the signature?
33. In four sharp removes, what tones are displaced?
34. What new tones take their places?
35. Which of these is the last new sharp, and where is it placed in the signature?
36. What is the commencing, closing and prevailing key of a tune called?
37. What are the other keys called?
38. What are transitions from and to the Principal key called?
39. What are the transitions between the Subordinate keys called?

PRACTICE.

40. Follow the Examiner's pointing in a voluntary containing transitions of two or three removes.
41. Sing your part in Exs. 340, 342, 344, which the Examiner may select.
42. Sing your part in Exs. 351, 353, 354, which the Examiner may select.
43. Sing your part in Exs. 355, 359, which the Examiner may select.
44. Sol-fa and point on the modulator from memory an example containing transitions of two and three removes.
45. Write from memory a similar example.

MISCELLANEOUS.

SLUMBER SWEETLY.

(SERENADE.)

Wm. Mason, Mus. Doc., by per.

Key B♭. *Dolce. Sempre e legato.*

m, :f, :fe,	s, :d :m	r :— :d	t, :— :l,	s, :— :t,.l,	s, :f :m	r :— :d	s, :— :
d, :r, :re,	m, :— :s,	se, :— :l,	s, :— :f,	r, :re, :m,	f, :l, :s,	m, :f, :m,	d, :r, :re,
Slum - -	- ber	sweet - ly,	dear - est,	Close	thy	wea - ry	eyes.
d :t, :l,	s, :m :d	t, :— :d	f :d :l,	t, :d :de	r :t, :s,	s, :l, :s,	m, :f, :fe,
d, :— :—	— :— :d,	f, :— :—	f, :— :—	s, :— :—	s,, :— :—	d, :— :—	— :— :—
Slum - -	- bor	sweet -	ly,	Close	thine	eyes,	

F.t.

m, :f, :fe	s, :d :m	^{m}l :— :s	s :— :f	m :d :f	m :— :r	d :— :—	— :— :
m, :r, :re,	m, :— :s,	^{fe,}t, :d :de	r :t, :s,	d :— :d	d :l, :t,	d :— :l,	s, :— :
Guard - ian an -	gels	round thee ho -	ver	Till the	morn - ing	rise,	
s, :t, :l,	s, :m :d	^{l,}r :re :m	f :r :t,	d :m :l	s :fe :f	m :— :f	m :— :
d, :— :d,	d, :— :d,	^{r,}s, :— :s,	s, :— :s,	d, :— :d,	s, :— :s,	d :— :—	— :— :

f.B♭.

^{s}r :— :de	r :f :m	r :d :l,	s, :— :d	s, :— :s,	s, :fe, :s,
^{t_s,}f, :— :m,	f, :l, :s,	m, :— :m,	m, :r, :d,	t,, :d, :de,	r, :— :r,
Then may	love on	air - y	pin - ions,	Bear thy	heart in
^{m}t, :s, :le,	t, :s, :t,	d :— :d	d :s, :m,	s, :l, :le,	t, :l, :s,
^{d,}s,, :— :s,,	s,, :— :s,,	d, :m, :s,	d, :— :d,	s,, :— :s,,	s,, :— :s,,

l, :s, :fe,	s, :— :	m, :f, :fe,	s, :d :m	r :— :d	t, :d :l,
re, :m, :re,	m, :— :	d, :r, :re,	m, :— :s,	se, :— :l,	se, :l, :f,
trans - port	bound,	To its	own do -	min - ions,	Where no
fe, :s, :l,	s, :— :	d :t, :l,	s, :m :d	t, :— :d	r :d :d
d, :— :d,	d, :— :	d, :— :d,	d, :— :d,	f, :— :f,	f, :— :f,

Ritard.

s, :d :m	r :— :s,	d :— :—	s :— :s	s :— :—	s, :m, :s,	d :— :—	— :— :
m, :— :s,	fe, :— :f,	m, :— :—	s, :l, :t,	d :— :—	m, :— :r,	d, :— :—	— :— :
earth - ly	care is	found;	Maid - en	sleep,	Maid - en	sleep.	
d :— :d	l, :— :t,	d :— :—	t, :d :r	m :— :—	s, :— :f,	m, :— :—	— :— :
s, :— :s,,	s,, :r, :s,	d, :— :—	s,, :— :s,,	d, :— :—	s,, :— :s,,	d, :— :—	— :— :

MY DREAM.

KEY A♭. (SONG WITH VOCAL ACCOMPANIMENT.) T. F. SEWARD, by per.

	.s_1 :d .r	m :- .d :t_1 .d	r :- .s_1 :r .m	f :- .l :s .f	m : .s_1 :d .r
	1. In light and	shade the soft winds	played, Where clo-ver	blooms a-long the	stream; Bent low the
	2. And bask-ing	there in perfumed	air, And in the	sun - -shine's golden	beam, Two hearts a -
SOP.	:	*pp* s_1 .s_1 :s_1 :s_1	s_1 .s_1 :s_1 :s_1	s_1 .s_1 :s_1 :s_1	s_1 .s_1 :s_1 :s_1
ALTO.	:	m_1 .m_1 :m_1 :m_1	f_1 .f_1 :f_1 :f_1	r_1 .r_1 :r_1 :r_1	m_1 .m_1 :m_1 :m_1
		La la la la	la la la la	la la la la	la la la la
TENOR.	:	d .d :d :d	t_1 .t_1 :t_1 :t_1	t_1 .t_1 :t_1 :t_1	d .d :d :d
BASE.	:	d_1 .d_1 :d_1 :d_1	s_1 .s_1 :s_1 :s_1	s_1 .s_1 :s_1 :s_1	d_1 .d_1 :d_1 :d_1

m :- .d :t_1 .d	l_1 :- .l :s .f	m :-.re,m :f .t_1	d :— :- .m	m,f.m,f:m .se :t .m
sip with hon-ied	lip. The fleeting	bub - ble's laughing	gleam. And	all day long their
lone, two hands as	one. Went wand'ring	by the list'ning	stream. And	murm'ring flow and
s_1 .s_1 :s_1 :s_1	l_1 .l_1 :l_1 :l_1	s_1 .s_1 :s_1 :s_1	s_1 .s_1 :s_1 :	t_1 .t_1 :t_1 :t_1
m_1 .m_1 :m_1 :m_1	f_1 .f_1 :f_1 :f_1	m_1 .m_1 :m_1 :r_1 .f_1	m_1 .m_1 :m_1 :	se_1 .se_1 :se_1 :se_1
la la la la	la la la la	la la la la	la la la	La la la la
d .d :d :d	d .d :d :d	d .d :d :r	d .d :d :	m .m :m :m
d_1 .d_1 :d_1 :d_1	f_1 .f_1 :f_1 :f_1	s_1 .s_1 :s_1 :s_1	d_1 .d_1 :d_1 :	m_1 .m_1 :m_1 :m_1

m,f.m,f:m .d :l_1 .d	r,m.r,m:r .s :fe .l	s :- .s_1 :d .r	m :- .d :t_1 .d	r :- .s_1 :r .m
sweet wild song. The	birds were chanting in my	dream. In light and	shade the soft winds	played, Where clo-ver
whis-pers low, Were	strangely mingled in my	dream. And basking	there in perfumed	air, And in the
d .d :d :d	*ff* t_1 .t_1 :t_1 :d	t_1 : :	*pp* s_1 .s_1 :s_1 :s_1	s_1 .s_1 :s_1 :s_1
l_1 .l_1 :l_1 :l_1	s_1 .s_1 :s_1 :l_1	s_1 : :	m_1 .m_1 :m_1 :m_1	f_1 .f_1 :f_1 :f_1
la la la la	la la la la	la.	La la la la	la la la la
m .m :m :m	r .r :r :r	r : :	d .d :d :d	t_1 .t_1 :t_1 :t_1
l_1 .l_1 :l_1 :l_1	r .r :r :r_1	s_1 : :	d_1 .d_1 :d_1 :d_1	s_1 .s_1 :s_1 :s_1

f :- .l :s .f	m :- .s_1 :d .r	m :- .d :t_1 .d	l_1 :- .l :s .f	m :-.re,m :f .t_1
blooms a-long the	stream; Bent low to	sip with hon-ied	lip. The fleet-ing	bub - ble's laughing
sun - shine's golden	beam, Two hearts a -	lone, two hands as	one, Went wand'ring	by the list'ning
s_1 .s_1 :s_1 :s_1	s_1 .s_1 :s_1 :s_1	s_1 .s_1 :s_1 :s_1	l_1 .l_1 :l_1 :l_1	s_1 .s_1 :s_1 :s_1
r_1 .r_1 :r_1 :r_1	m_1 .m_1 :m_1 :m_1	m_1 .m_1 :m_1 :m_1	f_1 .f_1 :f_1 :f_1	m_1 .m_1 :m_1 :r_1 .f_1
la la la la	la la la la	la la la la	la la la la	la la la la
t_1 .t_1 :t_1 :t_1	d .d :d :d	d .d :d :d	d .d :d :d	d .d :d :r
s_1 .s_1 :s_1 :s_1	d_1 .d_1 :d_1 :d_1	d_1 .d_1 :d_1 :d_1	f_1 .f_1 :f_1 :f_1	s_1 .s_1 :s_1 :s_1

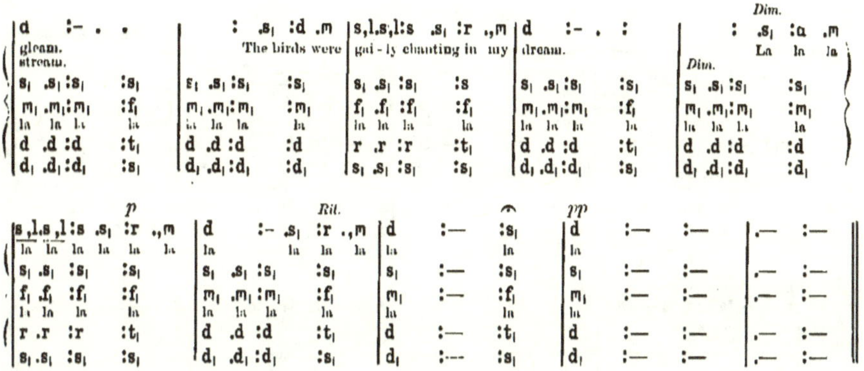

Dim.

d :- . .	: .s, :d .m	s,l.s,l:s .s, :r .,m	d :- . :	: .s, :d .m
gleam. / stream.	The birds were	gai - ly chanting in my	dream.	La la la
s, .s, :s, :s,	s, .s, :s, :s,	s, .s, :s, :s	s, .s, :s, :s,	s, .s, :s, :s,
m, .m, :m, :f,	m, .m, :m, :m,	f, .f, :f, :f,	m, .m, :m, :f,	m, .m, :m, :m,
la la la la	la la la la	la la la la	la la la la	la la la la
d .d :d :t,	d .d :d :d	r .r :r :t,	d .d :d :t,	d .d :d :d
d, .d, :d, :s,	d, .d, :d, :d,	s, .s, :s, :s,	d, .d, :d, :s,	d, .d, :d, :d,

p s,l.s,l:s .s, :r .,m	*Rit.* d :- .s, :r .,m	d :— :s,	*pp* d :— :—	.— :—
la la la la la la	la la la la	la la	la	
s, .s, :s, :s,	s, .s, :s, :s,	s, :— :s,	s, :— :—	.— :—
f, .f, :f, :f,	m, .m, :m, :f,	m, :— :f,	m, :— :—	.— :—
la la la la	la la la la	la la	la	
r .r :r :t,	d .d :d :t,	d :— :t,	d :— :—	.— :—
s, .s, :s, :s,	d, .d, :d, :s,	d, :— :s,	d, :— :—	.— :—

Key Ab.

SUPPORT.

E. Cornhill.

mf d :— |d :d	d :— |d :—	d :d |d :d	r :— |— :—	*p Dim.* m :— |m :m
s, :— |l, :l,	s, :— |d :—	d :l, |s, :fe,	s, :— |— :—	s, :— |t, :t,
1. Here, Lord, by	faith, I	see Thee face to	face,	Here would I
2. I have no	help but	Thine, nor do I	need	An - oth - er
3. I have no	wis - dom	save in Him, who	is	My wis - dom
m :— |f :f	m :— |m :—	s :f |m :r	r :— |— :—	d :— |m :r
d :— |f, :f,	d :— |d, :—	m, :f, |s, :l,	t, :— |— :—	d :— |se, :se,

m :— |m :—	m :r |d :t,	d :— |— :—	m :— |m :m	m :— |s, :—
l, :— |l, :—	l, :l, |s, :s,	s, :— |— :—	s, :— |s, :s,	s, :— |m, :—
touch and	han-dle things un -	seen;	Here grasp, with	firm - er
arm save	Thine to lean up -	on;	It is e -	nough, my
and my	teach-er both in	one;	No wis - dom	can I
d :— |d :—	f :t |m :r	m :— |— :—	d :— |d :d	d :— |d :—
l, :— |l, :—	f, :f, |s, :s,	d :— |— :—	d :— |d :d	d :— |d, :—

l, :l, |la, :la,	s, :— |— :—	s :— |s :s	s, :ta, |l, :r	m :— |r :—	d :— |— :—
f, :f, |f, :f,	m, :— |— :—	d :— |d :d	d :m, |f, :l,	d :— |t, :—	d :— |— :—
hand th' e-ter - nal	grace,	And all my	wea - ri - ness up -	on Thee	lean.
Lord, enough, in -	deed,	My strength is	in Thy might, Thy	might a - -	lone.
lack while Thou art	wise,	No teach - ing	do I crave save	Thine a - -	lone.
d :d |d :d	d :— |— :—	s :— |s :s	s :d |d :f	s :— |f :—	m :— |— :—
f, :f, |f, :f,	d, :— |— :—	m, :— |m, :m,	m, :d, |f, :r,	s, :— |s, :—	d :— |— :—

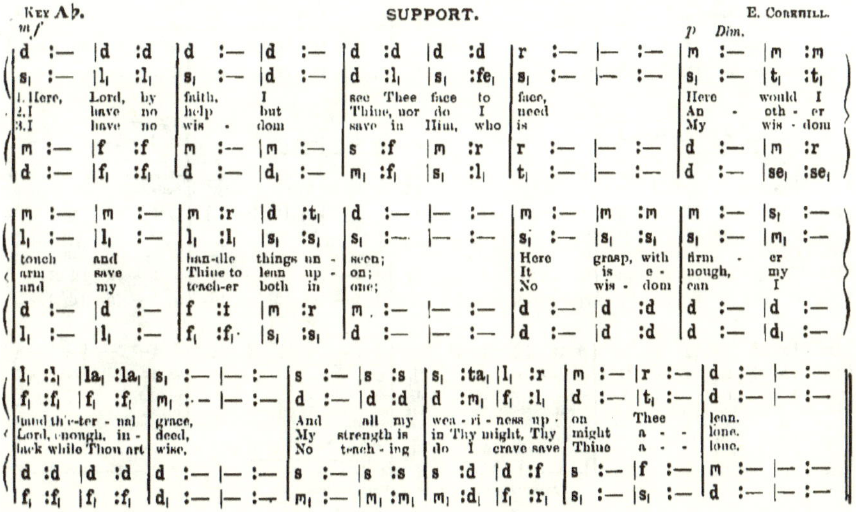

THE FAIRY'S ISLE.

MARY LADD. THEO. F. SEWARD.

pp KEY B♭.

:s, |s, :— :— |— :l, :s, |s, :— :— |— :— :s,.s, |d :— :— |— :f. :m |r :— :— |— :—

1. In eve - - - ning's smile This lit - - - - tle isle,
2. The moon - - - beams here, Fall soft and clear,
3. O mor - - - tal, come, To our fair - - - - y home,

:m, |m, :— :m, |f, :— :f,.f, |m, :— :m, |m, :— :m, |m, :— :m, |m, :l, :s,.s, |s, :— :s, |s, :—

1. In eve - ning's smile This lit - tle isle, In eve - ning's smile This lit - tle isle,
2. The moon - beams here, Fall soft and clear, The moon - beams here, Fall soft and clear,
3. O mor - tal, come, To our fair - y home, O mor - tal, come, To our fair - y home,

:s, |s, :— :s, |s, :— :s,.s, |s, :— :s, |s, :— :d |d :— :d |d :— :d.d |t, :— :t, |t, :—

:d, |d, :— :d, |t, :— :t,.t, |d, :— :d, |d, :— :d, |d, :— :d, |d, :— :d,.d, |s, :— :s, |s, :—

F.t. *pp* *Cres.* *f*

:ʳs |s :— :s |s :— :s |s :d' :t |l :s :f |m :— :m |r :d :r |d :— :— |— :—

Gleams fair a - mong the waves, Gleams fair a - mong the waves,
And stars blink with de - light, And stars blink with de - light,
We'll guide you through the lake, We'll guide you through the lake,

:ˢd |d :— :d |r :— :r |d :— :— |— :— :d |d :— :d |t, :d :t, |d :— :— |— :—

Gleams fair a - mong the waves, Gleams fair a - mong the waves,
And stars blink with de - light, And stars blink with de - light,
We'll guide you through the lake, We'll guide you through the lake,

:ᵗm |m :— :m |f :— :f |m :l :s |f :m :l |s :— :s |f :m :f |m :— :— |— :—

:ˢd |d :— :d |t, :— :t, |d :— :— |— :— :f, |s, :— :s, |s, :— :s, |d :— :— |— :—

f.C.

:ᵈs, |s, :— :— |— :t, :d |r :— :— |— :— :s, |s, :— :— |— :d :r |m :— :— |— :—

That toss their spray, And bound a - way,
And men in green, And gold - - - - en sheen,
O'er pearl - - - y shells, And lil - - - - y bells,

:ᵈs, |f, :— :f, |f, :— :f, |f, :— :f, |f, :— :f, |m, :— :m, |m, :— :f, |s, :— :s, |s, :—

That toss their spray, And bound a - way, That toss their spray, And bound a - way,
And men in green, And gold - en sheen, And men in green, And gold - en sheen,
O'er pearl - y shells, And lil - y bells, O'er pearl - y shells, And lil - y bells,

:ᵐt, |t, :— :t, |t, :r :d |t, :— :t, |t, :— :t, |d :— :— |d :— :d |d :— :d |d :—

:ᵈs, |s, :— :s, |s, :— :s, |s, :— :s, |s, :— :s, |d, :— :— |d, :— :d, |d, :— :d, |d, :—

:m |m :f :m |r :m :r |d :r :d |l, :f :r |d :— :— |t, :l, :t, |d :— :— |— :—

:s, |s, :l, :s, |f, :s, :f, |m, :— :m, |f, :l, :l, |s, :— :— |— :— :f, |m, :— :— |— :—

To hid - den el - fin caves, To hid - den el - - - - fin caves,
Dance in the sil - ver night, Dance in the sil - - - - ver night,
That lie be - neath the brake, That lie be - neath the brake,

:d |d :— :d |t, :— :t, |d :— :d |d :— :d |m :— :— |r :d :r |d :— :— |— :—

:d, |d :— :d |s, :— :s, |l, :— :l, |f, :— :f, |s, :— :— |— :— :s, |d, :— :— |— :—

From "The Singer," by per. of Biglow & Main.

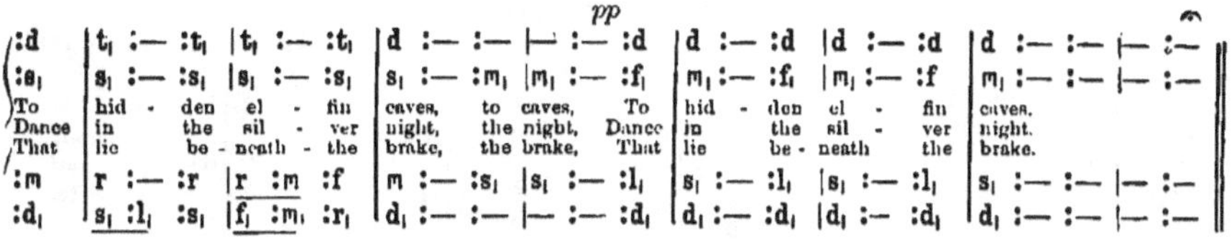

pp

:d | t, :— :t, | t, :— :t, | d :— :— | — :— :d | d :— :d | d :— :d | d :— :— | — :— ||
:s, | s, :— :s, | s, :— :s, | s, :— :m, | m, :— :f, | m, :— :f, | m, :— :f | m, :— :— | — :— ||
To | hid - den | el - fin | caves, to | caves, To | hid - den | el - fin | caves.
Dance | in the | sil - ver | night, the | night, Dance | in the | sil - ver | night.
That | lie be - | neath - the | brake, the | brake, That | lie be - | neath the | brake.
:m | r :— :r | r :m :f | m :— :s, | s, :— :l, | s, :— :l, | s, :— :l, | s, :— :— | — :— ||
:d, | s, :l, :s, | f, :m, :r, | d, :— :— | — :— :d, | d, :— :d, | d, :— :d, | d, :— :— | — :— ||

THROUGH THE DAY.

KEY E♭. B. C. UNSELD.

m :— :f | m :r :d | s :— :l | s :f :m | m :— :r | d :— :d | r :d :r | m :— :
d :— :d | d :— :d | d :— :d | d :— :d | d :— :t, | d :— :l, | t, :l, :t, | d :— :
1.Through the | day Thy | love hath | spared us; | Now we | lay us | down to | rest,
2.Pil - grims | here, on | earth, and | strang - ers, | Dwell - ing | in the | midst of | foes,
s :— :l | s :f :m | m :— :f | m :l :s | s :— :f | m :— :fe | s :— :s | s :— :
d :— :d | d :— :d | d :— :d | d :— :d | d :— :s, | l, :— :l, | s, :— :s, | d :— :

m :— :f | m :r :d | s :— :l | s :f :m | m :— :m | m :l :s | fe :m :fe | s :— :
d :— :d | d :— :d | d :— :d | d :— :d | d :— :r | d :— :d | d :— :d | t, :— :
Through the | si - lent | watch - es | guard us, | Let no | foe our | peace mo - | lest.
Us and | ours pre - | serve from | dan - gers, | In Thy | love may | we re - | pose.
s :ta :l | s :f :m | m :— :f | m :l :s | s :— :se | l :m :ma | r :s :l | s :— :
d :— :d | d :— :d | d :— :d | d :— :d | d :— :t, | l, :— :d | r :— :r | s, :— :

s :— :l | s :f :m | m :— :r | d :— :— | d :— :d | d :l :s | s :r :m | d :— :—
d :— :d | d :— :d | t, :— :t, | d :— :— | d :— :ta, | l, :d :d | t, :— :t, | d :— :—
Je - sus, | Thou our | guard - ian | be; | Sweet it | is to | rest in | Thee.
And when | time's short | day is | past, | Rest with | Thee in | heaven at | last.
m :— :f | m :l :s | s :— :f | m :— :— | m :— :m | f :— :m | r :f :s | m :— :—
d :— :d | d :— :d | s, :— :s, | l, :— :— | l, :— :s, | f, :— :s, | s, :— :s, | d :— :—

s :— :l | s :d' :— | d' :— :l | s :m :— | m :— :m | s :f :r | d :— :t, | d :— :— ||
d :— :d | d :m :— | f :— :f | m :d :— | d :— :ta, | l, :— :l, | s, :— :s, | s, :— :— ||
O, 'tis | sweet, | O, 'tis | sweet, | O, 'tis | sweet to | rest in | Thee.
m :— :f | m :s :ta | l :— :d' | d' :s :m | m :— :m | r :— :f | m :— :r | m :— :— ||
d :— :d | d :— :— | f :— :f | d :— :— | l, :— :s, | f, :— :f, | s, :— :s, | d :— :— ||

O LOVE DIVINE.

O. W. HOLMES. MENDELSSOHN, arr. by T. F. S.

p KEY F. *Andante.*

:s, | d :- .s, :d .r | r :m :s | f :m :r | s :— :m | d :t, :d
:s, | s, :— :s, .t, | t, :d :d | d :— :d | d :— :s, | l, :— :l,
O | Love Di - | vine, that | stooped to | share Our | sharp - - est
:m | m :— :m .f | f :s :ta | l :s :f | m :— :m | m :r :m
:d | d :— :d | d :— :d | d :— :d | d :— :d | l, :— :l,

| d :r :m | f :- .m :r .d | d :t, :s, | d :- .s, :d .r | r :m :s
| l, :— :d | r :- .d :l, | s, :— :s, | s, :— :s, .t, | t, :d :d
pang, our | bit - - t'rest | tear, On | Thee we | cast each
| f :— :s | l :- .s :f .m | m :r :f | m :— :m .f | f :s :ta
| f, :— :m, | r, :- .m, :f, .fe, | s, :— : | d :d :d | d :— :d
On Thee

| f :m :r | s :— :m | d :t, :d | d :r :m | f :- .r :d .t,
| d :— :d | d :— : | fe, :fe, :fe, | s, :t, :ta, | l, :— :s,
earth - - born | care, We | smile at | pain while | Thou art
| l :s :f | m :— : | r :r :r | r :s :s | f :— :m .r
| d :— :d | d :— : | r, :r, :r, | s, :— :d | f, :— :s,
We smile at pain

| d :— :s, | s :- .m :r .m | f :- .m :r .d | t, :d :l, | fe, :s, :s,
| s, :— :s, | m :- .d :t, .d | d :— :s, | s, :— :l, | fe, :s, :s,
near, Though | long the | wea - - ry | way we | tread, And
| m :— : | : .s :s .s | l :- .s :f .m | r :m :d | d :t, :
| d :— : | : : | : : | : : | : :
Tho' long the

| s :- .m :r .m | s .f :- .m :r .d | t, :d :m | m :r : | .s, :t, :d
| m :- .d :t, .d | d :— :s, | s, :— :d | d :t, : | .s, :s, :—
sor - - row | crown each | ling - - 'ring | year, | (Inst.)
| : .s :s .s | l :- .s :f .m | r :m :m .fe | s :— : | :f :m
| : : | : : | : : | : : | s, :— :—
And sor-row

f

| m :r :s | s :— :s | s :— :s | d' :— :d' | s :— :m | d :t, :d |
| d :t, :t, | d :— .s, :d .r | r :m :s | f :m :r | d :— : | fe, :fe, :fe, |
No path we shun, no dark - ness dread, O Love Di -
| s :— :f | m :— :m .f | f :s :ta | l :s :f | m :— : | r :r :r |
| — :— : | d :d :d | d :— :d | d :— :d | d :— : | r, :r, :r, |
No path O Love

Rit.

| d :r :m | f :— .r :d .t, | d :— . : | : .m :m .m | r :— :m | f :— .r :d .t, | d :— |
| s, :t, :ta, | l, :— :s, | s, :— . : | : .d :d .d | t, :— :d | d :— .l, :s, | s, :— |
vine, while Thou art near, while Thou art near, while Thou art near, While Thou art near.
| r :s :s | f :— :m .r | m :— .s :s .s | s :— :— | — :— :ta | l :— .f :m .r | m :— |
| s, :— :d | f, :— :s, | d :— . : | : : | : :d | f, :— :s, | d :— |

FOREST SONG. EVENING.

MARY A. LATHBURY. T. F. SEWARD.

KEY B♭.

| m, .f, :fe, .s, | l, .s, :s, | s, .l, :t, .d | d .t, :t, | t, .f :l, .t, |
| d, .r, :re, .m, | re, .m, :m, | f, .f, :f, .s, | f, .f, :f, | f, :f, .f, |
1. Soft thro' the fad - ing light, Falls the twi - light's pur-ple veil! Far o'er the
2. Arms of the for - est trees, Rock the rest - less winds to sleep; Si - lent the
3. Fold, then, your wea - ry wings, Troubled heart and bus - y brain, "Rest, rest," the
| d .t, :l, .s, | fe, .s, :s, | t, .d :r .m | r .r :r | r :r .r |
| d, :d, .d, | d, .d, :d, | s, .s, :s, .s, | s, .s, :s, | s, :s, .s, |

| l, .s, :s, | fe, .s, :t, .l, | s, :— .f, | m, .f, :fe, .s, | l, .s, :s, |
| m, .m, :m, | r, .r, :r, .r | r, .m, :f, .r, | d, .r, :re, .m, | re, .m, :m, |
wa - ters bright Flits a sun - lit sail. Hush! while the day-light dies;
birds and bees, Sink in slum - ber deep. "Rest," sings the for - est, "rest,"
for - est sings, Rest from care and pain. "Rest," sings the woodland still,
| d .d :d | d .t, :r .d | t, .d :r .t, | d .t, :l, .s, | fe, .s, :s, |
| d, .d, :d, | r, .r, :r, .r, | s, :— .s, | d, :d, .d, | d, .d, :d, |

Rit. *pp*

| s, .l, :t, .d | d .t, :t, | t, .f :l, .t, | l, .s, :m | m .f :r .m | d :— |
| f, .f, :f, .s | f, .f, :f, | f, :f, .f, | m, .m, :s, | s, .l, :f, .s, | m, .f, :m, |
Ev'ning sounds thro' all the air, Soft on the si-lence rise, Like an an - gel's prayer.
List - en to her lul - la - by, "Rest" on the Father's breast, 'Neath His watchful eye.
While the si - lent shadows fall, "Rest, rest from ev - ery ill, God is o - ver all.
| t, .d :r .m | r .r :r | r :r .r | d .d :d | d .d :t, .t, | d .l, :s, |
| s, .s, :s, .s, | s, .s, :s, | s, :s, .s, | d, .d, :d, | s, .s, :s, .s, | d, :— |

AUTUMN SONG.

EMMA S. STILLWELL.

T. F. SEWARD, by per.

KEY A♭.

```
:s1 | s1 :- .d :m .d | d .,t1 :t1 :d | r :- .s1 :l1 .s1 | s1 :d :s1 | s1 :- .d :m .d
:m1 | m1 :- .m1 :s1 .m1 | f1 .,f1 :f1 :m1 | f1 :- .f1 :f1 .f1 | m1 :— :m1 | m1 :- .m1 :s1 .m1
1.O | wav - ing, moaning | autumn trees, Say | where - fore do ye | sigh? Ye | weave yourselves such
2.O | faint, faint life, O | doubting soul! These | leaf - lets that I | tread Send | forth sweet incense
3.O | wav - ing, moaning | autumn trees, 'Tis | meet that ye should | sigh, While | lov - lier things than
:d | d :- .d :d .d | r .,r :r :d | t1 :- .t1 :t1 .t1 | d :— :d | d :- .d :d .d
:d1 | d1 :- .d1 :d1 .d1 | s1 .,s1 :s1 :s1 | s1 :- .s1 :s1 .s1 | d1 :— :d1 | d1 :- .d1 :d1 .d1

d .,t1 :t1 :t1 | t1 :- .t1 :d .fe1 | s1 :— :s1 | t1 :- .r :f .l | s .,fe :s :m
s1 .,s1 :s1 :s1 | s1 :- .s1 :fe1 .r1 | r1 :— :s1 | s1 :- .s1 :s1 .t1 | d .,d :d :s1
royal robes, It | must be sweet to | die; Clad | in more lavish | beauty now Than
as they fade, Per - | fume their low - ly | bed,— And | teach sweet truth, if | we will read What
autumn leaves Do | fade and droop and | die; Yet | change your dirge-notes | to a psalm,— They
m .,r :r :r | r :- .r :r .d | t1 :— :s1 | s1 :- .t1 :r .f | m .,re :m :d
s1 .,s1 :s1 :s1 | r1 :- .r1 :r1 .r1 | s1 :— :s1 | s1 :- .s1 :s1 .s1 | d .,d :d :d

f .,m :f :r | m :— :s1 | t1 :- .r :f .l | s .,fe :s :m | r :- .t1 :l1 .t1
s1 .,s1 :s1 :s1 | s1 :— :s1 | s1 :- .t1 :r .f | m .,re :m :s1 | s1 :- .s1 :fe1 .fe1
drapes the west ern | sky, Clad | in more lavish | beauty now Than | drapes the western
every leaf has | said, And | teach sweet truth, if | we will read What | ev - ery leaf has
bloom again on | high; Yet | change your dirge-notes | to a psalm,— They | bloom a - gain on
r .,de :r :t1 | d :— :s1 | s1 :- .s1 :s1 .t1 | d .,d :d :d | t1 :- .r :d .r
s1 .,s1 :s1 :s1 | d :— :s1 | s1 :- .s1 :s1 .s1 | d .,d :d :d1 | r1 :- .r1 :r1 .r1

s1 :— :s1 | s1 :- .d :m .d | d .,t1 :t1 :d | r :- .s1 :l1 .s1 | s1 :d :s1 .
O | wav - ing, moaning | autumn trees, Say | where - fore do ye | sigh? Ye
s1 :— : | m1 :— :— | f1 :— :m1 | f1 :— :— | m1 :— :—
sky. / said. / high. | Hm.........................................................
t1 :— : | d :— :— | r :— :d | t1 :— :— | d :— :—
s1 :— : | d1 :— :— | s1 :— :— | s1 :— :— | d1 :— :—

s1 :- .d :m .s | s .,f :f .f :m .r | d :— :— | — .m :l .s :m .d | d .t1 :l1 :t1 | d :—
weave yourselves such | royal robes. It must be | sweet,............ | ....... It must be | sweet to | die.
— :— :s1 .ta1 | l1 :- . : | : .l1 :l1 .l1 | s1 . : .s1 :s1 .s1 | f1 :— :f1 | m1 :—
.......................... | ........ | It must be | sweet. It must be | sweet to | die.
— :— :— | — :- . : | : .d :r .re | m . : .m :m .m | r :— :r | d :—
— :— :— | f1 :- . : | : .fe1 :fe1 .fe1 | s1 . : .s1 :s1 .s1 | s1 :— :s1 | d1 :—
```

SWEET AND LOW.

TENNYSON. J. BARNBY.

pp KEY C. *Larghetto.* M. 100.

| m :— :m | l :— :— | s :— :s | d' :— :— | d' :t :l | s :-.s :fe |
| m :— :m | re :— :— | m :— :m | f :— :— | m :m :m | r :-.r :r |
1.Sweet and low, Sweet and low, Wind of the west - - ern
2.Sleep and rest, Sleep and rest, Fa - ther will come to thee
| s :— :s | fe :— :— | s :— :s | l :— :— | s :r' :d' | t :-.t :l |
| d :— :d | d :— :— | d :— :d | d :— :— | d :d :d | r :-.r :r |

| l :— :— | s :— :— | m :— :— | l :— :l | s :— :ᵐl, | r :— :— |
| r :— :— | — :— :— | m :— :— | re :— :re | m :— :ᵐl, | t, :— :— |
sea, Low, low, breathe and blow,
soon; Rest, rest on moth - - er's breast,
| d' :— :— | t :— :— | s :— :— | fe :— :fe | s :— :ᵐl | s :— :— |
| s :— :— | — :— :— | d :— :— | d :— :d | d :— :ᵈf, | f :— :— |

p

| s :m :f | r :-.r :m | r :— :— | d :— : |
| d :d :d | d :-.d :t, | t, :— :— | d :— : |
Wind the west - - ern sea,
Fa-ther will come to thee soon.
| s :s :f | l :-.l :s | f :— :— | m :— : |
| m :d :l, | f, :-.f, :s, | d :— :— | — :— : |

f.C. *mf*

| ᵈs :t :l | s :l :s | s :d' :l | s :— :— |
O - ver the roll - ing wa - - ters go,
| ᵗᵃf :— :— | f :— :f | m :m :re | m :— :— |
O - - - ver the wa - - ters go,
Fa - - - ther will come to his babe,
| ˢr' :t :d' | r' :d' :r' | d' :d' :d' | d' :— :— |
Fa ther will come to his babe in the nest,
| ᵐt :s :l | t :l :t | d' :m :fe | s :— :— |

pp

| s :t :l | s :l :s | s :d' :fe | s :— :— |
Come from the dy - - ing moon and blow,
| f :— :f | f :— :f | m :— :re | m :— :— |
Come from the moon and blow,
Sil - ver sails out of the west,
| t :s :l | t :l :t | d' :s :l | s :— :— |
Sil - - ver sails all out of the west,
| s, :— :s, | s, :— :s, | d :— :d | d :— :— |

f

| d' :d' :d' | d' :— :t | l :— :— | la :— :— |
| d :m :l | se :— :se | l :— :— | d :— :— |
Blow him a - gain to me,
Un-der the sil - - ver moon,
| l :d' :m' | m' :— :r' | d' :— :— | ma' :— :— |
| l, :l, :d | m :— :m | f :— :— | fe :— :— |

p *rall. e dim.*

| s :— :s | s :-.l :s | s :— :s | s :-.l :s |
| d :— :m | r :-.r :r | d :— :d | d :-.f :f |
While my lit - tle one, while my pret - ty one
Sleep, my lit - tle one, sleep, my pret - ty one,
| m' :— :d' | t :-.t :t | d' :— :d' | t :-.t :ta |
| s :— :s | f :-.f :f | m :— :ma | r :-.r :ra |

pp

| d' :— :— | — :— :— | — :— :— | — :— : |
| m :— :— | f :— :— | m :— :— | — :— : |
sleeps.........................
sleep..........................
| ta :— :— | l :— :la | s :— :— | — :— : |
| d :— :— | — :— :— | — :— :— | — :— : |

GRANDEUR.

KEY E♭. *With the utmost dignity and firmness.* ART. from WAGNER

```
:s  | d'  :—  :s      | m  :—  :m.f,s      | s   :l   :s   | s   :f   :l  | r'  :—  :d'  |
:m  | m   :—  :d      | d  :—  :d          | d   :—   :d   | de  :r   :f  | fe  :—  :fe  |
1.Now  may  the  God  of  grace  and  power,  At - tend  His
2.Then save us,  Lord,  from  slav - - ish  fear,  And  let  our
:s  | s   :—  :m      | m  :—  :s          | s   :f   :s   | l   :—   :l  | l   :—  :l   |
:d  | d   :—  :m,     | l, :—  :s,.f,.m,   | m,  :f,  :m,  | r,  :—   :r  | r   :—  :r   |
```

```
| t   :—  :s.l.t    | d'  :l   :s .,m  | m   :r   :s   | l   :s   :l   | l   :—  :s  |
| s   :r  :t,.d.r   | d   :—   :d      | d   :t,  :r   | r   :—   :m   | f   :—  :m  |
peo - ple's  hum - ble  cry,  De - fend  them  in  the
trust  be  firm  and  strong,  Till  Thy  sal - va - - tion
| s   :—  :s        | s   :m   :s      | s   :—   :t   | l   :t   :d'  | l   :f  :s  |
| f   :—  :f        | m   :d   :m,     | s,  :—   :s   | f   :—   :m   | r   :—  :m  |
```

```
| l  :s  :l  | l   :—  :l   | s  :—  :s.l.t    | d'  :t   :l    | s    :f   :m    | r   :—     :r   | d  :—  ||
| f  :—  :m  | re  :—  :re  | m  :f  :f        | m   :—   :f .d | -.m  :r   :d    | d   :t,.l, :t,  | d  :—  ||
need - ful  hour,  And  send  de - liv - - - - - 'rance  from  on  high.
shall  ap - pear,  And  hymns  of  peace  con - clude  our  song.
| t  :—  :l  | fe  :—  :fe  | s  :t  :t.d'.r'  | d'  :—   :- .f  | s    :l   :l    | s   :—     :f   | m  :—  ||
| r  :—  :d  | t,  :—  :t,  | d  :r  :s,       | l,  :s,  :f,    | m,   :f,  :fe,  | s,  :—     :s,  | d  :—  ||
```

TRUST.

KEY B♭. T. F. SEWARD, by per.

```
:s,  | s,  :fe,  :s,  | l,  :s,  :s,  | s,  :d   :r   | m   :—  :m   | m   :re   :m   | f   :m   :m   | r   :—    :r   | r   :—  :r   |
:m,  | m,  :re,  :m,  | f,  :m,  :m,  | m,  :s,  :s,  | s,  :—  :s,  | s,  :fe,  :s,  | l,  :s,  :s,  | s,  :fe,  :l,  | s,  :—  :f,  |
1.O  Love  Di - vine!  that  stooped  to  share  Our  sharp - est  pang,  our  bit - t'rest  tear,  On
2.Tho'  long  the  wea - ry  way  we  tread,  And  sor - row  crown  each  ling - 'ring  year,  No
3.When  droop - ing  pleas - ure  turns  to  grief,  And  trem - bling  faith  is  changed  to  fear,  The
:d   | d   :—    :d   | d   :—   :d   | d   :—   :t,  | d   :—  :d   | d   :—    :d   | d   :—   :d   | t,  :l,   :d   | t,  :—  :t,  |
:d,  | d,  :—    :d,  | d,  :—   :d,  | d,  :m,  :s,  | d,  :—  :d,  | d,  :—    :d,  | d,  :—   :d,  | r,  :—    :r,  | s,  :—  :s,  |
```

```
| r   :m   :r   | d   :s,  :d   | r   :m   :r   | d   :—  :d   | m   :f   :m   | r   :l,  :l,  | s,  :l,  :t,  | d   :—  ||
| f,  :s,  :f,  | m,  :—   :m,  | f,  :s,  :f,  | m,  :—  :m,  | s,  :l,  :s,  | f,  :—   :f,  | f,  :—   :f,  | m,  :—  ||
Thee  we  cast  each  earth - born  care,  We  smile  at  pain,  while  Thou  art  near.
path  we  shun,  no  dark - ness  dread,  Our  hearts  still  whisp - 'ring,  Thou  art  near.
murm - 'ring  wind,  the  quiv - 'ring  leaf  Shall  soft - ly  tell  us  Thou  art  near.
| t,  :—   :t,  | d   :—   :d   | t,  :—   :t,  | d   :—  :d   | de  :—   :de  | r   :—   :r   | t,  :d   :r   | d   :—  ||
| s,  :—   :s,  | d,  :—   :d,  | s,  :—   :s,  | d,  :—  :d   | l,  :—   :l,  | r,  :—   :t,  | s,  :—   :s,  | d,  :—  ||
```

BOAT SONG.

Mary A. Lathbury.
Theo. F. Seward.

Key F.

s :— :— |m :— : | s :— :— |r :— : | s :l :s |f :m :r | d :— :m |s :— :—
d :— :— |d :— : | t, :— :— |t, :— : | m :f :m |r :d :t, | d :— :d |d :— :—

1. Float - - ing, float - - ing, Gai - - ly sing - ing as we row,
2. Float - - ing, float - - ing, Through the shad - ows soft and deep,
3. Float - - ing, float - - ing, See the moon a - bove the lake,
D.C. *Float - ing, float - - ing, Gai - ly sing - ing as we row.*

m :— :— |s :— : | s :— :— |s :— : | s :— :s |s :— :f | m :— :s |m :— :—
d :— :— |d :— : | s, :— :— |s, :— : | s, :— :s, |s, :— :s, | d :— :d |d :— :—

s :— :— |m :— :— | s :— :— |r :— : | s :l :s |f :m :r | d :— :— |— :— :
d :— :— |d :— :— | t, :— :— |t, :— : | m :f :m |r :d :t, | d :— :— |— :— :

Rock - ing, rock - - ing, In the sun - set glow.
Rock - ing, rock - - ing, With the waves to sleep.
Rock - ing, rock - - ing, In her sil - - ver wake.
Rock - ing, rock - - ing, In the sun - - set glow.

m :— :— |s :— :— | s :— :— |s :— : | s :— :s |s :— :f | m :— :— |— :— :
d :— :— |d :— :— | s, :— :— |s, :— : | s, :— :s, |s, :— :s, | d :— :— |— :— :

FINE.

d :— :— |l :— : | s :— :— |m :— : | s :— :r |r :m :f | m :— :r |d :— :
l, :— :— |d :— : | d :— :— |d :— : | t, :— :t, |t, :d :r | d :— :t, |d :— :

Soft - - ly steal - ing O'er the wa - ters far a - way;
Day is end - ing, Star - ry eyes a - bove us beam;
Drift - - ing, drift - ing, From the shad - ow - haunt - ed land;

f :— :— |f :— : | m :— :— |s :— : | s :— :s |s :— :s | s :— :f |m :— :
f, :— :— |f, :— : | d :— :— |d :— : | s, :— :s, |s, :— :s, | d :— :d |d :— :

C.t.

d :— :— |l :— :— | s :— :— |m :— : | rs :— :s |s :l :t | d' :— :d' |r' :m' :r'
l, :— :— |d :— :— | d :— :— |d :— : | t,m :— :m |f :— :f | m :— :m |f :— :f

Bells are peal - - ing For the dy - ing day, the dy - - ing
All hearts blend - - ing In a hap - - py dream, a hap - py
Drift - ing, drift - - ing In - - to fair - - y land, to fair - y

f :— :— |f :— :— | m :— :— |s :— : | sd' :— :d' |r' :— :r' | d' :— :d' |t :— :t
f, :— :— |f, :— :— | d :— :— |d :— : | rs :— :s |s :— :s | d :— :d |s :— :s

f.F. D.C.

d' :— :d' |r' :m' :r' | d's :— :— |— :— :— | — :— :— |— :— :— | — :— :— |— :— :—
m :— :m |f :— :f | mt, :— :— |d :— :— | r :— :— |d :— :— | t, :— :— |— :— :—

day, the dy - - ing day, the dy - - ing day.
dream, a hap - py dream, a hap - py dream.
land, to fair - y land, to fair - y land.

d' :— :d' |t :— :t | d's :— :— |m :— :— | f :— :— |m :— :— | r :— :— |— :— :—
d :— :d |s :— :s | ds, :— :— |s, :— :— | s, :— :— |s, :— :— | s, :— :— |— :— :—

EVENING HYMN.

mp KEY D. DANIEL BATCHELLOR.

| s :- .f | m .f :s .l | s :— | f :— | *p* f :- .m | r .m :f .s | m :— | — : |
| m :- .r | d .r :m .f | m :— | r :— | r :- .d | t, .d :r .t, | d :— | — : |

1. Day - light from the sky has fad - ed, Shad - ows fall on land and sea;
2. Flow'rs a - mid the calm of e - - ven, Lift their heads refreshed with dew;
3. Babes their trusting eyelids clos - ing, Slum - ber on their mother's breast;

| d' :- .d' | s .s :d' .d' | l :— | l :— | s :- .s | s .s :s .s | s :— | — : |
| d :- .d | d .d :d .d | de :— | r :— | s, :- .s, | s, .s, :s, .s, | d :— | — : |

| s :- .f | m .f :s .l | s :— | *mf* l :— | t :- .d' | t .l :s .fe | s :— | — : |
| m :- .r | d .d :m .f | m :— | m :— | r :- .r | r .r :r .d | t, :— | — : |

Ere in sleep our eyes are sha - - ded, Lord, we raise our hearts to Thee!
Wea - ry hearts look up to heav - en, There to find our strength a-new,
Lit - tle birds in peace re-pos - ing, Un - der parent wings find rest.

| d' :- .d' | s .s :d' .d' | d' :— | d' :— | s :- .l | s .d' :t .l | s :— | — : |
| d :- .d | d .d :d .d | d :— | l, :— | r :- .r | r .r :r .r | s, :— | — : |

| *mp* f :- .m | r .m :f .s | f :— | m : | *Cres* r :- .de | r .m :f .fe | s :— | — :— |
| r :- .d | t, .d :r .t, | r :— | d : | l, :- l, | l, .l, :r .d | t, :d | r .m :f |

Take not Thou Thy light a-way, Fair - er than the light of day;
Thus we thirst for Thee, O Lord! Let Thy grace on us be poured;
Whith - er shall Thy children flee, Heav'n - ly Father, but to Thee?

| s :- .s | s .s :s .s | s :— | — : | l :- .s | f .l :l .l | s :l | t .d' :r' |
| s, :- .s, | s, .s, :s, .s, | s, :l, .t, | d : | f :- .m | r .de :r .r | s .— | — :— |

| s :- .f | m .f :s .l | s :m' | r' .d' :t .l | s :- .l | t .d' :r .m | *Dim - e - rit.* s :f | m :— |
| m :- .r | d .r :m .f | m :s | f :f | m :- .f | f .m :r .d | t, :— | d :— |

Fa - ther, let thy presence cheer us, Dark-ness flies when thou art near us.
Cleanse and pardon and re-store us, Shed the dew of blessing o'er us.
Thou wilt watch while in thy keep - - - ing, Calm and peaceful we are sleep - ing.

| d' .- .d' | s .s :d' .d' | d' :— | l :r' .d' | d' :- .d' | s .s :l .s | s :— | s :— |
| d :- .d | d .d :d .d | d :— | f :f | d :- .d | r .m :f .m | r :s, | d :— |

FABEN.

KEY C. J. H. WILLCOX.

| :s .s | s :- .m' :r' .m' | d' :s :s .s | f :- .l :s .f | f :m :f .f | s :- .m' :r' .m' |
| :m .m | m :- .s :f .f | m :m :d .d | r :- .f :m .r | r :d :t, .t, | d :- .s :f .f |

1. Love di-vine, all love ex-cel - ling, Joy of heaven, to earth come down, Fix in us Thy humble
2. Come Al-might - y to de-liv - er, Let us all Thy life re-ceive, Sudden - ly re-turn and
3. Finish then Thy new cre-a - tion, Pure and spot - less let me be, Let us see Thy great sal-

| :d' .d' | d' :- .s :l .t | d' :d' :d' .d' | d' :- .d' :t .t | d' :s :s .s | s :- .s :l .t |
| :d .d | d :- .d :d .d | d :d :m .m | s :- .s :s .s | d :— :r .r | m :- .d .d .d |

```
d' :s :d' .d' | t :- .l :s .fe | s :— :s .s | l :- .l :t .t | d' :d' :l .l
m :m :m .m | r :- .r :r .d | t, :— :r .r | m :- .m :f .f | m :m :m .m
dwell-ing, All Thy faith-ful mer-cies crown: Je-sus, Thou art all com-pas-sion, Pure, un-
nev-er, Nev-er more Thy temples leave. Thee we would be al-ways bless-ing, Serve Thee
va-tion Per-fect-ly se-cured in Thee: Changed from glo-ry in-to glo-ry, Till in
d' :d' :d' .l | s :- .d' :t .l | s :— :t .t | d' :- .d' :r' .r' | d' :d' :d' .d'
d :d :l, .l, | r :- .r :r .r | s, :— :s .s | s :- .s :s .s | l :l :l .l

l :- .d' :t .l | l :se :s .s | s :- .m' :r' .m' | d' :s :se .se | l .r' .d' :t | d' :—
re :- .re :re .re | m :— :f .f | m :- .s :f .m | m :d :r .r | d .f :m :r | m :—
bound-ed love Thou art, Vis-it us with Thy sal-va-tion, En-ter every trem-bling heart.
as Thy hosts a-bove, Pray and praise Thee without ceas-ing, Glo-ry in Thy per-fect love.
heav'n we take our place, Till we cast our crowns be-fore Thee, Lost in wonder, love and praise.
d' :- .l :t .d' | d' :t :t .t | d' :- .d' :t .t | l :s :t .t | l .l :s :s | s :—
f :- .f :f .f | m :— :s .s | d :- .d :s .se | l :m :m .m | f .r :s :s, | d :—
```

H. P. M. & Grace J. Frances.

GOOD-NIGHT, MY DARLING.

(For Male Voices.)

Key D. Hubert P. Main.

```
:s | d' : :d' | d' : :m' | r' :d' :— | — : :s | l :— :d' | d' :— :r' | t :— :— | — :
:m | s : :s | s : :d' | t :d' :— | — : :m | f :— :l | s :— :s | s :— :— | — :
1. Good night, good night, my dar-ling; May earth-ly cares now cease,
2. Good night, good night, my dar-ling; May smiles from eyes a-bove,
3. Good night, good night, my dar-ling; Sweet dreams I ask for Thee;
4. Good night, good night, my dar-ling; Till morn a-gain shall break,
:d | m : :m | m : :s | f :m :— | — : :d | d :— :d .r | m :— :f | r :— :— | — :
:d | d : :d | d : :d | s, :d :— | — : :d | f, :— :f, | s, :— :s, | s, :— :— | — :

:s | s :— :d' | m' :— :r' | r' :— :— | — : :s | d' : :d' | d' : :l | s :m :— | — :
:f | m :— :s | d' :— :d' | t :— :— | — : :s | s : :ta | l : :f | m :d :— | — :
God give thee rest and peace. Good night, good night, my dear-est,
Look down on thee in love. Good night, etc.
O think and dream of me. Good night, etc.
And thou from sleep a-wake. Good night, etc.
:r | d :— :m | fe :— :fe | s :— :— | — : :f | m : :s | f : :d | d :d :— | — :
:t, | d :— :d | l, :— :r, | s, :— :— | — : :t, | d : :m, | f, : :f, | d :d :— | — :

:s | l :d' :— | d' :— :m' | r' :— :— | d' :— :s | d' :— :— | — :— :— | — :— :— | — :
:m | f :l :— | s :— :d' | t :— :— | d' :— : | : :ta | l : :la | l :— :— | — :
My precious love, my dar-ling; Good night, good night, good night.
:d | d :— :r | m :— :s | f :— :— | m :— : | : :s | f : :r | m :— :— | — :
:d | f, :— :f, | s, :— :s, | s, :— :— | d :— : | : :m, | f, : :f, | d, :— :— | — :
```

JESUS, I COME TO THEE.

KEY C. T. F. SEWARD, by per.

m :m :m	s :- .f :m	f :f :f	f :— :—	t :t :t
d :d :d	m :- .r :d	r :r :r	r :— :—	r :r :r
1. Je - sus, I	come to Thee,	no one be -	side	Cares for the
2. Far from the	nar - row way	long have I	strayed,	Dark clouds have
3. Back to Thy	dear love for	shel - ter and	rest,	Flee I, O
s :s :s	s :- .s :s	s :s :s	s :— :—	s :s :s
d :d :d	d :- .d :d	s, :s, :s,	s, :— :—	s, :s, :s,

r' :- .d' :t	d' :m :l	s :— :—	m :m :m	s :- .f :m
f :- .m :r	m :d :f	m :— :—	d :d :d	m :- .r :d
sor - row I'm	try - ing to	hide;	Help - less and	des - o - late,
cov - ered me	where I have	prayed;	Now to Thy	mer - cy I
Lord, like a	bird to its	nest;	Noth - ing I	bring Thee, but
s :- .s :s	s :d' :d'	d' :— :—	s :s :s	d' :- .d' :d'
s, :- .s, :s,	d :d :d	d :— :—	d :d :d	d :- .d :d

d' :d' :d'	l :— :—	l :r' .d' :t .l	s :l .t :d'	s .f :m :r
m :m :m	f :— :—	f :t .l :s .f	m :f :m	m .r :d :t,
tired with my	sin,	O - pen Thine	arms to me	Lord, take me
come with my	sin,	Pit - y and	com - fort me,	Lord, take me
sor - row and	sin,	O - pen Thine	arms for me,	Lord, take me
d' :d' :d'	d' :— :—	d' :l :t .d'	d' :s :s	s .l :s :f
l :l :l	f :— :—	f :f :f	m :r :d	m .f :s :s,

d :— :—	s .s :s .s :s .s	s :— :—	l .l :l .l :r' .d'	t :— :—
d :— :—	m .m :m .m :r .f	m :— :—	f .f :f .f :fe .fe	s :— :—
in. in. in.	Open now Thine arms to	me,	Pity, Lord, and comfort	me;
m :— :—	d' .d' :d' .d' :t .r'	d' :— :—	d' .d' :l .l :l .l	s :— :—
d :— :—	d .d :d .d :s, .s,	d :— :—	f .f :f .f :r .r	s :— :—

d' .d' :r' .d' :t .l	s :l .t :d'	s .f :m :r	d :— :—
m .m :f .m :s .f	m :f :m	m .r :d :t,	d :— :—
O - pen now Thine arms for	me, for me,	Lord, take me	in.
s .s :s .s :s .s	s :d' :d'	d' .l :s :s .f	m :— :—
d .d :d .d :d .d	d :d :d	m .f :s :s,	d :— :—

STAND BY THE FLAG.

KEY D. *Maestoso e marcato.* HENRY TUCKER.

| d :m .,f | s :– .s | l .t :d' .r' | d' :t .s | d' :t | l :s |
| d :m .,f | s :– .s | f .f :s .f | m :r .s | m :re | m :m |
1. Stand by the flag; its folds have waved in glo - ry, To foes a fear, to
2. Stand by the flag; though death shot round it rat - tle, And un - der - neath its
| d :m .,f | s :– .d' | d' .s :s .l | s :s .t | l :l | l :l |
| d :m .,f | s :– .m | f .r :m .f | s :s, .s, | l, :t, | d :de |

| f .m :r .d | m :r . | d :m .,f | s :– .s | l .t :d' .r' | d' :t .r' |
| r .d :d .d | d :t, . | d :m .,f | s :– .s | f .f :s .f | m :r .l |
friends a guardian robe, And spread to na - - tions round the joyful sto - ry, Of
waving folds have met, In all the dread ar - ray of sanguine bat - tle, The
| l .l :l .l | s :– . | d :m .,f | s :– .s | d' .s :s .l | s :s .l |
| r .m :f .fe | s :– . | d :m .,f | s :– .s | f .r :m .f | s :s .f |

A.t.

| m' :r' | d' :f' | m' .r' :d' .t | d' :— | r's :s .,s | s :– .f |
| se :m | m :f | s .l :s .f | m :— | sd :t, .,t, | d :– .r |
Free - dom's tri - umph o - ver all the globe. Stand by the flag on
point - ed lance and glitt'ring bay - o - net. Stand by the flag all
| t :t | d' :r' | d' .f' :m' .r' | d' :— | tm :f .,f | m :– .f |
| m :se | l :r | m .f :s .s, | d :— | tm :r .,r | d :– .r, |

f.D.

| m .r :d .t, | d :s, . | s :s .,s | s :– .f | m .r :d .t, | d :— | f.d :m .,f |
| d .l, :s, .s, | s, :s, . | d :t, .,t, | d :– .r | d .l, :s, .f, | m, :— | f.d :m .,f |
land and ocean bil - - low; By it your fa - - thers stood, unmoved and true, Liv - ing de-
doubt and treason scorn - ing, Trust - ing with cour - age firm, and faith sublime, That it will
| s .f :m .r | m :m . | s :f .,f | m :– .f | s .f :m .r | d :— | f.d :m .,f |
| m, .f, :s, .s, | d :d . | m :r .,r | d :– .r, | m, .f, :s, .s, | d :— | f.d :m .,f |

Rall.

| s :– .s | l .t :d' .r' | d' :t .r' | m' :r' | d' :f' | m' .r' :d' .t | d' :— ||
| s :– .s | f .f :s .f | m :r .l | se :m | m :f | s .l :s .f | m :— ||
fend - ed. dying, from their pil - low, With their last bless - ing passed it un-to you.
float un - til th'e - ternal morn - ing Pales in its glo - ries all the light of time.
| s :– .d' | d' .s :s .l | s :s .l | t :t | d' :r' | d' .f' :m' .r' | d' :— ||
| s :– .m | f .r :m .f | s :s .f | m :se | l :r | m .f :s .s, | d :— ||

FAITHFUL AND TRUE.

RICHARD WAGNER.

p KEY B♭.

| s, :d .,d | d :- . | s, :r .,t, | d :- . | s, :d .,f | f :m .,r
| s, :s, .,s, | s, :- . | s, :s, .,s, | s, :- . | s, :m, .,l, | l, :s, .,s,
Faith - ful and | true | now rest ye | here, | Where love tri - | umph - ant shall
| m :m .,m | m :- . | m :f .,r | m :- . | m :d .,d | d :d .,f
| d :d .,d | d :- . | d :s, .,s, | d :- . | d :d .,d | d :—

| d :t, .,d | r :- . | s, :d .,d | d :- . | s, :r .,t, | d :- .
| s, :fe, .,fe, | s, :- . | s, :s, .,s, | s, :- . | s, :s, .,s, | s, :- .
crown ye with | joy! | Star of re- | nown, | flow'r of the | earth,
| m :r .,d | t, :- . | m :m .,m | m :- . | m :f .,r | m :- .
| — :l, .,l, | s, :- . | d :d .,d | d :- . | d :s, .,s | d :- .

| s, :d .,m | s :m .,d | l, :r .,m | d :- . | f :m .r | l, :l,
| s, :s, .,s, | t, :l, .,l, | l, :f, .,s, | m, :- . | d :t, .l, | f, :f,
Blest be ye | both, far from | all life's an - | noy, | Champ - ion vic - | to - - rious,
| m :m .,m | m :d .,m | r :t, .,t, | d :- . | l :s .f | r :r
| d :d .,d | m, :l, .,l, | f, :s, .,s, | d :- . | : | :

p G t.m.l.

| t, :d .,r | r :- . | f :m .r | l, :l, | l.d :r .,m | m :—
| s, :s, .,s, | s, :- . | d :t, .l, | f, :f, | m.s, :t, .,d | d :—
now rest thee | here! | Maid bright and | glo - rious, | now rest thee | here!
| r :m .,t, | t, :- . | l :s .f | r :r | de.m :s .,s | s :—
| s, :s, .,s, | s, :- . | : | : | l.d :s, .,d | d :- .d
The

ye have for - sak - en,
| s :l .s | f :m | s .fe :f .m | m :r | s :l .t | d' :m
| d :d .d | r .t, :d | t, :t, | t, :t, | d :d .d | d :d
Mirth's nois - y | rev - - el | ye've for - - | sak - en, | Ten - der de - | lights for
| m :f .m | l .la :s .m | r :r .s | f :f | s :s .s | m :m
| d :— | — :d | s, :- .s, | s, :s, | m, :m, .m, | l, :l,
rev - - - - - - el

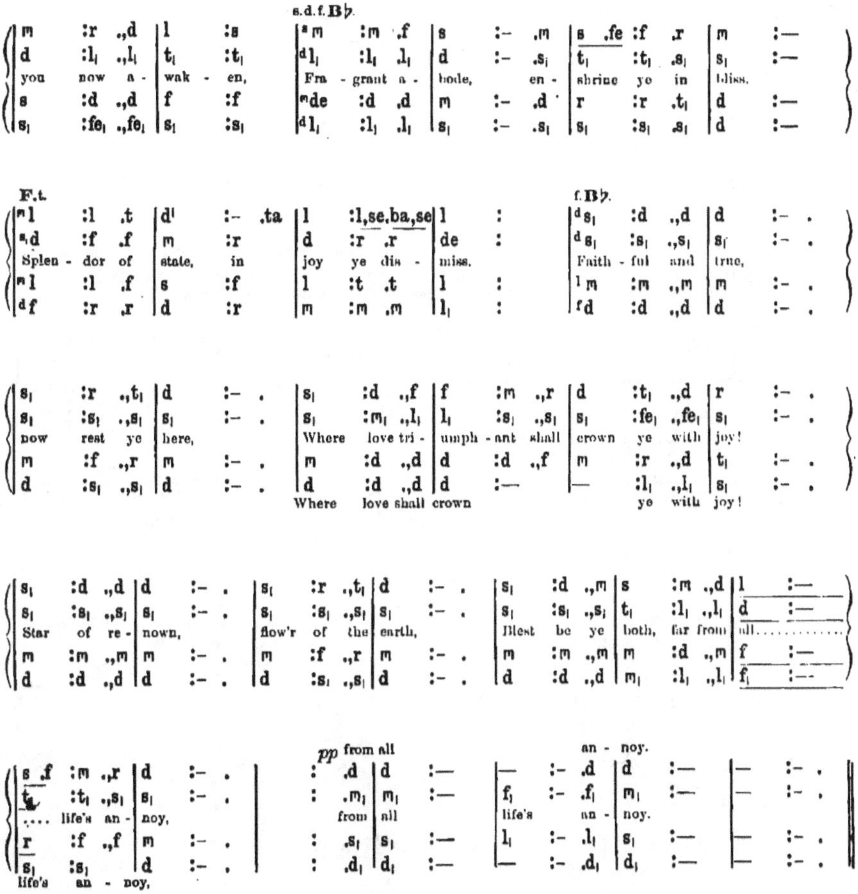

s.d.f. B♭.

| m :r .,d | l :s | [s]m :m .f | s :– .m | s .fe :f .r | m :— |
| d :l_1 .,l_1 | t_1 :t_1 | [d]l_1 :l_1 .l_1 | d :– .s_1 | t_1 :t_1 .s_1 | s_1 :— |
you now a - wak - en, Fra - grant a - bode, en - shrine ye in bliss.
| s :d .,d | f :f | [m]de :d .d | m :– .d | r :r .t_1 | d :— |
| s_1 :fe_1 .,fe_1 | s_1 :s_1 | [d]l_1 :l_1 .l_1 | s_1 :– .s_1 | s_1 :s_1 .s_1 | d :— |

F.t.

| [m]l :l .t | d' :– .ta | l :l,se.ba,se | l : | f.B♭. [d]s_1 :d .,d | d :– . |
| [s]d :f .f | m :r | d :r .r | de : | [d]s_1 :s_1 .,s_1 | s_1 :– . |
Splen - dor of state, in joy ye dis - miss. Faith - ful and true,
| [m]l :l .f | s :f | l :t .t | l : | [l]m :m .,m | m :– . |
| [d]f :r .r | d :r | m :m .m | l_1 : | [f]d :d .,d | d :– . |

| s_1 :r .,t_1 | d :– . | s_1 :d .,f | f :m .,r | d :t_1 .,d | r :– . |
| s_1 :s_1 .,s_1 | s_1 :– . | s_1 :m_1 .,l_1 | l_1 :s_1 .,s_1 | s_1 :fe_1 .,fe_1 | s_1 :– . |
now rest ye here, Where love tri - umph - ant shall crown ye with joy!
| m :f .,r | m :– . | m :d .,d | d :d .,f | m :r .,d | t_1 :– . |
| d :s_1 .,s_1 | d :– . | d :d .,d | d :— | — :l_1 .,l_1 | s_1 :– . |
Where love shall crown ye with joy!

| s_1 :d .,d | d :– . | s_1 :r .,t_1 | d :– . | s_1 :d .,m | s :m .,d | l :— |
| s_1 :s_1 .,s_1 | s_1 :– . | s_1 :s_1 .,s_1 | s_1 :– . | s_1 :s_1 .,s_1 | t_1 :l_1 .,l_1 | d :— |
Star of re - nown, flow'r of the earth, Blest be ye both, far from all............
| m :m .,m | m :– . | m :f .,r | m :– . | m :m .,m | m :d .,m | f :— |
| d :d .,d | d :– . | d :s_1 .,s_1 | d :– . | d :d .,d | m_1 :l_1 .,l_1 | f_1 :— |

pp from all an - noy.
| s .f :m .,r | d :– . | | : .d | d :— | — :– .d | d :— | — :– . ||
| t_1 :t_1 .,s_1 | s_1 :– . | | : .m_1 | m_1 :— | f_1 :– .f_1 | m_1 :— | — :– . ||
..... life's an - noy, from all life's an - noy.
| r :f .,f | m :– . | | : .s_1 | s_1 :— | l_1 :– .l_1 | s_1 :— | — :– . ||
| s_1 :s_1 | d :– . | | : .d_1 | d_1 :— | — :– .d_1 | d_1 :— | — :– . ||
life's an - noy,

MINOR MODE PHRASES,

SELECTED FROM WELL-KNOWN COMPOSERS.

For the 5th requirement of the Intermediate Certificate, any one of Nos. 11 to 22, taken by lot, must be Sol-faed in correct tune and time. Two attempts allowed. The key may be changed when necessary.

No. 1. KEY G. *Lah is E.* — From "'Tis when to sleep." SIR H. BISHOP.

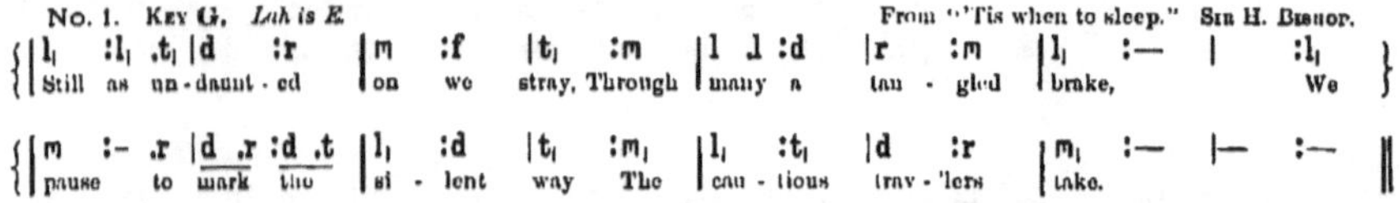

```
|l,   :l,  .t, |d    :r     |m    :f     |t,   :m      |l  .l :d    |r    :m     |l,   :—   |     :l,
 Still as  un-daunt - ed     on    we     stray, Through many  a     tan  - gled  brake,          We

|m    :-  .r   |d .r :d .t  |l,   :d     |t,   :m,     |l,   :t,    |d    :r     |m,   :—   |—    :—   ||
 pause    to    mark  the     si - lent   way   The      cau - tious  trav - 'lers  take.
```

No. 2. KEY B♭ *Lah is G.* — From the "Turkish Drinking Song." MENDELSSOHN.

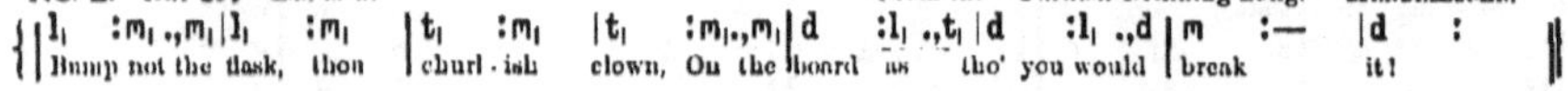

```
|l,   :m, .,m, |l,   :m,    |t,   :m,    |t,   :m, .,m, |d   :l, .,t, |d   :l, .,d |m    :—    |d    :    ||
 Bump not the   flask, thou   churl - ish  clown, On the  board as      tho' you would break        it!
```

No. 3. KEY A. *Lah is F♯.* — From a Part-Song. W. BOYD.

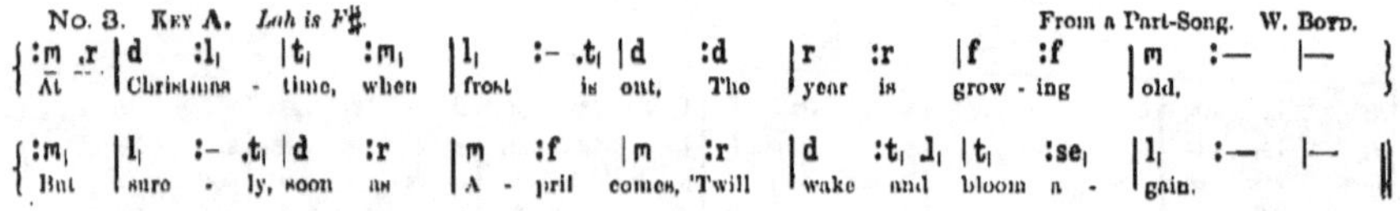

```
:m  .r |d    :l,    |t,   :m,   |l,   :-  .t, |d    :d    |r    :r    |f    :f     |m    :—   |—
 At     Christmas -  time, when   frost    is    out,  The   year  is    grow - ing   old,

:m,    |l,   :-  .t, |d    :r    |m    :f     |m    :r      |d    :t, .l, |t,   :se,  |l,   :—   |—   ||
 But    sure  - ly,  soon  as     A  - pril    comes, 'Twill  wake   and    bloom a  -   gain.
```

No. 4. KEY C. *Lah is A.* — From "The Dawn of Day." WELSH AIR.

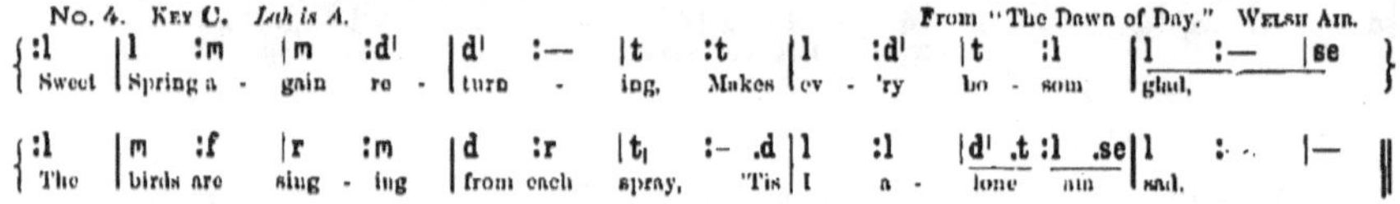

```
:l     |l    :m    |m    :d'   |d'   :—    |t    :t      |l    :d'   |t    :l    |l    :—   |se
 Sweet  Spring a -  gain  re -  turn  -     ing,  Makes   ev -  'ry   bo -  som  glad,

:l     |m    :f    |r    :m    |d    :r     |t,   :-  .d  |l    :l    |d' .t :l  .se |l    :-   |—   ||
 The    birds are   sing - ing  from each    spray,  'Tis   I     a -   lone   an     sad.
```

No. 5. KEY A. *Lah is F.* — From "There are good fish in the sea." J. R. THOMAS.

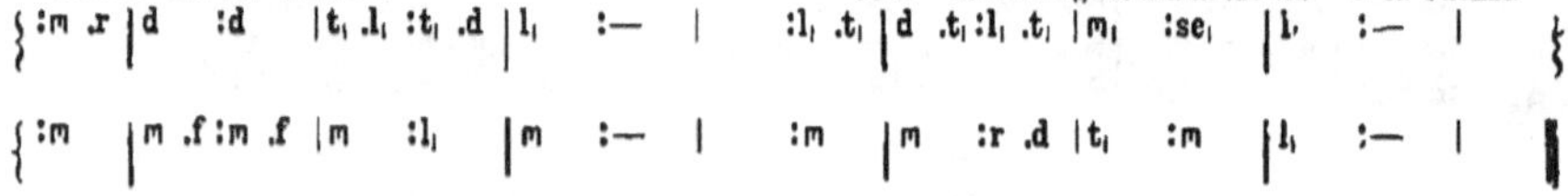

```
:m  .r |d    :d    |t, .l, :t, .d |l,   :—   |     :l, .t, |d .t, :l, .t, |m,   :se,  |l,   :—   |

:m     |m .f :m .f |m    :l,      |m    :—   |     :m      |m    :r  .d   |t,   :m    |l,   :—   |    ||
```

No. 6. KEY D♭. *Lah is B♭.* — From "Of noble race was Shenkin." WELSH AIR.

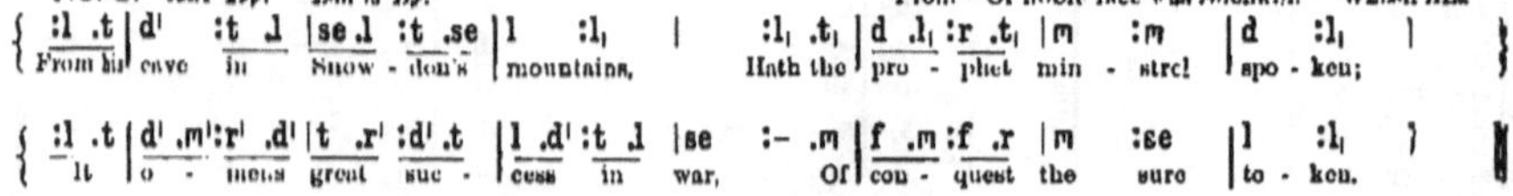

```
:l  .t  |d'   :t  .l  |se .l :t  .se |l    :l,    |     :l, .t,  |d .l, :r .t, |m    :m     |d    :l,   |
 From his cave  in      Snow - don's   mountains,         Hath the  pro -  phet   min - strel  spo - ken;

:l  .t  |d' .m' :r' .d' |t  .r' :d' .t |l .d' :t .l |se   :-  .m |f .m :f .r |m    :se   |l    :l,   ||
 It      o  -    mens    great   suc -   cess   in    war,     Of  con - quest  the   sure   to - ken.
```

No. 7. KEY C. *Lah is A.* From a Part-Song. H. LAHEE.

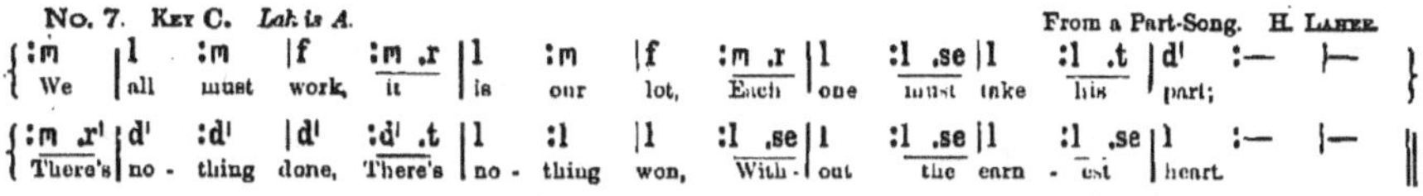

{ :m | l :m | f :m .r | l :m | f :m .r | l :l .se | l :l .t | d' :— | — }
We all must work, it is our lot, Each one must take his part;

{ :m .r' | d' :d' | d' :d' .t | l :l | l :l .se | l :l .se | l :l .se | l :— | — ‖
There's no - thing done, There's no - thing won, With - out the earn - est heart.

No. 8. KEY A. *Lah is F♯.* From a Part-Song. C. G. ALLEN.

{ :m, | d :— | t, :l, | t, :— | m, :m, | m :— | r :d | t, :— | — }
The sad leaves are dy - ing, the sweet birds have flown,

{ :m, | l, :— | t, :d | t, :se, | m, :m, | d :— | r :d | t, :— | — }
O'er ev - 'ry fair blos - som once bloom - ing and bright,

{ :t, | m :— | r :d | r :— | d :l, | m, :— | l, :se, | l, :— | — }
The frost spi - rit lays her cold fin - - gers to - night.

No. 9. KEY B♭. From "Judas." HANDEL.

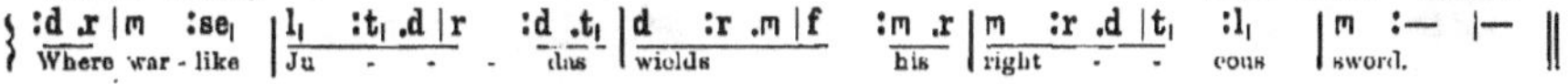

{ :d .r | m :se, | l, :t, .d | r :d .t, | d :r .m | f :m .r | m :r .d | t, :l, | m :— | — ‖
Where war - like Ju - - - - das wields his right - - eous sword.

No. 10. KEY F. *Lah is D.* From "The Owl." J. R. THOMAS.

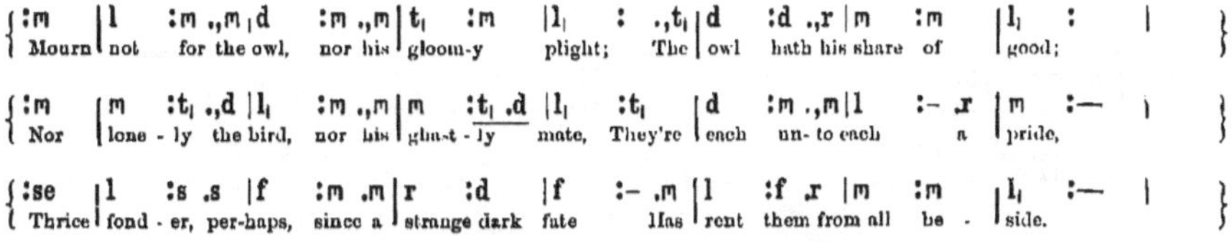

{ :m | l :m .,m | d :m .,m | t, :m | l, : .,t, | d :d .,r | m :m | l, : | }
Mourn not for the owl, nor his gloom-y plight; The owl hath his share of good;

{ :m | m :t, .,d | l, :m .,m | m :t, .d | l, :t, | d :m .,m | l :- .r | m :— | }
Nor lone - ly the bird, nor his ghast - ly mate, They're each un- to each a pride,

{ :se | l :s .s | f :m .m | r :d | f :- .m | l :f .r | m :m | l, :— | }
Thrice fond - er, per-haps, since a strange dark fate Has rent them from all be - side.

No. 11. KEY B♭. *Lah is G.* From "Good night, thou glorious sun." HENRY SMART.

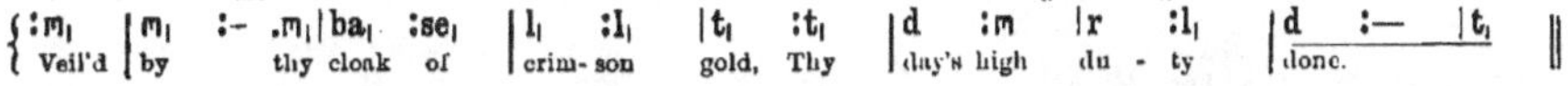

{ :m, | m, :- .m, | ba, :se, | l, :l, | t, :t, | d :m | r :l, | d :— | t, ‖
Veil'd by thy cloak of crim- son gold, Thy day's high du - ty done.

No. 12. KEY C. *Lah is A.* From the tune "Hereford." P. LA TROBE.

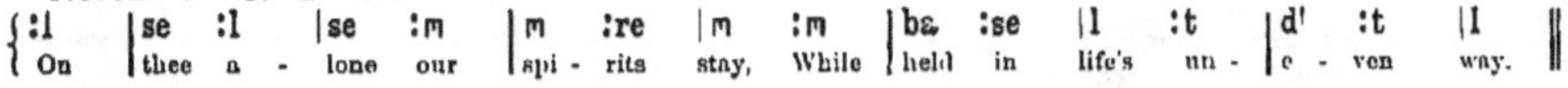

{ :l | se :l | se :m | m :re | m :m | ba :se | l :t | d' :t | l ‖
On thee a - lone our spi - rits stay, While held in life's un - e - ven way.

No. 13. KEY D. *Lah is B.* From "Jephtha." HANDEL.

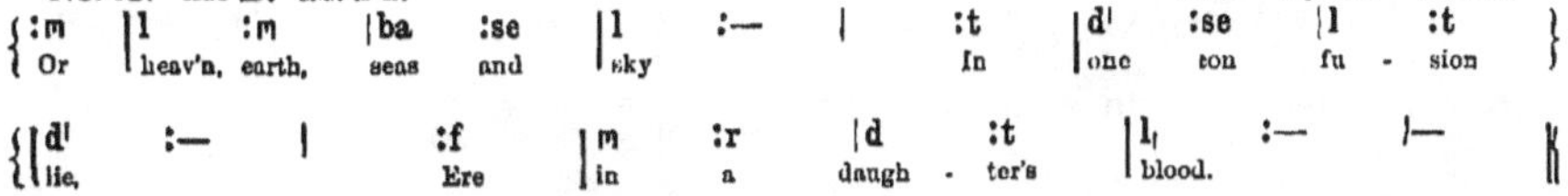

{ :m | l :m | ba :se | l :— | :t | d' :se | l :t }
Or heav'n, earth, seas and sky In one con fu - sion

{ d' :— | :f | m :r | d :t | l, :— | — ‖
lie, Ere in a daugh - ter's blood.

No. 14. KEY D. *Lah is B.* From "The Lady of the Lea." HENRY SMART.

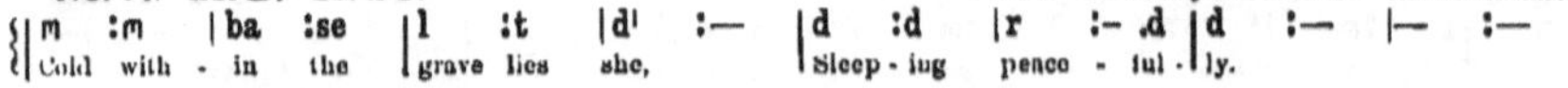

| m :m | ba :se | l :t | d^1 :— | d :d | r :– .d | d :— | — :—
Cold with - in the grave lies she, Sleep - ing peace - ful - ly.

No. 15. KEY D. *Lah is B.* From "Black-eyed Susan." LEVERIDGE.

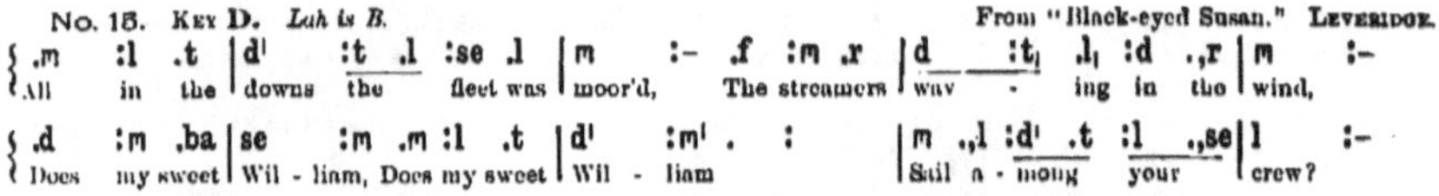

.m :l .t | d^1 :t .l :se .l | m :– .f :m .r | d :t$_1$ .l$_1$:d .,r | m :–
All in the downs the fleet was moor'd, The streamers wav - ing in the wind,

.d :m .ba | se :m .m :l .t | d^1 :m^1 . : | m .,l :d^1 .t :l .,se | l :–
Does my sweet Wil - liam, Does my sweet Wil - liam Sail a - mong your crew?

No. 16. KEY C. *Lah is A.* From "Now May is here." HENRY SMART.

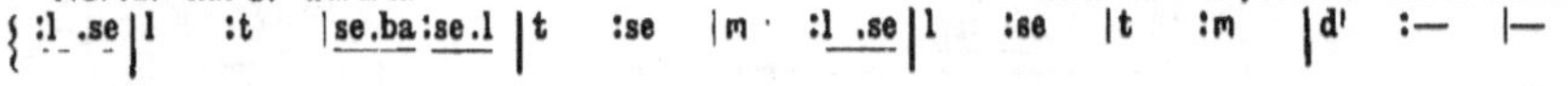

:l .se | l :t | se .ba :se .l | t :se | m :l .se | l :se | t :m | d^1 :— | —

No. 17. KEY A. *Lah is F♯* From the same.

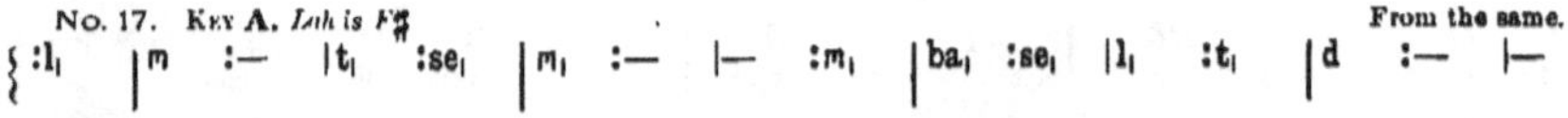

:l$_1$ | m :— | t$_1$:se$_1$ | m$_1$:— | — :m$_1$ | ba$_1$:se$_1$ | l$_1$:t$_1$ | d :— | —

No. 18. KEY C. *Lah is A.* From "Achieved is the glorious work." HAYDN.

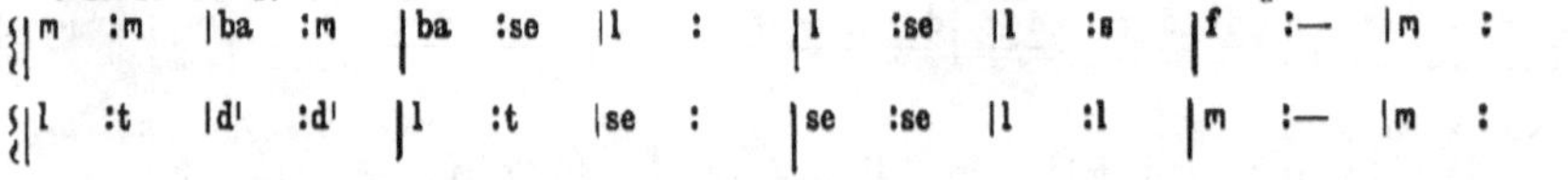

| m :m | ba :m | ba :se | l : | l :se | l :s | f :— | m :

| l :t | d^1 :d^1 | l :t | se : | se :se | l :l | m :— | m :

No. 19. KEY C. *Lah is A.* From "Esther." HANDEL.

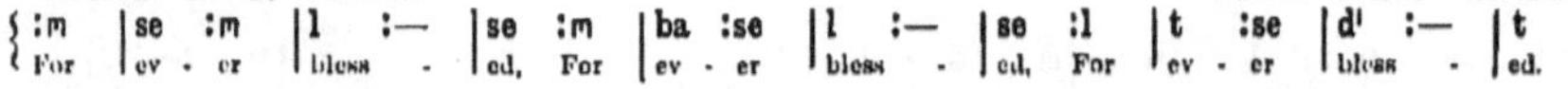

:m | se :m | l :— | se :m | ba :se | l :— | se :l | t :se | d^1 :— | t
For ev - er bless - ed, For ev - er bless - ed, For ev - er bless - ed.

No 20. KEY B♭. *Lah is G.* From "Jack Frost." J. L. HATTON.

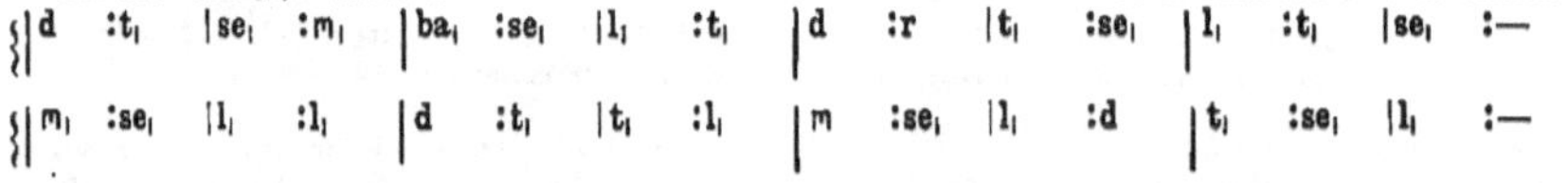

| d :t$_1$ | se$_1$:m$_1$ | ba$_1$:se$_1$ | l$_1$:t$_1$ | d :r | t$_1$:se$_1$ | l$_1$:t$_1$ | se$_1$:—

| m$_1$:se$_1$ | l$_1$:l$_1$ | d :t$_1$ | t$_1$:l$_1$ | m :se$_1$ | l$_1$:d | t$_1$:se$_1$ | l$_1$:—

No. 21. KEY C. *Lah is A.* From "The Three Fishers." G. A. MACFARREN.

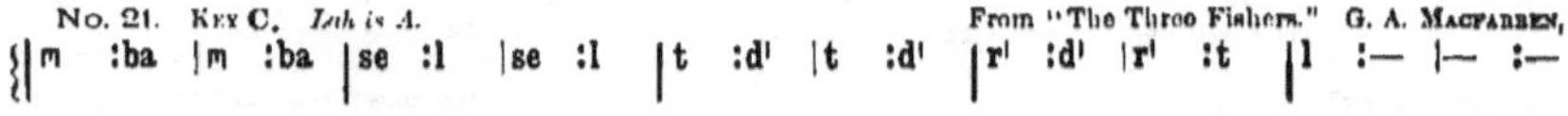

| m :ba | m :ba | se :l | se :l | t :d^1 | t :d^1 | r^1 :d^1 | r^1 :t | l :— | — :—

No. 22. KEY E♭. *Lah is C.* Phrases from "Israel in Egypt." HANDEL.

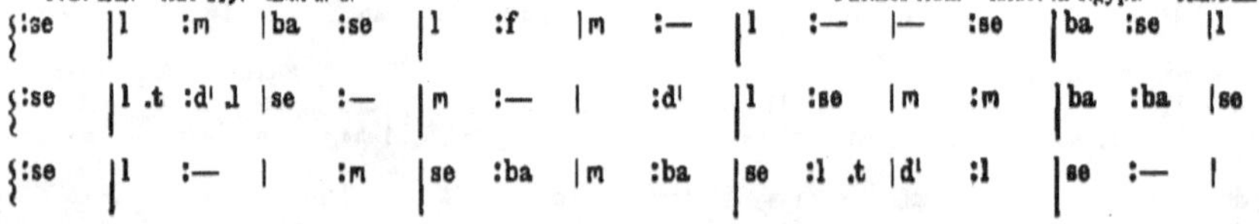

:se | l :m | ba :se | l :f | m :— | l :— | — :se | ba :se | l

:se | l .t :d^1 .l | se :— | m :— | :d^1 | l :se | m :m | ba :ba | se

:se | l :— | :m | se :ba | m :ba | se :l .t | d^1 :l | se :— |

Voice training naturally divides itself into three departments—the training of the chest, the training of the larynx and the training of the mouth; in other words, the control of the breath, the proper use of the registers and the production of good tone. There must be exercises for training and strengthening the muscles of the chest, to obtain control over the slow emission of the breath; exercises for developing and strengthening the registers, and exercises for placing and purifying or beautifying the tone. Only the general principles of voice training are given here. More complete instructions will be found in the Standard Course and Teachers' Manual. Behnke's "Mechanism of the Human Voice" and Webb and Allen's "Voice Culture" are also recommended, especially the latter for exercises and studies.

The vocal organ is a wind instrument, the machinery of which consists of—

THE BELLOWS.—The *Chest* and *Lungs*—which supplies the motive-power—breath.

THE TONE-PRODUCER.—The *Larynx*—which creates the tone.

THE RESONATOR.—The *Throat* and *Mouth*—which gives color or quality to the tone.

The Bellows.—The apparatus of breathing may be thought of as a wind-chest, having at the back the back-bone, at the sides and in front the ribs and breast-bone, and at the bottom a movable floor called the diaphram. This diaphram is a muscular membrane placed across the body, forming a flexible partition between the chest and abdomen. It is arched upward like an inverted basin. During inhalation it flattens and descends, thus increasing the capacity of the chest. The lungs, which fill the greater part of this wind-chest, are like two great sponges, full of cells, containing air. Respiration consists of two acts—namely, inspiration, taking in the air, and expiration, giving it out. The forces by which these acts are carried on are the natural elasticity of the lungs and the muscular action of the ribs and diaphram. It is not necessary for our present purpose to describe all the actions of the muscles used in breathing, it is enough for the singer to know that such muscles exist and that they need to be trained and strengthened. *The Wind-pipe* is a tube or passage-way for the air to and from the lungs. On the top of the wind-pipe is placed

The Tone-Producer—The instrument of voice, which is in every person's throat, is called the *Larynx* or *Voice-box*. It is a very complex structure, consisting of various cartilages and ligaments, and may be described as resembling a funnel, the bowl of which has been bent into a triangular shape. The most prominent angle forms the protuberance, which may be seen and felt on the outside of the throat, commonly known as Adam's apple. Inside the larynx are—

The Vibrators or real producers of the voice. They are two elastic cushions, or lips, with sharp edges, called rather inappropriately the "vocal cords." They are attached to the walls of the larynx, one on each side, and in ordinary breathing are drawn apart, thus allowing the air to pass up and down freely. When the voice is to be produced they are brought together in the middle of the larynx, thus closing the passage, so that the air from the the lungs being forced past the vocal cords, sets them in vibration and thus produces a tone. The *pitch* of the tone produced is according to the *thickness*, the *tightness*, and the *length* of the vocal cords set in vibration. The thicker, looser and longer the cords are the lower is the tone produced; and the thinner, tighter and shorter they are the higher is the pitch of the tone. Let it be clearly understood that the voice *originates* in the larynx, its pitch is varied there, its quality, good or bad, it gets in the mouth.

The Registers are caused by the *quantity*, that is, the thickness and length, of the vibrating membranes put in use. A register is a series of tones produced by the same mechanism—by the same adjustment or action of the vocal cords. In the lowest or *Thick* register the tones are produced by the vibration of the vocal cords through their whole length and *thickness*. The sensation is as though the tones were produced in the chest, and for this reason this series of tones is called by many teachers the "Chest" register. In the middle or *Thin* register the tones are produced by the *thin* edges of the vocal cords alone vibrating. The sensation is that of a vibration in the throat, for this reason this series is called by many teachers the "Medium" or "Falsetto" register. For the tones of the highest or *Small* register the vocal cords are *shortened*, leaving only about one third of their length to vibrate. The sensation is as though the tones were produced in the head, hence the term "Head" register. The physical cause of the change of register is this: as the voice ascends in the Thick register the cords are stretched more and more tightly for each higher tone. When this process of tightening has been carried as far as the cartilages will bear the strain, the register is changed, and the thin edges of the cords vibrate, producing a higher sound with less effort. As the voice ascends, the process of tightening once more commences, and goes on until again the cartilages have reached the utmost point of tension. Beyond this point the voices of men do not go, but women have a still higher register, which is produced by shortening the cords. These doctrines of the registers are not founded upon mere conjecture, but are based upon facts obtained by actual observation, by means of the laryngoscope,* of the action of the vocal cords in the living throat.

The point at which the vocal cords naturally change from the *Thick* to the *Thin* register is just below the pitch G, most commonly the break occurs at E or F. This break is at the same point of absolute pitch in all voices, whether of men or women. It is in the higher part of the male voice and lower part of the female voice. The change from the Thin to the Small register occurs only in the upper part of the female voice, about the pitch of g', top of the treble staff. The change from the Lower Thick into the Upper Thick, and from the Lower Thin into the Upper Thin are changes of quality more than changes of mechanism or action of the larynx.

* The laryngoscope (*larynx-seer*) is a small mirror with a slender handle. By placing it in the back of the mouth, over the throat, and with a properly adjusted light, the whole machinery of the larynx may be plainly seen.

The diagram shows the ordinary range of the human voice, the compass of the different voices and the divisions of the registers. It will be noticed that the Tenors and Basses use the Thick register almost exclusively. Men naturally use this register in speaking. Very rarely a man may be heard speaking in his Thin register, with a thin, squeaking quality. The constant use of the Thick register in speech is the reason why men are tempted to strain their voices upward, and to neglect the cultivation of their Thin register. Tenors should carefully train the upper tones of the Thick and Lower tones of the Thin register. Women commonly speak in their Thin register—occasionally a woman is heard to speak in the rough Lower Thick. It is this common habit of using the Thin register in speech which tempts them, in singing, to employ it downward more than is necessary, and so, to neglect and ignore the better tones of the Thick register. In women's voices it is the Thick register which is commonly found to be uncultivated. Many soprano singers do not know what it is, and even contraltos are afraid to employ what they think is a man's voice. In men it is the Thin register which is usually untrained, and Tenors hesitate to use what they think is a woman's voice.

It is never safe to force a lower register higher than the limit here given. The upper register may and should be carried downward, over or through several tones of the lower register. It is in this way that a blending or equalization of the registers is accomplished. A good singer should be able to pass from one register to another without allowing the difference to be noticed. The three tones of the Upper Thick register, D, E, F, which may be sung in either the Thick or the Thin register, are called optional tones, and the pupil is advised to exercise both registers on these three tones in order to equalize their quality and power and to use either register interchangeably.

We now come to the third and last part of our instrument, namely—

The Resonator—The throat and mouth. *Quality of Voice* (that which makes the difference between a hard, wiry voice, a soft, clear voice, a muffled, hollow voice, a full, rich voice, etc.), depends chiefly upon the mouth, though to some extent on the management of the breath and the natural peculiarity of the larynx. The mouth can be put into a great variety of positions, so as to enlarge, lessen, or alter its cavity. The different positions produce the different vowels—"oo," "ah," "ee," etc. It is the shaping of the mouth more than all that determines the quality of the tone produced; and the physical part of voice training, besides strengthening the lungs and bringing the vocal cords under the will of the singer, consists in learning to strengthen the good and suppress the bad elements of which every sound is made up.

The direction of the breath is an important point. The cardinal rule is "throw the breath forward." Do not let it strike at the back of the mouth, or pass up through the nostrils, but try to direct it upon the roots of the upper front teeth. Think of the tone as being produced, apparently, between the lips, rather than in the throat. The quality of the tone depends greatly upon the *habit* of throwing the air-stream *forward* in the mouth. Certain vowels naturally favor this habit more than others. In English, "*ee*," "*ai*," "*o*" and "*oo*" (as in "*peel*," "*pail*," "*pole*" and "*pool*"), are all "forward" vowels. These vowels, however, do not promote the proper opening of the mouth. The most useful vowel in vocal practice, that which opens the mouth properly and places the tongue most favorably, is the open vowel "*ah*" (as in *father, bar, far*, etc.). But this vowel is commonly formed by most persons far back in the mouth. To bring it forward, begin the tone with "*oo*" placed well forward, upon the lips, then change the "*oo*" to "*o*," keeping the tone forward and finally change the "*o*" to "ah," keeping the "*ah*" forward. It is better to precede these "*oo, oh, ah*" exercises with staccato exercises upon the syllable "*koo*" to secure a *clear attack*; they also throw the tone forward and make the throat supple.

Voice Training in Class.—It is only to a small extent that voice training can be carried out in class, but the experience gained in a well trained class will encourage many pupils to seek additional practice in private lessons under a competent teacher. Only when the pupils themselves are intelligent and observant students of their own voices can voice training in class be profitable. In ignorant and careless hands it may destroy voices by forcing them up into unnatural registers. No teacher should attempt to carry his pupils far into these studies, who has not himself studied and been trained in them. It is well for the student to know at once that the secret of success will not be in the particular form of his exercises, or in the multitude of them, or in their being written by this man or the other,—but in their being frequently used and perfectly worked through. Every one should seek to have a *cultivated* voice. The cultivated voice is known from another by its first sound. There is no mistaking the master of his instrument.

a.—The double horizontal lines at *a* shows the places of the great break between the Thick and Thin registers.

b.—The single lines at *b, c* and *d* show the places of the lesser breaks

e.—The dotted lines show the average places of the breaks.

Only the ordinary compass of voices is given in the above diagram. Many voices are capable of carrying the tones several degrees higher or lower than the limit here assigned. In practice, however, it is best never to force the extreme tones. The pupil should confine his practice to those tones that can be reached with comparative ease.

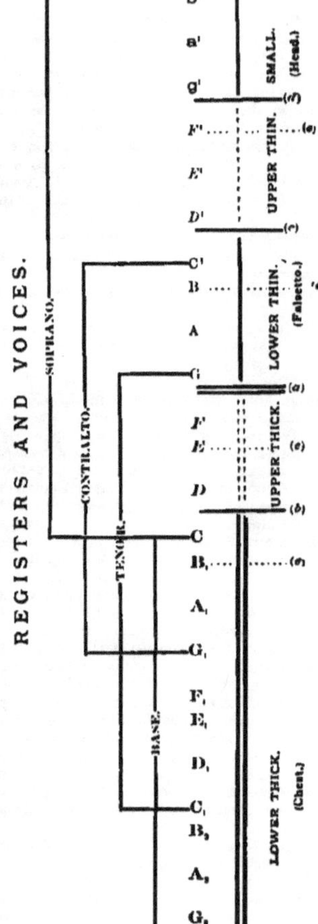

Breathing Exercises.—Position: Pupils standing, arms akimbo, hands upon the waist, fingers in front.

I. *Inhale* slowly as the teacher raises his hand.

Draw in the breath through a small opening in the nearly closed lips, as though sipping hot soup. Expand the waist and lower part of the chest but do not raise the shoulders.

Exhale suddenly as the teacher drops his hand.

Expel the air through the wide open mouth, as in a heavy sigh.

Repeat a number of times.

II. *Inhale* as above. Hold the breath while the teacher's hand remains up, about four seconds.

The breath must be held, not by closing the throat, but by keeping the chest distended—the mouth and throat open.

Exhale as above. Several repetitions.

III. *Inhale* rapidly and deeply, through the nostrils, as the teacher raises his hand with a quick movement.

Exhale slowly and steadily as the teacher gradually lowers his hand.

Expel the air through a small orifice in the lips, as though "blowing the fire," or cooling the hot soup. The air must not ooze out, as it were, of its own weight, but should be forced out with more or less pressure from the chest. Repetitions.

IV. *Inhale* quickly as in III.

Exhale slowly through the closed teeth forming the sound of *s* (as in *hiss*). This may also be done with *f*, *th*, *sh*, also changing from *s* to *f*, etc., without stopping the flow of breath.

Repetitions.

V. *Inhale* as in III.

Exhale sustaining the tone G, vowel *Ah*, while the teacher slowly counts eight; again ten, and again twelve, etc. Increase the length of tone at each lesson until it reaches twenty or more counts.

It is not intended that *all* of the above exercises are to be done at each lesson, only one or two should be done at a time. They should be introduced in the order given, and when all of them have been practiced the teacher will vary the exercises so as to avoid sameness and mere routine.

1. KEYS **D, E, F.** May be used in First Step. To be taught by pattern.

| d : | d : | d .d :d .d | d : | d :— | — :— | — :— | — : |
| Koo, † | koo † | koo, koo, koo, koo, | koo, † | Oo.......... | Oh............ | Ah.......... | .... † |

| m : | m : | m .m :m .m | m : | m :— | — : - | — :— | — : |
| Koo, | koo | koo, koo, koo, koo, | koo, | Oo.......... | Oh............ | Ah.......... | .... |

| s : | s : | s .s :s .s | s : | s :— | — :— | -- :— | — : |
| Koo, | koo | koo, koo, koo, koo, | koo, | Oo.......... | Oh............ | Ah.......... | .... |

| s : | m : | d .d :d .d | d : | d :— | — :— | — :-- | — : ||
| Koo | koo | koo, koo, koo, koo, | koo, | Oo.......... | Oh............ | Ah.......... | .... ||

1. KEYS **E, F, G.** May be used in Second Step.

| d :— | — : † | r :— | — : † | m :— | — : ||

Koo......oh........ah † Koo.....oh........ah † Koo......oh........ah

2. KEYS **E, F, G.**

| d :— | — : | d :r | m :r | d :r | m :r | d :r | m :r | d :— | — : ||

Oo................. † Oo...

Oo,...oh........... † Oh...

Oo,...oh....ah...... † Ah..

Koo................. † Oo.......................oh....................ah...............................

3. KEYS **E, F, G.**

| d :— | — : | d.r :d.r | m.r :m.r | d.r :d.r | m.r :m.r | d.r :m.r | m.r :m.r | d :— | — : ||

Oo................. † Oo...

Oo....oh........... † Oh...

Oo....oh....ah..... † Ah..

Oo................. † Oo.......................Oh....................Ah...............................

4. KEYS **D, E♭.** For Third Step.

| d :— † | r :— † | m :— † | f :— † | s :— † | l :— ||

Koo-oh-ah, † Koo-oh-ah, † Koo-oh-ah, † Koo-oh-ah, † Koo-oh-ah, † Koo-oh-ah,

† If a piano or organ is available the following exercise may be used instead of No. 1 and 2, page, 179, and Nos. 1 and 4, page, 180. May also be used with the time-form of No. 1, page, 179.

Koo-oh-ah, etc.
May be carried up to E at the discretion of the teacher.

At first the practice to be confined to the limit here given. Later on, at the discretion of the teacher, the compass to be extended up to G' and down to, G_2 in the proper registers.

1. KEYS E, F, F♯, G.

| d :–̂ . | d .r :m .f | s .f :m .r | d .r :m .f | s .f :m .r | d .r :m .f | s .f :m .r | d :— | — : ‖

Koo....... † Oo..
Koo, .oh... † Oh..
Koo-oh-ah.. † Ah..
Koo....... † Oo.........................Oh.........................Ah.....................................

2. KEYS E, F, F♯, G.

| d :–̂ . | d .m :r .t | m .s :f .r | d .m :r .f | m .s :f .r | d .m :r .f | m .s :f .r | d :— | — : ‖

Koo....... † Oo..
Koo, .oh... † Oh..
Koo-oh-ah.. † Ah..
Koo....... † Oo.........................Oh.........................Ah.....................................

3. KEYS D, E♭, E, F.

| d :–̂ . | 𝄋 d :r .m :f .s | l :s .f :m .r D.S. | d :— :— | : : ‖
Koo, etc. Oo, etc.

4. KEYS C, D♭, D, and higher at the discretion of the teacher.

| d :–̂ | 𝄋 d :r .m | f .s :l .t | d' :t .l | s .f :m .r D.S. | d :— | — : ‖
Koo, etc. † Oo, etc.

5. KEY A, A♭, G down to D. For Thin register, male voice.

Thick.......................... *Thin* *Thin*
| d :— | m :s | d' :— | — : | d' :d' | d' : | t :t | t : |
Koo koo koo *Koo* *Koo koo koo* *Koo koo koo*

| d' :t | l :s | l :t | d' :— | d' :— | t :— | d' :— | — : ‖
Koo koo koo koo Koo koo koo Koo koo Koo.

6. KEYS E♭, E, F, F♯, G. For Thin register, male voice.

| d :— | m :s | d' :— | — : | d' :t | l :s | d' :t | l :s | d' :r' | m' :r' | d' :t | d' :— ‖
Koo kȯo, koo, *Koo.........* † *Koo koo koo koo* etc.

7. KEYS E♭, D, D♭, C. For Thin register, male voice. May be sung by ladies and gentlemen together, ladies singing an octave lower than written.

| m' :f' | m' :r' | m' :f' | m' :r' | m' :f' | s' :f' | m' :r' | d' :— ‖
Koo, koo koo koo, etc.

KEYS D, E♭, E, F. For blending the registers.

1. LADIES. 2. GENTLEMEN.

```
  Thick.                 Thin.                       Thick.                  Thin.
{|d   :—  |—  :    † |d   :—  |—  :   ||  {|d'  :—  |—  :    † |d'  :—  |—  :
 |Koo - oh - ah      |Koo - oh - ah       |Koo - oh - ah       |Koo - oh - ah
```

3. KEYS D to F. For blending registers, female voice.

```
  Thick.   Thin.    Thick.             Thick.  Thin.    Thick.              Thick.  Thin.    Thick.
{|d' :— |m  :— |d  :— |— :  † |d  :— |s  :— |d  :— |— :  † |d  :— |d' :— |d  :— |— :
 |Ah...........|....          |Ah...........|....          |Ah...........|....
```

4. KEYS C, C♯, D, E♭. For blending registers, male voice.

```
  Thick.   Thin.    Thick.             Thick.  Thin.    Thick.              Thick.  Thin.    Thick.
{|d' :— |r' :— |d' :— |— :  † |d' :— |m' :— |d' :— |— :  † |d' :— |s' :— |d' :— |— :
 |Ah...........|....          |Ah...........|....          |Ah...........|....
```

5. KEYS C to E, for female voice. KEYS A to D♭, for male voice.

```
  Thick.     Thin.                              Thick.     Thin.
{|d   :—   |m   :—   |s   :—  |—  :          |d   :—   |f   :—   |l   :—  |—  :
 |Ah.................|....                    |Ah.................|....

  Thin.                                         Thin.
{|s   :—   |f   :—   |m   :—  |—  :          |m   :—   |r   :—   |d   :—  |—  :
 |Ah.................|....                    |Ah.................|....
```

6. KEYS D to F.

```
{|d  :-. |m  :-. |s  :-. |d' :-. |d' :-. |s  :-. |m  :-. |d  :-.
  Oo      oh      ah      ai      ai      ah      oh      oo.
  Oh      ah      ai      ee      ee      ai      ah      oh.
```

7. KEYS C to E♭.

```
{|d :-. |m :-. |s :-. |d' :-. |m' :— |— :   |m' :-. |d' :-. |s :-. |m :-. |d :— |— :
 |Oo     oh    |ah     ai     |ee           |ee      ai     |ah     oh    |oo.
```

pp 8. KEYS F, E, E♭ D.

```
                                            pp
{|d  .t,  :d  .r   |m      :          |m  .r   :m  .f   |s      :
 |Oo  oh   ah  ai  |ee                |oo  oh   ah  ai  |ee

                                                        <  >
{|s  .s   :s  .f   |m      :          |s  .s   :l  .t   |d'     :—
 |Oo  ah   ah  ai  |ee                |oo  oh   ah  ai  |ee
```

1. KEYS B♭, A, A♭ and G. For the *Thick* register. Sing slowly, with full, deep, resonant tones.

| m_1 :f_1 | m_1 :r_1 | m_1 :f_1 | m_1 :r_1 | m_1 :f_1 | m_1 :r_1 | d_1 :— | — : ||
Ah..........

2. KEYS G, A♭, A and B♭.

| s_1 :f_1 | m_1 :f_1 | s_1 :f_1 | m_1 :f_1 | m_1 :— | r_1 :— | d_1 :— | — : ||
Ah..........

3. KEYS G, A♭ and A. *Small* register only. Sing softly, use very little breath.

| d' :t | l :s | d' :t | l :s | d' :t | l :t | d' :— | — : ||
Ah..........

4. KEYS G, A♭ and A.

Thin.......... *Small*.......... *Thin*..........
| d :— | m :f | s :— | — : | d' :— | t :l | s : | — : | f :— | m :r | d :— | — : ||

5. KEYS D, E♭, E and F.

Thin.......... *pp* *Small*.......... *Thin*..........
| d :m | s :d' | m' :— | — :d' | s :m | d :— ||
Ah..........
Oo, oh, ah, ai, ee,.......... ai, ah, oh, oo.

6. Different keys for different voices.

| d :m | s :— | s .l :s .f | m :— | m .f :m .r | d :— | d .t :l_1 .t_1 | d :— ||
Oo oh ah.......... Ah.......... Ah.......... Ah..........
Ah oh oo.......... Oo.......... Oo.......... Oo..........
Ah ai ee.......... Ee.......... Ee.......... Ee..........

pp 7. KEYS C, C♯, D.

| d .m :s .m | d .m :s .m † | f .l :d' .l | f .l :d' .l † | *m* s .t :r' .t | s .t :r' .t | *f* d' :— | — :— ||
Ah..........
| d :— | — :— | f :— | — :— | s :— | — :— | d' .s :m .s | d :— ||

8. KEYS F to A for female voices KEYS B♭ to E♭ for male voices.

p
| s_1 :— | — :d | m :— | — :r | d :— | — : | *m* s_1 :— | — :r | f :— | — :m |
Ah.......... Ah..........

| r :— | — : | *f* s_1 :— | — :m | s :— | — :f | m :— | — : | *m* s_1 :— | — :r |
.... Ah.......... Ah..........

| f :— | — :m | r :— | — : | *p* s_1 :— | — :d | m :— | — :r | d :— | — : ||
.... Ah..........

1. KEYS C to G. Sing the first measure three times.

D.C. twice.

{| d ,r .m ,f :s ,l .f ,r | d : ||
Ah........................ ...

2. KEYS C to G.

D.C. twice.

{| d ,r .m ,s :l ,s .f ,r | d :
Ah.................... ... ...

4. KEY C to G. Basses and Altos not higher than E♭.

D.C. twice.

{| d ,d' .t ,l :s ,f .m ,r | d : ||
Ah...................... ...

3. KEYS C to G.

D.C. twice.

{| d',d .r ,m :f ,s .l ,t | d' :
Ah ....

5. KEYS C to G.

D.C. | Sing the first and fourth measures twice. 𝄋 D.S.

{| d .r,m:f .m,r | d .r,m:f ,s.l ,t | d' : | d' .t,l :s .l ,t | d' .t ,l :s ,f .m,r | d :
Ah........ Ah... ....

6. KEYS C to G. D.C. twice.

{| d .m :s .d' :s .m | d :— : ||
Ah.......................... ..

7. KEYS C to G. D.C. twice.

{| d ,m .s ,d' :t ,s .f ,r | d :
Ah............................ ..

8. KEY D.

{| d .m :r .f | m .s :f .l | s .t :l .d' | t .r' :d' † | d' .l :t .s | l .f :s .m | f .r :m .d | r .t, :d
Ah........ Ah............ ...

9. KEY D.

{| d .r :m .d | r .m :f .r | m .f :s .m | f : | s .l :t .s | l .t :d' .l | t .d' :r' .t | d' :
La la la la la la la, La......... la.......... la.......... la,

{| d' .r' :m' .d' | t .d' :r' .t | l .t :d' .l | s : | f .s :l .f | m .f :s .m | r .m :f .r | d :
La.......... .... La.. ....

10. KEYS B♭ up to F. M. 60 to 132.

{:d ,r ,m | r ,m ,f :m ,f ,s | f ,s ,l :s ,l ,t | l ,t ,d' :t ,d' ,r' | d' || m' ,r' ,d' | r' ,d' ,t :d' ,t ,l | t ,l ,s :l ,s ,f | s ,f ,m :f ,m ,r | d
Ah..... ......

11. KEYS B up to E. M. 60 to 132.

{:d ,t, ,d | r ,d ,r :m ,r ,m | f ,m ,f :s ,f ,s | l ,s ,l :t ,l ,t | d' || d' ,r' ,d' | t ,d' ,t :l ,t ,l | s ,l ,s :f ,s ,f | m ,f ,m :r ,m ,r | d
Ah..... ......

12. KEYS B up to E. M. 60 to 160.

{| d .m :r .d | r .f :m .r | m .s :f .m | f .l :s .f | s .t :l .s | l .d' :t .l | t .r' :d' .t | d' :—
Ah.............

{| d' .m' :r' .d' | t .r' :d' .t | l .d' :t .l | s .t :l .s | f .l :s .f | m .s :f .m | r .f :m .r | d :—
Ah...............

1. KEYS C to F, changing registers.

{| d .r,m:f,s .l ,t | d' :r' | m' :— | r',d'.t,l :s ,f.m,r | d :d' | d :— ||

2. KEYS F down to B♭.

{| d' .t ,l:s ,f.m,r | d :t₁ | l₁ :— | t₁,d.r,m :f ,s.l ,t | d' :d | d' :— ||

3. KEYS G, A♭ and A. To be sung *legato* to "ah". The parts may afterwards sing simultaneously, making three octaves

SOPRANOS.

{| d' :t .l | s .f :m .r | d :— | t₁ :— ||

CONTRALTOS and TENORS.

{| d :t₁ .l₁ | s₁ .f₁ :m₁ .r | d :— | t₂ :— ||
| d' :t .l | s .f :m .r | d :— | t₁ :— ||

BASSES.

{| d :t₁ .l₁ | s₁ .f₁ :m₁ .r₁ | d₁ :— | t₂ :— | d₁ : | — :— ||

4. KEYS C to E, changing registers.

{| d ,t₁ ,d :m ,r ,d | r ,d ,r :f ,m ,r | m ,r ,m :s ,f ,m | ᶠf ,m ,f :l ,s ,f | s ,f ,s :t ,l ,s }

{| l ,s ,l :d' ,t ,l | t ,l ,t :r' ,d' ,t | d' :— | d' ,t ,d' :m' ,r' ,d' | t ,l ,t :r' ,d' ,t }

{| l ,s ,l :d' ,t ,l | ˢs ,f ,s :t ,l ,s | f ,m ,f :l ,s ,f | m ,r ,m :s ,f ,m | r ,d ,r :f ,m ,r | d :— ||

5. KEYS G to B♭, changing registers.

BASSES.

{| d₁ :r₁ .m₁ | f₁ .s₁ :l₁ .t₁ | d :— | t₁ :l₁ |

D.t. TENORS.

| ˢd :r .m | f .s :l .t | d' :— | t :l }

A.t. ALTOS.

{| ˢd₁ :r₁ .m₁ | f₁ .s₁ :l₁ .t₁ | d :— | t₁ :l₁ |

E.t. SOPRANOS.

| ˢd :r .m | f .s :l .t | d' :— | — : }

SOPRANOS.

{| d' :t .l | s .f :m .r | d :— | r :m |

f.A ALTOS.

| ᶠd :t₁ .l₁ | s₁ .f₁ :m₁ .r₁ | d₁ :— | r₁ :m₁ }

f.D. TENORS.

{| ᶠd' :t .l | s .f :m .r | d :— | r :m |

f.G. BASSES.

| ᶠd :t₁ .l₁ | s₁ .f₁ :m₁ .r₁ | d₁ :— | — : ||

SOLFEGGIOS.

1. KEY G. D t.

{|d :— |m :s |l, :— |f :r |d :t, |l, :s, |d :— | :ʳs |l :— |t :— }

{|d' :— |— :l |s :— |f :r |d :— | : f.G. |ˢr :— |m :— |f :— |— :s }

{|m :d |l, :r |s, :— | : |d :— |r :— |m :s |l, :r |s, :— |t, :— |d :— |— : ‖

2 KEY C. G.t.

{|d :— |m :-.f |s :— |d : |d' :— |t :-.l |s :— |m : |ˢd :— |s, :— }

{|l, :— |d :— |t, :-.d |r :-.m |d :— |— : f.C. |ᶠd :— |m :-.f |s :— |d : }

{|d' :— |t :-.l |s :— |m : |d' :m |f :s |l :— |d' :— |s :m |f :r |d :— |— : ‖

3. KEY E♭. *Lah is C.*

{:m |l :— :d' |t :— :se |*m* l :— :— |*p* m :— :d |r :— :m |*m* d :— :m |t, :— :— |m :— †}

{:se |l :— :d' |t :— :se |*m* l :— :— |m :— † *p* :d |f :— :r |m :— :— |l, :— :— |— :— *pp* D.C. ‖

{𝄋 :m |t :— :se |m :— :se |l :— :— |m :— † :d |f :— :— |t, :— :— |t, :— :— |— :— †}

{:m |l :— :d' |t :— :se |l :— :— |r : † :re |m :— :— |— :— :— |*pp* l, :— :— |— :— D.S. ‖

KEY F.

ETUDES.

From WEBB & ALLEN'S VOICE CULTURE,* by per.

| d,r.d,r:m . | d,r.d,r:m . | r,m.r,m:f . | r,m.r,m:f . | m,f.m,f:s . | f,m.f,m:r . |
Ah.................. (and other vowels.)

| d,r.d,r:m,r.m,r | d : | D.C. 𝄋: r,m.r,m:r,m.r,m | r . : | m,f.m,f:m,f.m,f | m . : |

| f ,s .f ,m:r . | m ,f .m ,r :d | r .m ,r :m ,r .m ,r | d : D.S. ||

2. KEY F. From WEBB & ALLEN'S VOICE CULTURE, by per.

| d ,r .d ,r:m ,f .m,f | s :m . | f ,s .f ,m:r . | m,f .m ,r :d | d,r .m,r :d ,r .m,f |
Ah.... etc.

| s :m . | r .s :- ,fe.m,fe | s : | D.C. 𝄋: f ,s .f ,m :f ,s .f ,m | f :r . |

| m,f.m,r :m,f.m,r | m :d . | r,m.f,m:s ,f .m,r | d† .m,r :f ,m.r,d | s :f,m.f ,r | d : D.S. ||

3. KEY D. From WEBB & ALLEN'S VOICE CULTURE, by per.

| d ,r .d ,r :d ,r .d ,r | d :m . | s ,l .s ,l :s ,l .s ,l | s :d' . | t ,d'.t ,d':t ,d'.t ,d' |

| l ,t .l ,t :l ,t .l ,t | s :t .,l | s : | s ,l .s ,l :s ,l .s ,l | s :r' . |

| s ,l .s ,l :s ,l .s ,l | s :d' . | l ,t.l ,t :l ,t .l ,d' | t,d'.t ,d':t,d'.t,r | d',r'.d',r':d',r'.d',r' | d' : ||

4. KEY D. From WEBB & ALLEN'S VOICE CULTURE, by per.

| d ,r .m ,f :s .d' | d ,r .m ,f :s .d' | r',d'.t ,l :s . | r',d'.t ,l :s . | d,r .m ,f :s .d' |

| r ,m.f ,s :l .r' | s ,d'.r',d':t ,s .f ,r | d :d' . D.C. FINE. A.t. || d,r .m,f :s .l | s,f .m,r :d . |

| l_1,t_1.d ,r :m .f | m,r.d,t_1:l_1 . | r,m.f ,s :l . | d,r,m,f:s . | s_1,l_1.t_1,d:r .m | f.D. ds : . D.C. ||

* "Voice Culture."—A complete method of theory and practice for the cultivation and development of the voice, by George James Webb and Chester G. Allen. Published by The Biglow & Main Co., 76 East Ninth St., New York. In this work, which contains nearly 200 large pages, the laws governing the use and development of the human voice are fully and carefully explained. The position of the vocal organs in using the different registers of the voice is illustrated by means of diagrams. The book contains also the largest and best variety of Exercises and Etudes of any now in use.

Pronunciation.—A pure and exact enunciation, making every word stand out clear and distinct, is an essential feature of good singing. This can only be secured by special practice upon the vowels and consonants. Vowels are ways of emitting the breath; consonants are ways of interrupting it. Both require *definite* positions and movements of the lips and tongue. Musical tones cannot be prolonged upon consonants, the vowels are therefore the more important to the singer in the production of a good tone. But distinctness of utterance depends upon a sharp, clean delivery of the consonants. Some of the vowels have already been practiced in connection with the voice exercises, and will be studied more fully presently. In first attracting the attention of the pupil to the action of the articulating organs it is easier to begin with the consonants. *An articulation* is a joint. A joint implies in this case both a separation and a connection of spoken sounds. The lips may come into contact with one another, or the lip touch the upper teeth, or the tongue touch teeth or palate. There may be thus an absolute or nearly absolute stopping of the vowel sounds. And these points of separation are also made points of junction. They are joints or articulations. The muscles of articulation are chiefly in the lips and tongue, for the teeth are comparatively stationary.

The work has to be done by the *Lips*, and by *Tip*, *Middle* and *Back* of the tongue. Properly devised exercises in articulation are intended to give special practice to these muscles. Thus the teacher will arrange a group of consonants to give exercise to the lips, another group to exercise the lips and teeth, and so on.

The teacher will arrange groups for Tip-tongue, such as, *To, No, Lo, Do.* For the Mid-and Back tongue, *Jo, Go, Yo, Ko.* Various groupings may be made, as *Bo, Co, Fo, Lo; Mo, No, Po, To*, etc. Various forms of melody may be used instead of the scale. The consonants may also be arranged as *finals* instead of *initials*, thus, *ōp, ōm, ōb, ōv*, etc (long sound of ō, *ope, ome*, etc.) Again as both initial and finals thus, *Pōp, Mōm, Bōb, Vōv*, etc. And again as double articulations, thus, *op-po, om-mo, ob-bo, ov-vo*, etc. Consonantal diphthongs should also be practiced, such as *Blo, Clo, Flo, Glo*, etc. The limits of this book will not admit of a full list of such combinations. The teacher will construct such as he may think useful in his work. In these exercises the movements of the articulating muscles should be decided and energetic, considerably exaggerating the consonant element.

Vowels are produced by giving certain fixed forms to the cavity between the larynx and the lips. When the tongue, palate and lips are properly adjusted, the shape of the cavity thus formed becomes a mold into which the vowel is cast. Any change in the shape of the cavity will modify the character of the vowel. For the *Simple vowels*— those in which there is no change from beginning to end—the mouth remains fixed in one position. For the *Compound vowels*—those which end with a glide into another vowel—the mouth changes from one position to another. A common fault is to make the change too soon—thus, for "day" is heard "*da-ee;*" "great" becomes "*gra-eet;*" "high," "*hi-ee;*" "bow," "*bow-oo,*" etc. In singing a compound vowel the position taken for the first element must be steadily held until just at the close, and then an easy glide made into the vanishing sound. The teacher will arrange different successions of vowels, as *oh, ah, ai, ee*, or *oo, aw, u* (at) *e* (let), and others, and sing them to the scale, ascending and descending, as suggested in the exercise below.

LONG VOWELS.

aa	(ah)	in	*bah,*	*far.*
au	(aw)	"	*Paul,*	*law.*
oa	(oh)	"	*load,*	*pole.*
oo	....	"	*cool,*	*pool.*
ai	(ay)	"	*paid,*	*pay.*
ee	....	"	*bee,*	*fee.*

SHORT VOWELS.

u	....	in	*but,*	*cut.*
a	....	"	*bat,*	*cat.*
e	....	"	*bet,*	*get.*
i	....	"	*bit,*	*sit.*
uo	(u)	"	*full,*	*pull.*

DIPHTHONGS.

ei	(I)	in	*height,*	*pine.*
oi	(oy)	"	*boil,*	*boy.*
ou	(ow)	"	*out,*	*how.*
eu	(ew)	"	*feud,*	*few.*

CONSONANTS.

LIPS.

P	in	*pine,*	*pipe.*
B	"	*bay,*	*babe.*
Wh	"	*wheel,*	*when.*
W	"	*weal,*	*way.*
M	"	*may,*	*maim.*

LIPS and TEETH.

F	in	*file,*	*fife.*
V	"	*vile,*	*revive.*

TONGUE and TEETH.

Th	in	*thin,*	*teeth.*
Dh	"	*then,*	*bathe.*

TIP-TONGUE.

T	in	*tin,*	*tint.*
D	"	*deal,*	*deed.*
L	"	*lean,*	*leal.*
N	"	*nut,*	*nun.*
R	"	*roll,*	*roar.*

MID-TONGUE.

S	in	*sell,*	*less.*
Z	"	*zone,*	*nose.*
Sh	"	*shine,*	*dash.*
Zh	"	*azure,*	*treasure.*
Ch	"	*churn*	*church.*
J	"	*just*	*judge.*
Y	"	*you,*	*due.*

BACK-TONGUE.

K	in	*keen,*	*kick.*
G	"	*game,*	*gag.*
N	"	*sing,*	*song.*

ASPIRATE.

H	in	*hail,*	*ha-ha.*

KEY C. The scale, ascending and descending.

d	:d	|d	:d	|r	:r	|r	:r	|m	:m	|m	:m	|f	:f	|f	:f, etc.
Po,	Mo,	Bo,	Wo,	Po,	Mo,	Bo,	Wo, etc.								
Oh,	ah,	ai,	ee,	oh,	ah,	ai,	ee, etc.								

Make different groupings—ascending with one series and descending with another. Various forms of melody and different groups of vowels will suggest themselves to the teacher. Prefix a consonant to each vowel, thus, *Boh, Bah, Bai, Bee*, etc. Suffix a consonant, thus, *ohb, ahb, aib, eeb*, etc. Then both prefix and suffix—thus, *bohb, bahb, baib, beeb*, etc.

THE STAFF NOTATION.

It is recomended that instruction in the Staff Notation be defered until the Third, or better still, the Fourth Step of Tonic Sol-fa has been passed. But for the sake of those teachers who may find it expedient or who may be *compelled* to introduce the staff early in their lessons, the exercises are arranged to correspond with the steps of the method, so that the staff *may be* taught concurrently with the Tonic Sol-fa. Nothing in the staff notation should be taught until the corresponding matter in Tonic Sol-fa has been learned. Music is a thing apart from Notation, and the more thoroughly pupils understand the principles of *music*, the more easily will they master the staff notation.

FIRST STEP.

1. The Staff.

2. Degrees.

added line above.
space above.
5th line.
4th line.
3rd line.
2nd line.
1st line.
4th space.
3rd space.
2nd space.
1st space.
space below.
added line below.

The teacher may have the pupils name the degrees as he points, thus—"First line," "Third space," "Second line," etc.

First Rule.—When *Doh* is on a line, *Me* and *Soh* are on the next two lines above. When *Doh* is in a space, *Me* and *Soh* are in the next two spaces above. *Doh*, *Me* and *Soh* are *similarly* placed—all on lines, or all in spaces.

The place of *Doh* is shown by the square character (■) at the beginning of each exercise. The staff *without the clef*, as in the following exercises, does not represent absolute pitch, therefore, any pitch suitable for the voices may be taken for the key-tone. The letters in parenthesis suggest the pitch which may be taken for *Doh*.

As a preliminary exercise the pupils may name the degrees in the order in which the notes are placed, thus in No. 3, the pupils will say, "First line, second line, third line, second line," and so on. The pupils may next "read the notes," that is, name the Sol-fa syllables in the speaking voice. After this the exercise is to be sung—sol-faed.

The bars are used in these exercises mainly to help the eye to keep the place in reading. The measures are numbered as a convenience in calling attention to certain notes, correcting errors, etc.

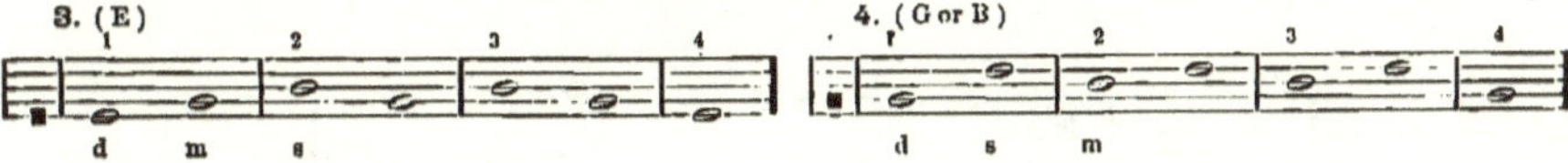

Second Rule.—Octaves are *dis*-similarly placed. When *Doh*, *Me* and *Soh* are on lines, their octaves, above or below, are in spaces. When they are in spaces, their octaves are on lines.

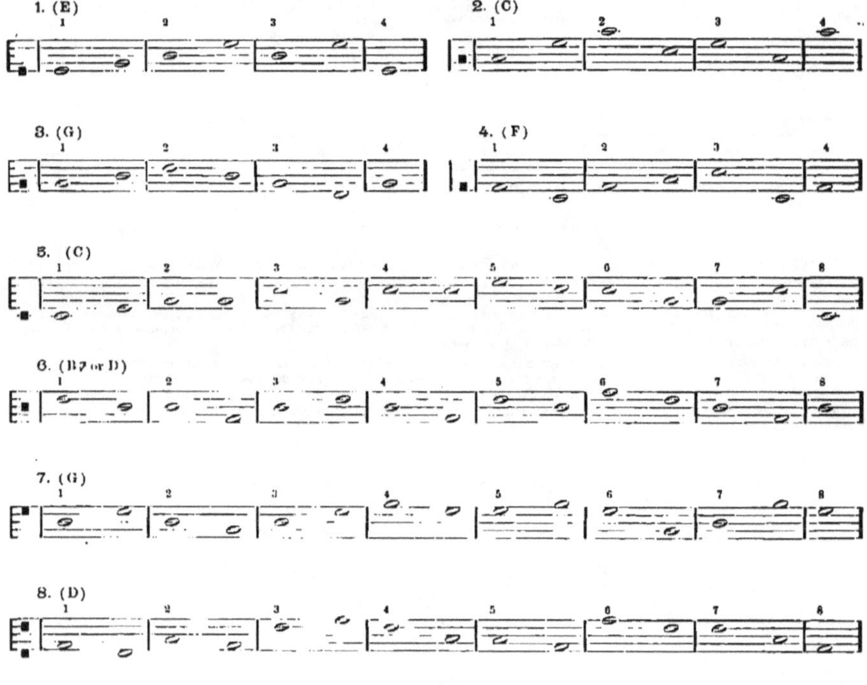

Writing Exercises. Copy into the staff notation any of the exercises from Nos. 9 to 26, pages 9 and 10, selected by the teacher, or similar ones supplied by him. They should also be sung from the staff copies.

Copy into the Sol-fa notation any of the foregoing staff exercises, and then rewrite them on the staff from the sol-fa copy, placing *Doh* differently from the printed copy.

The place of *Doh* for key D, space below, or third line; key C, added line below, or second space; key E, first line or third space; key F, first space or fourth line; key G, second line or fourth space; key A, second space.

Time.—In the Staff Notation the relative length of tones is represented by notes of different shapes for the different lengths. The notes in common use are:

WHOLE. HALF. QUARTER. EIGHTH. SIXTEENTH.

Notes have two uses: 1. To indicate by their position on the staff, which tones are to be sung. 2. By their shape, the length of each tone. Notes have no fixed or absolute value, they represent relative length only. The names of the notes indicate their relative values. A Whole note represents a tone twice as long as a Half note, or four times as long as a Quarter note, and so on.

Any note may be taken to represent the time of a pulse. The notes commonly used as pulse-notes, are the Half, the Quarter, and the Eighth. The different kinds of measures and the kind of note taken as the pulse-note are indicated by the *Measure Signature*, consisting of two figures in the form of a Fraction. The upper figure denotes the number of pulses in the measure, and the lower figure the kind of note that goes to a pulse.

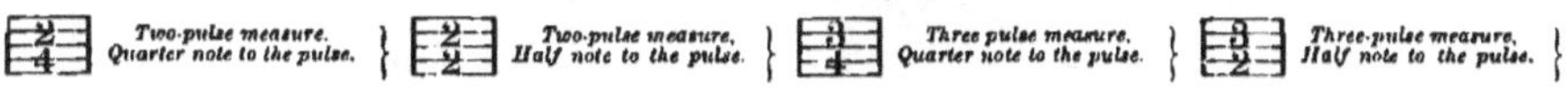

The bar indicates the strong accent, but there are no marks for the weak and medium accents.

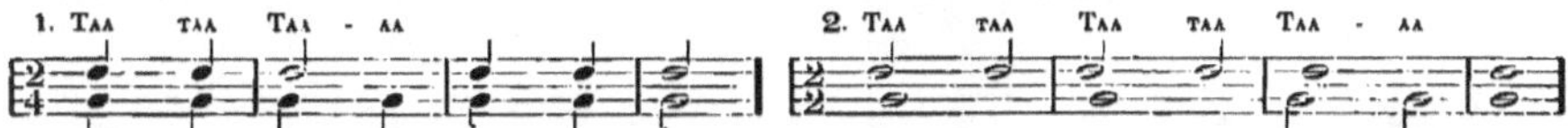

Each part to be tantaied as a separate exercise, then the two continuously as one.

The **Tie** indicates the continuation of the tone for the time of both notes. The **Dot** increases the value of any note one half.

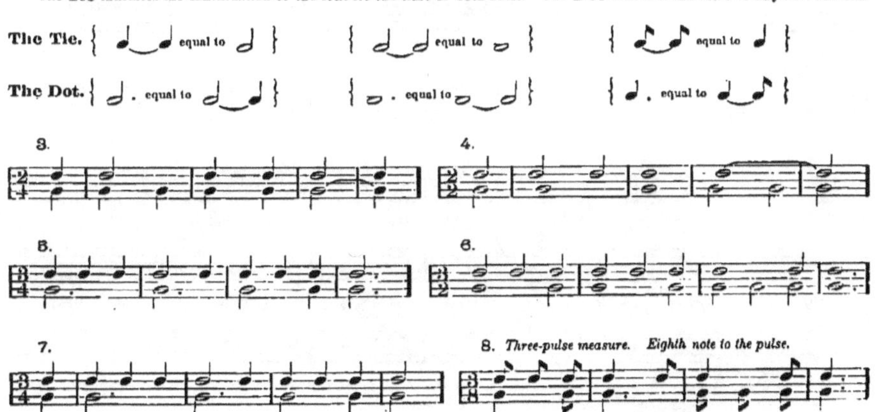

Writing Exercises.—Copy into Staff notation, quarter note to the pulse, Exercises 38, 39, 43; half note to the pulse, Exs. 40, 44, pages, 14 and 15. Copy into Sol-fa notation, Exs. 1, 2, 4, 5, page, 192.

Half-pulses.

1. Quarter-note to the pulse.
TAA TAA TAA - TAI TAA
2. Half-note to the pulse.
TAA TAA - TAI TAA TAA
Each part to be taataied as a separate exercise, then the two continuously as one.
3. TAA TAA TAA - - TAI TAA
4. TAA - TAI TAA TAA - TAI TAA
5. (C)
6. (G)
Now we have some fas-ter notes, Eighth notes we call them; We can "taatai" from the staff, Taa-tai, taa - tai, do not laugh.
7. (F)
8. (C)

Writing Exercises.—Copy into the Staff notation, quarter note to the pulse, Exs. 48 and 50; half note to pulse, Ex. 49, page, 16. Copy into Sol-fa notation, Exs. 5, 6 and 8, page, 193.

SECOND STEP.

Third Rule.—*Ray* is placed next above *Doh*, and *Te* next below *Doh*.

Writing Exercises.—Copy into the Staff notation, quarter note to the pulse, Exs. 59, 60, 61; half note to the pulse, Ex. 62, page, 20. Copy into Sol-fa Exs. 1, 2, 3 and 4, page, 194.

Four-pulse and Six-pulse Measures.

MEASURE SIGNATURES.

Writing Exercises.—Copy into Staff notation, quarter note to the pulse, Exs. 76, 79, page, 25; eighth note to the pulse, Ex. 83, page, 26. Copy into Sol-fa, Exs. 5, 6, 7, page, 195.

The Clefs and Key Signatures are explained on page 200. At present no notice need be taken of them, unless the pupils have passed the Third Step in Tonic Sol-fa, in which case the teacher may explain as much of the subject as will answer present purposes.

CHORAL SONG.

1. GOD IS LOVE. U.

THIRD STEP.

Fourth Rule.—The place of *Fah* is next above *Me; Lah* next above *Soh.* Or, *Lah* is one degree above *Soh*, and *Fah* one degree below.

Fifth Rule.—Alternate tones of the scale are *similarly* placed. *Doh*, *Me*, *Soh* and *Te* are placed alike; *Ray*, *Fah*, *Lah* and *Doh*' are placed alike. When d, m, s and t are on lines, r, f, l and d' are in spaces. When d, m, s and t are in spaces, r, f, l and d' are on lines.

Writing Exercises.—Copy into Staff notation, quarter note to the pulse, exs. 111, 112, 116; eighth note to the pulse, exs. 113, 117. Copy into Sol-fa notation, exs. 1, 2, 4, p. 198; 2, 3, 4, p. 199.

The Clefs.

The Treble, or G clef. The Base, or F clef. The Tenor, or C clef.

THE POSITION OF THE LETTERS AS FIXED BY THE CLEFS.

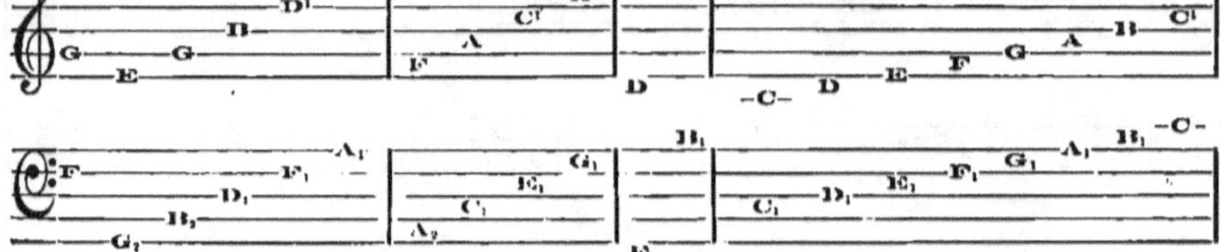

THE STANDARD SCALE AND PITCH OF VOICES.

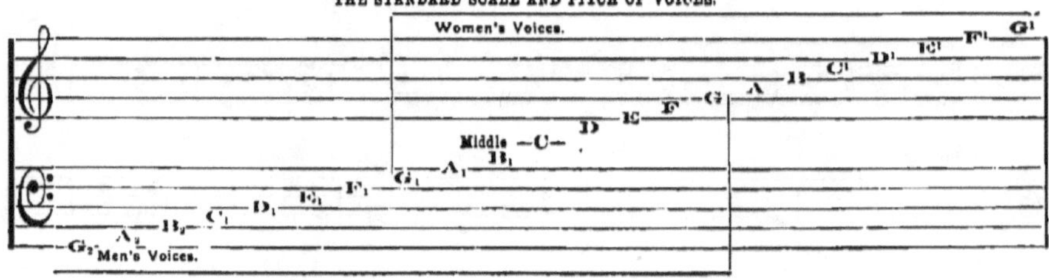

THE REAL PITCH OF THE CLEFS.

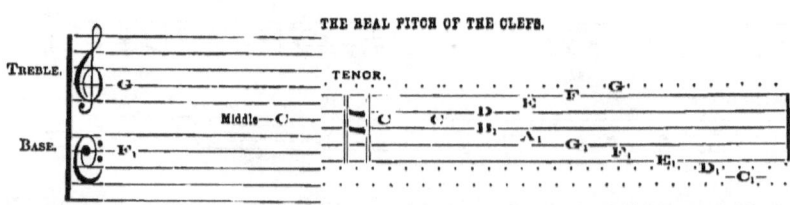

TREBLE. BASE. TENOR. Middle—C—

The Treble clef represents the G *above* Middle C. The Base clef represents the F *below* Middle C. The Tenor clef represents Middle C.

NOTE.—This use of the C clef is not the same as its use in orchestral scores. Its proper place is upon a line—the first line for Soprano, second line for Mezzo Soprano, third line for Contralto and fourth line for Tenor. It has been thought best to adopt the practice which is followed extensively in this country, and to place it in the third space, thus making the arrangement of the letters the same as that with the Treble clef and indicating the pitches which are really sung by the male voice when reading from the Treble clef.

The following five exercises are to be read by letter, not to be sung.

Writing Exercises.—Copy the following in notes on the Treble Staff.

6. | C F | D A | G E | B D' | A C' | G' E' | F' D' | C' ||

Copy the following on the Base Staff.

7. | G F, | B_2 D, | G_2 E, | A_2 G, | B, C | A, D, | F_2 G_2 | C, ||

Table of Key Signatures.

Rules for finding Doh.—Without sharps or flats, key C, *Doh* is on the added line below, Treble staff, and second space, Base staff. *With sharps*, the last sharp to the right is *Te*. *Doh* is on the next degree above. *With two or more flats*, the flat next to the last is *Doh*. With only one flat, that flat is *Fah*, *Doh* is on the fourth degree below.

Writing Exercises.—Write the signatures for the following keys,—both Treble and Base clefs—and place a note showing the position of *Doh* or write the scale in each key—D. E, G, A, E♭, F, A♭, B♭.

Rests.—Silences are indicated by *Rests.* Each note has a rest of corresponding value.

1. Round for two parts.
Come, come, come, the Sum-mer now is here; Come, come, come, the Sum-mer now is here.
Half-pulse Continuations.
2. Quarter note to the pulse.
TAA - AA - TAI TAA - AA - TAI
3. Half-note to the pulse.
TAA - AA - TAI TAA - AA - - TAI
4. Round for three parts.
Nor love thy life nor hate, Nor love thy l fe nor hate, But what thou liv'st live well, But
what thou liv'st live well; How long or short per - mit, per - mit to heav'n.
THE GOLDEN CORN.
T. F. S.
1. Heap high the far - mer's win - try hoard! Heap high the gold - en corn!
2. Thro' vales of grass and meads of flow'rs, Our ploughs their fur - rows made,
3. All through the long bright days of June, Its leaves grew bright and fair,
4. And now with Au - tumn's moon - lit eves, Its har - vest time has come,
No rich - er gift has Au - tumn poured From out her lav - ish horn!
While on the hill the sun and show'rs Of change - ful A - pril played.
And waved in hot mid - sum - mer noon, Its soft and yel - low hair.
We pluck a - way its frost - ed leaves, And bear its treas - ures home.

1. **Quarter Pulses.**

TAA TAI ta - fa - te - fe

2. **Quarter Continuations.**

TAA - te - fe TAA - e - fe

3.

4.

5. Round for three parts.

Bright, how bright the morn - ing light! oh!............................. how

6.

FINE. D.C.

EVENING.

NAEGELI

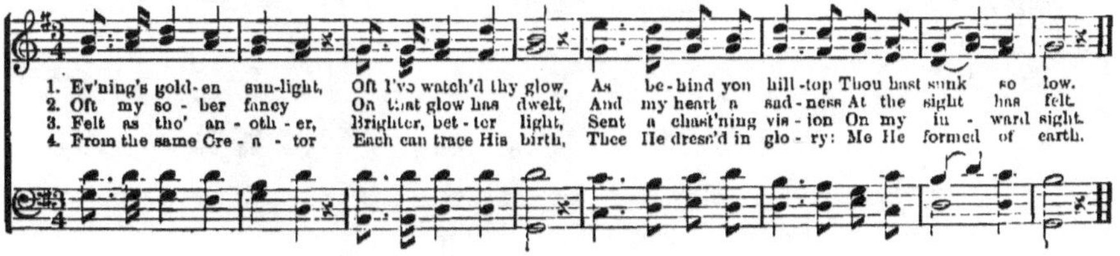

1. Ev'ning's gold - en sun - light, Oft I've watch'd thy glow, As be - hind yon hill - top Thou hast sunk so low.
2. Oft my so - ber fancy On that glow has dwelt, And my heart a sad - ness At the sight has felt.
3. Felt as tho' an - oth - er, Brighter, bet - ter light, Sent a chast'ning vis - ion On my in - ward sight.
4. From the same Cre - a - tor Each can trace His birth, Thee He dress'd in glo - ry: Me He formed of earth.

1.
FORTH WITH FOOTSTEPS LIGHT.
1. Forth, with foot - steps light, Up the mount-ain height; Winds fresh blow - ing, O - dors strew - ing, Wait to greet us there.
2. See the sun in state Rise at heav - ens gate: Forth to meet him, And to greet him, Soars the war - bling lark.
Cho.—Forth, forth, with foot - steps light, Let us scale the mount - ain height; Fresh in the morn - ing air, Na - ture seems most fair.
Forth, come forth with foot - steps light, And let us scale the mount - ain height, While fresh and bright in morn - ing air, All na - ture seems most fair.
2.
WHEN EARLY MORN SHALL WAKE US.
1. When ear - ly morn shall wake us To life and light a - new, Should drow - sy Sloth o'er-take us, Then Du - ty comes to shake us, And show us what to do, ... And show us what to do.
2. Birds war - ble their de - vo - tion In glad and thank-ful songs; Thro' wood, and field, and o - cean, All things are seen in mo - tion In gay and bus - y throngs, In gay and bus - y throngs.

FOURTH STEP.

Transition is sometimes indicated in the staff notation by a change of signature, but the general practice is to retain the old signature and indicate the distinguishing tones of the new key (*Fe* or *Ta*) as they are needed by the use of Accidentals (♯ ♭, ♮).

Sharp Fah (*fe*) means the first sharp key and should be called *Te*, unless contradicted by *Fah*. In key C and all keys with sharp signatures, *Fe* is expressed by a *sharp* on the degree that represents *Fah*. To restore *Fah* the natural is used. In all keys with flat signatures *Fe* is expressed by a *natural* on *Fah*. To restore *Fah* the flat is used.

Flat Te (*ta*) is the distinguishing tone of the first flat key and should be called *Fah*, unless contradicted by *Te*. In key C and all keys with flat signatures *Ta* is expressed by a *flat* on the degree that represents *Te*. To restore *Te* a *natural* is used. In all sharp keys *Ta* is indicated by a *natural* on *Te*. To restore *Te* a sharp is used,

Duration of Accidentals.—The influence of an accidental continues to the end of the measure in which it occurs, unless contradicted by another sign. It affects the line or space upon which it is placed, not merely the note that follows it.

Cautionary Accidentals.—The pupil must be careful to distinguish between accidentals that are of *real* effect and those which are merely put in as a caution to the player. If an accidental, contradicting some other accidental in a *previous measure*, merely repeats what is in the signature it is only cautionary.

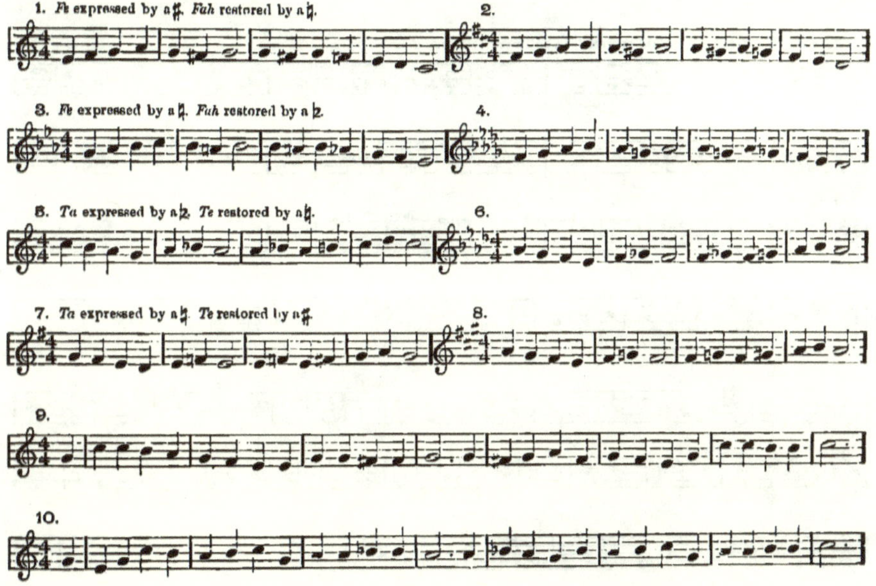

1. Transition with change of signature.
sd t, d s,
ds s l
2. Without change of signature.
sd t, d s,
or—s fe s r
ds s l
3.
rs
ds
4.
rs s l
or—r r m
5. Should be sol-faed by both "perfect" and "imperfect" methods.
6.
7.
8.
ml s,
ds d'
9.
10.

BARNARD. C. M.
D. C. UNSELD.
1. Come let us sing the song of songs— The saints in heav'n be - gan the strain,
2. To Him en - throned by fil - ial right, All pow'r in heav'n and earth pro - claim,
3. ong as we live, and when we die, And while in heav'n with Him we reign;
The hom - age which to Christ be - longs, "Wor - thy the Lamb, for He was slain."
Hon - or maj - es - ty and might, "Wor - thy the Lamb, for He was slain."
This song our song of songs shall be; "Wor - thy the Lamb, for He was slain."
SILVER SPRING. C. M.
DR. LOWELL MASON.
1. There is a name I love to hear, I love to sing its worth;
2. It tells me of a Sav - iour's love, Who died to set me free;
3. This name shall shed its fra - grance still A - long this thorn - y road;
It sounds like mu - sic in mine ear, The sweet - est name on earth.
It tells me of His pre - cious blood, The sin - ner's per - fect plea.
Shall sweet - ly smooth the rug - ged hill That leads me up to God.

1.
RELIANCE.
Theo. F. Seward, by per.
D.C. 1. O Je - sus! Friend un - fail - ing, How dear Thou art to me! Are cares or fears as - sail - ing? I find my strength in Thee!
2. Why should I droop in sor - row? Thou'rt ev - er by my side! Why, trembling, dread the mor - row, What ill can e'er be - tide?
Fine.
Why should my feet grow wea - ry Of this my pil - grim way? Tho' rough the path and drea - ry, It ends in per - fect day!
If I my cross have tak - en, 'Tis but to fol - low Thee; If scorn'd, despised, for - sak - en, Naught sev - ers Thee from me!
D.C.
2.
SUBMISSION.
Dr. Lowell Mason, by per.
1. O Lord! my best de - sires ful - fill, And help me to re - sign Life, health, and com - fort to Thy will, And make Thy pleas - ure mine.
2. Why should I shrink at Thy com - mand, Thy love for - bids my fears; Why trem - ble at Thy gra - cious hand, That wipes a - way my tears?

1.
THERE'S A CHARM IN SPRING.
Theo. F. Seward, by per.
1. There's a charm in spring, when ev - ery-thing Is burst-ing from the ground, from the ground, When pleasant show'rs bring
forth the flow'rs, And all is life a - round; In Summer's day, the fra - grant bay Most sweet-ly scents the
breeze, And it is still, save murm'ring rill, Or sound of humming bees.
2.
When Autum's come, with rusty gun,
In quest of birds we roam;
Unerring aim, we mark the game,
And proudly bear it home.
Old Winter's night has its delight,
Around old stories go,
Old Winter's day we're blithe and gay,
Defying ice and snow.
2.
SURRENDER.
Chester G. Allen, by per.
1. Vain, de - lu - sive world, a - dieu, With all of creature good:
On - ly Je - sus I pur - sue, Who bought me with His blood:
All Thy pleas-ures I fore - go;
I tram - ple on Thy wealth and pride; On - ly Je - sus will I know, And Je - sus cru - ci - fied.

Writing Exercises.—Copy into Staff notation quarter-note to the pulse, with change of signature, Nos. 175 176, 177; without change of signatures, Nos. 178, 179, 181, p. 68. Copy into Sol-fa, "perfect" method, Nos. 1, 5, 7; "imperfect" method Nos. 4, 6, 10, p. 208.

1. Chromatic Scale.
d de r re m f fe s se l le t d' d' t ta l la s sa f m ma r ra d
2.
3. The ♮ as a ♯.
4.
5. The ♮ as a ♭.
6.
7.

Writing Exercises.—Copy into Staff notation, quarter note to the pulse, Nos. 220 in keys D and E, 221 in keys G and A♭, 225 in keys D and D♭, 227 in keys C, D♭ and E. Copy into Sol-fa notation Nos. 2, 3, 5, page, 212; Nos. 3 and 4, page, 213.

1.
WILBUR.
Theo. F. Seward, by per.
1. How ten - der is Thy hand, O Thou be - lov - ed Lord;
2. How gen - tle was the rod That chast - ened us for sin!
3 A Fa - ther's hand we felt, A Fa - ther's heart we knew;
Af - flic - tions come at Thy com - mand, And leave us at Thy word.
How soon we found a smil ing God, Where deep dis - tress had been.
With tears of pen - i - tence we knelt, And found His word was true.
2.
CURTISS.
Wm. F. Sherwin, by per.
1. Cease, ye mourn - ers, cease to lan - guish O'er the grave of those you love;
2. While our si - lent steps are stray - ing, Lone - ly through night's deep - 'ning shade,
3. Light and peace at once de - riv - ing, From the hand of God most high,
Pain and death and night and an - guish En - ter not the world a - bove.
Glo - ry's bright - est beams are play - ing Round the hap - py Christ - ian's head.
In His glo - rious pres - ence liv - ing, They shall nev - er, nev - er die.

1 Syncopation.
2.
3.
IN GROVES OF FRAGRANT LARCHES.
SOPRANO.
1. In groves of fra - grant lar - ches, We soft - ly pace a - long, While all the for - est arch - es Re -
2. The air - y mu - sic meets us Like pass - ing spir - it voice, With tri - nd ly mean-ing greets us, And
CONTRALTO.
3. And why should not the prais - es Of hu - man lips be heard, When grate-ful in - stinct rais - es The
4. We too, the ech - oes wak - ing, Our glad - ness will ex - press, All gloom - y thoughts for - sak-ing, The
TENOR.
BASE.
sound with cheerful song. La la la la la la, etc.
bids our hearts re - joice.
trill - ings of the bird. La la la la la la, etc.
Lord of life to bless.
La la la la la la la, etc.
La la la la la la, etc.

1. **Quarter-pulse Silence. Sixteenth Rest.**

FIFTH STEP.

In the Staff notation the Minor Mode is represented as an appendage of the relative major. The minor mode is named from the pitch of the tone *Lah*. Thus the relative minor of the key C is *A minor;* the relative minor of the key G is *E minor*, and so on. Each signature indicates a major key and its relative minor. Thus the signature of one sharp indicates the keys of G major and *E minor*. The notational difficulties are with *Se* and *Ba*, chiefly with *Ba*.

The Sharp Seventh of the minor mode (*Se*) is always written as the sharp of *Soh*.

The Sharp Sixth of the minor mode (*Ba*) is always written as the sharp of *Fah*. There is no sign in the staff notation by which *Ba* can be distinguished from *Fe*. It is easily mistaken for *Fe* unless it stands in immediate relation with *Se*. When *Fah sharp* is followed by *Soh sharp*, and when *Soh sharp* is followed by *Fah sharp*, the *Fah sharp* must always be called *Ba*.

Writing Exercises.—Copy into Staff notation, quarter note to the pulse. Nos. 272, 271, 280, 281, 283. Copy in Sol-fa notation, Nos. 2, 4, 5, page, 217.

SIXTH STEP.

Transitions of more distant removes.—Singing from the staff notation is easy so long as the music does not change key, or when there is a change of but one remove. But reading remote transitions and modulations, in which the singer is confronted by a bewildering army of accidentals, is not easy. The difficulty is to some extent in the music, but to a much greater extent in the notation. Occasionally passages are met with which seem to be nothing but a wilderness of sharps, flats and naturals. Nearly every note is altered, the signature is not the slightest guide to the key, and the singer is apt to despair of finding it. Without a knowledge of harmony it is impossible to be perfectly certain in the power of deciding the key at a glance. The harmonist reads the key most quickly by watching the movement of the Base, especially in cadences. The ordinary singer, reading music at first sight, has not time to compare one part with another, to notice the movement of the Base, to mark the various accidentals and their resolutions. He must watch for the characteristic melodic shapes and phrases. All decided changes of key are felt most positively in cadences. The mental affects are there most strongly asserted; therefore, by "looking ahead" to the close and noticing the mental effects, the singer will be aided in deciding the key. The most expert readers sometimes find it necessary to analyze the whole phrase before they can be positively certain of the key.

Rules for finding the key.—The order of the sharps or flats as they occur in signatures should be memorized. A signature is the sharps or flats necessary in transitions from key C to other keys placed in *compact order;* the same sharps or flats occurring as accidentals are simply the *signature dispersed.* It will be remembered that the last sharp in a signature is *Te,* the last flat is *Fah;* this same rule holds good in the case of accidentals (except as to chromatics, to be mentioned later).

Order of the sharps.

1	2	3	4	5	6
F♯	C♯	G♯	D♯	A♯	E♯

It should be remembered that the first sharp in the above table indicates the key G; the first, and second key D; the first, second and third key A, and so on. To adopt a convenient phrase, "C♯ is sharper than F♯; G♯ is sharper than C♯," and so on. Or, we may say that F♯ is the nearest sharp; C♯ is a farther sharp, G♯ a still farther sharp, and so on through the whole series. From t is we deduce the rule—"Find the *sharpest* or *farthest* sharp and call it *Te.*"

Order of the flats.

1	2	3	4	5	6
B♭	E♭	A♭	D♭	G♭	C♭

With the flats we notice that B♭ is the nearest flat; E♭ is a farther flat; A♭ a still farther flat, and so on. The rule for flats is —"Find the *flattest* or *farthest* flat and call it *Fah.*"

Naturals in keys with flat signatures are the same as sharps, and in keys with sharp signatures, naturals are the same as flats. The rules of the *last sharp* and the *last flat* are now applied to the natural. In flat signatures the last *natural* is *Te.* In sharp signatures the last *natural* is *Fah.* The last sharp or flat is the *farthest* one to the *right;* the last natural is the *nearest* one to the *left.*

Order of naturals in keys with flat signatures.

6	5	4	3	2	1
B♮	E♮	A♮	D♮	G♮	C♮

Order of naturals in keys with sharp signatures.

6	5	4	3	2	1
F♮	C♮	G♮	D♮	A♮	E♮

The mode of search is now reversed. In the above table it is seen that the *farthest* natural is C♮; G♮ is a nearer natural; D♮ is still nearer, and so on. The rule is, with flat signatures—"Find the *nearest* natural and call it *Te.*" With sharp signatures—"Find the nearest natural and call it *Fah.*" Another rule—The farthest sharp in the signature left uncancelled is *Te.* The furthest flat left uncancelled is *Fah.*

Sometimes, when a passage does not contain either a *Te* or a *Fah* the rule of the farthest flat or sharp or nearest natural will not give the clue. The key must then be decided by the melodic shape, the cadence and the mental effect of the passage.

Chromatic Tones.—Care must be taken to distinguish between accidentals that indicate transition and those used for mere passing chromatic effects. If an accidental is repeated through several measures, wherever the same tone occurs, no doubt the key is changed. But if it is not repeated, or if it is contradicted, it is a chromatic tone, or a very brief transition. If the farthest sharp or flat be immediately contradicted it is a chromatic tone, and the next farthest must be looked for to decide the key.

Unmarked Accidentals.—In transition it sometimes happens that *Fe Ba,* and *Ta,* which would otherwise be expressed by a natural contradicting some sharp or flat in the signature, will have *nothing* to distinguish them, and are often a source of difficulty to the pupil. *Fe* and *Ba* in all first flat removes are the same as *Te* of the old key and remain unmarked. *Ta* in all first sharp removes is the same as *Fah* of the old key and remains unmarked.

Sharp Removes, departing with sharps.

1 2 3 4 5 6

Flat Removes, returning with naturals.

1 2

? unmarked accidental.

3 4 5 6

Flat Removes, departing with flats.

1 2 3

? unmarked accidental.

4 5 6

Sharp Removes, returning with naturals.

1 2 3 4 5 6

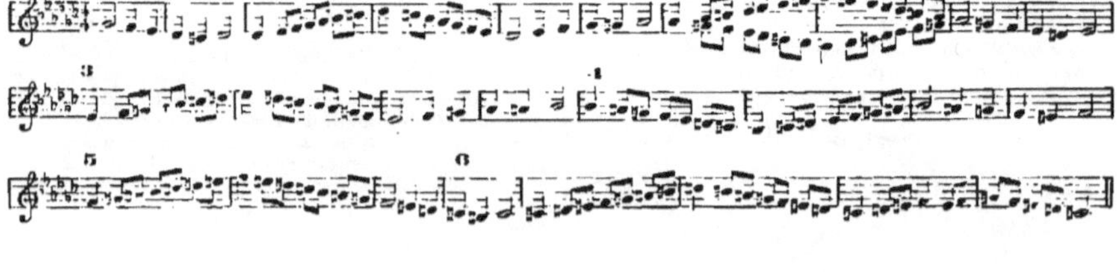

1. Unmarked accidentals, *Fe, Ba, Ta.*
?
2.
?
3.
?
4.
?
5. Transition—what Removes?
From J. Barnby.
6.
From J. B. Dykes.

1.
f
m
f
2.
3.
4.
5.

3.

INDEX.—Part II.

For Index to Part I, see page 112.

www.ingramcontent.com/pod-product-compliance
Lightning Source LLC
Chambersburg PA
CBHW021844230426
43669CB00008B/1080
9783337218577